Mastering ASP.NET Core 2.0

MVC patterns, configuration, routing, deployment, and more

Ricardo Peres

BIRMINGHAM - MUMBAI

Mastering ASP.NET Core 2.0

First published: November 2017

Production reference: 1141117

Published by Packt Publishing Ltd.
Livery Place
35 Livery Street
Birmingham
B3 2PB, UK.

ISBN 978-1-78728-368-8

www.packtpub.com

Credits

Author
Ricardo Peres

Reviewer
Alvin Ashcraft

Commissioning Editor
Merint Mathew

Acquisition Editor
Karan Sadawana

Content Development Editor
Siddhi Chavan

Technical Editor
Abhishek Sharma

Copy Editor
Safis Editing

Project Coordinator
Prajakta Naik

Proofreader
Safis Editing

Indexer
Tejal Daruwale Soni

Graphics
Abhinash Sahu

Production Coordinator
Aparna Bhagat

About the Author

Ricardo Peres is a Portuguese developer, blogger, and occasionally, an e-book author. He has over 17 years of experience in software development, using technologies such as C/C++, Java, JavaScript, and .NET. His interests include distributed systems, architectures, design patterns, and general .NET development.

He currently works for the London-based Simplifydigital as a technical evangelist, and was first awarded as an MVP in 2015.

Ricardo maintains a blog, *Development With A Dot*, where he regularly writes about technical issues. You can read it here: `http://weblogs.asp.net/ricardoperes`.

He wrote *Entity Framework Core Cookbook - Second Edition* and was the technical reviewer for *Learning NHibernate 4* by Packt.

Ricardo also contributed to Syncfusion's *Succinctly* collection of e-books with titles on NHibernate, Entity Framework Code First, Entity Framework Core, multitenant ASP.NET applications, and Microsoft Unity.

You can catch up with him on Twitter at `http://twitter.com/rjperes75`.

I would like to thank my son, Francisco, and daughter, Madalena, for all their love; they are the reason why I wrote this book.

Couldn't have done it without my friends GC and PJ; thank you for all your friendship and support!

In memory of my parents, Irene and Jorge Peres.

About the Reviewer

Alvin Ashcraft is a software developer living near Philadelphia, PA. He has dedicated his 22-year career to building software with C#, Visual Studio, WPF, ASP.NET, HTML/JavaScript, UWP, and Xamarin apps and SQL Server. He was awarded as a Microsoft MVP eight times, once for Software Architecture in 2009 and the seven subsequent years for C# and Visual Studio and Tools. You can read his daily links for .NET developers on his blog at `alvinashcraft.com` and UWP App Tips blog at `www.uwpapp.tips`.

He currently works as a Principal Software Engineer for Allscripts, developing clinical healthcare software. He has previously been employed with several large software companies, including Oracle, Genzeon, and Corporation Service Company. There, he helped create software solutions for financial, business, and healthcare organizations using Microsoft platforms and solutions.

He was a technical reviewer for *NuGet 2 Essentials* by Packt.

> *I would like to thank my wonderful wife, Stelene, and our three amazing daughters for their support. They were very understanding while I read and reviewed these chapters on evenings and weekends to help deliver a useful, high-quality book for the ASP.NET Core developers.*

www.PacktPub.com

For support files and downloads related to your book, please visit www.PacktPub.com.

Did you know that Packt offers eBook versions of every book published, with PDF and ePub files available? You can upgrade to the eBook version at www.PacktPub.com and as a print book customer, you are entitled to a discount on the eBook copy. Get in touch with us at service@packtpub.com for more details.

At www.PacktPub.com, you can also read a collection of free technical articles, sign up for a range of free newsletters and receive exclusive discounts and offers on Packt books and eBooks.

www.packtpub.com/mapt

Get the most in-demand software skills with Mapt. Mapt gives you full access to all Packt books and video courses, as well as industry-leading tools to help you plan your personal development and advance your career.

Why subscribe?

- Fully searchable across every book published by Packt
- Copy and paste, print, and bookmark content
- On demand and accessible via a web browser

Customer Feedback

Thanks for purchasing this Packt book. At Packt, quality is at the heart of our editorial process. To help us improve, please leave us an honest review on this book's Amazon page at https://www.amazon.com/dp/1787283682.

If you'd like to join our team of regular reviewers, you can e-mail us at customerreviews@packtpub.com. We award our regular reviewers with free eBooks and videos in exchange for their valuable feedback. Help us be relentless in improving our products!

Table of Contents

Preface

ASP.NET Core is relatively new in the development scenario, but it builds on ASP.NET, which is an old relative. It has been around for so many years, and has been so popular that one might think: why change it?

However, some things need to change; the enterprise world has changed, and the arrival of the cloud has changed things dramatically. A developer is not just a Windows developer or a Linux developer, but, quite often is both, as the business demands it. That is why a need in the .NET world was in order.

ASP.NET Core was built from scratch; it is not just an improvement of the venerable ASP.NET framework, it is something new. Web Forms are now gone, as the technology trends seem to go in the direction of the Model-View-Controller paradigm, and not just in .NET. Developer communities are embracing new techniques, such as Test-Driven Development (TDD), which fit perfectly with MVC.

Because .NET Core is entirely open source, it has benefited from the community as well, with pull requests being submitted for new features, and lead developers are discussing the roadmap openly on the internet. These are exciting times!

This book will guide you through the features of ASP.NET Core; some you may recognize from pre-Core versions, but a good number are new. Even previously existing features are somewhat new, as they are built on a totally different infrastructure that more modular, lightweight, and extensible.

Here, you will find material on ASP.NET Core, but also on .NET Core itself, as it's the framework that ASP.NET sits upon. Both seasoned ASP.NET developers and .NET Core newcomers should hopefully be able to find something for them.

What this book covers

Chapter 1, *Getting Started with ASP.NET Core*, introduces .NET Core and ASP.NET Core and explains some of the core (no pun intended) concepts.

Chapter 2, *Configuration*, talks about the new configuration system of .NET Core.

Chapter 3, *Routing*, describes how routes are used to match incoming requests to controllers and actions.

Chapter 4, *Controllers and Actions*, explains all about the classes (controllers) and methods (actions) that are used to process requests.

Chapter 5, *Views*, takes you through the HTML views and the new Razor Pages functionality of ASP.NET Core 2.

Chapter 6, *Using Forms and Models*, shows how HTML inputs are turned into models and how to generate HTML for model properties.

Chapter 7, *Security*, discusses some of the security aspects of ASP.NET Core, including authorization and authentication.

Chapter 8, *Reusable Components*, guides us through the different ways we can write reusable code for different purposes.

Chapter 9, *Filters*, presents the interception capabilities of ASP.NET Core.

Chapter 10, *Logging, Tracing, and Diagnostics*, demonstrates how we can capture information about our apps.

Chapter 11, *Testing*, walks us through writing tests to verify the functioning of our apps and modules.

Chapter 12, *Client-Side Development*, teaches you how to integrate Visual Studio and ASP.NET Core with popular scripting technologies.

Chapter 13, *Improving the Performance and Scalability*, guides you through improving the performance and scalability of your web applications.

Chapter 14, *Real-Time Communication*, teaches you how to use SignalR for server-to-client communication.

Chapter 15, *Other Topics*, is the chapter where some features of ASP.NET Core that couldn't find a place in other chapters are explained.

Chapter 16, *Deployment*, the last chapter. You will learn about the different deployment options available for ASP.NET Core applications.

What you need for this book

To follow the example code in this book, you'll need a computer running a reasonably recent version of Windows, macOS, or Linux. You'll also need a text editor to edit the code; I highly recommend using a text editor that allows you to open multiple files at a time and switch between them easily. Visual Studio 2015 or 2017 or Visual Studio Code come to my mind immediately. The latter is open source and is available on Windows, macOS, and Linux, and is a lightweight editor that nevertheless offers quite interesting features. Visual Studio should be well known to seasoned .NET developers and offers enterprise-level features, including rich debugging capabilities and code refactoring. It is available in different editions, ranging from Enterprise to Community, also with different costs associated, the Community edition is free, but, as can be expected, offers fewer less features than its paid counterpart. However, rest assured that to follow this book you can use any of them without any problems.

Who this book is for

If you are a .NET developer who has been writing ASP.NET applications and you want to migrate to .NET Core, you are the perfect audience for this book. It will tell you about all of the features of the recent releases of ASP.NET Core, 1.1 and 2.0, in a structured way, each chapter covering a different subject.

This book assumes you are familiar with .NET and the C# programming language and have written some code before. It also assumes you are comfortable with the command-line interface in your operating system of choice. The commands you need to run will be provided in this book.

Conventions

In this book, you will find a number of text styles that distinguish between different kinds of information. Here are some examples of these styles and an explanation of their meaning.

Code words in text, database table names, folder names, filenames, file extensions, pathnames, dummy URLs, user input, and Twitter handles are shown as follows: "We'll first call the `GetContacts()` method on an instance of `ContactUtil` to get the hardcoded `Contact` list."

A block of code is set as follows:

```
if (this.TempData.ContainsKey("key"))
{
  var value = this.TempData["key"];
}
```

Any command-line input or output is written as follows. The input command might be broken into several lines to aid readability, but needs to be entered as one continuous line in the prompt:

```
dotnet restore
```

New terms and **important words** are shown in bold. Words that you see on the screen, for example, in menus or dialog boxes, appear in the text like this: "You add a TypeScript file to your project by clicking **Add New Item** | **Visual C#** | **ASP.NET Core** | **Web** | **Scripts** | **TypeScript File**."

Warnings or important notes appear like this.

Tips and tricks appear like this.

Reader feedback

Feedback from our readers is always welcome. Let us know what you think about this book--what you liked or disliked. Reader feedback is important for us as it helps us develop titles that you will really get the most out of.

To send us general feedback, simply email `feedback@packtpub.com`, and mention the book's title in the subject of your message.

If there is a topic that you have expertise in and you are interested in either writing or contributing to a book, see our author guide at `www.packtpub.com/authors`.

Customer support

Now that you are the proud owner of a Packt book, we have a number of things to help you to get the most from your purchase.

Downloading the example code

You can download the example code files for this book from your account at `http://www.packtpub.com`. If you purchased this book elsewhere, you can visit `http://www.packtpub.com/support` and register to have the files emailed directly to you.

You can download the code files by following these steps:

1. Log in or register to our website using your email address and password.
2. Hover the mouse pointer on the **SUPPORT** tab at the top.
3. Click on **Code Downloads & Errata**.
4. Enter the name of the book in the **Search** box.
5. Select the book for which you're looking to download the code files.
6. Choose from the drop-down menu where you purchased this book from.
7. Click on **Code Download**.

Once the file is downloaded, please make sure that you unzip or extract the folder using the latest version of:

- WinRAR / 7-Zip for Windows
- Zipeg / iZip / UnRarX for macOS
- 7-Zip / PeaZip for Linux

The code bundle for the book is also hosted on GitHub at `https://github.com/PacktPublishing/Mastering-ASP.NET-Core-2.0`. We also have other code bundles from our rich catalog of books and videos available at `https://github.com/PacktPublishing/`. Check them out!

Errata

Although we have taken every care to ensure the accuracy of our content, mistakes do happen. If you find a mistake in one of our books--maybe a mistake in the text or the code--we would be grateful if you could report this to us. By doing so, you can save other readers from frustration and help us improve subsequent versions of this book. If you find any errata, please report them by visiting http://www.packtpub.com/submit-errata, selecting your book, clicking on the **Errata Submission Form** link, and entering the details of your errata. Once your errata are verified, your submission will be accepted and the errata will be uploaded to our website or added to any list of existing errata under the Errata section of that title.

To view the previously submitted errata, go to https://www.packtpub.com/books/content/support and enter the name of the book in the search field. The required information will appear under the **Errata** section.

Piracy

Piracy of copyrighted material on the internet is an ongoing problem across all media. At Packt, we take the protection of our copyright and licenses very seriously. If you come across any illegal copies of our works in any form on the internet, please provide us with the location address or website name immediately so that we can pursue a remedy.

Please contact us at copyright@packtpub.com with a link to the suspected pirated material.

We appreciate your help in protecting our authors and our ability to bring you valuable content.

Questions

If you have a problem with any aspect of this book, you can contact us at questions@packtpub.com, and we will do our best to address the problem.

1

Getting Started with ASP.NET Core

Welcome to my new book on ASP.NET Core!

.NET and ASP.NET Core are relatively new in the technological landscape, as they have been officially released only last August. Having the .NET part in the name, it would seem that these would probably only be new versions of the highly popular .NET Framework, but that is not the case, we are talking about something that is truly new!

It's not just multi-platform support (howdy, Linux!), but it's so much more. It's the new modularity in everything, the transparent way by which we can now change things, the source code just in front of our eyes teasing us to contribute to it, to make it better, is indeed a lot different!

In this first chapter, we are going to talk a bit about what changed in ASP.NET and .NET in the Core versions, and also about the new underlying concepts, such as OWIN, runtime environments and dependency injection. Then I'll present in brief the sample project that will accompany us through the book.

In this chapter, we will cover the following topics:

- History of ASP.NET Core
- Introduction to .NET Core
- Inversion of control and dependency injection
- OWIN
- The MVC pattern

- Hosting
- Environments
- The sample project

Introducing ASP.NET Core

Microsoft ASP.NET was released 15 years ago, in 2002, as part of the then shiny new .NET Framework. It inherited the name **ASP** (**Active Server Pages**) from its predecessor, with whom it barely shared anything else, other than being a technology for developing dynamic server-side contents for the internet, which ran on Windows platforms only.

ASP.NET gained tremendous popularity, one has to say, and competed hand-to-hand with other popular web frameworks such as **Java Enterprise Edition** (**JEE**) and **PHP**. In fact, it still does, with sites such as **BuiltWith** giving it a share of 21% (ASP.NET and ASP.NET MVC combined), way ahead of Java (`https://trends.builtwith.com/framework`). ASP.NET was not just for writing dynamic web pages. It could also be used for **XML** (**SOAP**) web services, which, in early 2000, were quite popular. It benefited from the .NET Framework and its big library of classes and reusable components, which made enterprise development almost seem easy!

Its first version, ASP.NET 1, introduced **Web Forms**, an attempt to bring to the web the event and component model of desktop-style applications, shielding users from some of the less friendly aspects of HTML, HTTP, and state maintenance. To a degree, it was highly successful, one could easily, using Visual Studio, create a data-driven dynamic site in just a few minutes! A great deal of stuff could be accomplished merely through markup, with no code changes (read, compile) needed.

Version 2 came along a few years afterwards, and among all the other goodies, brought with it extensibility in the form of a provider model. A lot of its functionality could be adapted by the means of custom providers. Later on it received the addition of the AJAX Extensions which made AJAX-style effects astonishingly easy. It set the standard for years to come, leaving only room for more components.

Precisely, following versions 3.5, 4, and 4.5 only offered more of the same, with new specialized controls for displaying data and charts for retrieving and manipulating data and a few security improvements. A big change was that some of the framework libraries were released as open source.

Between versions 3.5 and 4, Microsoft released a totally new framework, based on the **Model-View-Controller** (**MVC**) pattern, and mostly open source. Although it sits on top of the infrastructure laid out by ASP.NET, it offered a whole new development paradigm, which this time fully embraced HTTP and HTML. It seemed to be the current trend for web development across technologies, and the likes of PHP, Ruby and Java, and .NET developers were generally pleased with it. ASP.NET developers had now two choices, Web Forms and MVC, both sharing the ASP.NET pipeline and .NET libraries but offering two radically different approaches to getting contents to the browser.

In the meantime, the now venerable .NET Framework had grown adult in an ever changing world. In the modern enterprise, the needs have changed, and sentences such as *runs on Windows only* or *we need to wait XX years for the next version* became hardly acceptable. Acknowledging this, Microsoft started working on something new, something different that would set the agenda for years to come ... enter .NET Core!

In late 2014, Microsoft announced .NET Core. It was meant to be a platform-independent, language-agnostic, free and open source full rewrite of the .NET Framework. It's main characteristics were as follows:

- The base class libraries of .NET were to be rewritten from scratch, while keeping the same (simplified) public APIs, which meant not all of them would be available initially
- Being able to also run on non-Windows operating systems, specifically, several Linux and macOS flavors, and in mobile devices, so all Windows-specific code (and APIs) would be discarded
- All of its components were to be delivered as NuGet packages, meaning that only a small bootstrap binary would need to be installed in the host machine
- There was no longer a dependency (or, let's say, a very close relationship) with IIS, it should be able to run auto-hosted or inside a hosting process, like, well, IIS
- It would be open source, and developers would be able to influence it, either by creating tickets or by submitting change requests

This eventually took place in July 2016, when version 1.0 of .NET Core was released. The .NET developers could now write once and deploy (almost) everywhere and they finally had a say on the direction the framework was taking!

Rewriting from scratch the whole .NET Framework is a task of epic proportions, so Microsoft had to make decisions and define priorities. One of them was to ditch ASP.NET Web Forms and to only include MVC. So gone were the days when ASP.NET and Web Forms were synonyms, and the same happened with ASP.NET Core and MVC, it's now just ASP.NET Core! And it's not just that the ASP.NET Web API, which used to be a different thing, is now merged with ASP.NET Core as well, a wise decision from Microsoft, as basically the two technologies, MVC and Web API, had a lot of overlap and even had classes with the same name for pretty much the same purpose.

So, what does this mean for developers? Here are my personal thoughts:

- C# only, no Visual Basic.NET for the time being; not a bad thing, in my opinion.
- Open source is great! If you want to change anything, just grab the code from **GitHub** and make the changes yourself! If they're good enough, chances are, others may be interested in them too, so why not submit a pull request to have them integrated?
- We don't need to decide upfront if we want to use MVC or the Web API, it's just a matter of adding one or two NuGet packages anytime and adding a couple of lines to the `Startup.cs` file; the same controller can serve both API and web requests seamlessly.
- Attribute routing is built-in, so there's no need for any explicit configuration.
- ASP.NET Core now uses **Open Web Interface for .NET (OWIN)** based middleware and configuration, so you will need to change (significantly) your modules and handlers so that they fit into this model; MVC/Web API filters are basically the same.
- No dependency on IIS or Windows, meaning, we can easily write our apps in good old Windows/Visual Studio and then just deploy them to Azure/AWS/Docker/Linux/macOS. It's actually pretty cool to debug our app in Docker/Linux from Visual Studio! It can run self-hosted in a console application too.
- A consequence of the latter, no more **IIS Manager** or `web.config`/`machine.config` files.
- Not all libraries are already available for .NET Core, meaning, you will either need to find replacements or implement the features yourself. The site `https://icanhasdot.net/Stats` has a good list of whatever is/is not available for .NET Core and there is also a list in the project's roadmap at `https://github.com/dotnet/core/blob/master/roadmap.md`.

- Even the core (pun intended) .NET Core classes are still lacking some methods that used to be there, take, for example the `System.Environment` class.
- You need to handpick the NuGet packages for the libraries you want to use, including for classes that you took for granted in the old days. For .NET; this includes for example, `System.Collections` (https://www.nuget.org/packages/System.Collections), as they are not automatically referenced. Sometimes it's hard to find out which NuGet package contains the classes you want, when this happens `http://packagesearch.azurewebsites.net` may come in handy;
- No more Web Forms (and the visual designer in Visual Studio), now it's MVC all the way!

.NET Core

Talking about ASP.NET Core without explaining .NET Core is somewhat cumbersome. .NET Core is the framework everyone is talking about, and for good reasons. ASP.NET Core is probably its most interesting API now, as it no longer (for the time being, that is) includes any other productivity/graphical user interface library. You heard it right, no more Windows Forms or Windows Presentation Framework or even Windows Services!

And why is that? Well, all these APIs relied heavily on Windows native features; in fact, Windows Forms was merely a wrapper around the Win32 API that has accompanied Windows since its early days. Because .NET Core is multi-platform, it would be a tremendous effort to have versions of these APIs for all supported platforms. By all means this doesn't mean, of course, that it won't happen; it's just that it hasn't happened yet.

With .NET Core, a host machine only needs a relatively small bootstrap code to run an application; the app itself needs to include all the reference libraries it needs to operate. Interestingly, it is possible to compile a .NET Core application to native format, thus producing a machine-specific executable that includes in it all the dependencies, and can even be run in a machine without the .NET Core bootstrapper.

As I said previously, .NET Core was written from scratch, which unfortunately means that not all the APIs that we were used to have been ported. Specifically, as of .NET Core 1.1 and 2.0, the following features are still missing:

- ASP.NET Web Forms (`System.Web.UI`)
- XML Web Services (`System.Web.Services`)
- LINQ to SQL (`System.Data.Linq`)

- Windows Forms (`System.Windows.Forms`)
- Windows Presentation Foundation (`System.Windows` and `System.Xaml`)
- Windows Communication Foundation server-side classes (`System.ServiceModel`)
- Windows Workflow Foundation (`System.Workflow` and `System.Activities`)
- .NET Remoting (`System.Runtime.Remoting`)
- Some ADO.NET APIs, such as `DataSet`/`DataView` (`System.Data`), and parts of the ADO.NET provider model (`System.Data.Common`)
- Code generation (`System.CodeDom`)
- Distributed transactions (`System.Transactions`)
- Active Directory/LDAP (`System.DirectoryServices`)
- Enterprise Services (`System.EnterpriseServices`)
- Email (`System.Net.Mail`)
- XML and XSD (`System.Xml.Xsl` and `System.Xml.Schema`)
- IO ports (`System.IO.Ports`)
- Managed Addin Framework (`System.Addin`)
- Speech (`System.Speech`)
- Configuration (`System.Configuration`), this one was replaced by a new configuration API
- Windows Management Instrumentation (`System.Management`)
- Drawing functionality (`System.Drawing`), although some structures exist
- Application Domains and sandboxing (`System.AppDomain`)
- Windows Registry (`Microsoft.Win32`)

This is by no means an exhaustive list. As you can see, there are a lot of features missing. Still, it is quite possible to achieve pretty much whatever we need to, provided we do things in a different way and handle the extra burden!

The following APIs are new or still around and are safe to use:

- MVC and Web API (`Microsoft.AspNetCore.Mvc`)
- Entity Framework Core (`Microsoft.EntityFrameworkCore`)
- Roslyn for code generation and analysis (`Microsoft.CodeAnalysis`)
- All Azure APIs
- Managed Extensibility Framework (`System.Composition`)

- Text encoding/decoding and regular expressions processing (`System.Text`)
- JSON serialization (`System.Runtime.Serialization.Json`)
- Low-level code generation (`System.Reflection.Emit`)
- Most of ADO.NET (`System.Data`, `System.Data.Common`, `System.Data.SqlClient`, `System.Data.SqlTypes`)
- LINQ and Parallel LINQ (`System.Linq`)
- Collections, including concurrent (`System.Collections`, `System.Collections.Generic`, `System.Collections.ObjectModel`, `System.Collections.Specialized`, `System.Collections.Concurrent`)
- Threading, inter-process communication and task primitives (`System.Threading`)
- Input/Output, compression, isolated storage, memory-mapped files, pipes (`System.IO`)
- XML (`System.Xml`)
- Windows Communication Foundation client-side classes (`System.ServiceModel`)
- Cryptography (`System.Security.Cryptography`)
- Platform Invoke and COM Interop (`System.Runtime.InteropServices`)
- Universal Windows Platform (`Windows`)
- Event Tracing for Windows (`System.Diagnostics.Tracing`)
- Data Annotations (`System.ComponentModel.DataAnnotations`)
- Networking, including HTTP (`System.Net`)
- Reflection (`System.Reflection`)
- Maths and numerics (`System.Numerics`)
- Reactive Extensions (`System.Reactive`)
- Globalization and localization (`System.Globalization`, `System.Resources`)
- Caching (including in-memory and Redis) (`Microsoft.Extensions.Caching`)
- Logging (`Microsoft.Extensions.Logging`)

Again, not the full list, but you get the picture. These are just Microsoft APIs made available for .NET Core; there are obviously thousands of others from different vendors.

 And why are these APIs supported? Well, because they are specified in a **.NET Standard**, and .NET Core implements this standard! More on this in a moment.

In .NET Core, there is no more a **Global Assembly Cache (GAC)**, but there is a centralized location (per user) for storing NuGet packages, `%HOMEPATH%.nugetpackages`, which prevents you from having duplicate packages locally for all of your projects. .NET Core 2.0 introduced the **runtime store**, which is somewhat similar to GAC. Essentially, it is a folder on a local machine where some packages are made available and compiled for the machine's architecture. Packages stored there are never downloaded from NuGet; they are instead referenced locally and do not need to be included with your app. A welcome addition, I may add! Read more about metapackages and the runtime store here: `https://docs.microsoft.com/en-us/aspnet/core/fundamentals/metapackage`.

The `Microsoft.AspNetCore.All` metapackage (a set of packages) includes:

- All supported packages by the ASP.NET Core team
- All supported packages by the Entity Framework Core
- Internal and third-party dependencies used by ASP.NET Core and Entity Framework Core

Visual Studio templates for .NET Core 2 already reference this metapackage.

NuGet packages are at the heart of .NET Core, and mostly everything needs to be obtained from NuGet. Even projects in the same Visual Studio solution are referenced from one another as NuGet packages. When using .NET Core, you will need to explicitly add the NuGet packages that contain the functionality that you wish to use. It is likely that you may come across some of the following packages in some of your projects:

Package	Purpose
`Microsoft.EntityFrameworkCore`	Entity Framework Core
`Microsoft.Extensions.Caching.Memory`	In-memory caching
`Microsoft.Extensions.Caching.Redis`	Redis caching
`Microsoft.Extensions.Configuration`	General configuration classes
`Microsoft.Extensions.Configuration.EnvironmentVariables`	Configuration from environment variables
`Microsoft.Extensions.Configuration.Json`	Configuration from JSON files

`Microsoft.Extensions.Configuration.UserSecrets`	Configuration in user secrets (`https://docs. microsoft.com/ en-us/aspnet/ core/security/ app-secrets`)
`Microsoft.Extensions.Configuration.Xml`	Configuration in XML
`Microsoft.Extensions.DependencyInjection`	Built-in dependency injection framework
`Microsoft.Extensions.Logging`	Logging base classes
`Microsoft.Extensions.Logging.Console`	Logging to the console
`Microsoft.Extensions.Logging.Debug`	Logging to debug
`System.Collections`	Collections
`System.ComponentModel`	Classes and interfaces used in the definition of components and data sources
`System.ComponentModel.Annotations`	Data annotations for validation and metadata
`System.Data.Common`	ADO.NET
`System.Globalization`	Globalization and localization APIs
`System.IO`	Input/Output APIs
`System.Linq.Parallel`	Parallel LINQ
`System.Net`	Networking APIs
`System.Reflection`	Reflection

`System.Security.Claims`	Security based upon claims
`System.Threading.Tasks`	Tasks implementation
`System.Xml.XDocument`	XML APIs

Again, not an exhaustive list, but you get the picture. You may not see references to all these packages, because adding one package that has dependencies will bring all these dependencies along, and **big** packages have a lot of dependencies.

There are no more `.exe` files; now all assemblies are `.dll`, which means they need to be run using the `dotnet` command line utility. All .NET Core applications start with a static `Main` method, as the *old* Console and Windows Forms did, but now we need the dotnet utility to run them. dotnet is a very versatile tool, and can be used to build, run, deploy, and restore NuGet packages, execute unit tests, and create NuGet packages from a project. As I said, it is also possible to compile an assembly to the native format, but we won't be covering it here.

.NET Core ships with built-in **dependency injection (DI)**, logging, and a flexible configuration framework, which allows you to plug in your own providers if you so wish to. All of the new APIs (such as Entity Framework Core and ASP.NET Core) use these services uniformly. For the very first time, we see a coherent behavior across APIs.

Also, most productivity APIs like ASP.NET and Entity Framework allow replacing the services they're built upon by customized versions, allowing you to have them work the exact way you want them, provided, of course, you know what you are doing, and these services are generally based upon interfaces. Everything is much more modular and transparent.

Unit testing got first-class citizenship in .NET Core. Most new APIs were designed with testability in mind (think for example of the new in-memory provider for Entity Framework Core), and the tooling (**dotnet**) has an explicit option for executing unit tests, which can be written in any framework (presently, xUnit, NUnit, MbUnit and Microsoft, among others, have released unit test frameworks compatible with .NET Core). We will cover unit testing in this book in more detail.

Platforms

.NET Core works in the following platforms:

- Windows 7 SP1 or higher
- Windows Server 2008 R2 SP1 or higher
- Red Hat Enterprise Linux 7.2 or higher
- Fedora 23 or higher
- Debian 8.2 or higher
- Ubuntu 14.04 LTS/16.04 LTS, or higher
- Linux Mint 17 or higher
- openSUSE 13.2 or higher
- Centos 7.1 or higher
- Oracle Linux 7.1 or higher
- macOS X 10.11 or higher

This covers all modern Windows, Linux and macOS distributions (Windows 7 SP1 was released in 2010). It may well work in other distributions, but these are the ones that have been thoroughly tested by Microsoft.

So, how does this work? It turns out that whenever you request a NuGet package that needs native libraries, not included in the operating system, these are also included in the `.nupkg` archive. .NET Core uses **Platform Invoke (P/Invoke)** to call the operating system-specific libraries. This means that you do not have to worry about it, the process to locate, add a NuGet package, and publish the project is the same no matter what the target operating system will be.

Keep in mind that platform independence is transparent to you, the developer, unless of course you also happen to be a library author, in which case you may need to care about it.

Dependencies and frameworks

Inside a .NET Core project, you specify the frameworks that you wish to target. What are these frameworks? Well, .NET Core itself, but the *classic* .NET Framework as well, Xamarin, **Universal Windows Platform (UWP)**, **Portable Class Libraries (PCL)**, Mono, Windows Phone, and more.

In the early days of .NET Core, you would either target .NET Core itself or/as well as, one of these other frameworks. Now it is advisable to target standards instead. According to Immo Landwerth of Microsoft (`https://blogs.msdn.microsoft.com/dotnet/2016/09/26/introducing-net-standard`):

.NET Standard solves the code sharing problem for .NET developers across all platforms by bringing all the APIs that you expect and love across the environments that you need: desktop applications, mobile apps & games, and cloud services:

- **.NET Standard** *is a set of APIs that all .NET platforms have to implement. This unifies the .NET platforms and prevents future fragmentation.*
- **.NET Standard 2.0** *is implemented by* **.NET Framework, .NET Core, Mono,** *and* **Xamarin.** *For .NET Core, this adds many of the existing APIs that have been requested.*
- **.NET Standard 2.0** *includes a compatibility shim for .NET Framework binaries, significantly increasing the set of libraries that you can reference from your .NET Standard libraries.*
- **.NET Standard** *will replace* **Portable Class Libraries** *(**PCLs**) as the tooling story for building multi-platform .NET libraries.*

Put in a different way:

- **.NET Standard** is a specification that covers which APIs a .NET platform has to implement
- **.NET Core** is a concrete .NET platform and implements the .NET Standard
- The latest .NET Standard will always cover the highest .NET full framework released

David Fowler (`https://twitter.com/davidfowl`) of Microsoft came up with the following analogy:

```
interface INetStandard10
{
  void Primitives();
  void Reflection();
  void Tasks();
  void Collections();
  void Linq();
}
interface INetStandard11 : INetStandard10
{
  void ConcurrentCollections();
  void InteropServices();
}
```

```
interface INetFramework45 : INetStandard11
{
  // Platform specific APIs
  void AppDomain();
  void Xml();
  void Drawing();
  void SystemWeb();
  void WPF();
  void WindowsForms();
  void WCF();
}
```

It should make it very easy to understand. As you can see, all .NET APIs that need Windows (WPF, Windows Forms, Drawing) are only available in a specific platform (.NET 4.5), not a standard. Standards are for cross-platform functionality.

 For more information, please refer to https://docs.microsoft.com/en-us/dotnet/articles/standard/library.

So instead of targeting a specific version, such as .NET 4.5.1, .NET Core 1.0, Mono, Universal Windows Platform 10, or Windows Phone 8.1, you target a .NET standard. Your project is guaranteed to work on all platforms that support that standard (or a higher one), either existing or waiting to be created. You should try to keep your dependency to the lowest standard possible, to increase the number of platforms where your app will work, if that is important to you.

The following table lists all the .NET Standards and the platforms they support:

.NET Standard	1.0	1.1	1.2	1.3	1.4	1.5	1.6	2.0
.NET Core	1.0	1.0	1.0	1.0	1.0	1.0	1.0	2.0
.NET Framework	4.5	4.5	4.5.1	4.6	4.6.1	4.6.1 4.6.2	4.6.1 vNext	4.6.1
Mono	4.6	4.6	4.6	4.6	4.6	4.6	4.6	5.4
Xamarin.iOS	10.0	10.0	10.0	10.0	10.0	10.0	10.0	10.14
Xamarin.Mac	3.0	3.0	3.0	3.0	3.0	3.0	3.0	3.8
Xamarin.Android	7.0	7.0	7.0	7.0	7.0	7.0	7.0	7.5
Universal Windows Platform	10.0	10.0	10.0	10.0	10.0	vNext	vNext	vNext
Windows	8.0	8.0	8.1					

.NET Standard	1.0	1.1	1.2	1.3	1.4	1.5	1.6	2.0
Windows Phone	8.1	8.1	8.1					
Windows Phone Silverlight	8.0							

This table represents the current mapping between the different .NET frameworks and the .NET Standard they implement at the time this book was written, and the latest version is always available at: `https://github.com/dotnet/standard/blob/master/docs/versions.md`.

Each .NET Standard version features some APIs and each higher version supports more, as you can see in the following table:

Version	#APIs	Growth %
1.0	7,949	
1.1	10,239	+29%
1.2	10,285	+0%
1.3	13,122	+28%
1.4	13,140	+0%
1.5	13,355	+2%
1.6	13,501	+1%
2.0	32,638	+142%

.NET Core 2.0 and .NET Standard 2.0 were made available in August 2017 and now four frameworks target .NET Standard 2.0:

- .NET Framework **full**
- .NET Core 2.0
- Xamarin
- Mono

You can have your dependencies specified per target or for all targets. In the former case, all the dependencies need to support all targets and in the latter, we can have different dependencies for each target. You'll probably want a mix of the two, with common libraries as global dependencies and more specialized libraries specified only where available. If you target more than one standard (or framework), pay attention, because you may have to resort to conditional defines (`#if`) to target those features that only exist in one of them.

The .NET Standard FAQ is available in GitHub: `https://github.com/dotnet/standard/blob/master/docs/faq.md`.

Targeting .NET Core or the full .NET framework

It is important that you know that you can target the full .NET framework in an ASP.NET Core application! However, if you do it, you lose the platform independency, that is, you can only run it on Windows.

By default, an ASP.NET Core project targets `netcoreapp1.0` or `netcoreapp2.0`, depending on whether you are targeting ASP.NET Core 1.x or 2.x, but you can change it in the `.csproj` file. If you just want to target one framework, modify the `TargetFramework` element like this:

```
<TargetFramework>net461</TargetFramework>
```

Or, if you want to target more than one, replace `TargetFramework` for `TargetFrameworks`:

```
<TargetFrameworks>netcoreapp2.0;net461</TargetFrameworks>
```

For more info, please refer to the Microsoft documentation: `https://docs.microsoft.com/en-us/dotnet/core/tools/csproj`.

Understanding the MVC pattern

Going back to ASP.NET now. So, for those of you that were still working with Web Forms, what is this MVC thing anyway, and where did it come from?

Let's face it, it was pretty easy in Web Forms to do terrible things, such as adding lots of/sensitive code in the page (which wouldn't be compiled until the page was accessed by the browser), adding complex business logic to a page class, having several megabytes of code in View State going back and forth on every request, and so on. There was no mechanism at all, other than the developer's discretion, to do things the right way. Plus, it was terrible to unit test it, because it relied on browser submission (`POST`) and JavaScript to have things working properly, such as binding actions to event handlers and submitted values to controls. There had to be a different solution, and in fact there was.

The **Model-View-Controller** (**MVC**) design pattern was defined in the late 1970s and early 1980s of the past century (scary, isn't it?). It was conceived as a way to properly segregate things that shouldn't conceptually be together, such as the code to render a **user interface** (**UI**) and the code that contains the business logic and data access that will feed and control that UI. In the MVC paradigm (and its offspring), we have controllers which expose public actions. Inside each action, the controller applies any business logic it needs to and then decides which view it should render, passing it enough information (the model) so that it can do its job. A controller knows nothing about UI elements, it just takes the data and execution context it needs to operate inside the action and goes from there. Likewise, a view will not know anything about databases, web services, connection strings, SQL, and the like, it just renders data, possibly taking simple decisions about the way to do it. As for the model, it's basically anything you want that contains the information required by the view, including lists of records, static user information, and more. This strict separation makes things much easier to manage, test and implement. By all means, the MVC pattern is not specific to the web, it can be used whenever this separation of concerns is useful, such as when we have a user interface and some code to control it.

The following diagram presents the relationship between views, controllers and models:

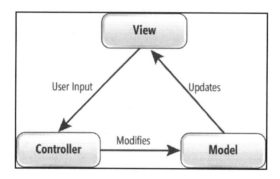

MVC is normally associated with **Object-Oriented Programming** (**OOP**), but there are implementations in a myriad of languages, including JavaScript and PHP. The .NET MVC implementation has the following basic characteristics:

- **Controller** classes are either **Plain Old CLR Object** (**POCO**) or inherit from a base class, Controller. Inheriting from Controller is not required (unlike in previous versions), but it does make things slightly easier. Controller classes are instantiated by the ASP.NET Core **dependency injection** (**DI**) framework, which means they can have the services they depend upon passed into them.

- **Actions** are public methods in a controller; they can take parameters, of both simple types as well as complex ones (POCOs); MVC uses what is called model binding to translate information sent from the browser (the query string, headers, cookies, forms, dependency injection, and other locations) into method parameters. The choice of which method from which controller to invoke from the request URLs and submitted parameters is achieved by a mix of a routing table, conventions, and helper attributes.

- The **model** is sent from the controller to the view in the return of an action method and it can be basically anything (or nothing); of course, action methods for API calls do not return views, but can return a model together with an HTTP status code. Other ways exist to pass data to the view, namely, the view bag, which is essentially an untyped dictionary of data; the difference between the two is that the model is normally typed. A model is automatically validated and bound to the action method parameters.

- **Views** consist of **Domain-Specific Languages (DSL)** files that are interpreted by a view engine and turned into something that the browser can interpret, such as HTML. ASP.NET Core features an extensible view engine framework but includes a single implementation, **Razor**. Razor offers a simple syntax that allows developers to mix HTML and C# to get hold of the model passed in and make decisions on what to do with it. Views can be constrained by layouts (Web Forms developers can think of layouts as master pages) and they can include other partial views (similar to web user controls in Web Forms). A view for the Razor view engine has the `.cshtml` extension, and cannot be accessed directly, only as the result of an action invocation. Views can be pre-compiled, so that syntax errors are detected sooner.

- **Filters** are used to intercept, modify, or fully replace the request; built-in filters include preventing access to unauthenticated users or redirecting to an error page in the event of an exception occurring.

Now, there are other patterns similar in purpose to MVC, such as **Model-View-Presenter (MVP)** or **Model-View-ViewModel (MVVM)**. We will only focus on Microsoft's implementation of MVC and its specifics. In particular, the version of MVC that ships with ASP.NET Core is version 6, because it builds on version 5 which was previously available for the .NET full framework, but both add and drop a couple of features. Because it now sits on the new .NET Core framework, it is fully based on **OWIN**, so there's no more `Global.asax.cs` file. More on this later on.

MVC, the way it is implemented in ASP.NET, focuses on:

- **URLs**: They are now more meaningful and **Search Engine Optimization (SEO)** friendly
- **HTTP verbs**: The verb now exactly states what the operation is supposed to do, like, GET for idempotent operations, POST for new contents, PUT for full content updates, PATCH for partial content updates, DELETE for removals, and more
- **HTTP status codes**: For returning operation result codes, which is more important in the case of Web APIs

For example, issuing a GET request to http://somehost/Product/120 is likely to return a view for a product with id 120 and a DELETE request for the same URL will probably delete this product and return either some HTTP status code or a nice view informing us of the fact. URLs and their binding to controllers and actions are configurable through routes, and it is likely that this URL will be handled by some controller called ProductController and some action method that is configured to handle GET or DELETE requests. Views cannot be extracted from the URL because they are determined inside the action method.

We will cover Microsoft's implementation of MVC in depth in the following chapters. Being a .NET Core thing, obviously all of its components are available as NuGet packages. Some of those you will likely find are:

Package	Purpose
Microsoft.AspNetCore.Antiforgery	Anti-forgery APIs
Microsoft.AspNetCore.Authentication	Authentication base classes
Microsoft.AspNetCore.Authentication.Cookies	Authentication through cookies
Microsoft.AspNetCore.Authorization	Authorization APIs
Microsoft.AspNetCore.Diagnostics	Diagnostics APIs
Microsoft.AspNetCore.Hosting	Hosting base classes
Microsoft.AspNetCore.Identity	Identity authentication
Microsoft.AspNetCore.Identity.EntityFrameworkCore	Identity with Entity Framework Core as the store

Microsoft.AspNetCore.Localization.Routing	Localization through routing
Microsoft.AspNetCore.Mvc	The core MVC features
Microsoft.AspNetCore.Mvc.Cors	Support for **Cross Origin Request Scripting (CORS)**
Microsoft.AspNetCore.Mvc.DataAnnotations	Validation through data annotations
Microsoft.AspNetCore.Mvc.Localization	Localization based APIs
Microsoft.AspNetCore.Mvc.TagHelpers	Tag helpers functionality
Microsoft.AspNetCore.Mvc.Versioning	Web API versioning
Microsoft.AspNetCore.ResponseCaching	Response caching
Microsoft.AspNetCore.Routing	Routing
Microsoft.AspNetCore.Server.IISIntegration	IIS integration
Microsoft.AspNetCore.Server.Kestrel	Kestrel server
Microsoft.AspNetCore.Server.WebListener (Microsoft.AspNetCore.Server.HttpSys in ASP.NET Core 2)	WebListener server (now called HTTP.sys). See https://docs.microsoft.com/en-us/aspnet/core/fundamentals/servers/httpsys.
Microsoft.AspNetCore.Session	Session functionality
Microsoft.AspNetCore.StaticFiles	Ability to serve static files

You may or may not need all these packages, but you should make yourself familiar with them.

In ASP.NET Core 2.0, there is the `Microsoft.AspNetCore.All` NuGet metapackage. This includes most of the individual packages you will need, so you can add just this one. Mind you, it targets `netcoreapp2.0`.

Getting one's context

You will probably remember the `HttpContext` class from ASP.NET. The current instance of this class would represent the current context of execution, which included both the request information and the response channel. It was ubiquitous, even though in Web Forms it was sometimes hidden, it was the way by which the web application communicated with the client.

Of course, ASP.NET Core also has an `HttpContext` class, but there is a big difference, there is no longer a `Current` static property that lets us get hold of the current context, instead, the process is a bit more convoluted. Anyway, all of the **infrastructure** classes--controllers, views, view components, tag helpers, and filters, allow easy access to the current context.

So, besides `Request` and `Response` properties, which are mostly similar to their pre-core counterparts, we also have:

- A `Features` collection, which exposes all of the features implemented by the current hosting server (Kestrel, WebListener/`HTTP.sys`, and more)
- A `RequestServices` property, which gives us access to the built-in dependency injection framework, more on it in the next chapters
- A `TraceIdentifier` property, which uniquely identifies a request, in ASP.NET Core 2.x; in earlier versions, we had to access it through a feature
- A `Connection` object, from where we can obtain relevant information about the client connection such as any client certificates, for example:
  - The `Authentication` object, giving easy access to security primitives such as sign in, sign out, deny, and more
  - The `Session` object, which is implemented by the `ISessionFeature` feature, and is exposed directly by the `HttpContext`

The context is a vital part of an ASP.NET Core application, as we will see.

The OWIN pipeline

Previous versions of ASP.NET had a very close relation with **Internet Information Services (IIS)**, Microsoft's flagship web server that ships with Windows. In fact, IIS was the only supported way to host ASP.NET.

Wanting to change this, Microsoft defined the **Open Web Interface for .NET (OWIN)** specification, which you can read about at http://owin.org. In a nutshell, it is a standard for decoupling server and application code, and for the execution pipeline for web requests. Because it is just a standard and knows nothing about the containing web server (if any), it can be used to extract away its features.

.NET Core borrowed heavily from the OWIN specification. There are no more Global.asax, web.config, or machine.config configuration files, modules or handlers. What we have is:

- Some bootstrap code declares a class that contains a convention-defined method (Startup will be used, if no class is declared)
- This conventional method, which should be called Configure, receives as its sole parameter a pointer to an IApplicationBuilder instance
- You then start adding middleware to the IApplicationBuilder; this middleware is what will handle your web requests

A simple example is in order. First, the bootstrap class, which should probably be named Program:

```
public class Program
{
  public static void Main()
  {
    var host = new WebHostBuilder()
        .UseKestrel()
        .UseStartup<Startup>()
        .Build();
        host.Run();
  }
}
```

Things can get more complicated, but don't worry too much about it now. Later on, I will explain what this all means. For the time being, it's enough to know that we are leveraging a WebHostBuilder to host Kestrel, and passing a conventional class called Startup. This Startup class goes like this:

```
public class Startup
```

```
{
  public void Configure(IApplicationBuilder app)
  {
    app.Run(async (context) =>
    {
      await context.Response.WriteAsync("Hello, OWIN World!");
    }
  }
}
```

There are a couple of things here that deserve an explanation. First, you will notice that the `Startup` class does not implement any interface or inherit from some explicit base class. This is because the `Configure` method does not have a predefined signature, other than its name, and taking as its first parameter an `IApplicationBuilder`. For example, the following is also allowed:

```
public void Configure(IApplicationBuilder app,
  IHostingEnvironment env) { /* ... */ }
```

This version even gives you more than what you asked for. But I digress.

The `IApplicationBuilder` interface defines a `Run` method. This method takes a `RequestDelegate` parameter, which is a delegate definition that accepts an `HttpContext` (remember this one?) as its sole parameter, and returns a `Task`. In my example, we made it asynchronous by adding `async` and `await` keywords to it, but it needs not be so. All you have to care about is to extract whatever you want from the `HttpContext` and write whatever you want to it, this is your web pipeline. It wraps both the HTTP request and response objects and we call it `middleware`.

The `Run` method is a full-blown pipeline on its own, but we can plug other steps (middleware) to the pipeline, by using the (pun intended) `Use` method:

```
app.Use(async (context, next) =>
{
  await context.Response.WriteAsync("Hello from a middleware!");
  await next.Invoke();
}
```

This way, we can add multiple steps, and they all will be executed in the order they were defined:

```
app.Use(async (context, next) =>
{
  await context.Response.WriteAsync("step 1!");
  await next.Invoke();
}
```

```
app.Use(async (context, next) =>
{
  await context.Response.WriteAsync("step 2");
  await next.Invoke();
}
```

Just keep in mind that the order does matter here!

The `Use` method takes as its parameters an `HttpContext` instance and returns a `Func<Task>`, which is normally a call to the next handler, so that the pipeline proceeds.

We could extract the lambda to its own method, like this:

```
async Task Process(HttpContext context, Func<Task> next)
{
  await context.Response.WriteAsync("Step 1");
  await next.Invoke();
}

app.Use(Process);
```

It is even possible to extract the middleware to its own class, and apply it using the generic `UseMiddleware` method:

```
public class Middleware
{
  private readonly RequestDelegate _next;
  public Middleware(RequestDelegate next)
  {
    this._next = next;
  }
  public async Task Invoke(HttpContext context)
  {
    await context.Response.WriteAsync("This is a middleware class!");
    await this._next.Invoke(context);
  }
}

app.UseMiddleware<Middleware>();
```

In this case, the constructor needs to take as its first parameter a pointer to the next middleware in the pipeline, as a `RequestDelegate` instance.

I think you got the picture, OWIN defines a pipeline to which you can add handlers which are then called in sequence. The difference between `Run` and `Use` is that the former ends the pipeline, that is, it won't call anything after itself.

The following diagram (from Microsoft) clearly shows this:

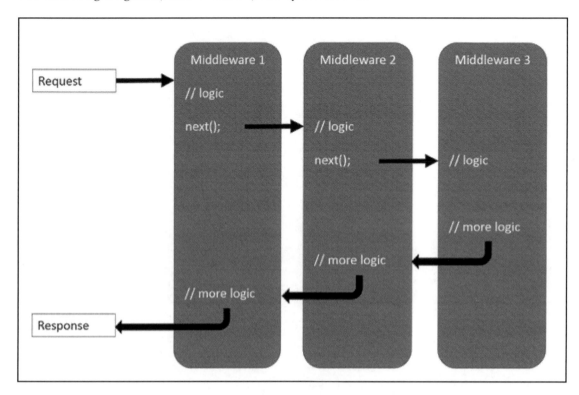

The first middleware, in a way, wraps all of the next ones. For example, imagine you want to add exception handling to all the steps in the pipeline; you could do something like this:

```
app.Use(async (context, next) =>
{
  try
  {
    await context.Response.WriteAsync("inside an exception handler");
    await next.Invoke();
  }
  catch (Exception ex)
  {
    //do something with the exception
  }
  await context.Response.WriteAsync("outside an exception handler");
}
```

The call to `next.Invoke()` is wrapped in a `try...catch` block, so any exception that may be thrown by another middleware in the pipeline, as long as it was added after this one, will be caught.

You can read more about Microsoft's implementation of OWIN at: `https://docs.microsoft.com/en-us/aspnet/core/fundamentals/owin`.

Why is OWIN important? Well, because ASP.NET Core (and its MVC implementation) are built on it. We will see later that in order to have an MVC application we need to add the MVC middleware to the OWIN pipeline in the `Startup` class' `Configure` method, normally like this:

```
app.UseMvc();
```

Hosting

You probably noticed, when we talked about OWIN, that I mentioned that the sample app was hosted in **Kestrel**. Kestrel is the name of a platform-independent web server fully written in .NET Core (of course, using the native libraries of your operating system). You need to host your web application somewhere, and .NET Core offers the following options:

- **Kestrel**: Platform independent, your host of choice in case you want to have your code run on any platform
- **WebListener**: A Windows-only host, offering significant performance advantages over Kestrel, but also the disadvantage that it needs Windows; starting with ASP.NET Core 2, it is now called `HTTP.sys`
- **IIS**: As in the past, you can continue to host your web app in IIS, on Windows, benefiting from the *old* pipeline and configuration tools

A server in this context is merely an implementation of `IServer`, an interface defined in the `Microsoft.AspNetCore.Hosting` NuGet package. This defines the base contract that a server offers, which can be described as:

- A `Start` method, where all the fun begins, it is responsible for creating the `HttpContext`, setting up the `Request` and `Response` properties, and calling the conventional `Configure` method.
- A collection of `Features` that are supported by the implementation. There are dozens of features, but, at the very least, a server needs to support `IHttpRequestFeature` and `IHttpResponseFeature`.

Each of these server implementations are provided in NuGet packages:

Server	Package
Kestrel	`Microsoft.AspNetCore.Server.Kestrel`
WebListener	`Microsoft.AspNetCore.Server.WebListener` (`Microsoft.AspNetCore.Server.HttpSys` from ASP.NET Core 2)
IIS	`Microsoft.AspNetCore.Server.IISIntegration`

IIS cannot be used on its own. IIS is, of course, a Windows native application and is therefore not available through NuGet, but the `Microsoft.AspNetCore.Server.IISIntegration` package includes the IIS ASP.NET Core Module, which needs to be installed in IIS so that it can run ASP.NET Core apps with Kestrel (WebListener is not compatible with IIS). There are, of course, other server implementations by third-party providers (take, as an example, Nowin, available at `https:/ /github.com/Bobris/Nowin`).

So, what is there to know about these, and how can we select one of these hosting servers?

Kestrel

Kestrel is the *default*, multi-platform, web server. It offers acceptable performance, but lacks lots of features that are expected in real-life:

- No buffering
- No support for Windows authentication (as time passes, this is less of a problem)
- No WebSockets
- No HTTP/2
- No direct file transmission
- No strong security protection (large requests, and more)

From this, it should be clear that Kestrel is not meant to be used in production, unless sitting behind a reverse proxy (such as Nginx, Apache, or IIS). It is configured at bootstrap through the `UseKestrel` extension method and, if you need to configure its options, you will need to supply an additional lambda:

```
var host = new WebHostBuilder()
    .UseKestrel(opt =>
    {
        opt.ThreadCount = 10;
```

```
    })
    //rest goes here...
```

Read more about it at: https://docs.microsoft.com/en-us/aspnet/core/fundamentals/servers/kestrel.

WebLisTener

This one is for Windows only, as it is a wrapper around HTTP.sys, the Windows subsystem that handles web requests. It offers by far the best performance, supports HTTP/2, WebSockets, Windows Authentication, direct file transmission, port sharing, response caching and mostly anything that you can think of. The disadvantage, of course, is that it requires Windows 7 or Windows Server 2008 R2 and later. At bootstrap, use the UseWebListener extension method to add it to the host builder, possibly with a configuration parameter:

```
.UseWebListener(opt =>
    {
        opt.ListenerSettings.Authentication.AllowAnonymous = false;
    })
```

As of ASP.NET Core 2.0, WebListener is now called HTTP.sys.

IIS

We already know about IIS. IIS can be used as a reverse proxy for Kestrel, or to add features that the host does not support, such as Windows Authentication. For that, we should include support for IIS, by calling UseIISIntegration. Here, the configuration should be done through the Web.config file, which, in this case, is a requirement (Visual Studio will add this file to the root of your project).

Nginx

Nginx is a UNIX and Linux reverse proxy that can be used with ASP.NET Core. We will talk a bit more about Nginx in Chapter 16, *Deployment*.

Apache

Apache, the popular UNIX and Linux server (which actually also runs in Windows) can also act as a reverse proxy. More info in `Chapter 16`, *Deployment*.

Configuration

As we've seen, usually, the server is chosen using a `WebHostBuilder` instance. As a minimum, you need to tell it which server to use and what is the root directory:

```
var host = new WebHostBuilder()
    .UseKestrel()
    .UseContentRoot(Directory.GetCurrentDirectory())
    .UseIISIntegration()
    .UseStartup<Startup>()
    .Build();
```

Features

Different servers will offer different features. Here are some of the features that are included out of the box:

Interface	Feature
IHttpRequestFeature	Access to the request object and collections (form, headers, cookies, query string, and more)
IHttpResponseFeature	Access to the response object and collections (headers, cookies, content, and more)
IHttpAuthenticationFeature	Authentication based on claims and principals
IHttpUpgradeFeature	Support for HTTP Upgrades (see `https://tools.ietf.org/html/rfc2616.html#section-14.42`)
IHttpBufferingFeature	Response buffering
IHttpConnectionFeature	Properties for local host calls
IHttpRequestLifetimeFeature	Detecting if a client has disconnected, and the ability to actually disconnect it
IHttpSendFileFeature	The ability to directly send a file as a response
IHttpWebSocketFeature	WebSockets

IHttpRequestIdentifierFeature	Uniquely identifying requests
ISessionFeature	Supplies the session functionality. Needs to be added by the session middleware, not available otherwise
ITlsConnectionFeature	Retrieving client certificates
ITlsTokenBindingFeature	Working with TLS tokens

All of these features can be obtained through the IServer's `Features` property or from the `HttpContext`, by requesting their interface. This is one way to obtain access to the functionality that the feature supplies, but for some features, there are workarounds. For example, the ASP.NET `Session` object can be obtained directly from the `HttpContext`. Features are essentially how the `HttpContext` class gets the behavior it exposes; for example, request and response objects, sessions, and more.

Launch configuration

Visual Studio can have more than one configuration per project, meaning, it can launch your project in several ways and there's a toolbar button that shows just this:

In particular, we can choose whether to launch our web application using IIS (or IIS Express) as the host, or use whatever (Kestrel or WebListener) is specified in the code. The launch settings are stored in the `PropertieslaunchSettings.json` file, which gets created by default by Visual Studio. This file has the following (or similar) contents:

```
{
  "iisSettings": {
    "windowsAuthentication": true,
    "anonymousAuthentication": true,
    "iisExpress": {
      "applicationUrl": "http://localhost:24896/", "sslPort": 0
    }
```

```
    },
    "profiles": {
      "IIS Express": {
        "commandName": "IISExpress",
        "launchBrowser": true,
        "environmentVariables": {
          "ASPNETCORE_ENVIRONMENT": "Development"
        }
      },
      "Web": {
        "commandName": "Project",
        "launchBrowser": true,
        "launchUrl": "http://localhost:5000",
        "environmentVariables": {
          "ASPNETCORE_ENVIRONMENT": "Development"
        }
      }
    }
  }
}
```

Here we can see the default ports plus the environment name to be used (to be discussed shortly). This file does not need to be changed by hand (although it can), you can see it in visual form through project properties:

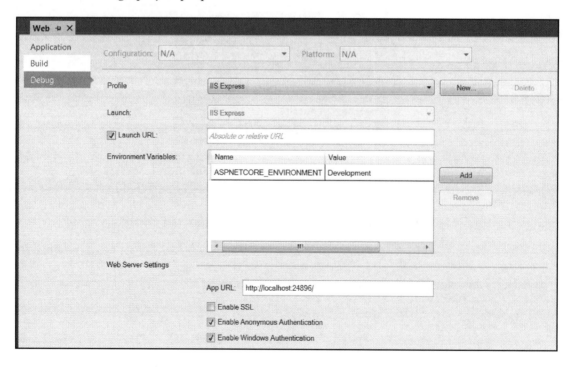

Inversion of control and dependency injection

Inversion of Control (IoC) and **dependency injection (DI)** are two related but different patterns. The first tells us that we should not depend on actual, concrete, classes, but instead on abstract base classes or interfaces that specify the functionality we're interested in. Depending on its registrations, the IoC framework will return a concrete class that matches our desired interface or abstract base class. DI on the other hand, is the process by which when a concrete class is built, the dependencies it needs are then passed to its constructor (constructor injection, although there are other options). These two patterns go very well together, and throughout the book, I will use the terms IoC or DI container/framework to mean the same thing.

.NET always had support for a limited form of inversion of control, Windows Forms designers used it at design time to get access to the current designer's services for example, and Windows Workflow Foundation also used it to get registered extensions at runtime. But in .NET Core, Microsoft centralized it and made it a first-class citizen of the ecosystem. Now virtually everything is dependent on the inversion of control and dependency injection framework. It is made available in the `Microsoft.Extensions.DependencyInjection` NuGet package.

An inversion of control and dependency injection container allow services (classes) to be registered and accessed by their abstract base class or an interface they implement. Application code does not need to care about what is the actual class that implements the contract, this makes it very easy to switch the actual dependencies in the configuration or at runtime. Other than that, it also injects dependencies into the actual classes that it is building. Say, for example, you have this scenario:

```
public interface IMyService
{
  void MyOperation();
}
public interface IMyOtherService
{
  void MyOtherOperation();
}
public class MyService : IMyService
{
  private readonly IMyOtherService _other;
  public MyService(IMyOtherService other)
  {
    this._other = other;
  }
```

```
    public void Operation()
    {
      //do something
    }
}
```

If you register a MyService class to the dependency injection container, when it builds an actual instance it knows that it will also need to build an instance of IMyOtherService to pass to the MyService constructor, and this cascades for every dependency in the actual IMyOtherService implementation.

The WebHostBuilder, when it is building the host, also initializes an IServiceCollection instance, which is then passed to the Startup class' ConfigureServices method. This is a conventional method that should be used for our own registrations.

Now, a service registration has three components:

- The type under which it will be registered (the key of the registration)
- The lifetime of it
- The actual instance factory

A lifetime can be one of:

- Scoped: A new instance of the service will be created per each web request (or scope), and the same instance will always be returned for the same request (scope) whenever we ask the DI framework for it
- Singleton: The instance to be created will be kept in memory, and it will always be returned
- Transient: A new instance will be created whenever it is requested

The instance factory can be:

- An actual instance; of course, this cannot be used with the Transient or Scoped lifetimes
- A concrete Type, which will then be instantiated as needed
- A Func<IServiceProvider, object> delegate, that knows how to create instances of the concrete type, after receiving a reference to the dependency injection container

There are several extension methods that allow us to do registrations; all of the following are identical:

```
services.AddScoped<IMyService, MyService>();
services.AddScoped<IMyService>(sp => new MyService((IMyOtherService)
  sp.GetService(typeof(IMyOtherService))));
services.AddScoped(typeof(IMyService), typeof(MyService));
services.Add(new ServiceDescriptor(typeof(IMyService),
  typeof(MyService), ServiceLifetime.Scoped));
```

The same goes for all other lifetimes.

The dependency injection framework has the concept of scopes, to which scoped registrations are bound. We can create new scopes and have our services associated with them. There is the IServiceScopeFactory interface which is automatically registered and it allows us to do things like this:

```
var serviceProvider = services.BuildServiceProvider();
var factory = serviceProvider.GetService<IServiceScopeFactory>();

using (var scope = factory.CreateScope())
{
   var svc = scope.ServiceProvider.GetService<IMyService>();
}
```

Any scope-bound service returned from the service provider inside the CreateScope inner scope is destroyed with the scope. Interestingly, if any scope-registered service implements IDisposable, its Dispose method will be called at the end of the scope.

Now, you need to keep in mind a few things:

- The same Type can only be registered once, it is not possible to have multiple registrations, even for different lifetimes
- You cannot register a Singleton service that takes a dependency that is Scoped, as it wouldn't make sense, by definition Scoped changes every time
- You cannot pass an instance to a Scoped or Transient registration
- You can only resolve, from the factory delegate, services that have themselves been registered; the factory delegate, however, will only be called after all services have been registered, so you do not need to worry about the registration order

- You can have several implementations registered for the same `Type`, and they will be returned in a call to `GetServices<T>`
- The resolution will return `null` if no service by the given `Type` is registered
- Only the last registered implementation for a given `Type` is returned by `GetService/GetService<T>`

Several .NET Core APIs supply extension methods that do their registrations; for example, `AddMvc` or `AddSession`.

After all the registrations are done, eventually, the actual dependency framework will be built from the `IServiceCollection` instance. It's public interface is none other than the *venerable* `IServiceProvider`, which has been around since .NET 1.0. It exposes a single method, `GetService`, which takes as its single parameter a `Type` to resolve. There are however, available in the `Microsoft.Extensions.DependencyInjection` package and namespace, a few useful generic extension methods:

- `GetService<T>()`: Returns an instance of the service type already cast appropriately, if one is registered, or `null` otherwise
- `GetRequiredService<T>()`: Tries to retrieve a registration for the given service type, and throws an exception if none is found
- `GetServices<T>()`: Returns all of the services whose registration key matches (is identical, implements, is a subclass) of the given service key

You can register multiple services for the same `Type`, but only the last being registered will be retrievable using `GetService()`. Interestingly, all of them will be returned using `GetServices()`!

> Keep in mind that the latest registration for a `Type` overrides any previous one, meaning you will get the latest item when you do a `GetService`, but all of the registrations are returnable by `GetServices`.

Although the most common usage will probably be constructor injection, where the dependency injection framework creates a concrete type passing it all of its dependencies in the constructor, it is also possible to request at any given time an instance of the service we want, by a reference to a `IServiceProvider`, like the one available in the context:

```
var urlFactory =
    HttpContext.RequestServices.GetService<IUrlHelperFactory>();
```

Finally, I need to talk about something else. People have been using third-party dependency injection and inversion of control frameworks for ages. .NET Core, being as flexible as it is, certainly allows us to use our own, which may offer additional features to what the built in one provides. All it takes is that our DI provider of choice also exposes an `IServiceProvider` implementation; if it does, we just need to return it from the `ConfigureServices` method:

```
public IServiceProvider ConfigureServices(IServiceCollection services)
{
  //AutoFac
  var builder = new ContainerBuilder();
  //add registrations from services
  builder.Populate(services);
  return new AutofacServiceProvider(builder.Build());
}
```

All in all, it's very good to see inversion of control and dependency injection. This is just the basics, we will talk about dependency injection in pretty much all of the book.

Knowing the environments

.NET Core has the notion of environment. An environment is basically a runtime setting in the form of an environment variable called **ASPNETCORE_ENVIRONMENT**. This variable can take one of the following values (case-sensitive):

- **Development**: A development environment, which probably does not need much explaining
- **Staging**: A pre-production environment used for testing
- **Production**: The environment (or as similar as possible) where the application will live once it is released

To be correct, you can pass any value, but these have particular significance to .NET Core. There are several ways by which you can access the current environment, but you're most likely to use one of the following methods, extensions methods and properties of the `IHostingEnvironment` interface:

- `IsDevelopment()`
- `IsProduction()`
- `IsStaging()`
- `IsEnvironment("SomeEnvironment")`
- `EnvironmentName`

The `IsDevelopment`, `IsProduction`, and `IsStaging` extension methods are just convenience methods using the `IsEnvironment` method. Based on the actual environment you can make decisions on the code, such as pick a different connection string, web service URL, and so on. It is important to point out that this has nothing to do with **Debug** or **Release** compiler configurations.

You normally get an instance of `IHostingEnvironment` from the `Configure` method:

```
public void Configure(IApplicationBuilder app,
    IHostingEnvironment env) { /* ... */ }
```

But also from the constructor of the `Startup` class:

```
public Startup(IHostingEnvironment env) { /* ... */ }
```

Or even from the dependency injection framework, which is available from the `HttpContext` class, among other places:

```
var env =
    HttpContext.RequestServices.GetService<IHostingEnvironment>();
```

A final note, service configuration plays well with environments. Instead of a single `ConfigureServices` method, we can have multiple methods, named `ConfigureDevelopmentServices`, `ConfigureStagingServices`, and `ConfigureProductionServices`. A nice feature that can help us better organize our code!

A sample project

Throughout the book, I will be providing examples based upon a fictitious online shopping application: Book Store. This application will have the following basic requirements:

- It shall have a public as well as a private section
- Access to the private section shall be granted after successful authentication
- It shall be possible to search the books in the database by simple criteria
- A book shall have a picture together with its information and the number of ratings
- It shall be possible for authenticated users to rate books
- The application shall produce usage logs
- It shall be translatable to different languages

The app will consist of ASP.NET Core code but also CSS, JavaScript, JSON, images and other files.

Structure

Our solution will be split by various projects, for better encapsulating our conceptual application layers:

- `Web`: The core of the web app
- `DomainModel`: The Entity Framework Core domain model
- `WebComponents`: Reusable components
- `UnitTests`: Unit tests

The following diagram describes the relationship between the different projects in the sample project:

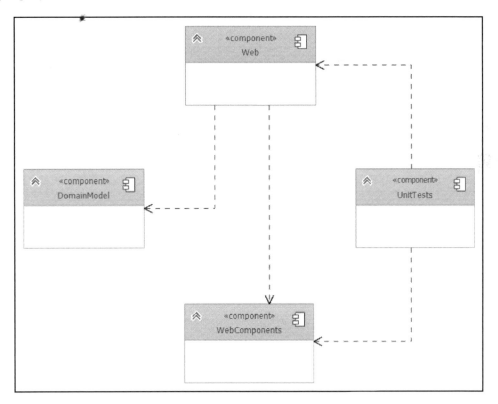

The `Web` project shall contain the bootstrap code, controllers, views and static files.

The `DomainModel` and `WebComponents` projects can probably be shared by other projects, even some that may not be web applications but use the same domain model.

A sample domain model could be:

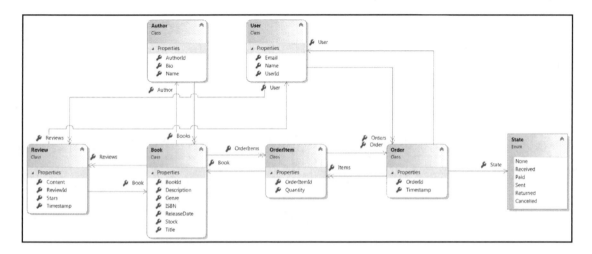

This will serve as the basis for the sample app we will be building. Here we have:

- The `Book` is the main entity, it has the basic properties you'd expect in a book
- A `Book` can have one or more `Authors`, possibly some `Reviews` and a few other properties
- An `Order` will have a creation timestamp, a current state, and contain at least one `OrderItem`, but possibly more, and is associated with a `User` (the user will be managed by ASP.NET Identity, of which we'll see more in a few chapters)
- A `Review` awards stars to a book and needs to be filed by a registered `User`

This should be more than enough for our purpose, which is to explain ASP.NET Core with a simple example.

Summary

In this first chapter, we went through some of the biggest changes in ASP.NET Core and .NET Core. I introduced you to some of the key concepts around .NET Core:

- The NuGet distribution model
- The OWIN pipeline
- The hosting model
- Environments
- The improved context
- The built-in dependency framework

Also, we had a brief introduction to the sample project that we will be developing throughout the book. In the course of the next chapters, we will dive more and more into it.

2
Configuration

Previous versions of .NET had a relatively simple configuration system, where all settings went into XML files with the `.config` extension. There was a basic schema that could handle both system settings and untyped key-value pairs. There was also some degree of inheritance, as some of the settings could be defined machine-wide, and then overridden per application, and even in virtual applications underneath an IIS application. It was possible to define custom sections with typed settings and complex structures, by writing and registering .NET classes.

However, as convenient as this would seem, it turns out it had its limitations, namely:

- Only XML files were supported; it was not possible to have other configuration sources out of the box
- It was difficult to have different configuration files/configuration sections per environment (staging, QA, production, and more)
- It was not possible to receive notifications when the configuration changed
- It was tricky to save changes

Moreover, as dependency injection was not part of the core .NET infrastructure, there was no way to have configuration values injected into its our services automatically.

Configuration in .NET Core

Realizing this, Microsoft made configuration a first-order concept in .NET Core and did so in quite a flexible, extensible way. It all starts with a builder instance; we add providers to it and when we're happy we just ask it to build a configuration object, which will hold all the values loaded from each provider in memory.

This configuration object will be capable of returning configuration settings from any of the added providers transparently, which means that regardless of the source, we use the same syntax for querying configuration options. It will hold an in-memory representation of all the values loaded from all registered providers, and will allow you to change them, or add new entries.

The base class model for the configuration API in .NET Core goes like this:

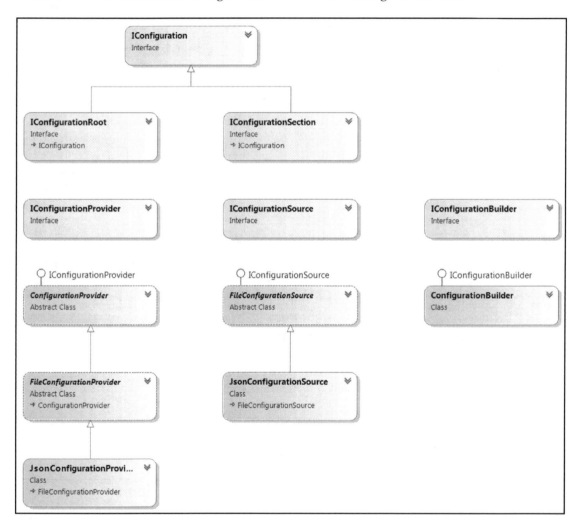

So the provider mechanism is split into two base interfaces and their implementations:

- `IConfigurationSource`: is responsible for creating a concrete instance of an `IConfigurationProvider`; each of the available providers (coming next) implement this interface
- `IConfigurationProvider`: specifies the contract for actually retrieving values, reloading, and more; the root class that implements this is `ConfigurationProvider`, and there's also particular implementation that serves as the root for all file-based providers, `FileConfigurationProvider`

`ConfigurationBuilder` itself is just a specific implementation of the `IConfigurationBuilder` interface and there are no other implementations. Its contract specifies how we can add providers and build the configuration from them:

```
var builder = new ConfigurationBuilder()
    .Add(source1)
    .Add(source2);

var cfg = builder.Build();
```

As for the configuration itself, there are three base interfaces:

- `IConfiguration`: This specifies the methods for retrieving and setting configuration values, reloading, monitoring changes, and more
- `IConfigurationRoot`: This adds a method for reloading the configuration to `IConfiguration`
- `IConfigurationSection`: This is a configuration section, meaning that it can be located somewhere beneath the configuration root in a location identified by a path (the keys of all of the parent sections up to and including its own key) and a key that uniquely identifies that section in its parent

We will shortly see the ways by which we can use the configuration values, but for now it is worth mentioning that we can retrieve and set individual settings through the overloaded `[]` operator in `IConfiguration`:

```
cfg["key"] = "value";
string value = cfg["key"];
```

This takes a string as the `key` and returns a string as the `value`, and in the next sections we will see how we can circumvent this limitation. If no entry for the given key exists, it returns `null`.

All keys are case-insensitive. A path is the dot (.) combined set of keys and sub-keys that can be used to get to a specific value.

For the record, the core configuration API is implemented in the `Microsoft.Extensions.Configuration` and `Microsoft.Extensions.Configuration.Binder` Nuget packages, which are automatically included by other packages, like those of the specific providers. Let us now have a look at the available providers.

ASP.NET Core 2.x automatically registers the `IConfiguration` instance in the dependency injection framework; for previous versions, you need to do this manually.

Providers

The available Microsoft configuration providers (and their NuGet packages) are:

- JSON files: `Microsoft.Extensions.Configuration.Json`
- XML files: `Microsoft.Extensions.Configuration.Xml`
- INI files: `Microsoft.Extensions.Configuration.Ini`
- User secrets: `Microsoft.Extensions.Configuration.UserSecrets`
- Azure Key Vault: `Microsoft.Extensions.Configuration.AzureKeyVault`
- Environment variables: `Microsoft.Extensions.Configuration.EnvironmentVariables`
- Command line: `Microsoft.Extensions.Configuration.CommandLine`
- Memory: `Microsoft.Extensions.Configuration`
- Docker secrets: `Microsoft.Extensions.Configuration.DockerSecrets`

Some of these are based upon the `FileConfigurationProvider` class: JSON, XML and INI.

When you reference these packages, you automatically make their extensions available. So for example, if you want to add the JSON provider you have two options as follows:

You can either add a `JsonConfigurationSource` directly:

```
var jsonSource = new JsonConfigurationSource { Path = "filename.json" };
builder.Add(jsonSource);
```

Or use the `AddJsonFile` extension method:

```
builder.AddJsonFile("filename.json");
```

Most likely, the extension methods are what you need. As I said you can have any number of providers at the same time, for example:

```
builder
    .AddJsonFile("appsettings.json")
    .AddEnvironmentVariables()
    .AddXmlFile("web.config");
```

You just need to keep in mind that if two providers return the same configuration setting, the order by which they were added matters; the result you get will come from the last provider added as it will override the previous ones. So for example, imagine you are adding two JSON configuration files, one that is common across all environments (development, staging, and production) and the other for a specific environment; in this case you would likely have the following:

```
builder
    .AddJsonFile("appsettings.json")
    .AddJsonFile($"appsettings.{env.EnvironmentName}.json");
```

This is so the environment-specific configuration file takes precedence.

Each provider, of course, will feature different properties for setting up; all file-based providers will require, for instance, a file path, but that doesn't make sense when we're talking about environment variables.

File-based providers

Both JSON, XML, and INI configuration sources are based upon files, therefore, their classes inherit from the abstract base class `FileConfigurationSource`. This class offers the following configuration properties:

- `Path`: The actual, fully-qualified physical path where the file is to be found; this is a required setting
- `Optional`: A Boolean flag for specifying whether or not the absence of the file causes a runtime error (`false`) or not (`true`); the default is `false`
- `ReloadOnChange`: Here, you decide whether to automatically detect changes to the source file (`true`) or not (`false`); the default is `false`
- `ReloadDelay`: The delay, in milliseconds, before reloading the file in the event that a change was detected (`ReloadOnChange` set to `true`); the default is 250 milliseconds
- `OnLoadException`: A delegate to be called should an error occur while parsing the source file; this is empty by default
- `FileProvider`: The file provider that actually retrieves the file; the default is an instance of `PhysicalFileProvider`, set with the folder of the `Path` property

All of the extension methods allow you to supply values for each of these properties, except `OnLoadException`. You are also free to specify your own concrete implementation of an `IFileProvider`, which you should do if you have specific needs, such as getting files from inside a Zip file. `ConfigurationBuilder` has an extension method, `SetBasePath`, that sets a default `PhysicalFileProvider` pointing to a folder on your file system, so that you can pass relative file paths to the configuration source's `Path` property.

If you set `ReloadOnChange` to true, .NET Core will start an operating system-specific file that monitors watch on the source file; because these things come with a cost, try not to have many watches.

A typical example would be as follows:

```
builder
    .SetBasePath(@"C:\Configuration")
    .AddJsonFile(path: "appsettings.json", optional: false, reloadOnChange:
true)
    .AddJsonFile(path: $"appsettings.{env.EnvironmentName}.json", optional:
true,
        reloadOnChange: true);
```

This would result in the `appsettings.json` file being loaded from the
`C:\Configuration` folder (and throwing an exception if it is not present), and then
`appsettings.development.json` (this time, ignoring it if the file doesn't exist).
Whenever there's a change in either file, they are reloaded and the configuration is updated.

If however we wanted to add an error handler, we need to add the configuration source
manually, as follows:

```
var jsonSource = new JsonConfigurationSource { Path = "filename.json" };
jsonSource.OnLoadException = (x) =>
    {
        if (x.Exception is FileNotFoundException)
        {
            Console.Out.WriteLine("File not found");
            x.Ignore = true;
        }
    };
builder.Add(jsonSource);
```

This way we can prevent certain errors from crashing our application.

All file-based providers are added by an extension method with the name `AddxxxFile`,
where `xxx` is the actual type, `Json`, `Xml`, or `Ini`, and always taking the same parameters
(`path`, `optional`, and `reloadOnChange`).

JSON provider

We typically add a JSON configuration file using the `AddJsonFile` extension method. The
JSON provider will load a file containing JSON contents and make its structure available for
configuration using a dotted notation. A typical example could be:

```
{
  "ConnectionStrings": {
      "DefaultConnection": "Server=(localdb)mssqllocaldb;
      Database=aspnetcore; Trusted_Connection=True;
      MultipleActiveResultSets=true"
  }
}
```

Any valid JSON content will work. As of now, it is not possible to specify a schema.

An example for loading a configuration value would be:

```
var defaultConnection = cfg["ConnectionStrings:DefaultConnection"];
```

XML provider

XML is becoming less and less common, with JSON inversely becoming more and more popular, however there are still good reasons to use XML. So we add an XML file using the `AddXmlFile` extension method, and in what configuration is concerned, we need to wrap our XML contents in a `settings` node; the XML declaration is optional, as follows:

```
<settings Flag="2">
    <MySettings>
        <Option>10</Option>
    </MySettings>
</settings>
```

Again, as of now, it is not possible to specify a validating schema.

Two examples of this are as follows:

```
var flag = cfg["Flag"];
var option = cfg["MySettings:Option"];
```

INI provider

INI files are a thing of the past, but, for whatever reason, Microsoft is still supporting them. In case you're not familiar with its syntax, this is what it looks like:

```
[SectionA]
Option1=Value1
Option2=Value2

[SectionB]
Option1=Value3
```

You add INI files to the configuration through the `AddIniFile` extension method.

> One word of advice: both XML and JSON file formats support anything that INI files do, so unless you have a very specific requirement you're better off with either JSON or XML.

A single example is as follows:

```
var optionB2 = cfg["SectionB:Option1"];
```

Other providers

Besides file-based providers, there are other ways to store and retrieve configuration information. Here we list the current available options in .NET Core.

User secrets

.NET Core introduced **user secrets** as a means of storing sensitive information per user. The benefit of this is that it is kept in a secure manner, out of configuration files, and is not visible by other users. A user secrets store is identified (for a given user) by userSecretsId, which the Visual Studio template initializes as a mix of string and GUID, like aspnet-Web-f22b64ea-be5e-432d-abc6-0275a9c00377. Secrets in a store can be listed, added or removed through the dotnet executable:

```
dotnet user-secrets list                --lists all the values in the
store
dotnet user-secrets set "key" "value"   --set "key" to be "value"
dotnet user-secrets remove "key"        --remove entry for "key"
dotnet user-secrets clear               --remove all entries
```

You will need the Microsoft.Extensions.SecretManager.Tools package. The command dotnet user-secrets will only work when in the presence of a project file that specifies the userSecretsId store id. The AddUserSecrets extension method is what we use to add user secrets to the configuration, and it will either pick up this userSecretsId setting automatically, or you can provide your own at runtime as follows:

```
builder.AddUserSecrets(userSecretdId: "[User Secrets Id]");
```

Another option is to get the user secrets id from an assembly, which in that case needs to be decorated with the UserSecretsIdAttribute attribute as follows:

```
[assembly: UserSecretsId("aspnet-Web-f22b64ea-be5e-432d-abc6-0275a9c00377")
```

In this case, the way to load it is like this:

```
builder.AddUserSecrets<Startup>();
```

Be warned: if you have more than one assembly with the same user secret id (by mistake), the application will throw an exception when loading them.

Yet another way to specify user secrets (in ASP.NET Core 2.x) is through the `.csproj` file, by using a `UserSecretsId` element:

```
<PropertyGroup>
  <TargetFramework>netcoreapp2.0</TargetFramework>
  <UserSecretsId>9094c8e7-0000-0000-0000-c26798dc18d2</UserSecretsId>
</PropertyGroup>
```

Regardless of how you specify the user secrets ID, as with all the other providers, the way to load a value is:

```
var value = cfg["key"];
```

In case you are interested, you can read more about .NET Core user secrets here: https://docs.microsoft.com/en-us/aspnet/core/security/app-secrets.

Azure Key Vault

Azure Key Vault is an Azure service that you can leverage for enterprise-level secure key-value storage. The full description is outside the scope of this book, but you can read about it here: https://azure.microsoft.com/en-us/services/key-vault. It is sufficient to say that you add the Azure Key Vault provider through the `AddAzureKeyVault` extension method, as depicted in this line of code:

```
builder.AddAzureKeyVault(vault: "https://[Vault].vault.azure.net/",
    clientId: "[Client ID]", clientSecret: "[Client Secret]");
```

After this, all are added to the configuration object and you can retrieve them in the usual way.

Command line

Another very popular way to get configuration settings is the command line. Executables regularly expect information to be passed in the command line, so as to dictate what should be done or to control how it should happen.

The extension method to use is `AddCommandLine`, and it expects a required and an optional parameter as follows:

```
builder.AddCommandLine(args:
Environment.GetCommandLineArgs().Skip(1).ToArray());
```

The `args` parameter will typically come from `Environment.GetCommandLineArgs()`, and we take the first parameter out, as it is the entry assembly's name. If we are building our configuration object in `Program.Main`, we can use its `args` parameter too.

Now there are several ways to specify parameters:

```
Key1=Value1
--Key2=Value2
/Key3=Value3
--Key4 Value4
/Key5 Value5
```

An example would be:

```
dotnet run MyProject Key1=Value1 --Key2=Value2 /Key3=Value3 --Key4 Value4
/Key5 Value5
```

If the value has spaces in it, you need to wrap it in quotes ("). You can't use – (single dash), as it would be interpreted as a parameter to `dotnet` instead.

The optional parameter to `AddCommandLine`, `switchMappings`, is a dictionary that can be used to create new keys that will duplicate those from the command line, as follows:

```
var switchMappings = new Dictionary<string,
string>(StringComparer.OrdinalIgnoreCase)
    { { "--Key1", "AnotherKey" } };

builder.AddCommandLine(
    args: Environment.GetCommandLineArgs().Skip(1).ToArray(),
    switchMappings: switchMappings);
```

These keys can even have special characters in them, for example `--a:key` and `/some.key` are valid keys.

Again, use the same syntax for retrieving their values.

Environment variables

Environment variables exist in all operating systems and can also be regarded as a source of configuration. Many tools out there, like Docker, rely on environment variables for getting their operating context.

Adding environment variables to a .NET Core configuration is straightforward, you just need to call `AddEnvironmentVariables`. By default, this will bring all the existing environment variables into configuration, but we can also specify a prefix, and filter out all variables that do not start with it:

```
builder.AddEnvironmentVariables(prefix: "ASPNET_");
```

So this will add both `ASPNET_TargetHost` and `ASPNET_TargetPort`, but not `PATH` or `COMPUTERNAME`.

Memory

The memory provider is a convenient way of specifying values dynamically at runtime and for using dictionary objects. We add the provider with the `AddInMemoryCollection` extension method as follows:

```
var properties = new Dictionary<string, string> { { "key", "value" } };
builder.AddInMemoryCollection(properties);
```

The advantage of this approach is that it is easy to populate a dictionary with whatever values we want, particularly in unit tests.

Docker

The ability to have secrets coming from Docker-stored files is relatively new in .NET Core. Basically, it will try to load text files in a specific directory inside a Docker instance as the values where the key is the file name itself. This is an actual feature of Docker, of which you can read more here: https://docs.docker.com/engine/swarm/secrets.

The `AddDockerSecrets` extension method takes two optional parameters, the user secrets directory and whether or not this directory itself is optional, in other words just ignore it if it's not there:

```
builder.AddDockerSecrets(secretsPath: "/var/lib/secrets", optional:
true);
```

It is possible to specify these two parameters plus an ignore prefix and a delegate for filtering out files by their names, if we use the overload that takes a configuration object:

```
builder.AddDockerSecrets(opt =>
    {
        opt.SecretsDirectory = "/var/lib/secrets";
        opt.Optional = true;
        opt.IgnorePrefix = "ignore.";
        opt.IgnoreCondition = (filename) =>
    !filename.Contains($".{env.EnvironmentName}.");
    });
```

Here, we are filtering out both files starting with `ignore.` as well as those that do not contain the current environment name (for example, `.Development.`). Pretty cool!

Creating a custom provider

Although we have several options for storing configuration values, you may have your own specific needs. For example, if you are using Windows, you might want to store your configuration settings in the Registry. For that, you need a custom provider. Let's see how we can build one.

First, you need to add the `Microsoft.Win32.Registry` NuGet package to your project. Then, we start by implementing `IConfigurationSource`:

```
public sealed class RegistryConfigurationSource : IConfigurationSource
{
    public RegistryHive Hive { get; set; } = RegistryHive.CurrentUser;

    public IConfigurationProvider Build(IConfigurationBuilder builder)
    {
        return new RegistryConfigurationProvider(this);
    }
}
```

As you can see, the only configurable property is `Hive`, by which you can specify a specific Registry hive, with `CurrentUser` (HKEY_CURRENT_USER) being the default.

Next, we need an `IConfigurationProvider` implementation. Let's inherit from the `ConfigurationProvider` class, as this takes care of some of the basic implementations, like reloading (which we do not support as we go directly to the source):

```
public sealed class RegistryConfigurationProvider : ConfigurationProvider
{
    private readonly RegistryConfigurationSource _configurationSource;

    public RegistryConfigurationProvider(RegistryConfigurationSource
configurationSource)
    {
        _configurationSource = configurationSource;
    }

    private RegistryKey GetRegistryKey(string key)
    {
        RegistryKey regKey;
        switch (_configurationSource.Hive)
        {
          case RegistryHive.ClassesRoot:
            regKey = Registry.ClassesRoot;
            break;

          case RegistryHive.CurrentConfig:
            regKey = Registry.CurrentConfig;
            break;

          case RegistryHive.CurrentUser:
            regKey = Registry.CurrentUser;
            break;

          case RegistryHive.LocalMachine:
            regKey = Registry.LocalMachine;
            break;

          case RegistryHive.PerformanceData:
            regKey = Registry.PerformanceData;
            break;

          case RegistryHive.Users:
            regKey = Registry.Users;
            break;

          default:
            throw new InvalidOperationException($"Supplied hive
              {_configurationSource.Hive} is invalid.");
        }
```

```
            var parts = key.Split('');
            var subKey = string.Join("", parts.Where(
               (x, i) => i < parts.Length - 1));

            return regKey.OpenSubKey(subKey);
        }

    public override bool TryGet(string key, out string value)
    {
        var regKey = this.GetRegistryKey(key);
        var parts = key.Split('');
        var name = parts.Last();
        var regValue = regKey.GetValue(name);

        value = regValue?.ToString();

        return regValue != null;
    }

    public override void Set(string key, string value)
    {
        var regKey = this.GetRegistryKey(key);
        var parts = key.Split('');
        var name = parts.Last();

        regKey.SetValue(name, value);
    }
}
```

Finally, let's add a friendly extension method to make registration simpler:

```
public static class RegistryConfigurationExtensions
{
    public static IConfigurationBuilder AddRegistry(
        this IConfigurationBuilder builder,
        RegistryHive hive = RegistryHive.CurrentUser)
    {
        return builder.Add(new RegistryConfigurationSource { Hive = hive
});
    }
}
```

Now you can use this provider as follows:

```
builder
    .AddJsonFile("appsettings.json")
    .AddRegistry(RegistryHive.LocalMachine);
```

Nice and easy, don't you think?

Using configuration values

So we've now seen how to set up configuration providers, but how exactly can we use these configuration values?

Getting and setting values explicitly

Remember that the .NET Configuration allows you to set both reading and writing, both using the [] notation:

```
var value = cfg["key"];
cfg["another.key"] = "another value";
```

Of course, setting a value in the configuration object does not mean that it will get persisted into any provider, the configuration is kept in memory only.

It is also possible to try to have the value converted to some specific type, as follows:

```
cfg["count"] = "0";
var count = cfg.GetValue<int>("count");
```

 Do not forget that the value that you want to convert needs to be convertible from a string; in particular, it needs to have a TypeConverter defined for that purpose, which all .NET Core primitive types do. The conversion will take place using the current culture.

Configuration sections

It is also possible to use **configuration sections**. A configuration section is specified through a colon (:), as in section:subsection. An infinite nesting of sections can be specified. But, I hear you ask, what is a configuration section, and how do we define one? Well that depends on the configuration source you're using. In the case of JSON, a configuration section will basically map to a complex property. For example:

```
{
    "section-1": {
        "section-2": {
            "section-3": {
                "a-key": "value"
            }
        }
    }
}
```

Not all providers are capable of handling configuration sections or handle them in the same way. In XML, each section corresponds to a node, for INI files there is a direct mapping and for the Azure Key Vault, user secrets, memory (dictionaries), and environment variables providers, sections are specified as keys separated by colons (for example, ASPNET:Variable, MyApp:Variable, Data:Blog:ConnectionString and more). The example Registry provider I showed earlier does not, for example, support them.

We have a couple of sections here:

- The root section
- section-1
- section-2
- section-3

So, if we wanted to access value for key a-key, we would do so using the following syntax:

```
var aKey = cfg["section-1:section-2:section-3:a-key"];
```

Alternatively, we could ask for the `section-3` section and get the `a-key` value directly from it:

```
var section3 = cfg.GetSection("section-1:section-2:section-3");
var aKey = section3["a-key"];
var key = section3.Key;    //section-3
var path = section3.Path;  //section-1:section-2:section-3
```

A section will contain the path from where it was obtained; this is defined in the `IConfigurationSection` interface, which inherits from `IConfiguration`, thus making all of its extension methods available too.

By the way, you can ask for any configuration section and a value will always be returned, but this doesn't mean that it exists. You can use the `Exists` extension method to check for that possibility:

```
var fairyLandSection = cfg.GetSection("fairy:land");
var exists = fairyLandSection.Exists();   //false
```

A configuration section may have children and we can list them using `GetChildren`:

```
var section1 = cfg.GetSection("section-1");
var subSections = section1.GetChildren();   //section-2
```

.NET Core includes a shorthand for a typical configuration section, connection strings. This is the `GetConnectionString` extension method, and it basically looks for a connection string named `ConnectionStrings` and returns a named value from it. You can use the JSON schema introduced when we discussed the **JSON provider** as a reference:

```
var blogConnectionString = cfg.GetConnectionString("DefaultConnection");
```

Getting all values

It may not be that useful, but it is possible to get a list of all configuration values (together with their keys) present in a configuration object. We do this using the `AsEnumerable` extension method:

```
var keysAndValues = cfg.AsEnumerable().ToDictionary(kv => kv.Key, kv =>
kv.Value);
```

There's also a `makePathsRelative` parameter, which by default is `false`, and can be used in a configuration section to strip out the section's key from the returned entries' keys. Say, for example that you are working on section `section-3`, if you call `AsEnumerable` with `makePathsRelative` set to `true`, then the entry for `a-key` will appear as `a-key` instead of `section-1:section-2:section-3:a-key`.

Binding to classes

Another interesting option is to bind the current configuration to a class. The binding process will pick up any sections and their properties present in the configuration and try to map them to a .NET class. Let's say we have a JSON configuration of:

```
{
    "Logging": {
        "IncludeScopes": false,
        "LogLevel": {
          "Default": "Debug",
          "System": "Information",
          "Microsoft": "Information"
        }
    }
}
```

And a class as follows:

```
public class LoggingSettings
{
    public bool IncludeScopes { get; set; }
    public LogLevelSettings LogLevel { get; set; }
}
public class LogLevelSettings
{
    public LogLevel Default { get; set; }
    public LogLevel System { get; set; }
    public LogLevel Microsoft { get; set; }
}
```

> `LogLevel` comes from the `Microsoft.Extensions.Logging` namespace.

You can bind the two together like this:

```
var settings = new LoggingSettings {
    LogLevel = new LogLevelSettings() };
cfg.GetSection("Logging").Bind(settings);
```

The values of `LoggingSettings` will be automatically populated from the current configuration. Of course, this can be done for any configuration section, so if your settings are not stored at the root level, it will still work.

Another option is to have the configuration build and return a self-instantiated instance:

```
var settings = cfg.GetSection("Logging").Get<LoggingSettings>();
```

For this to work, the template class cannot be abstract and needs to have a public parameterless constructor defined.

 Don't forget that an error will occur if and only if a configuration value cannot be bound, either directly as a string, or through a `TypeConverter` to the target property in the POCO class. If no such property exists it will be silently ignored. The `TypeConverter` class comes from the `System.ComponentModel` NuGet package and namespace.

Injecting values

OK so we now know how to load configuration values from several sources, and we also know a couple of ways to ask for them explicitly. However, .NET Core relies heavily on dependency injection, so we might want to use that for configuration settings as well.

First, it should be fairly obvious that we can register the configuration object itself with the dependency injection framework:

```
var cfg = builder.Build();
services.AddSingleton(cfg);
```

Wherever we ask for an `IConfigurationRoot` object, we will get this one. We can also register it as the base `IConfiguration` which is safe as well, although we miss the ability to reload the configuration (we will cover this in more detail later on):

```
services.AddSingleton<IConfiguration>(cfg);
```

Note that ASP.NET Core 2.0 automatically registers the configuration object with the dependency injection framework.

We might also be interested in injecting some POCO class with configuration settings, in that case we use `Configure`:

```
services.Configure<LoggingSettings>(settings =>
    {
        settings.IncludeScopes = true;
        settings.Default = LogLevel.Debug;
    });
```

Here we are using the `Configure` extension method, which allows us to specify values for some POCO class to be created at runtime whenever it is requested. Rather than doing this manually we can ask the configuration object to do it:

```
services.Configure<LoggingSettings>(settings =>
    {
        cfg.GetSection("Logging").Bind(settings);
    });
```

We can even pass in the configuration root itself, or a sub-section of it, which is way simpler:

```
services.Configure<LoggingSettings>(cfg.GetSection("Logging"));
```

Of course, we might as well register our POCO class with the dependency injection framework as follows:

```
var cfg = builder.Build();
var settings = builder.GetSection("Logging").Get<LoggingSettings>();
services.AddSingleton(settings);
```

If we use the `Configure` method, the configuration instances will be available from the dependency injection framework as instances of `IOptions<T>`, where `T` is a template parameter of the type passed to `Configure`, as per this example, `IOptions<LoggingSettings>`.

The `IOptions<T>` interface specifies a `Value` property by which we can access the underlying instance that was passed or set in `Configure`. The good thing is, this is dynamically executed at runtime if and only if it is actually requested, meaning no binding from configuration to the POCO class will occur unless we explicitly want it.

A final note: before using `Configure`, we need to add support for it to the services collection as follows:

```
services.AddOptions();
```

This will require adding the `Microsoft.Extensions.Options` Nuget package first and will ensure that all required services are properly registered.

Reloading and handling change notifications

You may remember that when we talked about the file-based providers, we mentioned the `reloadOnChange` parameter. This sets up a file monitoring operation by which the operating system notifies .NET when the file's contents have changed. Even if we don't enable that, it is possible to ask the providers to reload their configuration. The `IConfigurationRoot` interface exposes a `Reload` method for just that purpose:

```
var cfg = builder.Build();
cfg.Reload();
```

So if we reload explicitly the configuration, we're pretty confident that when we ask for a configuration key, we will get the updated value in case the configuration has changed in the meantime. If we don't however, the APIs we've already seen don't ensure us that we get the updated version every time. For that, we can either:

- Register a change notification callback, so as to be notified whenever the underlying file content changes
- Inject a live snapshot of the data, whose value changes whenever the source changes too

For the first option, we need to get a handle to the reload token and then register our callback actions in it:

```
var token = cfg.GetReloadToken();
token.RegisterChangeCallback(callback: (state) =>
    {
        //state will be someData
        //push the changes to whoever needs it
    }, state: someData);
```

For the latter, instead of injecting `IOptions<T>`, we need to use `IOptionsSnapshot<T>`. Just by changing this we can be sure that the injected value will come from the current, up to date, configuration source, and not the one that was there when the configuration object was created. For example:

```
public class HomeController : Controller
{
    private readonly LoggingSettings _settings;

    public HomeController(IOptionsSnapshot<LoggingSettings> settings)
    {
        _settings = settings.Value;
    }
}
```

It is safe to use `IOptionsSnapshot<T>` instead of `IOptions<T>`, as the overhead is minimal.

Putting it all together

For the purpose of our online shop, our configuration needs are:

- Different connection strings per each environment (**development**, **staging**, and **production**)
- Different logging settings for the different environments
- All of these should be easily changeable, even at runtime

To solve this, we will stick with the JSON provider (or XML, if you prefer the syntax) and enable the reloading of the configuration upon changes. We'll add a common file first and then optional overrides for each of the different environments (beware the order in which you add each source).

We will use configuration sections to better organize the settings and we will also have POCO wrappers for them.

So, should you use `IOptions<T>` or our own POCO classes to inject configuration values? Well, if you do not want to pollute your classes or assemblies with references to .NET Core configuration packages, you should stick to your POCO classes. We're not too worried about this, so we recommend keeping the interface wrappers.

We will use `IOptionsSnapshot<T>` instead of `IOptions<T>`, so that we will always get the latest version of the configuration settings.

Summary

In this chapter we saw the many ways in which we can provide configuration to an ASP.NET Core application. We learned how to build a simple provider that takes configuration from the Windows Registry. We then discussed the many ways in which we can inject configuration settings using the built-in dependency injection framework and how to be notified of changes in the configuration sources. Finally, we presented some of the decisions we will be making for the sample *Book Shop* project.

3
Routing

In the old days of web applications, things were simple--if you wanted a page, you had to have a physical one. However, things have since evolved and ASP.NET Core is now an MVC framework. What does that mean? Well, in MVC, there is no such thing as physical pages (although this is not exactly true); instead, it uses routing to direct **requests** to route handlers. The most common route handlers in MVC are **controller actions**.

A request is just some relative URL, such as:

```
/Search/Mastering%ASP.NET%Core
/Admin/Books
/Book/1
```

This results in more readable URLs, and is also advantageous for search engines such as Google. The subject of optimizing a site--including its public URLs--for search engines is called **Search Engine Optimization (SEO)**.

When ASP.NET Core receives a request, one of two things can happen:

- There is a physical file that matches the request
- There is a route that accepts the request

In order for ASP.NET Core to serve physical files, it needs to be configured--for that, we use the `UseStaticFiles` extension method in `Configure`, that adds the static files processing middleware to the pipeline; the call to `UseStaticFiles` is included in the Visual Studio template for ASP.NET Core Web applications. If we don't enable static file serving, or if no file exists, the requests need to be handled by a **route handler**. The most common route handler in MVC is a **controller**.

A **controller** is a class that exposes an **action** that knows how to process a request. An **action** is a method that may take parameters and returns an **action result**. A **routing table** is what we use to direct **requests** to **controller actions**.

There are two APIs that we can use for registering routes:

- Fluent API
- Attributes

In previous versions, we had to explicitly add support for routing attributes, but they are now first-class citizens of .NET Core. Let us go through them, starting with the routing table concept.

Routing tables

In Chapter 1, *Getting started with ASP .Net Core*, we talked about the OWIN pipeline, explaining that we use middleware to build this pipeline. It turns out that there is an MVC middleware that is responsible for interpreting the requests and translating them into controller actions. To do this, we need a **routing table**. There is only one routing table and it is configurable through the UseMvc method, as can be seen in this example from the default Visual Studio template:

```
app.UseMvc(routes =>
    {
      routes.MapRoute(
        name: "default",
        template: "{controller=Home}/{action=Index}/{id?}");
    });
```

What do we see here? The UseMvc extension method of IApplicationBuilder has a parameter that is an instance of IRouteBuilder, which lets us add routes to it. A route is essentially comprised of the following components:

- A name (default)
- A template ({controller=Home}/{action=Index}/{id?})
- Optional default values for each routing parameter (Home, Index)

There are some optional parameters that weren't shown in this example:

- Optional routing parameter constraints
- Optional data tokens
- A route handler
- A route constraints resolver

We will go through all of these in this chapter. This is the default MVC template, and this call is identical to having:

```
app.UseMvcWithDefaultRoute();
```

As for the actual route, the *name* is just something that has meaning for us, and it is not used in any way. More interesting is the *template*, which we will see in a moment.

These extension methods `MapRoute` resolves to something like the following:

```
var inlineConstraintResolver = routes
    .ServiceProvider
    .GetRequiredService<IInlineConstraintResolver>();

routes.Routes.Add(new Route(
    routes.DefaultHandler,
    name,
    template,
    new RouteValueDictionary(defaults),
    new RouteValueDictionary(constraints),
    new RouteValueDictionary(dataTokens),
    inlineConstraintResolver));
```

So, a route is essentially an instance of the `Route` class, populated with the name, template and all other parameters.

Route templates

A template is a relative URL, so it mustn't start with a slash (/). In it, you define the structure of your site, or, more accurately, the structure that you intend to make available. Being as ASP.NET Core is an MVC framework, the template should tell it how to map the request to an action method in a controller. We can see that the template:

```
{controller=Home}/{action=Index}/{id?}
```

consists of sections separated by slashes, where each section has some tokens (inside curly braces).

Another example might be:

```
sample/page
```

Here it is not clear what we want, as there are no mentions of **controller** or **action**. However, this is a perfectly valid template, and the required information needs to come from elsewhere.

A template can have the following elements:

- Alphanumeric literals
- String fragments inside curly braces ({ }), which are named tokens and can be mapped to action method parameters
- Named tokens with equal assignments (=) have default values, in case the token is not supplied in the URL; it doesn't make sense to have a token with a default value followed by a required token without
- Tokens that end with a question mark (?), which are optional, meaning, they are not required; optional tokens cannot be followed by required tokens
- Tokens that start with a star (*), which are entirely optional and match anything; they need to be the last element in the template

Tokens are always alphanumeric character segments and can be separated by separator symbols (/, ?, -, (,), and so on). However, you don't need to use separators; the following is perfectly valid--notice the lack of a slash between the `action` and the `id` tokens:

```
{controller=Admin}/{action=Process}{id}
```

Another slightly more complex example, adding a catch-all token `querystring` as follows:

```
{controller=Admin}/{action=Process}/{?id}?{*querystring}
```

This template will match the following URLs:

URL	Parameters
`/`	controller: `Admin` action: `Process` id: N/A querystring: N/A
`/Account`	controller: `Account` action: `Process` id: N/A querystring: N/A

/Admin/Process	controller: `Admin` action: `Process` id: N/A querystring: N/A
/Admin/Process/1212	controller: `Admin` action: `Process` id: `1212`
/Admin/Process/1212?force=true	controller: `Admin` action: `Process` id: `1212` querystring: `force=true`

Yet another perfectly valid example would be:

```
api/{controller=Search}/{action=Query}?term={term}
```

Which would match:

```
api?term=.net+core
api/Search?term=java
api/Search/Query?term=php
```

Note that any literals must be present exactly in the URL, regardless of the casing.

Route parameter matching

Remember that a template needs to have a `controller` and an `action`; these are the only required tokens and have special meanings. A controller will match a controller class and an action will match one of its public methods. Any other parameter will match parameters of the same name in the action method. For example, a template of:

```
{controller=Search}/{action=Query}/{phrase}
```

Will map to this method in a class called `SearchController`:

```
public IActionResult Query(string phrase)
```

By convention, the name of the controller in a template does not take the `Controller` suffix.

If a route token is optional, then it must map to a parameter that has a default value:

```
{controller=Account}/{action=List}/{page?}
```

A matching method would have the following signature:

```
public IActionResult List(int page = 0)
```

Notice that the `page` parameter is an `int` that has a default value of `0`. This might be used, for example, for paging, where the default page is the first one (zero-based). This would be the same as having a token with a default of `0` and mapping it to a parameter without a default value.

So far, we've only seen how we can map simple values of strings or basic types; we will soon see how we can use other types.

We've mentioned that the `action` parameter is required, but, although this is true in a way, its value may be skipped. In this case, ASP.NET Core will use the value from the HTTP action header, such as--`GET`, `POST`, `PUT`, `DELETE`, and so on. This is particularly useful in the case of Web APIs and is often very intuitive. So, for example, a route with a template such as:

```
api/{controller}/{id}
```

For a request of:

```
GET /api/Values/12
```

Can be mapped to a method like this, in a controller named `ValuesController`:

```
public IActionResult Get(int id)
```

Route selection

ASP.NET Core, or rather, the routing middleware, will take the request URL and check for all the routes it knows about, if any matches the request. It will do so while respecting the route insertion order, so be aware that your request may accidentally fall into a route that isn't the one you were expecting. Always add the most specific ones first, then the generic ones.

After a template is found that matches the request, ASP.NET Core will check if there is an available action method on the target controller that does not have a NonActionAttribute, that forbids a method to be used as an action, or has an attribute inheriting from HttpMethodAttribute that matches the current HTTP verb. These are:

- HttpGetAttribute
- HttpPostAttribute
- HttpPutAttribute
- HttpDeleteAttribute
- HttpOptionsAttribute
- HttpPatchAttribute
- HttpHeadAttribute

If any of these is found, then the route will only be selected if the HTTP verb matches one of the verbs specified. There can be many attributes, meaning the action method will be callable using any of the HTTP verbs specified.

There are other HTTP verbs, but ASP.NET Core only supports these out of the box. If you wish to support others, you need to subclass HttpMethodAttribute and supply your list or use ActionVerbsAttribute.

Interestingly, ASP.NET Core--as before in, ASP.NET Web API--offered an alternative way of locating an action method--if the action token is not supplied, it will look for an action method whose name matches the current HTTP verb, regardless of the casing.

You can use these attributes to supply different action names, which allows you to use method overloading. For example, if you have two methods with the same name that take different parameters, the only way to differentiate between them is by using different action names:

```
public class CalculatorController
{
  //Calculator/CalculateDirectly
  [HttpGet(Name = "CalculateDirectly")]
  public IActionResult Calculate(int a, int b) { ... }

  //Calculator/CalculateByKey
  [HttpGet(Name = "CalculateById")]
  public IActionResult Calculate(Guid calculationId) { }
}
```

Or different target HTTP verbs:

```
//GET Calculator/Calculate
[HttpGet]
public IActionResult Calculate(int a, int b) { ... }

//POST Calculator/Calculate
[HttpPost]
public IActionResult Calculate([FromBody] Calculation calculation) { }
```

Of course, you can limit an action method--or the whole controller--so that it can only be accessed if the request is authenticated by using the `AuthorizeAttribute`. We won't go over that here, as it will be discussed in the chapter dedicated to security. It is worth noting, however, that even if the whole controller is marked with the `AuthorizeAttribute`, individual actions can still be accessible if they bear the `AllowAnonymousAttribute`:

```
[Authorize]
public class PrivateController
{
    [AllowAnonymous]
    public IActionResult Backdoor() { }
}
```

Another option is to constraint an action based on the content type of the request. You use `ConsumesAttribute` for that purpose, and you can apply as follows:

```
[HttpPost]
[Consumes("application/json")]
public IActionResult Process(string payload) { }
```

 For an explanation of what content types are please see `https://www.w3.org/Protocols/rfc1341/4_Content-Type.html`.

Another attribute that contributes to the route selection is `RequireHttpsAttribute`. If present in a method or controller class, a request is only accepted if it comes through HTTPS.

Finally, there are route constraints. These are generally used to validate the tokens passed in the request, but they can be used to validate the request as a whole. We will discuss them shortly.

So, the sequence is:

1. Find the first template that matches the request.
2. Check that a valid controller exists.
3. Check that a valid action method exists in the controller, either by action name or by verb matching.
4. Check that any constraints present are valid.
5. Check that any attributes that contribute to the route selection (`AuthorizeAttribute`, `NonActionAttribute`, `ConsumesAttribute`, `ActionVerbsAttribute`, `RequireHttpsAttribute`, and `HttpMethodAttribute`) all are valid.

We will see how constraints can affect the route selection shortly.

Special routes

The following routes are special:

- `[HttpGet("")]`: This is the controller's default action
- `[HttpGet("~/")]`: This is the application's default action for the default controller

Route defaults

We've seen how we can specify default values for route parameters in the template, but there's also another way, by overloading the `MapRoute` extension method that takes an object containing default values. Instead of supplying these defaults as strings, you can have:

```
app.UseMvc(routes =>
    {
        routes.MapRoute(
            name: "default",
            template: "{controller}/{action}/{id?}",
            defaults: new { controller = "Home", action = "Index" });
    });
```

This is valid even if you don't have the tokens in the route, as follows:

```
app.UseMvc(routes =>
    {
       routes.MapRoute(
         name: "default",
         template: "My/Route",
         defaults: new { controller = "My", action = "Route" });
    });
```

Remember that you do have to supply a `controller` and `action`, if they are not present in the template, they need to be supplied as defaults.

Route handlers

A **route handler** is what actually handles a request. ASP.NET Core allows us to specify a route handler per route, or to use the default, global, one. A route handler implements `IRouter`, and there is a class `Route` that does just that. However, this is not worth worrying about in most situations. If not supplied, the default route handler will be used; in the following example, it is `routes.DefaultHandler`:

```
var inlineConstraintResolver = routes
    .ServiceProvider
    .GetRequiredService<IInlineConstraintResolver>();

routes.Routes.Add(new Route(
    routes.DefaultHandler,
    name,
    template,
    new RouteValueDictionary(defaults),
    new RouteValueDictionary(constraints),
    new RouteValueDictionary(dataTokens),
    inlineConstraintResolver));
```

This is the actual implementation of `MapRoute`, and there is normally no reason to provide your own `IRouter` implementation—unless you need to do something before or after handling the request; in this case, however, filters are a better option.

The default route handler is an instance of `MvcRouteHandler`, which is the class that actually knows how to translate requests to controller actions. It wasn't designed for extensibility, but you can certainly wrap it inside a custom `IRouter` and delegate all heavy work to it.

Routing to inline handlers

There is a possibility in ASP.NET Core to handle a request directly, that is, to not route to a controller action. We define inline handlers by using an extension method that specifies the HTTP verb and the template to match, as follows:

- `MapGet`: HTTP Get
- `MapPost`: HTTP Post
- `MapPut`: HTTP Put
- `MapDelete`: HTTP Delete
- `MapVerb`: any named HTTP verb; for example; verb Get is the same as using MapGet

All of these methods offer two possible signatures (except for `MapVerb` that takes the HTTP verb), and take the following parameters:

- `template`: This is a route template
- `handler`: This is a handler that takes the current context (`HttpContext`) and returns a task
- `action`: This is an alternative to `handler` that instead takes the application builder instance (`IApplicationBuilder`)

Here are two examples, in the first, we are merely setting the response content type and writing some text to the output:

```
routes.MapGet(
    template: "DirectRoute",
    handler: async ctx =>
    {
      ctx.Response.ContentType = "text/plain";
      await ctx.Response.WriteAsync("Here's your response!");
    });
```

Now, we are adding a middleware to the response:

```
routes.MapGet(
    template: "DirectRoute",
    action: appBuilder =>
    {
      appBuilder.UseMiddleware<ResponseMiddleware>();
    });
```

The two approaches, using a handler or the application builder, are similar the former gives us direct access to the request context, while the latter allows us to add steps to the request pipeline for a particular route template. It all depends on what you want to do.

 You cannot mix direct handlers with controllers: the first handler that is picked up in the routing table will be processed, and no other, so for example, if you have a `MapGet` followed by a `MapRoute` for the same template, the handler or action specified in `MapGet` will be processed, but not the controller in `MapRoute`.

Route constraints

You can constrain a route in a number of ways, as follows:

- The request needs to match a given HTTP method
- The request needs to match a given content type
- Its parameters need to match certain rules

A constraint can be expressed in the route template or as a discrete object, using the `MapRoute` method. If you choose to use the route template, you need to specify its name next to the token to which it applies:

```
{controller=Home}/{action=Index}/{id:int}
```

Notice `{id:int}`: this constrains the `id` parameter to an integer, and is one of the provided constraints that we will talk about in a moment. Another option is to make use of the `defaults` parameter:

```
app.UseMvc(routes =>
{
    routes.MapRoute(
        name: "default",
        template: "{controller}/{action}/{id?}",
        defaults: new { controller = "Home", action = "Index" },
        constraints: new { id = new IntRouteConstraint() });
});
```

You should be able to guess that the anonymous class that is passed in the `constraints` parameter must have properties that match the route parameters.

Following on from this example, you can also pass constraints that are not bound to any route parameter, but instead perform some kind of bespoke validation, as follows:

```
routes.MapRoute(
    name: "default",
    template: "{controller}/{action}/{id?}",
    defaults: new { controller = "Home", action = "Index" },
    constraints: new { foo = new BarRouteConstraint() });
```

In this case, the constraint class `BarRouteConstraint` will still be called and can be used to invalidate a route selection.

HTTP methods

As we said earlier, in order to make an action method available to only some HTTP verbs or a specific content type, you can use one of the following:

- HttpGetAttribute
- HttpPostAttribute
- HttpPutAttribute
- HttpDeleteAttribute
- HttpOptionsAttribute
- HttpPatchAttribute
- HttpHeadAttribute
- ActionVerbsAttribute
- ConsumesAttribute

The names should be self-explanatory. You can add attributes for different verbs, and if any of them is present, the route will only match if its verb matches one of these attributes. `ActionVerbsAttribute` lets you pass a single method, or a list of methods, that you wish to support. `ConsumesAttribute` takes a valid content type.

Default constraints

ASP.NET Core includes the following constraints:

Constraint	Purpose	Example
alpha (AlphaRouteConstraint)	Limits the text to alphanumeric characters, that is, excluding symbols	{term:alpha}
bool (BoolRouteConstraint)	Is only true or false	{force:bool}
datetime (DateTimeRouteConstraint)	Gives a date or date and time pattern	{lower:datetime}
decimal (DecimalRouteConstraint)	Includes decimal values	{lat:decimal}
double (DoubleRouteConstraint)	Includes double precision floating point values	{precision:double}
exists (KnownValueRouteConstraint)	Forces a route token to be present	{action:exists}
float (FloatRouteConstraint)	Includes single precision floating point values	{accuracy:float}
guid (GuidRouteConstraint)	Includes GUIDs	{id:guid}
int (IntRouteConstraint)	Includes integer values	{id:int}
length (LengthRouteConstraint)	Includes a constrained string	{term:length(5,10)
long (LongRouteConstraint)	Includes a long integer	{id:long}

max (MaxRouteConstraint)	This is the maximum value for an integer	{page:max(100)}
min (MinRouteConstraint)	This is the minimum value for an integer	{page:min(1)}
maxlength (MaxLengthRouteConstraint)	Includes any alphanumeric string up to a maximum length	{term:maxlength(10)}
minlength (MinLengthRouteConstraint)	Includes any alphanumeric string with a minimum length	{term:minlength(10)}
range (RangeRouteConstraint)	Includes an integer range	{page:range(1,100)}
regex (RegexRouteConstraint)	A regular expression	{isbn:regex(^d{9}[d|X]$)}
required (RequiredRouteConstraint)	Includes a required value	{term:required}

A route parameter can take many constraints at once, such as:

```
Calculator/Calculate({a:int:max(10)},{b:int:max(10)})
```

In this example, parameters a and b need to be integers and have a maximum value of 10, at the same time. Another example is as follows:

```
Book/Find({isbn:regex(^d{9}[d|X]$)])
```

This will match an ISBN string starting with 9 digits and followed by either a trailing digit or the X character.

It is also possible to provide your own custom constraints.

Custom constraints

A constraint is any class that implements IRouteConstraint. If it is meant to be used inline in a route template, then it must be registered. Here's an example of a route constraint for validating even numbers:

```
public class EvenIntRouteConstraint : IRouteConstraint
{
  public bool Match(
    HttpContext httpContext,
    IRouter route,
    string routeKey,
    RouteValueDictionary values,
    RouteDirection routeDirection)
    {
      if ((values.ContainsKey(routeKey) == false) || (values[routeKey] ==
null))
      {
        return false;
      }

      var value = values[routeKey].ToString();
      int intValue;

      if (int.TryParse(value, out intValue) == false)
      {
        return false;
      }

      return (intValue % 2) == 0;
    }
}
```

You should be able to tell that all route parameters are provided in the values collection and that the route parameter name is in routeKey. If no route parameter is actually supplied, it will just return false, as it will if the parameter cannot be parsed into an integer. That's all there is to it.

If you wish to use a route constraint to validate a URL--or any of the request parameters--you can use a route constraint not bound to a route key:

```
public class IsAuthenticatedRouteConstraint : IRouteConstraint
{
  public bool Match(
    HttpContext httpContext,
      IRouter route,
      string routeKey,
      RouteValueDictionary values,
      RouteDirection routeDirection)
  {
    return httpContext.Request.Cookies.ContainsKey("auth");
  }
}
```

Granted, there are other (even better) ways to do this; this was only included as an example.

If we want to use inline constraints, we need to register the classes. Typically we do that in `ConfigureServices`, and we indicate a constraint code for them, as follows:

```
services.Configure<RouteOptions>(options =>
  {
    options.ConstraintMap.Add("evenint",typeof(EvenIntRouteConstraint));
  });
```

Now we can use it like this:

```
Calculator/Calculate({a:evenint},{b:evenint})
```

If on the other hand, you prefer to use the constraint classes directly in your `MapRoute` calls, you do not need to register them. Regardless, the route constraint collection is available as the `IInlineConstraintResolver` service:

```
var inlineConstraintResolver = routes
    .ServiceProvider
    .GetRequiredService<IInlineConstraintResolver>();
```

 If you wish to specify custom route constraints in routing attributes, you will need to register them.

Route data tokens

A **route data token**, as opposed to a **route token** or **route parameter**, is just some arbitrary data that you supply in a routing table entry and is available for use in the route handling pipeline, including the MVC action method. Unlike route tokens, route data tokens can be any kind of object, not just strings. They have absolutely no meaning for MVC, and will just be ignored.

You can pass a data token as follows:

```
app.UseMvc(routes =>
    {
        routes.MapRoute(
            name: "default",
            template: "{controller}/{action}/{id?}",
            defaults: new { controller = "Home", action = "Index" },
            constraints: null,
            dataTokens: new { foo = "bar", route = "default" });
    });
```

You can also retrieve them from the `RouteData.DataTokens` collection, as from inside a controller action:

```
public class HomeController : Controller
{
    public IActionResult Index()
    {
        var route = ControllerContext.RouteData.DataTokens["route"] as string;
        return this.View();
    }
}
```

Because the `DataTokens` values are prototyped as `object`, you need to know what you will be retrieving.

Areas

MVC has supported the concept of areas for a long time. Essentially, areas are for segregating and organizing controllers and views, so that, for example, you can have identically-named controllers in different areas.

Visual Studio lets you create folders in a project and then add controllers and views to them. You can mark these folders as areas.

Where routing is concerned, areas add another route token, appropriately named `area`, to `controller` and `action`. If you are to use areas, you will likely have another segment in your template, such as:

```
Products/Phones/Index
Reporting/Sales/Index
```

Here, `Products` and `Reporting` are areas. You need to map them to routes, so that they are recognized by MVC. You can use the `MapRoute` extension method, but you will need to supply the `area` token as follows:

```
app.UseMvc(routes =>
    {
        routes.MapRoute(
            name: "default",
            template: "{area:exists}/{controller}/{action}/{id?}",
            defaults: new { controller = "Home", action = "Index" });
    });
```

You can also use the `MapAreaRoute` extension method, which takes care of adding the `area` parameter:

```
routes.MapAreaRoute(
    name: "default",
    area: "Products",
    template: "List/{controller}/{action}/{id?}",
    defaults: new { controller = "Phones", action = "Index" });
```

This route will map a request of `List/Phones/Index` to an action method `Index` of a controller `PhonesController` inside the `Products` area.

Routing attributes

An alternative to adding routes to a routing table is to use **routing attributes**. Routing attributes existed before ASP.NET Core, and were even around in ASP.NET MVC and Web API, but we had to add support for them explicitly. We no longer have to do this.

Routes

These attributes are used to define routes, and are composable in nature--if we add a routing attribute to a class and another to one of its methods, the actual route will result from both of them.

The most obvious use of routing attributes would be to decorate an action method, as follows:

```
[Route("Home/Index")]
public IActionResult Index() { }
```

If, for example, you have many actions in the same controller and you wish to map them all using the same prefix (Home), you can do the following:

```
[Route("Home")]
public class HomeController
{
    [Route("Index")]
    public IActionResult Index() { }

    [Route("About")]
    public IActionResult About() { }
}
```

 In previous versions of MVC and Web API, you could use the RoutePrefixAttribute for this purpose. Now, RouteAttribute takes care of both cases.

As you can see, the route parameter in the HomeController class matches the conventional name for the controller (Home). Because of this, we can also use the [controller] special token:

```
[Route("[controller]")]
public class HomeController { }
```

Or, for an API controller:

```
[Route("api/[controller]")]
public class ServicesController { }
```

In addition, each of the actions are mapped with names that exactly match the method's names. Likewise, we can use [action]:

```
[Route("[action]")]
public IActionResult Index() { }
```

```
[Route("[action]")]
public IActionResult About() { }
```

Multiple route attributes can be passed, so that the action method will respond to different requests:

```
[Route("[action]")]
[Route("")]
[Route("Default")]
public IActionResult Index() { }
```

The `Index` method will be callable by any one of the following requests:

```
/Home
/Home/Index
/Home/Default
```

Notice that the `Home` part comes from the route attribute applied at the class level. If, on the other hand, you specify a slash in the template, you make the template absolute; this template will look as follows:

```
[Route("Default/Index")]
public IActionResult Index() { }
```

This can only be accessed as:

```
/Default/Index
```

If you want to take the controller into consideration, you should either name it explicitly in the template or use the `[controller]` special token:

```
[Route("[controller]/Default/Index")]
public IActionResult Index() { }
```

This will be accessible as:

```
/Home/Default/Index
```

Tokens `[controller]` and `[action]` are for when we want to use constants for routes. These constants have the potential to be used in lots of places, as they are not stuck to specific actions and controllers. They were not available in previous versions of ASP.NET MVC or Web API.

Defaults

With routing attributes you can specify the default controller by applying `RouteAttribute` with a blank template:

```
[Route("")]
public class HomeController { }
```

The default action in a controller will also be the one with an empty template as follows:

```
[Route("")]
public IActionResult Index() { }
```

If there is no method with an empty route template, ASP.NET Core will try to find one with a name matching the current HTTP method.

Constraints

You can also specify route constraints, and the syntax is identical to the one we've seen before:

```
[Route("Calculate({a:int},{b:int})")]
public IActionResult Calculate(int a, int b) { }
```

Areas

You can define routes that include areas too, by applying `AreaAttribute` to a controller:

```
[Area("Products")]
[Route("[controller]")]
public class ReportingController { }
```

Similar to `[controller]` and `[action]`, there is also the special token `[area]` that you can use in your templates to indicate the current area, as inferred from the filesystem:

```
[Route("[area]/Default")]
public IActionResult Index() { }
```

Action names

You can specify an action name for a controller method, either through an
`ActionNameAttribute`, as follows:

```
[ActionName("Default")]
public IActionResult Index() { }
```

You can do this through one of the HTTP verb selection attributes (`HttpGetAttribute`,
`HttpPostAttribute`, `HttpPutAttribute`, `HttpOptionsAttribute`,
`HttpPatchAttribute`, `HttpDeleteAttribute` or `HttpHeadAttribute`):

```
[HttpGet(Name = "Default")]
public IActionResult Index() { }
```

Please do remember that you cannot specify a route template and an
action name at the same time, as this will result in an exception being
thrown at startup time when ASP.NET Core scans the routing attributes.
Also, do not specify `ActionNameAttribute` and a verb selection attribute
at the same time as specifying the action name.

Non actions

If you want to prevent a public method in a controller class from being used as an action,
you can decorate it with the `NonActionAttribute`:

```
[NonAction]
public IActionResult Process() { }
```

Restrictions

When we talked about route constraints, we saw that we can restrict an action method so
that it is only callable if:

- It matches a given HTTP verb (`ActionVerbsAttribute`, `Http*Attribute`)
- It is called using HTTPS (`RequireHttpsAttribute`)
- It is called with a given content type (`ConsumesAttribute`)

We won't go into this in any further detail, as this has been explained before.

Route values

It is possible to supply arbitrary route values in an action method. This is the purpose of the abstract class `RouteValueAttribute`. You need to inherit from it:

```
public class CustomRouteValueAttribute : RouteValueAttribute
{
  public CustomRouteValueAttribute(string value) : base("custom",
    value) { }
}
```

And then apply and use it as follows:

```
[CustomRouteValue("foo")]
public IActionResult Index()
{
  var foo = ControllerContext.RouteData.Values["foo"];
  return this.View();
}
```

> `AreaAttribute` is an example of a class inheriting from `RouteValueAttribute`.
>
> There is no way to pass arbitrary route data tokens through attributes.

Dealing with errors

What do we do with errors, for example, when a resource is not found? You can use routing for this. Here, we will present two strategies:

- Adding a catch-all route
- Using the status code pages middleware

Catch-all route

You can add a catch-all route by adding an action method with a route that will always match if no other does. For example, we can use routing attributes as follows:

```
[HttpGet("{*url}", Order = int.MaxValue)]
public IActionResult CatchAll()
{
  this.Response.StatusCode = StatusCodes.Status404NotFound;
```

```
    return this.View();
  }
```

The same, of course, can be achieved with fluent configuration, in the `Configure` method:

```
app.UseMvc(routes =>
{
  //default routes go here

  routes.MapRoute(
    name: "CatchAll",
    template: "{*url}",
    defaults: new { controller = "CatchAll", action = "CatchAll" }
  );
});
```

Here, all you need to do is add a nice view with a friendly error message! Be aware that the other actions in the same controller also need to have routes specified, otherwise, the default route will become `CatchAll`!

Status code pages middleware

In order to use this middleware, call `UseStatusCodePagesWithReExecute` in the `Configure` method, just before `UseMvc`:

```
app.UseStatusCodePagesWithReExecute("/error/{0}");
app.UseMvc();
```

This instructs MVC to call a route starting with `/error/` and ending in the status code. There are two ways to match this, which we will look at in the following sections.

Specific status codes

You can add an action like this to a controller:

```
[Route("error/404")]
public IActionResult Error404()
{
  this.Response.StatusCode = StatusCodes.Status404NotFound;
  return this.View();
}
```

Now, either add an `Error404` view or instead call a generic view, passing it the `404` status code, perhaps through the view bag. Again, this route can be configured fluently, as follows:

```
routes.MapRoute(
  name: "Error404",
  template: "error/404",
  defaults: new { controller = "CatchAll", action = "Error404" }
);
```

Any status code

To catch-all errors in the same method, do the following instead:

```
[Route("error/{statusCode:int}")]
public IActionResult Error(int statusCode)
{
  this.Response.StatusCode = statusCode;
  this.ViewBag.StatusCode = statusCode;
  return this.View();
}
```

Here, we are calling a generic view called `Error` (inferred from the action name), so we need to pass it the originating status code, which we do through the view bag, as follows:

```
routes.MapRoute(
  name: "Error",
  template: "error/{statusCode:int}",
  defaults: new { controller = "CatchAll", action = "Error" }
);
```

Putting it all together

In real life, chances are you will mix code-based routing configuration and attributes. In our example, we will be using localization features, which require a lot of configuration, typically code-based configuration. Attribute routing also has its place, because we can directly define accessible endpoints that do not need to be restricted by general routing templates. Route constraints are very powerful and should be used.

Always start with the included default route template and go from there. It should be sufficient for around 80% of your needs. Others will either be defined through a custom route or routing attributes.

Security is something that needs to be taken into account, and using routing attributes for this purpose seems ideal, as we can immediately see what the security restrictions are by looking at controller methods.

Summary

In this chapter, we've seen the different ways by which we can configure routing; in other words, turning browser requests into actions. We looked at code-based and attribute-based routing and learned some of their strengths and limitations. We found out how we can restrict URL parameters to be of certain types or match certain requirements, as well as how to prevent an action method to be called unless it matches a specific verb, HTTPS requirement, or request content type. Finally, we looked at how to use routes to direct to status code or error specific actions so as to return friendly error pages.

Quite a few of the topics covered in this chapter will surface again in following chapters.

4

Controllers and Actions

This is where the actual code is, where you get things done, where you process the requests from the browser. We will talk about MVC controllers returning views but also about API-style controllers. But we also talk about persisting data across requests, injecting dependencies into our controllers and actions, action versioning and how to add localization support to the code. All in all, it's a very important chapter, so I ask for your full attention.

In this chapter, we will be talking about the most important aspects of an MVC application:

- Controllers
- Actions

Using controllers

In MVC, a controller is responsible for handling requests. It is where the business logic is located, where data is retrieved, request parameters validated, and so on. In object-oriented languages, such as those that support the .NET Framework, this is implemented in classes. Keep in mind that the MVC pattern advocates a strong separation of responsibilities, which makes all of its components particularly important; even if that is true, a controller is really the only required part of ASP.NET Core, as you can live without views, just think of web services that do not return any user interface, or models. This is a very important aspect of ASP.NET Core.

Controller base classes

ASP.NET Core (as with its predecessors) offers a base class `ControllerBase` that you can inherit from, although it is not strictly necessary. We will discuss this in more detail later on in this chapter. However, doing so has a number of advantages:

- Easy access to model validation

- Helper methods to return different results (redirect, JSON, views, text, and more)

- Direct access to the request and response infrastructure objects, including headers, cookies, and more

- Possibility to intercept/override action events

In reality, there is another class, `Controller`, that in turn inherits from `ControllerBase`, which you should inherit from in case you want to work with views. A case where you wouldn't need to work with views would be if you are writing a web service (web API).

The templates in Visual Studio always generate controllers that inherit from the `Controller` class, but you can change them to POCOs if you like. The only real requirement, unless you want to change the convention, is to add the `Controller` suffix to all your controllers. Namespace or physical location is irrelevant.

The `ControllerBase` class, among others, makes available the following properties:

- `ControllerContext` (`ControllerContext`): The execution context for the current controller and request, which includes the action descriptor (used to guess what action should be called) and value provider factories, from which the action parameters are obtained; it's an instance of the class

- `HttpContext` (`HttpContext`): The HTTP context, which includes the request and response objects, from which we can obtain and set all headers, cookies, status codes, authentication information, certificates, and more; also provides access to the dependency injection framework, framework features, the session state (if it's enabled) and the underlying connection properties

- `MetadataProvider` (`IModelMetadataProvider`): This is used to extract metadata--validators, textual descriptors, and editing information--for the class model

- `ModelBinderFactory` (`IModelBinderFactory`): This is an object that is used to create the binders that, in turn, are used to bind submitted request properties to a given class model
- `ModelState` (`ModelStateDictionary`): This is the submitted model's values and validation results
- `ObjectValidator` (`IObjectModelValidator`): This is an instance that is used to validate the submitted model
- `Request` (`HttpRequest`): This handles the convenience pointer to the same object inside the `HttpContext`
- `Response` (`HttpResponse`): This handles the convenience pointer to the same object inside the `HttpContext`
- `Url` (`IUrlHelper`): This is an instance that enables convenience methods to generate URL links to specific controller actions
- `User` (`ClaimsPrincipal`): This holds a reference to the current ASP.NET Core user; depending on the actual authentication mechanism in use, it will hold different values and claims, and even if not authenticated, this will never be **null**

The `Controller` class offers all of the above plus view-specific properties:

- `RouteData` (`RouteData`): This contains the MVC route data parameters
- `ViewBag`: (dynamic): This is a dynamic collection of data to make available in a view
- `ViewData` (`ViewDataDictionary`): This is identical to `ViewBag`, but strongly-typed, in the form of a key-value dictionary
- `TempData` (`ITempDataDictionary`): This is a strongly-typed dictionary for data to maintain until the next form submission

 It's safe and convenient to inherit from `Controller`, even if you do not use views, it won't harm.

Of course, your controller needs to offer at least one action method that can be used to perform some action and return something meaningful to the caller, be it an HTML view, some JSON content, or just an HTTP status code.

You also have a number of virtual methods that you can override so as to perform actions before, after, or instead of an action method being called. These are defined in the interfaces `IActionFilter` and `IAsyncActionFilter`, which are implemented by `Controller`:

- `OnActionExecuted` is called after an action is called
- `OnActionExecuting` is called synchronously just before an action is called
- `OnActionExecutingAsync` is called asynchronously before an action is called

These interfaces are the base of filters, which we will discuss in more detail later on.

I almost forgot: if a controller class has the `[NonController]` attribute applied to it, it is not considered and cannot be used as a controller.

POCO controllers

In Core, your controllers do not need to inherit from any base class or implement a particular interface. As we mentioned earlier, all they need is the `Controller` suffix, by convention, and to avoid the `[NonController]` attribute. The problem with this approach is that you lose all helper methods and context properties (`HttpContext`, `ControllerContext`, `ViewBag`, and `Url`), but you can have them injected.

If you add the `[Controller]` attribute to any POCO class, you can turn it into a controller, regardless of its name.

Adding context to POCO controllers

So, say for example, that you have a POCO controller `HomeController`. You don't have the various context and view bag-related properties, but with a couple of attributes applied to appropriately-typed properties, you can have the infrastructure inject them, as in the following example:

```
public class HomeController
{
  private readonly IUrlHelperFactory _url;

  public HomeController(IHttpContextAccessor ctx,
      IUrlHelperFactory url)
```

```
  {
    this.HttpContext = ctx.HttpContext;
    this._url = url;
  }

  [ControllerContext]
  public ControllerContext { get; set; }

  public HttpContext HttpContext { get; set; }

  [ActionContext]
  public ActionContext ActionContext { get; set; }

  [ViewDataDictionary]
  public ViewDataDictionary ViewBag { get; set; }

  public IUrlHelper Url { get; set; }

  public string Index()
  {
    this.Url = this.Url ??
      this._url.GetUrlHelper(this.ActionContext);
    return "Hello, World!";
  }
}
```

You will notice a few interesting things here:

- `ActionContext`, `ControllerContext`, and `ViewBag` are automatically injected just by adding the `[ActionContext]`, `[ControllerContext]`, and `[ViewDataDictionary]` attributes to properties of any name, and having types `ActionContext`, `ControllerContext` and `ViewDataDictionary`, respectively
- When the controller is instantiated by the ASP.NET Core infrastructure, the dependency injection framework injects the `IHttpContextAccessor` and `IUrlHelperFactory` objects
- The `HttpContext` object needs to be obtained from the passed `IHttpContextAccessor` instance
- In order to build an `IUrlHelper`, the `IUrlHelperFactory` needs an instance of `ActionContext`; because we don't have that at constructor time, we need to build it later on, for example, in an action method (in this example, `Index`)

However, to make this work, we need to tell ASP.NET Core to register the default implementations of `IHttpContextAccessor` and `IUrlHelperFactory`. This is normally done in the `ConfigureServices` method of the `Startup` class:

```
services.AddScoped<IHttpContextAccessor, HttpContextAccessor>();
services.AddScoped<IUrlHelperFactory, UrlHelperFactory>();
```

These properties will behave in exactly the same way as their non-POCO counterparts that are inherited from `ControllerBase` and `Controller`.

Intercepting actions in POCO controllers

If you want, you can also implement one of the filter interfaces so that you can interact with the request before or after an action is called, such as `IActionFilter`:

```
public class HomeController : IActionFilter
{
  public void OnActionExecuting(ActionExecutingContext context)
  {
    //before the action is called
  }

  public void OnActionExecuted(ActionExecutedContext context)
  {
    //after the action is called
  }
}
```

If you prefer to have an asynchronous handler, implement the asynchronous version (`IAsyncXXXFilter`) instead. We will talk more about filters in a couple of chapters.

Finding controllers

Regardless of whether you go for POCO or non-POCO controllers, ASP.NET Core applies the same rules for discovering controllers, which are as follows:

- They need to have the `Controller` suffix (strictly speaking, this can be changed, but we will leave this for now)
- They need to be instantiable classes (non-abstract, non-generic, and non-static)
- They cannot have the `[NonController]` attribute applied to them
- If they are POCO and do not have the `Controller` suffix, you can decorate them with the `[Controller]` attribute

By convention, the files that contain the controller classes are stored in a folder called `Controllers`, and also in a `Controllers` namespace, but this is just ignored.

Controller classes are looked up by the name in the route--the controller parameter--and they are searched in the assemblies registered for that purpose. By default, the currently executing assembly is included in the search, but all assemblies registered as **application parts** are too. You can register additional application parts when you add the MVC features to the dependency injection framework (`ConfigureServices` method) as follows:

```
services.AddMvc()
    .AddApplicationPart(typeof(MyCustomComponent).GetTypeInfo().Assembly);
```

Here, we are adding a reference to the assembly that contains a hypothetical class, `MyCustomComponent`. After we do that, any controllers that are located in it are available for use. In order to get the full list of found controllers, we can use `ControllerFeature` and populate it through `ApplicationPartManager`:

```
services.AddMvc()
    .AddApplicationPart(typeof(MyCustomComponent).GetTypeInfo().Assembly)
    .ConfigureApplicationPartManager(parts =>
        {
            var controllerFeature = new ControllerFeature();
            parts.PopulateFeature(controllerFeature);
            //controllerFeature.Controllers contains the list of discovered
controllers' types
        });
```

Controllers are only discovered once, at startup time, which is a good thing performance-wise.

If there are two controllers with the same name but in different namespaces, and they both expose an action method that matches the current request, ASP.NET won't know which one to pick and will throw an exception. If this happens, we need to give one of the classes a new controller name by applying a `[ControllerName]` attribute:

```
namespace Controllers
{
  public class HomeController
  {
  }

  namespace Admin
  {
    [ControllerName("AdminHome")]
```

```
    public class HomeController
    {
    }
  }
}
```

We could also change the action name, as we will see in a moment.

Now, let's see what happens once the controller type has been found.

Controller life cycle

After a controller's type is located, ASP.NET Core starts a process to instantiate it. The process is as follows:

1. The default controller factory (`IControllerFactory`) is obtained from the **dependency injection** (**DI**) framework and its `CreateController` method is called.

2. The controller factory uses the registered controller activator (`IControllerActivator`), also obtained from the DI, to obtain an instance to the controller (`IControllerActivator.Create`).

3. The action method is located using the `IActionSelector`, from the DI.

4. If the controller implements any filter interfaces (`IActionFilter`, `IResourceFilter`, and more), or if the action has any filter attributes, the appropriate methods are called upon it and on global filters.

5. The action method is called by the `IActionInvoker` from the `IActionInvokerProvider`, also obtained from the DI.

6. Any filter methods are called upon the controller, the action method's filters attributes, and also on global filters.

7. The controller factory releases the controller (`IControllerFactory.ReleaseController`).

8. The controller activator releases the controller (`IControllerActivator.Release`).

9. If the controller implements `IDisposable`, the `Dispose` method is called upon it.

Most of these components can be registered through the built-in DI framework; for example, suppose you want to replace the default `IControllerFactory` implementation, you could do this in the `ConfigureServices` method:

```
services.AddSingleton<IControllerFactory, CustomControllerFactory>();
```

Now, imagine you wanted to write an action selector that would redirect all calls to a specific method of a class. You could write a redirect action selector like as follows:

```
public class RedirectActionSelector : IActionSelector
{
  public ActionDescriptor SelectBestCandidate(
    RouteContext context,
    IReadOnlyList<ActionDescriptor> candidates)
  {
    var descriptor = new ControllerActionDescriptor();
      descriptor.ControllerName = typeof(MyController).Name;
      descriptor.MethodInfo =
        typeof(MyController).GetTypeInfo().GetMethod("MyAction");
      descriptor.ActionName = descriptor.MethodInfo.Name;
      return descriptor;
  }

  public IReadOnlyList<ActionDescriptor> SelectCandidates(RouteContext
context)
  {
    return new List<ActionDescriptor>();
  }
}
```

This will redirect any request to the `MyAction` method of the `MyController` class. Hey, it's just for fun, remember?

Actions

The action method is where all the action happens (pun intended). It is the entry point to the code that handles your request. The found action method is called from the `IActionInvoker` implementation; it must be a **physical**, non-generic, public instance method of a controller class. The action selection mechanism is quite complex and relies on the route **action** parameter.

The name of the action method should be the same as this parameter, but that doesn't mean that it is the physical method name; one can also apply the `[ActionName]` attribute to set it to something different, and this is of particular use if we have overloaded methods:

```
[ActionName("BinaryOperation")]
public IActionResult Operation(int a, int b) { ... }

[ActionName("UnaryOperation")]
public IActionResult Operation(int a) { ... }
```

Finding actions

After discovering a set of candidate controllers for handling the request, ASP.NET Core will check them all to see if they offer a method that matches the current route:

- It must be public, non-static, and non-generic
- Its name must match the route's action (the physical name may be different as long as it has an `[ActionName]` attribute)
- Its parameters must match the non-optional parameters specified in the route (those not marked as optional and without default values); if the route specifies an `id` value, there must be an `id` parameter and type, and if the `id` has a route constraint of `int`, like in `{id:int}`, then it must be of the `int` type
- The action method can have a parameter of type `IFormCollection`, `IFormFile`, or `IFormFileCollection`, as these are always accepted
- It cannot have a `[NonAction]` attribute applied to it

Synchronous and asynchronous actions

An action method can be synchronous or asynchronous. For the asynchronous version, it should be prototyped as follows:

```
public async Task<IActionResult> Index() { ... }
```

Of course, you can add any number of parameters you like, as with a synchronous action method. The key here, however, is to mark the method as `async` and to return `Task<IActionResult>` instead of just `IActionResult` (or another inherited type).

Why should you use asynchronous actions? Well, you need to understand this:

- Web servers have a number of threads that they use to handle incoming requests
- When a request is accepted, one of these threads is blocked waiting to process it
- If the request takes too long, this thread is unavailable to answer other requests

Enter asynchronous actions. With asynchronous actions, as soon as a thread accepts an incoming request, it immediately passes it along to a background thread that will take care of it, releasing the main thread. This is very handy, because it will be available to accept other requests. This is not related to performance, but instead scalability; using asynchronous actions allows your application to always be responsive, even if it is still processing requests in the background.

Getting the context

We've seen how in both POCO and controller-based controllers you can access the context. By context, we're talking about three things, in what action methods are concerned:

- The HTTP context, represented by the `HttpContext` class, from which you can gain access to the current user, the low level request and response properties, such as cookies, headers, and so on
- The controller context, an instance of `ControllerContext`, which gives you access to the current model state, route data, action descriptor, and so on
- The action context, of type `ActionContext`, which gives you pretty much the same information that you get from `ControllerContext`, but used in different places, so, if, in the future, some new feature is added to only one, it will not show up on the other

Having access to the context is important because you may need to make decisions based on the information you can obtain from it, or for example, set response headers or cookies directly. You can see that ASP.NET Core has dropped the `HttpContext.Current` property that had been around since the beginning of ASP.NET, so you don't have immediate access to it. However, you can get it from either `ControllerContext`, or `ActionContext`, or have it injected into your dependency injection-build component by having your constructor take an instance of `IHttpContextAccessor`.

Action constraints

The following attributes and interfaces, when implemented in an attribute applied to the action method, will possibly prevent it from being called:

- [NonAction]: The action is never called
- [Consumes]: If there are many candidate methods, for example, in the case of method overloading, this attribute is used to check if any of the methods accept the currently requested content type
- [RequireHttps]: If present, the action method will only be called if the request protocol is HTTPS
- IActionConstraint: If an attribute applied to an action method implements this interface, its Accept method is called to see if the action should be called or not
- IActionHttpMethodProvider: This is implemented by [AcceptVerbs], [HttpGet], [HttpPost], and other HTTP method selector attributes; if present, the action method will only be called if the current request's HTTP verb matches one of the values returned by the HttpMethods property
- IAuthorizeData: Any attribute that implements this interface, the most notorious of all being [Authorize], will be checked to see if the current identity (as specified by ClaimsPrincipal assigned to the HttpContext's User property) has the right policy and roles
- Filters: If a filter attribute is applied to the action, such as IActionFilter, or IAuthorizationFilter, for example, is invoked and may possibly either throw an exception or return an IActionResult, which prevents the action from being called (NotFoundObjectResult, UnauthorizedResult, and more)

This implementation of IActionConstraint will apply custom logic to decide whether a method can be called in its Accept method:

```
public class CustomAuthorizationAttribute: Attribute, IActionConstraint
{
  public int Order { get; } = int.MaxValue;

  public bool Accept(ActionConstraintContext context)
  {
    return context.CurrentCandidate.Action.DisplayName.Contains(
      "Authorized");
  }
}
```

The `context` parameter grants access to the route context, and from there, to the HTTP context and the current candidate method. These should be more than enough to make a decision.

The order by which a constraint is applied might be relevant, as the `Order` property of the `IActionConstraint` interface, when used in an attribute, will determine the relative order of execution of all the attributes applied to the same method.

Action parameters

An action method can take parameters. These parameters are, for example, submitted form values or query string parameters. There are essentially three ways by which we can get all submitted values:

- `IFormCollection`, `IFormFile`, and `IFormFileCollection`: A parameter of any of these types will contain the list of values submitted by an HTML form; they won't be used in a `GET` request as it is not possible to upload files with `GET`
- `HttpContext`: Directly accessing the context and retrieving values from either the `Request.Form` or `Request.QueryString` collections
- Adding named parameters that match values in the request that we want to access individually

The latter can either be of basic types, such as `string`, `int`, and more, or they can be of complex type. The way the values for them are injected is configurable and based on a provider model. `IValueProviderFactory` and `IValueProvider` are used to obtain the values for these attributes. ASP.NET Core offers developers a chance to inspect the collection of value provider factories through the `AddMvc` method:

```
services.AddMvc(options =>
    {
        options.ValueProviderFactories.Add(new CustomValueProviderFactory());
    });
```

Out of the box, the following value provider factories are available and registered in the following order:

- `FormValueProviderFactory`: Injects values from a submitted form, such as, `<input type="text" name="myParam"/>`
- `RouteValueProviderFactory`: Route parameters, for example, `[controller]/[action]/{id?}`

- `QueryStringValueProviderFactory`: Query string values, for example, `?id=100`
- `JQueryFormValueProviderFactory`: jQuery form values

The order, however, is important, because it determines the order in which value providers are added to the collection that ASP.NET Core uses to actually get the values. Each value provider factory will have its `CreateValueProviderAsync` method called and will typically populate a collection of value providers (for example, `QueryStringValueProviderFactory` will add an instance of `QueryStringValueProvider`, and more). This means that, for example, if you submitted a form value with the name `myField` and you are passing via a query string another value for `myField`, the first one is going to be used. However, many providers can be used at once, for example, if you have a route that expects an `id` parameter but can also accept query string parameters:

```
[Route("[controller]/[action]/{id}?{*querystring}")]
public IActionResult ProcessOrder(int id, bool processed) { ... }
```

This will happily access a request of `/Home/Process/120?processed=true`, where the `id` comes from the route and is processed from the query string provider.

Some methods of sending values allow them to be optional, for example, route parameters. With that being the case, you need to make sure that the parameters in the action method also permit the following:

- Reference types, including those that have a **null** value
- Value types, which should have a default value, such as `int a = 0`

For example, if you want to have a value from a route injected into an action method parameter, you could do it like this, if the value is mandatory:

```
[Route("[controller]/[action]/{id}")]
public IActionResult Process(int id) { ... }
```

Or like this, if it is optional:

```
[Route("[controller]/[action]/{id?}")]
public IActionResult Process(int? id = null) { ... }
```

Value providers are more interesting because they are the ones that actually return the values for the action method parameters. They try to find a value from its name--the action method parameter name. ASP.NET will iterate the list of supplied value providers, call its ContainsPrefix method for each parameter, and if the result is true, will then call the GetValue method.

Even if the supplied value providers are convenient, you might want to obtain values from other sources. I can think of, for example:

- Cookies
- Headers
- Session values

Imagine that you would like to have cookie values injected automatically into an action method's parameters. For that, you would write a CookieValueProviderFactory, which might well look like this:

```
public class CookieValueProviderFactory : IValueProviderFactory
{
  public Task CreateValueProviderAsync(ValueProviderFactoryContext context)
  {
    context.ValueProviders.Add(new
CookieValueProvider(context.ActionContext));
    return Task.CompletedTask;
  }
}
```

And then a CookieValueProvider to go along:

```
public class CookieValueProvider : IValueProvider
{
  private readonly ActionContext _actionContext;

  public CookieValueProvider(ActionContext actionContext)
  {
    this._actionContext = actionContext;
  }

  public bool ContainsPrefix(string prefix)
  {
    return
this._actionContext.HttpContext.Request.Cookies.ContainsKey(prefix);
  }

  public ValueProviderResult GetValue(string key)
  {
```

```
      return new
ValueProviderResult(this._actionContext.HttpContext.Request.Cookies[key]);
    }
}
```

After which, you would register it in the `AddMvc` method, in the `ValueProviders` collection of `MvcOptions`:

```
services.AddMvc(options =>
    {
        options.ValueProviderFactories.Add(new CookieValueProviderFactory());
    }):
```

Now you can have cookie values injected transparently into your actions without any additional effort.

 Don't forget that, because of C# limitations, you cannot have variables or parameters that contain – or other special characters, so you cannot inject values for parameters that have these in their names out of the box. In this cookie example, you won't be able to have a parameter for a cookie with a name like `AUTH-COOKIE`.

You can however, in the same action method, have parameters coming from different sources, as follow:

```
[HttpGet("{id}")]
public IActionResult Process(string id, Model model) { ... }
```

But what if the target action method parameter is not of the string type? The answer lies in **model binding**.

Model binding

Model binding is the process by which ASP.NET Core translates parts of the request including route values, query string, submitted forms, and more into strongly typed parameters. As is the case in most APIs of ASP.NET Core, this is an extensible mechanism. Do not get confused with model value providers, the responsibility of model binders is not to supply the values, but merely to make them fit into whatever class we tell them to!

Out of the box, ASP.NET can translate to:

- IFormCollection, IFormFile, and IFormFileCollection parameters
- Primitive/base types (which handle conversion to and from string)
- Enumerations
- POCO classes
- Dictionaries
- Collections
- Cancellation tokens (more on this later on)

The model binder providers are configured in the MvcOptions class, which is normally accessible through the AddMvc call:

```
services.AddMvc(options =>
    {
        options.ModelBinderProviders.Add(new CustomModelBinderProvider());
    });
```

Most scenarios that you will be interested in should already be supported. What you can also do is specify the source from which a parameter is to be obtained. So, let's see what we have.

Body

In case you are calling an action using an HTTP verb that lets you pass a payload (POST, PUT, and PATCH), you can ask for your parameter to receive a value from this payload by applying a [FromBody] attribute:

```
[HttpPost]
public IActionResult Submit([FromBody] string payload) { ... }
```

Besides using a string value, you can provide your own POCO class, which will be populated from the payload, if the format is supported by one of the input formatters configured (more on this in a second).

Form

Another option is to have a parameter coming from a specific named field in a submitted form, and for that we use the [FromForm] attribute:

```
[HttpPost]
public IActionResult Submit([FromForm] string email) { ... }
```

There is a Name property that, if supplied, will get the value from the specified named form field (for example, [FromForm(Name = "UserEmail")]).

Header

A header is also a good candidate for retrieving values, hence the [FromHeader] attribute:

```
public IActionResult Get([FromHeader] string accept) { ... }
```

The [FromHeader] attribute allows us to specify the actual header name (for example, [FromHeader(Name = "Content-Type")]), and if not specified, it will look for the name of the parameter that it is applied to.

Query

Or the query string, for which there is the [FromQuery] attribute:

```
public IActionResult Get([FromQuery] string id) { ... }
```

You can also specify the query string parameter name using the Name property: [FromQuery(Name = "Id")].

Route

The route parameters can also be a source of data, enter [FromRoute]:

```
[HttpGet("{id}")]
public IActionResult Get([FromRoute] string id) { ... }
```

Similarly to most other binding attributes, you can specify a name to indicate the route parameter where the value should come from (for example, [FromRoute(Name = "Id")]).

Dependency injection

You can also use a dependency injection, too, such as (`[FromServices]`):

```
public IActionResult Get([FromServices] IHttpContextAccessor accessor) {
... }
```

Of course, the service you are injecting needs to be registered in the DI framework in advance.

Custom binders

It is also possible to specify your own binder. There is the `[ModelBinder]` attribute, which takes an optional `Type` as its parameter. What's funny about this is that it can be used in different scenarios, such as the following:

- If you apply it to a property or field on your controller class, it will be bound to a request parameter coming from any of the supported value providers (query string, route, form, and more):

  ```
  [ModelBinder]
  public string Id { get; set; }
  ```

- If you pass a type of a class that implements `IModelBinder`, you can use this class for the actual binding process, but only for the parameter, property, or field you are applying it to:

  ```
  public IActionResult Process(
    [ModelBinder(typeof(CustomModelBinder))] Model model) { ... }
  ```

A simple model binder that does HTML formatting could be written as:

```
public class HtmlEncodeModelBinder : IModelBinder
{
  private readonly IModelBinder _fallbackBinder;

  public HtmlEncodeModelBinder(IModelBinder fallbackBinder)
  {
    if (fallbackBinder == null) throw new
    ArgumentNullException(nameof(fallbackBinder));

    _fallbackBinder = fallbackBinder;
  }

  public Task BindModelAsync(ModelBindingContext bindingContext)
```

```
    {
      if (bindingContext == null) throw new
ArgumentNullException(nameof(bindingContext));

        var valueProviderResult = bindingContext.ValueProvider.GetValue(
            bindingContext.ModelName);

        if (valueProviderResult.Length > 0)
        {
          var valueAsString = valueProviderResult.FirstValue;

          if (string.IsNullOrEmpty(valueAsString))
          {
            return _fallbackBinder.BindModelAsync(bindingContext);
          }

          var result = HtmlEncoder.Default.Encode(valueAsString);

          bindingContext.Result = ModelBindingResult.Success(result);
        }

        return TaskCache.CompletedTask;
      }
    }
```

 The code for this was written by Steve Gordon and is available at `https:/` `/www.stevejgordon.co.uk/html-encode-string-aspnet-core-model-` `binding.`

You can also add a model binding provider to the global list. The first one that handles the target type will be picked up. The interface for a model binding provider is defined by the `IModelBinderProvider` (who would say?), and it only specifies a single method, `GetBinder`. If it returns non-null, the binder shall be used.

Let's look at a model binder provider that would apply this model binder to string parameters that have a custom attribute:

```
public class HtmlEncodeAttribute : Attribute { }

public class HtmlEncodeModelBinderProvider : IModelBinderProvider
{
  public IModelBinder GetBinder(ModelBinderProviderContext context)
  {
    if (context == null) throw new ArgumentNullException(nameof(context));

    if ((context.Metadata.ModelType == typeof(string)) &&
```

```
(context.Metadata.ModelType.GetTypeInfo().IsDefined(typeof(HtmlEncodeAttrib
ute))))
    {
        return new HtmlEncodeModelBinder(new
SimpleTypeModelBinder(context.Metadata.ModelType));
    }

    return null;
    }
}
```

After this, we register it in `AddMvc`, to the `ValueProviderFactories` collection; this collection is iterated until a proper model binder is returned from `GetBinder`, in which case, it is used as follows:

```
services.AddMvc(options =>
    {
        options.ValueProviderFactories.Add(new
HtmlEncodeModelBinderProvider());
    });
```

We have created a simple marker attribute, `HtmlEncodeAttribute`, as well as a model binder provider, that checks if the target model is of the type string and has the `[HtmlEncode]` attribute applied to it. If so, it applies the `HtmlEncodeModelBinder`. It's as simple as that:

```
public IActionResult Process([HtmlEncode] string html) { ... }
```

We will be revisiting model binding later on in this chapter when we talk about HTML forms.

Input formatters

When you are binding some POCO class from the payload, by applying the `[FromBody]` attribute, ASP.NET Core will try to deserialize the POCO type from the payload as a string. For that, it uses an **input formatter**. Similar to **output formatters**, these are used to convert to and from common formats, such as JSON or XML. Support for JSON comes out of the box, but you will need to explicitly add support for XML. You can do so by including the NuGet package `Microsoft.AspNetCore.Mvc.Formatters.Xml` and explicitly adding support to the pipeline:

```
services.AddMvc()
    .AddXmlSerializerFormatters();
```

If you are curious, what this does is add an instance of XmlSerializerInputFormatter to the MvcOptions' InputFormatters collection. The list is iterated until one formatter is capable of processing the data. The included formatters are as follows:

- JsonInputFormatter, which can import from any JSON content (application/json)
- JsonPatchInputFormatter, which can import from JSON patch contents (application/json-patch+json)

Explicit binding

You can also fine tune which parts of your model class are bound, and how they are bound, by applying attributes. For example, if you want to exclude a property from being bound, you can apply the [BindNever] attribute:

```
public class Model
{
  [BindNever]
  public int Id { get; set; }
}
```

Alternatively, if you want to explicitly define which properties should be bound, you can apply [Bind] to a Model class:

```
[Bind("Name, Email")]
public class Model
{
  public int Id { get; set; }
  public string Name { get; set; }
  public string Email { get; set; }
}
```

Normally, if a value for a property is not supplied in the source medium, such as the POST payload or the query string, the property doesn't get a value. However, you can force this, as follows:

```
[BindRequired]
public string Email { get; set; }
```

If the Email parameter is not passed, then ModelState.IsValid will be false, and no exception is thrown.

You can also specify the default binding behavior at class level, and then override it on a property-by-property basis with a `[BindingBehavior]`:

```
[BindingBehavior(BindingBehavior.Required)]
public class Model
{
  [BindNever]
  public int Id { get; set; }
  public string Name { get; set; }
  public string Email { get; set; }
}
```

We should also mention that these attributes can be applied to action method parameters as follows:

```
public IActionResult Process(string id, [BindRequired] int state) { ... }
```

Cancelling requests

Sometimes, a request is cancelled by the client, such as when someone closes the browser, navigates to another page, or refreshes. The problem is, you don't know that it happened, and you continue to execute your action method not knowing that the answer will be discarded. To help in these scenarios, ASP.NET Core lets you add a parameter of the type `CancellationToken`. This is the standard way in .NET and .NET Core to allow the cancellation of asynchronous tasks. It works as follows:

```
public async Task<IActionResult> Index(CancellationToken cancel) { ... }
```

If for whatever reason the ASP.NET Core host (Kestrel, WebListener) detects that the client has disconnected, it fires the cancellation token (its `IsCancellationRequested` is set to `true`, the same for `HttpContext.RequestAborted`). This results in a `TaskCancelledException` being thrown, effectively interrupting your method's execution--unless, of course, you catch it, which you shouldn't. Another benefit is that you can pass this `CancellationToken` instance to any asynchronous methods you may be using (for example, `HttpClient.SendAsync()`, `DbSet<T>.ToListAsync()`, and more) and they will also be cancelled along with the client request!

Model validation

Once your model (the parameters that are passed to the action method) are properly built and their properties have had their values set, they can be validated. Validation itself is configurable.

All values obtained from all value providers are available in the `ModelState` property, defined in the `ControllerBase` class. For any given type, the `IsValid` property will say whether ASP.NET considers the model valid as per its configured validators, or not.

By default, the registered implementation relies on the registered model metadata and model validator providers, which include the `DataAnnotationsModelValidatorProvider`. This performs validation against the `System.ComponentModel.DataAnnotations` API, namely, all `ValidationAttribute`-derived classes (`RequiredAttribute`, `RegularExpressionAttribute`, `MaxLengthAttribute`, and more) but also `IValidatableObject` implementations. This is the *de facto* validation standard in .NET and it is capable of handling most cases.

When the model is populated, it is also automatically validated, but you can also explicitly ask for model validation by calling the `TryValidateModel` method in your action, for example, if you change anything in it:

```
public IActionResult Process(Model model)
{
  if (this.TryValidateModel(model))
  {
    return this.Ok();
  }
  else
  {
    return this.Error();
  }
}
```

As we have mentioned, `ModelState` will have the `IsValid` property set accordingly to the validation result, but we can also force re-validation.

If you want to check a specific property, you use the overload of `TryValidateModel` that takes an additional string parameter:

```
if (this.TryValidateModel(model, "Email"))
```

Behind the scenes, all registered validators are called and the method will return a Boolean flag with the result of all validations.

We will revisit model validation in an upcoming chapter. For now, let's see how we can plug in a custom model validator. We do this in ConfigureServices, through the AddMvc method:

```
services.AddMvc(options =>
    {
       options.ModelValidatorProviders.Add(new
CustomModelValidatorProvider());
    });
```

The CustomModelValidatorProvider looks as follows:

```
public class CustomModelValidatorProvider : IModelValidatorProvider
{
  public void CreateValidators(ModelValidatorProviderContext context)
  {
    context.Results.Add(new ValidatorItem { Validator = new
CustomModelValidator() });
  }
}
```

Simply, the main logic goes in CustomModelValidator:

```
public class CustomObjectModelValidator : IModelValidator
{
  public IEnumerable<ModelValidationResult> Validate(ModelValidationContext
context)
  {
    if (context.Model is ICustomValidatable)
    {
      //supply custom validation logic here and return
        a collection of ModelValidationResult
    }

    return Enumerable.Empty<ModelValidationResult>();
  }
}
```

The ICustomValidatable interface (and implementation) is left to you, dear reader, as an exercise. Hopefully, it won't be too difficult to understand.

This ICustomValidatable implementation should look at the state of its class and return one or more ModelValidationResults for any problems it finds.

Action results

Actions process requests and typically either return some content or an HTTP status code to the calling client. In ASP.NET Core, broadly speaking, there are two possible return types:

- An implementation of `IActionResult`
- Any .NET POCO class

`IActionResult` implementations wrap the actual response, plus a content type header and HTTP status code, and are generally useful. This interface defines only a single method, `ExecuteResultAsync`, which takes a single parameter of the type `ActionContext` that wraps all properties that describe the current request:

- `ActionDescriptor`: Describes the action method to call
- `HttpContext`: Describes the request context
- `ModelState`: Describes the submitted model properties and its validation state
- `RouteData`: Describes the route parameters

So you can see that `IActionResult` is actually an implementation of the command design pattern (`https://sourcemaking.com/design_patterns/command`) in the sense that it actually executes, not just stores data. A very simple implementation of `IActionResult` that returns a string and the HTTP status code `200` might be:

```
public class HelloWorldResult : IActionResult
{
  public async Task ExecuteResultAsync(ActionContext actionContext)
  {
    actionContext.HttpContext.Response.StatusCode = 200;
    await actionContext.HttpContext.Response.WriteAsync("Hello, World!");
  }
}
```

As we will see shortly, `IActionResult` is now the interface that describes HTML results as well as API-style results. The `ControllerBase` and `Controller` classes offer the following convenient methods for returning `IActionResult` implementations:

- `BadRequest` (`BadRequestResult`, HTTP code `400`): The request was not valid
- `Challenge` (`ChallengeResult`, HTTP code `401`): A challenge for authentication
- `Content` (`ContentResult`, HTTP code `200`): Any content
- `Created` (`CreatedResult`, HTTP code `201`): A result that indicates that a resource was created

- `CreatedAtAction` (`CreatedAtActionResult`, HTTP code 201): A result that indicates that a resource was created by an action
- `CreatedAtRoute` (`CreatedAtRouteResult`, HTTP code 201): A result that indicates that a resource was created in a named route
- `File` (`VirtualFileResult`, `FileStreamResult`, `FileContentResult`, HTTP code 200)
- `Forbid` (`ForbidResult`, HTTP code 403)
- `LocalRedirect` (`LocalRedirectResult`, HTTP code 302): Redirects to a local resource
- `LocalRedirectPermanent` (`LocalRedirectResult`, HTTP code 301): A permanent redirect to a local resource
- `NoContent` (`NoContentResult`, HTTP code 204): No content to deploy
- `NotFound` (`NotFoundObjectResult`, HTTP code 404): Resource not found
- `Ok` (`OkResult`, HTTP code 200): OK
- No method (`PartialViewResult`, HTTP code 200): Requested HTTP method not supported
- `PhysicalFile` (`PhysicalFileResult`, HTTP code 200): A physical file's content
- `Redirect` (`RedirectResult`, HTTP code 302): Redirect to a full URL
- `RedirectPermanent` (`RedirectResult`, HTTP code 301): Permanent redirect to an absolute URL
- `RedirectToAction` (`RedirectToActionResult`, HTTP code 302): A redirect to an action of a local controller
- `RedirectToActionPermanent` (`RedirectToActionResult`, HTTP code 301): A permanent redirect to an action of a local controller
- `RedirectToPage` (`RedirectToPageResult`, HTTP code 302, from ASP.NET Core 2): A redirect to a local Razor Page
- `RedirectToPagePermanent` (`RedirectToPageResult`, HTTP code 301): A permanent redirect to a local Razor Page
- `RedirectToPagePermanentPreserveMethod` (`RedirectToPageResult`, HTTP code 301): A permanent redirect to a local page preserving the original requested HTTP method
- `RedirectToPagePreserveMethod` (`RedirectToPageResult`, HTTP code 302): A redirect to a local page
- `RedirectToRoute` (`RedirectToRouteResult`, HTTP code 302): A redirect to a named route

- RedirectToRoutePermanent (RedirectToRouteResult, HTTP code 301): A permanent redirect to a named route
- SignIn (SignInResult): Signs in
- SignOut (SignOutResult): Signs out
- StatusCode (StatusCodeResult, ObjectResult, any HTTP code)
- No method (UnsupportedMediaTypeResult, HTTP code 415): Accepted content type does not match what can be returned
- Unauthorized (UnauthorizedResult, HTTP code 401): Not allowed to request the resource
- View (ViewResult, HTTP code 200, declared in Controller class): A view
- ViewComponent (ViewComponentResult, HTTP code 200): The result of invoking a view component

Some of these results also assign a content type, for example, ContentResult will return text/plain by default (this can be changed), and JsonResult will return application/json, and more. Some of the names are self-explanatory, others may require some clarification:

- There are always four versions of the Redirect methods--the regular (for temporary redirects), one for permanent redirects, and two additional versions that also preserve the original request HTTP method. It is possible to redirect to an arbitrary URL, the URL for a specific controller action, a Razor Page URL, and a local (relative) URL.
- Preserve method in a redirect means that the new request to be issued by the browser will keep the original HTTP verb.
- The File and Physical file methods offer several ways to return file contents, either through a URL, a Stream, a byte array, or physical file location. The Physical method allows you to directly send a file from a filesystem location, which may result in better performance. You also have the option to set an ETag or a LastModified date on the content you wish to transmit.
- ViewResult and PartialViewResult differ in that the latter only looks for partial views.
- Some methods may return different results, depending on the overload used (and its parameters, of course).
- SignIn, SignOut, and Challenge are related to authentication, and are pointless if not configured. SignIn will redirect to the configured login URL and SignOut will clear the authentication cookie.

- Not all of these results return contents, some of them only return a status code and some headers (for example, `SignInResult`, `SignOutResult`, `StatusCodeResult`, `UnauthorizedResult`, `NoContentResult`, `NotFoundObjectResult`, `ChallengeResult`, `BadRequestResult`, `ForbidResult`, `OkResult`, `CreatedResult`, `CreatedAtActionResult`, `CreatedAtRouteResult`, and all the `Redirect*` results). On the other hand, `JsonResult`, `ContentResult`, `VirtualFileResult`, `FileStreamResult`, `FileContentResult`, and `ViewResult` all return contents.

All the action result classes that return views (`ViewResult`) or parts of views (`PartialViewResult`) take a `Model` property which is prototyped as an `object`. You can use it to pass any arbitrary data to the view, but remember that the view must declare a model of a compatible type. Alas, you cannot pass anonymous types, as the view will have no way to locate its properties. In `Chapter 6`, *Using Forms and Models*, I will present a solution for this.

Returning an action result is probably the most typical use of a controller, but you can also certainly return any .NET object. To do this, you must declare your method to return whatever type you want:

```
public string SayHello()
{
   return "Hello, World!";
}
```

This is a perfectly valid action method. However, there are a few things you need to know:

- The returned object is wrapped in an `ObjectResult`, before any filters are called (`IActionFilter`, `IResultFilter`, for example)
- The object is formatted (serialized) by one of the configured **output formatters**, the first that says it can handle it
- If you want to change either the status code or the content type of the response, you will need to resort to the `HttpContext.Response` object

Why return a POCO class or an `ObjectResult`? Well, `ObjectResult` gives you a couple of extra advantages:

- You can supply a collection of output formatters (`Formatters` collection)
- You can tell it to use a selection of content types (`ContentTypes`)
- You can specify the status code to return (`StatusCode`)

Let's look at output formatters in more detail in regard to API actions. For now, let's look at an example action result, one that returns contents as XML:

```
public class XmlResult : ActionResult
{
  public XmlResult(object value)
  {
    this.Value = value;
  }

  public object Value { get; set; }

  public override Task ExecuteResultAsync(ActionContext context)
  {
    if (this.Value != null)
    {
      var serializer = new XmlSerializer(this.Value.GetType());
      using (var stream = new MemoryStream())
      {
        serializer.Serialize(stream, this.Value);
        var data = stream.ToArray();
        context.HttpContext.Response.ContentType =  "application/xml";
        context.HttpContext.Response.ContentLength = data.Length;
        context.HttpContext.Response.Body.Write(data, 0, data.Length);
      }
    }
    return base.ExecuteResultAsync(context);
  }
}
```

Here, you will need to add a reference to the `System.Xml.XmlSerializer` NuGet package for the `XmlSerializer` class.

API actions

Not all actions are meant to return HTML (such as views). Some return content is only suitable for non-human processing, such as some client API. In this case, other contents are more suitable than HTML--a **presentation** language namely, JSON or XML. Sometimes, it is only necessary to return an HTTP status code or some response headers. In the past, this was done with APIs outside ASP.NET MVC, such as with Microsoft's **ASP.NET Web API** (https://www.asp.net/web-api), **Nancy** (http://nancyfx.org), or **ServiceStack** (https://servicestack.net).

Let's pick up ASP.NET Web API. It has shared quite a few concepts and similarly-named (and purposed) APIs with MVC, but it was an entirely different project that used different assemblies and a different bootstrap mechanism (OWIN). Unsurprisingly, Microsoft made the decision, in ASP.NET Core, to unify MVC and Web API: now there is no more Web API, only MVC. The features are all here, however.

Output formatters

What does returning an object mean, in an HTTP response? Well, this object needs to be turned into something that can be transmitted over the wire. Some typical response types are as follows:

- `text/html`: For HTML content
- `text/plain`: For generic text content
- `application/json`: For JSON content
- `application/xml`: For XML content
- `binary/octet-stream`: For any binary content

Therefore, the object you return needs to be turned into something that can be sent using one of these content types. For this, ASP.NET Core uses the concept of an output formatter. An output formatter is essentially an implementation of `IOutputFormatter`.

Out of the box, ASP.NET Core includes the following output formatters:

- `HttpNoContentOutputFormatter` doesn't write any content at all; only returns an HTTP status code `204`
- `StringOutputFormatter` outputs strings as-is
- `StreamOutputFormatter` writes a `Stream` as a series of bytes
- `JsonOutputFormatter` serializes the object to JSON

There are also a couple of flavors of XML formatters that can be installed using the `Microsoft.AspNetCore.Mvc.Formatters.Xml` NuGet package and registered either through the `AddXmlDataContractSerializerFormatters` (for `DataContractSerializer`) or the `AddXmlSerializerFormatters` (for `XmlSerializer`).

Data contract and XML serializer use different approaches; for example, different attributes to control the output.

Output formatters can be configured using the `AddMvc` extension method overload that takes a parameter, as follows:

```
services.AddMvc(options =>
    {
        options.OutputFormatters.Insert(0, new MyOutputFormatter());
    })
```

So, how is an output formatter selected? ASP.NET Core iterates the list of configured outputters, and calls its `IOutputFormatter.CanWriteResult` method. The first formatter that returns `true` is the one that is used to serialize the object to the output stream (`WriteAsync` method).

Content negotiation

Content negotiation is the process by which the application returns data in a format that is requested by the client. This is usually for API-style invocations, and not requests that serve HTML. For example, a certain client might want data returned in a JSON format, and some might prefer XML. ASP.NET Core supports this.

There are essentially two ways to achieve this:

- Through a route or query string parameter
- Through the `Accept` request header

The first approach lets you specify on the URL the format that you're interested in. Let's see how this works first. Imagine you have this action method:

```
public Model Process() { ... }
```

Let's forget what `Model` actually is, as it's just a POCO class that contains the properties you're interested in. It could be as simple as this:

```
public class Model
{
    public int A { get; set; }
    public string B { get; set; }
}
```

Out of the box, ASP.NET Core includes a formatter for JSON, but you can add a NuGet package, also from Microsoft, that adds support for XML-- `Microsoft.AspNetCore.Mvc.Formatters.Xml`. As well as adding it to the services, you also need to tell ASP.NET what mapping to use; in this case, the `xml` format to the content type `application/xml`:

```
services.AddMvc(options =>
    {
        options.FormatterMappings.SetMediaTypeMappingForFormat("xml",
"application/xml");
    })
    .AddXmlSerializerFormatters();
```

There is already a mapping from `json` to `application/json`, so there is no need to add it as it will be the default.

Then, you need to decorate your action method with a route that specifies the `format` parameter:

```
[Route("[controller]/[action]/{format}")]
public Model Process() { ... }
```

You also need to decorate your controller class with the `[FormatFilter]` attribute, as follows:

```
[FormatFilter]
public class HomeController
{
}
```

Now, if you call your action with one of `json` or `xml`, you will get an answer properly formatted according to the format you specified:

```
<Model xmlns:xsi="http://www.w3.org/2001/XMLSchema-instance"
xmlns:xsd="http://www.w3.org/2001/XMLSchema">
    <A>1</A>
    <B>two</B>
</Model>
```

Or:

```
{"a":1,"b":"two"}
```

The other way is to use the request's `Accept` header, a standard way of specifying the content we're interested in receiving. API clients don't typically use it, but browsers do. In the `AddMvc` call, you need to activate the `RespectBrowserAcceptHeader` property:

```
services.AddMvc(options =>
    {
        options.RespectBrowserAcceptHeader = true;
    })
    .AddXmlSerializerFormatters();
```

Now, if you send an `Accept` header of either `application/xml` or `application/json` (this is the default), you will get the result in the desired format.

 For more information about the `Accept` header, please consult `https://developer.mozilla.org/en-US/docs/Web/HTTP/Headers/Accept`.

For the sake of completeness, the JSON formatter allows us to specify additional options, through the use of a `AddJsonOptions` extension method:

```
services.AddMvc()
    .AddJsonOptions(options =>
    {
        options.SerializerSettings.ContractResolver = new
CamelCasePropertyNamesContractResolver();
    });
```

This configures the resolver to use **camelCasing** instead of the default. There are too many options to discuss here, and since they're not really that relevant, we'll leave them be.

API versioning

Also related to API (web service)-style method invocations is versioning. By versioning your API, you can have multiple simultaneous versions of it, by possibly taking different payloads and returning different results. ASP.NET Core supports API versioning through the `Microsoft.AspNetCore.Mvc.Versioning` library.

Out of the box, you can apply the following techniques to specify the version that you're interested in:

- A URL parameter
- A header
- Any of the above, meaning, either the URL or a header

Let's say you have two controller classes of the same name, in two different namespaces:

```
namespace Controllers.V1
{
  [ApiVersion("1.0")]
  public class ApiController
  {
    public Model Get() { ... }
  }
}

namespace Controllers.V2
{
  [ApiVersion("2.0")]
  [ApiVersion("3.0")]
  public class ApiController
  {
    public Model Get() { ... }
  }
}
```

Here, you can see that we applied a couple of `[ApiVersion]` attributes to each, with each one specifying an API version that the controller supports. Let's see how we can implement versioning, starting with the route approach.

Header values

We will configure API versioning to infer the desired version from a header field. We configure versioning in the `ConfigureServices` method. Notice the `HeaderApiVersionReader` class:

```
services.AddApiVersioning(options =>
    {
      options.ApiVersionReader = new HeaderApiVersionReader(
        "api-version");
    });
```

Here, we're saying that the version should come from the header string called `api-version`. This is not a standard value, it's just some string we picked up.

Now, when calling your API at `/Api/Get`, while passing a header `api-version` with a value of `1.0`, the request will be handled by class `Controllers.V1.ApiController`. If you pass a value of `2.0` or `3.0`, however, it will be picked up by the class `Controllers.V2.ApiController`.

URL

In order to infer the version from the URL, we need to use the `QueryStringApiVersionReader` class, as follows:

```
services.AddApiVersioning(options =>
    {
        options.ApiVersionReader = new QueryStringApiVersionReader("api-
version");
    });
```

We also need to configure a route that takes this into account:

```
[Route("[controller]/{version:apiversion}")]
public Model Get() { ... }
```

Now, if we make a request to `/api/1.0`, we get version `1.0`, and the same goes for `2.0` and `3.0`.

If we want to be more flexible, we can use the `QueryStringOrHeaderApiVersionReader` class as the `ApiVersionReader`, and both approaches will work.

Deprecation

You can say that one version is obsolete by setting a flag to the `Deprecated` property:

```
[ApiVersion("1.0", Deprecated = true)]
```

Now, if you add the `ReportApiVersions` flag to `true`, you will receive, as part of the response, the versions that are supported and those that aren't:

```
services.AddApiVersioning(options =>
    {
        options.ReportApiVersions = true;
```

```
        options.ApiVersionReader = new QueryStringApiVersionReader("api-
version");
    });
```

This yields the following response headers:

```
api-deprecated-versions: 1.0
api-supported-versions: 2.0, 3.0
```

Default version

You can also specify a default version:

```
services.AddApiVersioning(options =>
    {
        options.AssumeDefaultVersionWhenUnspecified = true;
        options.DefaultApiVersion = new ApiVersion(2, 0);
        options.ApiVersionReader = new QueryStringApiVersionReader("api-
version");
    });
```

In this case, if you don't specify a version, it will assume that you want version 2.0.

Version mapping

As we've seen, the Controllers.V2.ApiController class is mapped to two versions--2.0 and 3.0. But what happens if you want to handle version 3.0 separately? Well, you simply add a [MapToApiVersion] attribute to a new method:

```
[MapToApiVersion("3.0")]
public Model GetV3() { ... }
```

Henceforth, all requests for version 3.0 will be handled by it.

Invalid versions

If an unsupported version is requested, not a deprecated one, an exception will be thrown and returned to the client as follows:

```
{
  "error":
  {
    "code": "ApiVersionUnspecified",
    "message":"An API version is required, but was not specified."
```

```
    }
  }
```

There are more options, but these should be more than enough to get you started.

API documentation

Web APIs have a specification that, initially had the name of **Swagger** but now goes by **OpenAPI** (`https://github.com/OAI/OpenAPI-Specification`), and is used to describe the endpoints and versions offered by some APIs. The Swagger v3.0 specification was contributed to the OpenAPI initiative, and thus Swagger has been merged with OpenAPI. It is still colloquially called Swagger in several places, and there is also an open source implementation for .NET called `Swashbuckle.AspNetCore` (`https://github.com/domaindrivendev/Swashbuckle.AspNetCore`). What this package does is inspect the action methods of your controllers and generate a JSON document that describes them. It also offers a simple web interface for invoking each of these action methods, how cool is that?

In order to use `Swashbuckle.AspNetCore`, we need to add a few NuGet packages-- `Swashbuckle.AspNetCore.SwaggerGen`, `Swashbuckle.AspNetCore.SwaggerUI`, and `Swashbuckle.AspNetCore`, where the latter is added automatically by the former. To use Swashbuckle, as with most ASP.NET Core APIs, we first need to register the required services to the dependency injection framework (`ConfigureServices`):

```
services.AddSwaggerGen(c =>
    {
        c.SwaggerDoc("v1", new Info {
            Title = "My API V1",
            Version = "v1",
            Contact = new Contact {
                Email = "rjperes@hotmail.com",
                Name = "Ricardo Peres",
                Url = "http://weblogs.asp.net/ricardoperes"
            }
        });
    });
```

We only register those that actually make use of them (in the `Configure` method), adding the Swagger middleware to the pipeline:

```
app.UseSwagger();

app.UseSwaggerUI(options =>
    {
        options.SwaggerEndpoint("/swagger/v1/swagger.json", "My API V1");
```

```
        });
```

The two calls, `UseSwagger` and `UseSwaggerUI`, refer to two different functionalities--the first is for the actual API documentation and the second is the user interface for invoking controller actions.

You can add as many calls to `AddSwaggerGen` as you like, with different API names or versions. Each version will generate a different API version document.

Swashbuckle works by introspecting all the controllers and their action methods, but, it will only find those that you explicitly want it to find, such as:

- Controllers marked with a `[Route]` attribute
- Action methods marked with `[Route]`, `[HttpGet]`, `[HttpPost]`, `[HttpPut]`, `[HttpDelete]`, `[HttpOptions]`, `[HttpPatch]`, or `[HttpMethod]` and, with an explicit route template

Now, when you access URL `/swagger/v1/swagger.json`, you get something like this:

```json
{
  "swagger": "2.0",
  "info": {
    "version": "v1",
    "title": "My API V1",
    "contact": {
        "name": "Ricardo Peres",
        "url": "http://weblogs.asp.net/ricardoperes",
        "email": "rjperes@hotmail.com"
    }
  },
  "basePath": "/",
  "paths": {
    "/Home": {
      "get": {
        "tags": [ "Home" ],
        "operationId": "HomeIndexGet",
        "consumes": [],
        "produces": [],
        "responses": {
          "200": {
            "description": "Success"
          }
        }
      }
    },
```

```
        "definitions": {},
        "securityDefinitions": {}
    }
```

Due to space constraints, we have only included one action method, `Index`, of the controller `Home`, in this sample output. However, you can see a single document, named `My API V1`, version `V1`. For each action method, Swashbuckle describes the HTTP methods it accepts, any content types that it accepts (these can be specified through the use of the `[Consumes]` attribute), returns (as set by `[Produces]`), and also the return status codes (`[ProducesContentType]` or `[SwaggerResponse]` attributes). If these are not specified, the defaults are used, which is `200` for the status code, no accept, or return content types.

> This version has nothing to do with the versioning schema discussed in the previous topic.

For each document you add with `AddSwaggerGen`, you get a different URL, such as `/swagger/v1/swagger.json`, `/swagger/v2/swagger.json`, and more.

Of more interest is the generated user interface, which can be accessed through the `/swagger` endpoint:

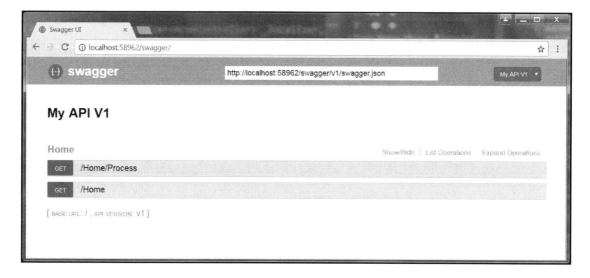

Here, we can see two actions (known as **operations**), /Home and /Home/Process. They are two action methods in the Home controller, and these are the routes to access each. For the sake of clarity, let's consider the Process action method to have the following signature:

```
[HttpGet("Process")]
[Produces("application/json")]
[SwaggerResponse(200, Description = "Processes some order", Type =
typeof(ProcessModel))]
public IActionResult Process(string id, int state) { ... }
```

Now, expanding the operations yields this:

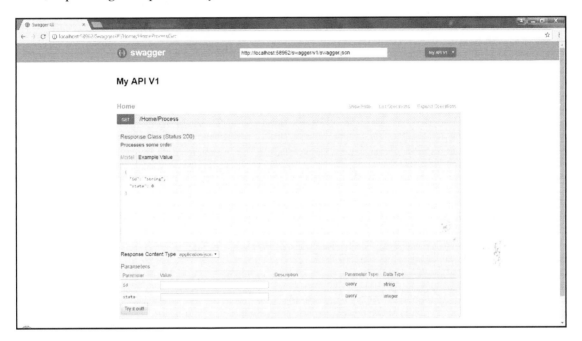

Here, you get a form that asks the parameters to `Process` and even shows you a sample response formatted as JSON. Brilliant! This sample response comes from the `Type` property applied to the `[SwaggerResponse]` attribute. If you fill them out and click on **Try it out!**, this is what you get:

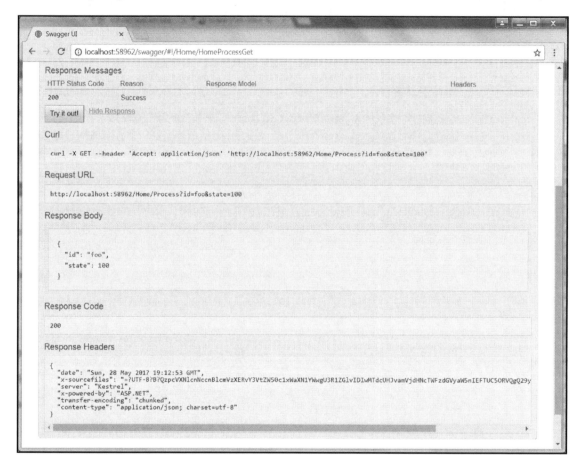

Here, you get the response payload plus all of the response headers. Pretty cool, right?

What remains to be shown is how we can customize the URLs for both the JSON documentation and the user interface. We do this through the `UseSwagger` and `UseSwaggerUI` extension methods as follows:

```
app.UseSwagger(options =>
    {
        options.RouteTemplate = "api-doc/{documentName}/swagger.json";
    });
```

The `RouteTemplate` property only needs to take a `{documentName}` token, the default being `swagger/{documentName}/swagger.json`. This token is replaced by whatever you add as the first parameter to the `SwaggerDoc` call in the `AddSwaggerGen` lambda. Don't forget that, if you change one, you need to change both:

```
app.UseSwaggerUI(options =>
    {
        options.SwaggerEndpoint("/api-doc/v1/swagger.json", "My API V1");
    });
```

 There are lots of other configuration options, so we advise you to take a look at the documentation available at `https://github.com/domaindrivendev/Swashbuckle.AspNetCore`.

Response caching

An action response of any type (HTML or JSON, for example) may be cached in the client in order to improve performance. Needless to say, this should only happen if the result it is returning rarely changes. This is specified in **RFC 7234**, **HTTP/1.1 Caching** (`https://tools.ietf.org/html/rfc7234`). Essentially, response caching is a mechanism by which the server notifies the client (the browser or some client API) to keep the response returned (including headers) for some URL for a certain amount of time and to use it, during that time, for all subsequent invocations of the URL. Only the `GET` HTTP verb can be cached, as it is designed to be idempotent; `PUT`, `POST`, `PATCH`, or `DELETE` cannot.

We add support for resource caching in `ConfigureServices` as follows:

```
services.AddResponseCaching();
```

We use it in `Configure`, which basically adds the response caching middleware to the ASP.NET Core pipeline:

```
app.UseResponseCaching();
```

We can also set a couple of options in the call to `AddResponseCaching`, such as:

- `MaximumBodySize` (`int`): This is the maximum size of the response that can be stored in the client response cache; the default is 64 KB
- `UseCaseSensitivePaths` (`bool`): This enables you to consider the request URL for the caching key as case-sensitive or not; the default is `false`

These can be used through an overload of the `AddResponseCaching` method:

```
services.AddResponseCaching(options =>
    {
        options.MaximumBodySize *= 2;
        options.UseCaseSensitivePaths = true;
    });
```

We can also have an action result cached by applying the `[ResponseCache]` attribute to either the action or the whole controller class. Following that, we have a couple of options-- we can either specify each of the cache parameters directly in the attribute or we can tell it to use a **cache profile**.

The options are as follows:

- `Duration` (`int`): The number of seconds to cache, the default is `0`
- `Location` (`ResponseCacheDuration`): The location of the cache (`Client`, `None`, `Any`); the default is `Any`
- `NoStore` (`bool`): Whether to prevent the storing of the result; the default is `false`
- `VaryByHeader` (`string`): The comma-separated list of headers for which an instance of the result is cached; the default is null
- `VaryByQueryKeys` (`string []`): A list of query string parameters for which an instance of the result is cached; the default is null
- `CacheProfileName` (`string`): The cache profile name, which is incompatible with the other options; the default is null

As we have mentioned, you either specify all of the individual options (or, at least, those that you need) or you specify a cache profile name. Cache profiles are defined at `Startup` in the `ConfigureServices` method, through the `AddMvc` extension method, as follows:

```
services.AddMvc(options =>
    {
        options.CacheProfiles.Add("5minutes", new CacheProfile {
            Duration = 5 * 60,
            Location = ResponseCacheLocation.Any,
            VaryByHeader = "Accept-Language" });
    });
```

This cache profile specifies that results are kept for five minutes, with different instances for different values of the `Accept-Language` header. After this, you only need to specify the name `5minutes`:

```
[ResponseCache(CacheProfileName = "5minutes")]
public IActionResult Cache() { ... }
```

The `VaryByHeader` and `VaryByQueryKeys` properties, if they have values, will keep different instances of the same cached response for each value of either the request header or the query string parameter (or both). For example, if your application supports multiple languages and you use the `Accept-Language` HTTP header to indicate which language should be served, the results are kept in cache for each of the requested language; that is, one for `pt-PT`, one for `en-GB`, and more.

It's generally preferable to use cache profiles, rather than providing all parameters in the attribute.

Maintaining state

What if you need to maintain a state, either from one component to the other in the same request, or across requests? Web applications have traditionally offered solutions for this, let's explore the options we have.

Request

Any object that you store in the request (in memory) will be available throughout its duration. Items are a strongly typed dictionary in the `HttpContext` class:

```
this.HttpContext.Items["timestamp"] = DateTime.UtcNow;
```

You can check for the existence of the item before accessing it; it is worth noting that this is case-sensitive:

```
if (this.HttpContext.Items.ContainsKey("timestamp")) { ... }
```

Of course you can also remove an item:

```
this.HttpContext.Items.Remove("timestamp");
```

Form

The `Form` collection keeps track of all values submitted by an HTML FORM, normally after a POST request. To access it, you use the `Form` property of the `Request` object of `HttpContext`:

```
var isChecked = this.HttpContext.Request.Form["isChecked"].Equals("on");
```

You can program defensively by first checking for the existence of the value (case-insensitive):

```
if (this.HttpContext.Request.Form.ContainsKey("isChecked")) { ... }
```

It is possible to obtain multiple values, and in that case, you can count them and get all their values:

```
var count = this.HttpContext.Request.Form["isChecked"].Count;
var values = this.HttpContext.Request.Form["isChecked"].ToArray();
```

Query string

Usually, you won't store data in the query string, but will rather get data from it, like in `http://servername.com?isChecked=true`. The `Query` collection keeps track of all parameters sent in the URL as strings:

```
var isChecked = this.HttpContext.Request.Query["isChecked"].Equals("true");
```

To check for the presence of a value, we use the following:

```
if (this.HttpContext.Request.Query.ContainsKey("isChecked")) { ... }
```

This also supports multiple values:

```
var count = this.HttpContext.Request.Query["isChecked"].Count;
var values = this.HttpContext.Request.Query["isChecked"].ToArray();
```

Route

As with the query string approach, you typically only get values from the route and do not write to them. Although you do have methods in the `IUrlHelper` interface, which is normally accessible through the `Url` property of the `ControllerBase` class, that generate action URLs, from which you can pack arbitrary values. Route parameters look like this-- `http://servername.com/admin/user/121`, and use a route template of `[controller]/[action]/{id}`.

To get a route parameter (a string), you do the following:

```
var id = this.RouteData.Values["id"];
```

And to check that it's there, use the following:

```
if (this.RouteData.ContainsKey("id")) { ... }
```

Cookies

Cookies have been around for a long time and are the basis of a lot of functionality on the web, such as authentication and sessions. They are specified in RFC 6265 (`https://tools.ietf.org/html/rfc6265`). Essentially, they are a way of storing small amounts of text in the client.

You can both read and write cookies. To read a cookie value, you only need to know its name; its value will come as a string:

```
var username = this.HttpContext.Request.Cookies["username"];
```

Of course, you can also check that the cookie exists with the following:

```
if (this.HttpContext.Request.Cookies.ContainsKey("username")) { ... }
```

To send a cookie to the client as part of the response, you need a bit more information, namely:

- `Name` (`string`): A name (what else?)
- `Value` (`string`): A string value
- `Expires` (`DateTime`): An optional expiration time stamp (the default is for the cookie to be session-based, meaning, it will vanish once the browser closes)
- `Path` (`string`): An optional path from which the cookie is to be made available (the default is /)

- Domain (string): An optional domain (the default is the current fully qualified host name)
- Secure (bool): An optional secure flag that, if present, will cause the cookie to only be available if the request is being served using HTTPS; the default is false
- HttpOnly (bool): Also an optional flag that indicates whether the cookie will be readable by JavaScript on the client browser; the default is also false

We add a cookie to the request object as follows:

```
this.HttpContext.Response.Cookies.Append("username", "rjperes",
    new CookieOptions {
        Domain = "packtpub.com",
        Expires = DateTimeOffset.Now.AddDays(1),
        HttpOnly = true,
        Secure = true,
        Path = "/"
    });
```

The third parameter, of the type CookieOptions, is optional, in which case the cookie assumes the default values.

The only way you can revoke a cookie is by adding one with the same name and an expiration date in the past.

> You mustn't forget that there is a limit to the number of cookies you can store per domain, as well as to the actual size of an individual cookie value; these shouldn't be used for large amounts of data. For more information, please consult RFC 6265.

Session

Sessions are a way to persist data per client. Typically, sessions rely on cookies, but it's possible (yet error-prone) to use query string parameters, and ASP.NET Core does not support this out of the box. In ASP.NET Core, sessions are opt-in; in other words, they need to be explicitly added. We need to add the NuGet package Microsoft.AspNetCore.Session and explicitly add support in the Configure and ConfigureServices methods of the Startup class:

```
public void ConfigureServices(IServiceCollection services)
{
    services.AddSession();
    //rest goes here
}
```

```
public void Configure(
    IApplicationBuilder app,
    IHostingEnvironment env,
    ILoggerFactory loggerFactory)
{
    app.UseSession();
    //rest goes here
}
```

After that, the `Session` object is made available in the `HttpContext` instance:

```
var value = this.HttpContext.Session.Get("key");  //byte[]
```

Probably a better approach is to use the `GetString` extension method, and serialize/deserialize to JSON:

```
var json = this.HttpContext.Session.GetString("key");
var model = JsonConvert.DeserializeObject<Model>(json);
```

Here, `Model` is just some POCO class and `JsonConvert` is a class from JSON.NET (`Newtonsoft.Json`) that has static methods for serializing and deserializing to and from JSON strings.

To store a value into the session, we use the `Set` or `SetString` methods:

```
this.HttpContext.Session.Set("key", value); //value is byte[]
```

The JSON approach is as follows:

```
var json = JsonConvert.SerializeObject(model);
this.HttpContext.Session.SetString("key", json);
```

Removing is achieved by either setting the value to `null` or calling `Remove`.

Similar to `GetString` and `SetString`, there are also the `GetInt32` and `SetInt32` extension methods. Use what best suits your needs, but never forget that the data is always stored as a byte array.

If you want to check for the existence of a value in the session, you should use the `TryGetValue` method:

```
byte[] data;
if (this.HttpContext.Session.TryGetValue("key", out data)) { ... }
```

That's pretty much it for using session as a general purpose dictionary. Now it's, configuration time! You can set some values, mostly around the cookie that is used to store the session, plus the idle interval, in a `SessionOptions` object:

```
services.AddSession(options =>
    {
        options.CookieDomain = "packtpub.com";
        options.CookieHttpOnly = true;
        options.CookieName = ".SeSsIoN";
        options.CookiePath = "/";
        options.CookieSecure = true;
        options.IdleTimeout = TimeSpan.FromMinutes(30);
    });
```

These can also be configured in the `UseSession` method in `Configure`:

```
app.UseSession(new SessionOptions { ... });
```

One final thing to note is that a session, by default, will use in-memory storage, which won't make it overly resilient or useful in real-life apps. However, if a distributed cache provider is registered before the call to `AddSession`, the session will use that instead! So, let's take a look at the next topic to see how we can configure it.

Before moving on, we need to keep in mind that:

- There's a bit of a performance penalty in storing objects in the session
- An object may be evicted from the session if the idle timeout is reached
- Accessing an object in the session prolongs its lifetime, that is, its idle timeout is reset

Cache

Unlike previous versions of ASP.NET, there is no longer built-in support for the cache; like most things in .NET Core, it is still available but as a pluggable service. There are essentially two kinds of cache in .NET Core:

- In-memory cache, which is represented by the `IMemoryCache` interface
- Distributed cache, which uses the `IDistributedCache` interface

.NET Core includes a default implementation of `IMemoryCache` and also one for `IDistributedCache`. The *caveat* for the distributed implementation is that it is also in-memory--it is only meant to be used in testing, but the good thing is that there are several implementations available, such as Redis (`https://redis.io/`) or SQL Server.

> In-memory and distributed caches can be used simultaneously, as they are unaware of each other.

Both the distributed and in-memory cache store instances as byte arrays (`byte[]`) but a good workaround is to first convert your objects to JSON and then use the method extensions that work with strings, as follows:

```
var json = JsonConvert.SerializeObject(model);
var model = JsonConvert.DeserializeObject<Model>(json);
```

In-memory cache

In order to use the in-memory cache, you need to register its service in `ConfigureServices` using the following default options:

```
services.AddMemoryCache();
```

If you prefer, you can also fine-tune them by using the overloaded extension method that takes a `MemoryCacheOptions` instance:

```
services.AddMemoryCache(options =>
    {
        options.Clock = new SystemClock();
        options.CompactOnMemoryPressure = true;
        options.ExpirationScanFrequency = TimeSpan.FromSeconds(5 * 60);
    });
```

The purposes of these properties is as follows:

- `Clock` (`ISystemClock`): This is an implementation of `ISystemClock` that will be used for the expiration calculation; it is useful for unit testing and mocking; there is no default
- `CompactOnMemoryPressure` (`bool`): This is used to remove the oldest objects from the cache when the available memory gets too low; the default is `true`

- ExpirationScanFrequency (TimeSpan): This sets the interval that .NET Core uses to determine whether to remove objects from the cache; the default is one minute

In order to use the in-memory cache, we need to retrieve an instance of IMemoryCache from the dependency injection:

```
public IActionResult StoreInCache(Model model, [FromServices] IMemoryCache cache)
{
    cache.Set("model", model);
    return this.Ok();
}
```

We will look at [FromServices] in more detail in the topic *Dependency injection*.

IMemoryCachesupports all the operations you might expect plus a few others, as follows:

- CreateEntry: Creates an entry in the cache and gives you access to expiration
- Get/GetAsync: Retrieves an item from the cache, synchronously or asynchronously
- GetOrCreate/GetOrCreateAsync: Returns an item from the cache if it exists, or creates one, synchronously or asynchronously
- Set/SetAsync: Adds or modifies an item in the cache, synchronously or asynchronously
- Remove: Removes an item from the cache
- TryGetValue: Tentatively tries to get an item from the cache, synchronously

That's pretty much it! The memory cache will be available for all requests in the same application and will go away once the application is restarted or stopped.

Distributed cache

The default out of the box implementation of the distributed cache is pretty much useless in real-life scenarios, but it might be a good starting point. Here's how to add support for it in ConfigureServices:

```
services.AddDistributedMemoryCache();
```

There are no other options, it's just that. In order to use it, ask the DI container for an instance of `IDistributedCache`:

```
private readonly IDistributedCache _cache;

public CacheController(IDistributedCache cache)
{
  this._cache = cache;
}

public IActionResult Get(int id)
{
  return this.Content(this._cache.GetString(id.ToString()));
}
```

The included implementation will behave in exactly the same ways as the in-memory cache, but there are also some good alternatives for a more serious usecase. The API it offers do the following:

- `Get`/`GetAsync`: Returns an item from the cache
- `Refresh`/`RefreshAsync`: Refreshes an item in the cache, prolonging its lifetime
- `Remove`/`RemoveAsync`: Removes an item from the cache
- `Set`/`SetAsync`: Adds an item to the cache, or modifies its current value

Be warned that because the cache is now distributed, and may take some time to synchronize, an item that you store in it may not be immediately available to all clients.

Redis

Redis is an open source distributed cache system. Its description is beyond the scope of this book, but it's sufficient to say that Microsoft has made a client implementation available for it in the form of the `Microsoft.Extensions.Caching.Redis` NuGet package. After you add this package, you get a couple of extension methods that you need to use to register a couple of services in `ConfigureServices`, which replaces `Configuration` and `InstanceName` properties with the proper values:

```
services.AddDistributedRedisCache(options =>
    {
        options.Configuration = "servername";
        options.InstanceName = "Shopping";
    });
```

And that's it! Now whenever you ask for an instance of `IDistributedCache`, you will get one that uses Redis underneath.

SQL Server

Another option is to use the SQL Server as a distributed cache. `Microsoft.Extensions.Caching.SqlServer` is the NuGet package that adds support for it. You can add support for it in `ConfigureServices` as follows:

```
services.AddDistributedSqlServerCache(options =>
    {
        options.ConnectionString =
           @"Data Source=.; Initial Catalog=DistCache; Integrated
Security=SSPI;";
        options.SchemaName = "dbo";
        options.TableName = "Cache";
    });
```

The rest is identical, so just get hold of an `IDistributedCache` from the DI, and off you go.

 ASP.NET Core no longer includes the `HttpApplication` and `HttpApplicationState` classes, which is where you could keep state applications. This mechanism had its problems, and it's better if you rely on either an in-memory or distributed cache instead.

Temporary data

The `Controller` class offers a `TempData` property of the type `ITempDataDictionary`. Temporary data is a way of storing an item in a request so that it is still available in the next request. It's provider-based, and currently there are two providers available:

- Cookie (`CookieTempDataProvider`)
- Session (`SessionStateTempDataProvider`)

For the latter, you need to enable session state support. To do this, you pick one of the providers and register it using the dependency injection framework, normally in the `ConfigureServices` method:

```
//only pick one of these
//for cookies
services.AddSingleton<ITempDataProvider, CookieTempDataProvider>();
//for session
```

```
services.AddSingleton<ITempDataProvider, SessionStateTempDataProvider>();
```

In ASP.NET Core 1, you need to configure the provider explicitly, but in ASP.NET Core 2 the `CookieTempDataProvider` is already pre-configured. If you use `SessionStateTempDataProvider`, you also need to enable sessions.

After you have selected one of the providers, you can add data to the `TempData` collection:

```
this.TempData["key"] = "value";
```

Retrieving and checking the existence is trivial, as follows:

```
if (this.TempData.ContainsKey("key"))
{
  var value = this.TempData["key"];
}
```

After you have enabled temporary data by registering one of the providers, you can use the `[SaveTempData]` attribute. When applied to a class that is returned by an action result, it will automatically be kept in temporary data.

The `[TempData]` attribute, if applied to a property in the model class, will automatically persist the value for that property in temporary data:

```
[TempData]
public OrderModel Order { get; set; }
```

Comparing state maintenance techniques

The following table provides a simple comparison of all the different techniques that can be used to maintain state among requests:

Technique	Storable objects	Is secure	Is shared	In process	Expiration
Request	`object`	Yes	No	Yes	No
Form	`string`	Yes (if using HTTPS)	No	Yes	No
Query String	`string`	No	Yes	Yes	No
Route	`string`	No	Yes	Yes	No
Cookies	`string`	Yes (if set to HTTPS only)	No	No	Yes

Session	byte[]	Yes	No	Maybe	Yes
Cache	object	Yes	Yes	Maybe	Yes
Temporary Data	string	Yes	No	No	Yes

Needless to say, not all these techniques serve the same purpose, instead, they are used in different scenarios.

Dependency injection

ASP.NET Core instantiates the controllers through its built-in **dependency injection (DI)** framework. Since it fully supports constructor injection, you can have any registered services injected as parameters to your constructor:

```
//ConfigureServices
services.AddSingleton<IHttpContextAccessor, HttpContextAccessor>();

//HomeController
public HomeController(IHttpContextAccessor accessor) { ... }
```

However, you can also request a service from the DI in a service locator way by leveraging the HttpContext.RequestServices property as follows:

```
var accessor =
this.HttpContext.RequestServices.GetService<IHttpContextAccessor>();
```

For the stronglytyped GetService<T> extension method you need to add a reference to the Microsoft.Extensions.DependencyInjection namespace.

In action methods, you can also inject a service by decorating its typed parameter with the [FromServices] attribute as follows:

```
public IActionResult Index([FromServices]
IHttpContextAccessor accessor) { ... }
```

Globalization and localization

If you need to build an application that will be used by people in different countries, you may want to have all of it or at least parts of it translated. It's not just that, though, you may also want to have decimal numbers and currency symbols presented in a way users would expect. The process by which an application is made to support different cultures is called **globalization** and **localization** is the process of adapting it to a specific culture, for example, by presenting it with text in a specific language.

ASP.NET Core, like previous versions, fully supports these two entwined concepts, by applying a specific culture to a request and letting it flow, and by having the ability to serve string resources according to the language of the requester.

We first need to add support for globalization and localization, and we do this by adding the `Microsoft.AspNetCore.Localization.Routing` package to the project. As far as this chapter is concerned, we want to be able to:

- Set the culture for the current request
- Hand resource strings that match the current culture

Let's configure localization in the `ConfigureServices` method with a call to `AddLocalization`. We'll pick the `Resources` folder as the source for resource files, as we'll see in a minute:

```
services.AddLocalization(options =>
{
  options.ResourcesPath = "Resources";
});
```

We create this `Resources` folder, and inside it a `Controllers` folder. Using Visual Studio, let's also create two resource files, one called `HomeController.en.resx` and the other `HomeController.pt.resx`. `resx`, which is a standard extension for resource files that are basically XML files containing key-value pairs. On each of these files, add an entry with the key `Hello` and the following value:

Portuguese	English
Olá!	Hello!

It should look like the following screenshot, notice that each file has the name of the controller class plus a two-letter culture identifier:

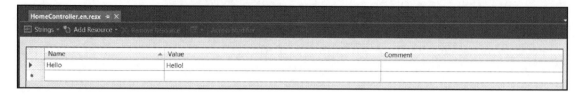

Now, let's define a range of cultures and languages to support. To make it simple, let's say that we will support **Portuguese (pt)** and **English (en)**:

```
var supportedCultures = new List<CultureInfo>
    {
        new CultureInfo("pt"),
        new CultureInfo("en")
    };
```

We are using pt and en, generic culture descriptors, but we could have also used pt-pt and en-gb for specific cultures. Feel free to add those you want.

We then configure `RequestLocalizationOptions` so as to have a default language:

```
services.Configure<RequestLocalizationOptions>(options =>
    {
        options.DefaultRequestCulture =
            new RequestCulture(supportedCultures.First().Name,
supportedCultures.First().Name);
        options.SupportedCultures = supportedCultures;
        options.SupportedUICultures = supportedCultures;
        options.RequestCultureProviders = new[] {
            new AcceptLanguageHeaderRequestCultureProvider {
                Options = options } };
    });
```

The process by which a culture is obtained from the browser is based upon a provider model. The following providers are available:

- `AcceptLanguageHeaderRequestCultureProvider` gets the culture from the `Accept-Language` **header**
- `CookieRequestCultureProvider` gets the culture from a cookie
- `QueryStringRequestCultureProvider` gets the culture from a query string parameter
- `RouteDataRequestCultureProvider` gets the culture from a route parameter

Just replace the `RequestCultureProviders` assignments in the previous code with the ones you want. As you can see, there are many options available, each featuring different features you need to set, such as the cookie name, the query string parameter, the route parameter name, and so on:

```
new CookieRequestCultureProvider { CookieName = "culture" }
new QueryStringRequestCultureProvider { QueryStringKey = "culture" }
new RouteDataRequestCultureProvider { RouteDataStringKey = "culture" }
```

In the second chapter, we looked at route constraints, so here we will introduce the culture route constraint:

```
public sealed class CultureRouteConstraint : IRouteConstraint
{
  public const string CultureKey = "culture";

  public bool Match(
    HttpContext httpContext,
    IRouter route,
    string routeKey,
    RouteValueDictionary values,
    RouteDirection routeDirection)
    {
      if ((!values.ContainsKey(CultureKey)) || (values[CultureKey] ==
null))
      {
        return false;
      }

      var lang = values[CultureKey].ToString();

      var requestLocalizationOptions = httpContext.RequestServices
          .GetRequiredService<IOptions<RequestLocalizationOptions>>();

      if ((requestLocalizationOptions.Value.SupportedCultures ==  null)
```

```
          || (requestLocalizationOptions.Value.SupportedCultures.Count ==
0))
      {
        try
        {
          new System.Globalization.CultureInfo(lang);  //if invalid, throws
an exception
          return true;
        }
        catch
        {
          //an invalid culture was supplied
          return false;
        }
      }

      //checks if any of the configured supported cultures matches the one
requested
      return requestLocalizationOptions.Value.SupportedCultures
          .Any(culture => culture.Name.Equals(lang,
StringComparison.CurrentCultureIgnoreCase));
    }
}
```

What this does is allow the verification of route values, such as {language:culture}, and
if the value is not a valid culture, you will get an exception. This route constraint needs to
be registered before it can be used, as follows:

```
services.Configure<RouteOptions>(options =>
    {
      options.ConstraintMap.Add(CultureRouteConstraint.CultureKey,
          typeof(CultureRouteConstraint));
    });
```

Now, we want our controller to respond to the browser's language settings. For example, in Chrome, we will configure this in **Settings** | **Languages** | **Language and input settings**:

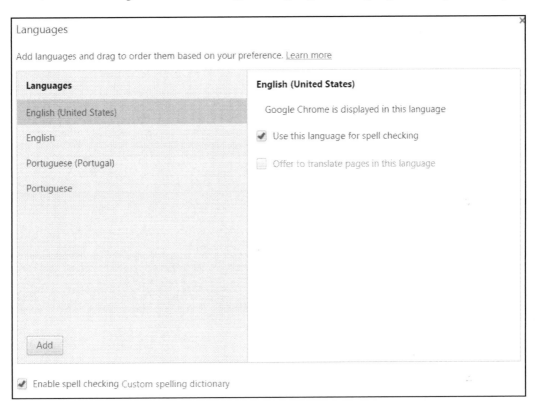

What this setting does is configure the `Accept-Language` HTTP header that the browser will send upon each request. We are going to take advantage of this to decide what language we will present.

Each controller that we wish to make localization-aware needs to be changed as follows:

- Add a middleware filter attribute so as to inject a middleware component
- Inject a string localizer that we can use to fetch appropriately translated resources

Here is what that should look like:

```
[MiddlewareFilter(typeof(LocalizationPipeline))]
public class HomeController
{
    private readonly IStringLocalizer<HomeController> _localizer;
```

```
public HomeController(IStringLocalizer<HomeController> localizer)
{
  this._localizer = localizer;
}
}
```

The `LocalizationPipeline` is actually an OWIN middleware component, and should look as follows:

```
public class LocalizationPipeline
{
  public static void Configure(IApplicationBuilder app,
      IOptions<RequestLocalizationOptions> options)
  {
      app.UseRequestLocalization(options.Value);
  }
}
```

Now if we want to access some specific resource in a culture-specific way, all we need to do is:

```
var hello = this._localizer["Hello"];
```

The returned string will come from the right resource file, based on the current culture, as originated from the browser. You can check this by looking at the `CultureInfo.CurrentCulture` and `CultureInfo.CurrentUICulture` properties.

There are a couple of final things to note:

- You can have several resource files per each language, or more accurately, per each specific (for example, en, pt) and generic language (for example, en-gb, en-us); if the browser requests a specific language (for example, en-gb, en-us), the localizer will try to find a resource file with that as a suffix, and if it cannot find one, it will try the generic language (for example, en). If this also fails, it will return the resource key provided (for example, `Hello`)
- The localizer never returns an error or a null value, but you can check if the value exists, for the current language with the following:

  ```
  var exists = _localizer["Hello"].ResourceNotFound;
  ```

Putting it all together

Using POCO controllers is not really needed, and it requires more work than whatever benefit we can take out of it, so let's have our controllers inherit from `Controller`.

Use asynchronous actions for improved scalability. This won't affect performance much, but your app will be more responsive.

You can forget about XML formatting, as JSON works perfectly, and is the standard way to send and process data on the web.

Use POCO classes as the model for your actions. The built-in model binders work well, as we'll see in upcoming chapters, but you can add the cookie value provider as it may come in handy.

As far as model validation is concerned, stick to the good old Data annotations API. If necessary, implement `IValidatableObject` in your model.

You will need sessions for the shopping cart functionality, so make sure you add support for it.

For our example, we would like to have localization support so as to have our shop available in both Portuguese and English (feel free to pick your own languages).

The Redis distributed cache system is very popular and is supported by both Azure and AWS. Redis should be your choice for a distributed cache where you would keep reference data; in other words, stuff that isn't changed often.

Performance-wise, response caching is also useful. The products page shouldn't change that much, so at least we can keep it in the cache for a few hours.

Summary

This was a long chapter where we covered controllers and actions, arguably the most important aspects of ASP.NET Core. We also covered parts of the model concept, such as binding, injection, and validation. We saw how we can maintain state and what the possible values that we can return from an action are. We also touched on API-style actions, namely, where in what versioning, content negotiation, and caching is concerned, and we also learned how to use resources for translation purposes. Some of these concepts will be revisited in future chapters; in the next one, we will be talking about views.

5

Views

Views are the **V** in **MVC**. They are the visual part of the application; typically a web app renders HTML pages, meaning HTML views. A view is a template that consists of a mix of HTML and possibly some server-side contents.

ASP.NET Core uses view engines to actually render the views, an extensible mechanism. Before Core times, there were several view engines available; although their purpose was always to generate HTML, they offered subtle differences in terms of syntax and the features they supported. Currently, ASP.NET Core only includes one view engine, called **Razor**, as the other one that used to be available, Web Forms, was dropped. Razor has been around for quite some time, and has been improved in the process of adding it to ASP.NET Core.

Razor files have the `cshtml` extension (for C# HTML) and by convention are kept in a folder called `Views` underneath the application, and below a folder with the name of the controller to which they apply, such as `Home`. There may be global and local views, and we will learn the distinction in a moment.

The typical way to have a controller action returning a view is by returning the result of executing the `View` method of the `Controller` class. This creates a `ViewResult`, and it can take a number of options:

- `ContentType` (`string`): An optional content type to return to the client; `text/html` is the default
- `Model` (`object`): Just any object that we want to make available to the view
- `StatusCode` (`int`): An optional status code to return; if none is provided, it will be `200`

- TempData (ITempDataDictionary): Strongly-typed temporary data to make available until the next request
- ViewData (ViewDataDictionary): A key-value collection of arbitrary data to pass to the view
- ViewName (string): The name of the view to render

The only required parameter is the ViewName and if it's not supplied, the current action name will be used; that is if we are executing in an action method named Index, and we want to return a view but don't supply its name, Index will be used:

```
public IActionResult Index()
{
  return this.View();   //ViewName = Index
}
```

There are some overloads to the View method which basically take either the viewName, the model, or both:

```
return this.View(
  viewName: "SomeView",
  model: new Model()
);
```

Beware, if your model is of the type string, .NET may mistakenly choose the View overload that takes a view name!

Now, imagine you want to return a view with a specific content type or status code. You can get the ViewResult object from the View method call and then change it:

```
var view = this.View(new Model());
view.ContentType = "text/plain";
view.StatusCode = 201;
return view;
```

Or, if we want to set some view data:

```
view.ViewData["result"] = "success";
```

View classes

A Razor view is actually a template that is transformed into a class that inherits from `RazorPage<T>`. The generic parameter is actually the type of the model, as we will see in a moment. This class inherits from `RazorPage`, which exposes a few useful properties:

- `IsLayoutBeingRendered` (`bool`): Whether currently a layout page is being rendered or not
- `BodyContent` (`IHtmlContent`): The resulting page's body contents; will only be available at a later time
- `TempData` (`ITempDataDictionary`): The temporary data dictionary
- `ViewBag` (`dynamic`): The view bag
- `User` (`ClaimsPrincipal`): The current user, as in `HttpContext.User`
- `Output` (`TextWriter`): The output writer, to which the HTML results are sent once the page is processed
- `DiagnosticSource` (`DiagnosticSource`): Allows logging diagnostic messages, covered here
- `HtmlEncoder` (`HtmlEncoder`): The HTML encoder used for encoding the results as they are sent in the response
- `Layout` (`string`): The current layout file
- `ViewContext` (`ViewContext`): The view context
- `Path` (`string`): The current view file path
- `Context` (`HttpContext`): The HTTP context

All of these properties can be used in a view.

We can, of course, define our own class that derives from `RazorPage<T>`, and have our view use it, by using `@inherits`:

```
public class MyPage : RazorPage<dynamic>
{
  public MyPage(IMyService svc)
  {
    this.Service = svc;
  }

  public IMyService Service { get; }
}
```

If we now inherit from this class:

```
@inherits MyPage
```

We can then use the `Service` property directly, in addition to all the other properties and methods:

```
@Service.Operation()
```

When an action signals that a view should be rendered, the following occurs (in a simplified way):

- The action returns a `ViewResult` object, because `ViewResult` implements `IActionResult`, its `ExecuteResultAsync` method is called asynchronously
- The default implementation attempts to find a `ViewResultExecutor` from the DI framework
- The `FindView` method is called on the `ViewResultExecutor`, which uses an injected `ICompositeViewEngine`, also obtained from the DI, to obtain an `IView` from the list of registered view engines
- The view engine chosen will be an implementation of `IRazorViewEngine` (which, on its turn, extends `IViewEngine`)
- The `IView` implementation uses the registered `IFileProviders` to load the view file
- The `ViewResultExecutor` is then asked to invoke the view, through its `ExecuteAsync` method, which ends up invoking the base `ViewExecutor's` `ExecuteAsync` methods
- The `ViewExecutor` builds and initializes some infrastructure objects such as `ViewContext` and ends invoking the `IView's` `RenderAsync` method
    - A Razor compilation service is obtained from the DI, (`IRazorCompilationService`) produces the C# code for the view (ASP.NET Core 1.x)
- Another service (`ICompilationService`) is used to compile the C# code
- The registered `IRazorPageFactoryProvider` creates a factory method for creating a .NET class that inherits from `IRazorPage` (ASP.NET Core 1.x and 2.x)
- The `IRazorPageActivator` is passed an instance of the new `IRazorPage`
- The IRazorPage's `ExecuteAsync` method is called

Here I didn't mention the filters, but they are here as well, except action filters, as I said.

Why is this important? Well, you may need to implement your own version of, say, the IRazorPageActivator, so that you can perform some custom initialization or dependency injection in the Razor view:

```
public class CustomRazorPageActivator : IRazorPageActivator
{
  private readonly IRazorPageActivator _activator;

  public CustomRazorPageActivator(
    IModelMetadataProvider metadataProvider,
    IUrlHelperFactory urlHelperFactory,
    IJsonHelper jsonHelper,
    DiagnosticSource diagnosticSource,
    HtmlEncoder htmlEncoder,
    IModelExpressionProvider modelExpressionProvider)
  {
    this._activator = new RazorPageActivator(metadataProvider,
      urlHelperFactory, jsonHelper, diagnosticSource, htmlEncoder,
modelExpressionProvider);
  }

  public void Activate(IRazorPage page, ViewContext context)
  {
    if (page is ICustomInitializable)
    {
      (page as ICustomInitializable).Init(context);
    }

    this._activator.Activate(page, context);
  }
}
```

All you need to do is register this implementation in ConfigureServices, for the IRazorPageActivator service:

```
services.AddSingleton<IRazorPageActivator, CustomRazorPageActivator>();
```

Locating views

When asked to return a view (ViewResult), the framework needs first to locate the view file.

The built-in convention for locating view files is:

- View files end with the `cshtml` extension
- View filenames should be identical to the view names, minus the extension (for example, a view of `Index` will be stored in a file named `Index.cshtml`)
- View files are stored in a `Views` folder and inside a folder named after the controller they are returned from, for example, `Views\Home`
- Global or shared views are stored in either the `Views` folder directly or inside a `Shared` folder inside of it, for example, `Views\Shared`

Actually, this is controlled by the `ViewLocationFormats` collection of the `RazorViewEngineOptions` class (Razor is the only included view engine). This has the following entries, by default:

- `/Views/{1}/{0}.cshtml`
- `/Views/Shared/{0}.cshtml`

 The `{1}` token is replaced by the current controller name and `{0}`, by the view name. The `/` location is relative to the ASP.NET Core application folder, not `wwwroot`.

If you want the Razor engine to look in different locations, all you need to do is tell it so through the `AddRazorOptions` method, that is usually called in sequence to `AddMvc`, in the `ConfigureServices` method:

```
services.AddMvc().AddRazorOptions(options =>
    {
        options.ViewLocationFormats.Add("/AdditionalViews/{0}.cshtml");
    });
```

The view locations are searched sequentially in the `ViewLocationFormats` collection, until one file is found.

The actual view file contents are loaded through `IFileProviders`. By default, only one file provider is registered (`PhysicalFileProvider`), but more can be added through the configuration:

```
services.AddMvc()
    .AddRazorOptions(options =>
        {
            options.FileProviders.Add(new CustomFileProvider());
        });
```

Adding custom file providers may prove useful, for example, if you want to load contents from non-orthodox locations, such as databases, ZIP files, assembly resources, and so on.

View location expanders

There is an advanced feature by which we can control, per request, the locations where to search the view files--it's called **view location expanders**. View location expanders are a Razor thing, and thus are also configured through `AddRazorOptions`:

```
services.AddMvc()
    .AddRazorOptions(options =>
        {
            options.ViewLocationExpanders.Add(new
ThemesViewLocationExpander("Mastering"));
        });
```

A view location expander is just some class that implements the `IViewExpander` contract. For example, imagine you want to have a theme framework, which would add a couple of folders to the views search path. You could write it as this:

```
public class ThemesViewLocationExpander : IViewLocationExpander
{
  public ThemesViewLocationExpander(string theme)
  {
    this.Theme = theme;
  }

  public string Theme { get; }

  public IEnumerable<string> ExpandViewLocations(
    ViewLocationExpanderContext context,
    IEnumerable<string> viewLocations)
  {
    var theme = context.Values["theme"];

    return viewLocations
      .Select(x => x.Replace("/Views/", "/Views/" + theme + "/"))
      .Concat(viewLocations);
  }

  public void PopulateValues(ViewLocationExpanderContext context)
  {
    context.Values["theme"] = this.Theme;
  }
}
```

The default search locations, as we've seen, are:

- `/Views/{1}/{0}.cshtml`
- `/Views/Shared/{0}.cshtml`

By adding this view location expander, for a theme called `Mastering`, these will become:

- `/Views/{1}/{0}.cshtml`
- `/Views/Mastering/{1}/{0}.cshtml`
- `/Views/Shared/Mastering/{0}.cshtml`
- `/Views/Shared/{0}.cshtml`

The `IViewLocationExpander` interface defines only two methods:

- `PopulateValues`: Used to initialize the view location expander; in this example, I used it to pass some value in the context
- `ExpandViewLocations`: This will be called to retrieve the desired view locations

View location expanders are queued, so they will be called in sequence, from the registration order; each `ExpandViewLocations` method will be called with all the locations returned from the previous one.

Both methods, through the `context` parameter, have access to all the request parameters (`HttpContext`, `RouteData`, and so on), so you can be as creative as you like, and define the search locations for the views according to whatever rationale you can think of.

View engines

I already mentioned that ASP.NET Core only includes one view engine, Razor, but nothing prevents us from adding more. This can be achieved through the `ViewEngines` collection of `MvcViewOptions`:

```
services.AddMvc()
    .AddViewOptions(options =>
        {
          options.ViewEngines.Add(new CustomViewEngine());
        });
```

A view engine is an implementation of `IViewEngine`, and the only included implementation is `RazorViewEngine`.

Again, view engines are searched sequentially, when ASP.NET Core is asked to render a view, and the first one that returns one, is the one that is used. The only two methods defined by `IViewEngine` are:

- `FindView` (`ViewEngineResult`): Tries to find a view from an `ActionContext`
- `GetView` (`ViewEngineResult`): Tries to find a view from a path

Both methods return `null` if no view is found.

A view is an implementation of `IView`, and the ones returned by `RazorViewEngine` are all `RazorView`. The only notable method in the `IView` contract is `RenderAsync`, which is the one responsible for actually rendering a view from a `ViewContext`.

 A view engine is not an easy task. You can find a sample implementation written by Dave Paquette in a blog post here: `http://www.davepaquette.com/archive/2016/11/22/creating-a-new-view-engine-in-asp-net-core.aspx`.

A Razor view is a template composed essentially of HTML, but it also accepts fragments-- which can be quite large, actually of server-side C# code:

- First, you may need to define the type of the model that your view receives from the controller. By default, it is dynamic, but you can change it with a `@model` directive:

        @model MyNamespace.MyCustomModel

- Doing this is exactly the same as specifying the base class of your view. This is accomplished by `@inherits`:

 Remember, the default is `RazorPage<dynamic>`

        @inherits RazorPage<MyNamespace.MyCustomModel>

 Don't forget, you cannot have at the same time `@inherits` and `@model`!

- If you don't want to write the full type name, you can add as many @using declarations as you want:

```
@using My.Namespace
@using My.Other.Namespace
```

- You can intermix HTML with Razor expressions, which are processed on the server side. Razor expressions always start with the @ character. For example, if you want to output the current logged in user, you could write this:

```
User: @User.Identity.Name
```

- You can output any method that returns either a string or an IHtmlContent directly:

```
@Html.Raw(ViewBag.Message)
```

- If you need to evaluate some simple code, you will need to include it inside parenthesis:

```
Last week: @(DateTime.Today - TimeSpan.FromDays(7))
```

Remember, if your expression has a space, you need to include it inside parenthesis, the only exception being the await keyword:

```
@await Component.InvokeAsync("Process");
```

- You can encode HTML (implicitly using the HtmlEncoder instance supplied in the HtmlEncoder property) like this:

```
@("<span>Hello, World</span>")
```

This will output an HTML-encoded string (see https://en.wikipedia.org/wiki/List_of_XML_and_HTML_character_entity_references for more information):

```
&lt;span&gt;Hello, World&lt;/span&gt;
```

More complex expressions, such as the definition of variables, setting values to properties or calling of methods that do not return a *stringy* result (`string`, `IHtmlContent`) need to go in a special block, in which you can put pretty much anything you would in a .NET method:

```
@{
    var user = @User.Identity.Name;
    OutputUser(user);
    Layout = "Master";
}
```

Sentences inside `@{}` blocks need to be separated by semicolons.

A variable defined this way can be used in any other place in the view--after the declaration, of course.

Let us look at conditionals (`if`, `else if`, `else` and `switch`) now, which are nothing special:

```
@if (this.User.Identity.IsAuthenticated)
{
  <p>Logged in</p>
}
else
{
  <p>Not logged in</p>
}

@switch (this.User.Identity.AuthenticationType)
{
  case "Claims":
    <p>Logged in</p>
    break;

  case null:
    <p>Not logged in</p>
    break;
}
```

Loops use a special syntax, where you can mix together HTML (any valid XML element) and code:

```
@for (var i = 0; i < 10; i++)
{
  <p>Number: @i</p>
}
```

Note that this will not work, because `Number` is not included inside an XML element:

```
@for (var i = 0; i < 10; i++)
{
  Number: @i
}
```

But this syntax (`@:`) would:

```
@:Number: @i
```

This makes the rest of the line to be treated as an HTML chunk.

The same syntax can be used in `foreach` and `while`.

Now `try/catch` blocks:

```
@try
{
  SomeMethodCall();
}
catch (Exception ex)
{
  <p class="error">An error occurred: @ex.Message</p>
  Log(ex);
}
```

`@using` and `@lock` blocks:

```
@using (Html.BeginForm())
{
  //the result is disposed at the end of the block
}

@lock (SyncRoot)
{
  //synchronized block
}
```

Now, what if you want to output the @ character? You need to escape it with another @:

```
<p>Please enter your username @@domain.com</p>
```

But Razor views recognize emails and do not force them to be encoded:

```
<input type="email" name="email" value="nobody@domain.com"/>
```

Finally, comments are also supported, single or multi-line:

```
@*this is a single-line Razor comment*@
@*
  this
  is a multi-line
  Razor comment
*@
```

Inside a @{} block you can add C# comments too:

```
@{
    //this is a single-line C# comment
    /*
    this
    is a multi-line
    C# comment
    */
  }
```

Of course, because a view is essentially HTML, you can also use HTML comments:

```
<!-- this is an HTML comment -->
```

 The difference between C#, Razor and HTML comments is that only HTML comments are left by the Razor compilation process, the others are discarded.

We can add functions (which are actually, in object-oriented terminology, methods) to our Razor views; these are just .NET methods that are only visible in the scope of a view. To create them, we need to group them inside a @functions directive:

```
@functions
{
  int Count(int a, int b) { return a + b; }

  public T GetValueOrDefault<T>(T item) where T : class, new()
  {
    return item ?? new T();
```

```
      }
   }
```

It is possible to specify the visibility. By default, this happens inside a class; it is called `private`. It is probably pointless to specify a visibility since the generated class is only known at runtime, and there is no easy way to access it.

The `@functions` name is actually slightly misleading, as you can declare fields and properties inside of it:

```
@functions
{
  int? _state;
  int State
  {
    get
    {
      if (_state == null)
      {
        _state = 10;
      }
      return _state;
    }
  }
}
```

Logging and diagnostics

As ususal, you can obtain a reference to an `ILogger<T>` from the DI framework and use it in your views:

```
@inject ILogger<MyView> Logger
```

But there is also another built-in mechanism, the `DiagnosticSource` class, and property, which is declared in the `RazorPage` base class. By calling its `Write` method, you can write custom messages to a diagnostics framework. These messages can be any .NET object, even an anonymous one, and there is no need to worry about its serialization:

```
@{
    DiagnosticSource.Write("MyDiagnostic", new { data = "A diagnostic" });
}
```

What happens with this diagnostic message is actually somewhat configurable. First, let us add the `Microsoft.Extensions.DiagnosticAdapter` NuGet package; let us now create a custom listener for the events generated for this diagnostic source:

```
public class DiagnosticListener
{
  [DiagnosticName("MyDiagnostic")]
  public virtual void OnDiagnostic(string data)
  {
    //do something with data
  }
}
```

We can add as many listeners as we want, targeting different event names. The actual method name does not matter, as long as it has a `[DiagnosticName]` applied to it that matches an event name. We need to register and hook it to the .NET Core framework, in the `Configure` method, by adding a reference to the `DiagnosticListener` service, so that we can interact with it:

```
public void Configure(IApplicationBuilder app, DiagnosticListener
diagnosticListener)
{
  var listener = new DiagnosticListener();
  diagnosticListener.SubscribeWithAdapter(listener);

  //rest goes here
}
```

Notice that the name in the `[DiagnosticName]` attribute and `DiagnosticSource.Write` call match and also the name `data` of the anonymous type in the `Write` call matches the parameter name (and type) of the `OnDiagnostic` method.

Built-in .NET Core classes produce diagnostics for the following:

- `Microsoft.AspNetCore.Diagnostics.HandledException`
- `Microsoft.AspNetCore.Diagnostics.UnhandledException`
- `Microsoft.AspNetCore.Hosting.BeginRequest`
- `Microsoft.AspNetCore.Hosting.EndRequest`
- `Microsoft.AspNetCore.Hosting.UnhandledException`
- `Microsoft.AspNetCore.Mvc.AfterAction`
- `Microsoft.AspNetCore.Mvc.AfterActionMethod`
- `Microsoft.AspNetCore.Mvc.AfterActionResult`

- `Microsoft.AspNetCore.Mvc.AfterView`
- `Microsoft.AspNetCore.Mvc.AfterViewComponent`
- `Microsoft.AspNetCore.Mvc.BeforeAction`
- `Microsoft.AspNetCore.Mvc.BeforeActionMethod`
- `Microsoft.AspNetCore.Mvc.BeforeActionResult`
- `Microsoft.AspNetCore.Mvc.BeforeView`
- `Microsoft.AspNetCore.Mvc.BeforeViewComponent`
- `Microsoft.AspNetCore.Mvc.Razor.AfterViewPage`
- `Microsoft.AspNetCore.Mvc.Razor.BeforeViewPage`
- `Microsoft.AspNetCore.Mvc.Razor.BeginInstrumentationContext`
- `Microsoft.AspNetCore.Mvc.Razor.EndInstrumentationContext`
- `Microsoft.AspNetCore.Mvc.ViewComponentAfterViewExecute`
- `Microsoft.AspNetCore.Mvc.ViewComponentBeforeViewExecute`
- `Microsoft.AspNetCore.Mvc.ViewFound`
- `Microsoft.AspNetCore.Mvc.ViewNotFound`

Hopefully the names should be self explanatory. Why would you use this mechanism over the `ILogger`-based one? This one makes it very easy to add listeners to a diagnostic source, with strongly-typed methods.

View compilation

Normally, a view is only compiled when it is first used, that is, a controller action returns a `ViewResult`. What this means is that any eventual syntax errors will only be caught at runtime, when the framework is rendering the page, plus, even if there are no errors, ASP.NET Core takes some time (in the millisecond order, mind you) to compile the view. This does not need to be so, however.

Microsoft makes available a NuGet package, `Microsoft.AspNetCore.Mvc.Razor.ViewCompilation`, that you can add as a reference to your project. After this, you can enable view compilation at publish time, and currently, the only way to do this is by manually editing the `.csproj` file. Look for the first `<PropertyGroup>` declared in it, the one that contains the `<TargetFramework>` element, and add a `<MvcRazorCompileOnPublish>` and a `<PreserveCompilationContext>` element. The result should look like this:

```
<PropertyGroup>
  <TargetFramework>netcoreapp1.1</TargetFramework>
```

```
    <MvcRazorCompileOnPublish>true</MvcRazorCompileOnPublish>
    <PreserveCompilationContext>true</PreserveCompilationContext>
  </PropertyGroup>
```

Now, whenever you publish your project, either using Visual Studio or the `dotnet publish` command, you will get errors such as this one, about an erroneous `Foo` method call:

```
Home/Index.cshtml(12,7): error CS0103: The name 'Foo' does not exist in the
current context [C:\Source\Mastering ASP.NET Core\Web\Web.csproj]
C:\Users\rjperes\.nuget\packages\microsoft.aspnetcore.mvc.razor.viewcompila
tion\1.1.1\build\netcoreapp1.1\Microsoft.AspNetCore.Mvc.Razor.ViewCompilati
on.targets(25,5): error MSB3073: The command "dotnet exec --runtimeconfig
"C:\Source\Mastering ASP.NET
Core\Web\bin\Debug\netcoreapp1.1\Web.runtimeconfig.json" --depsfile
"C:\Source\Mastering ASP.NET
Core\Web\bin\Debug\netcoreapp1.1\Web.deps.json"
"C:\Users\rjperes\.nuget\packages\microsoft.aspnetcore.mvc.razor.viewcompil
ation\1.1.1\build\netcoreapp1.1\..\../lib/netcoreapp1.1/Microsoft.AspNetCor
e.Mvc.Razor.ViewCompilation.dll"
@"obj\Debug\netcoreapp1.1\microsoft.aspnetcore.mvc.ra
 zor.viewcompilation.rsp"" exited with code 1. [C:\Source\Mastering ASP.NET
Core\Web\Web.csproj]
```

Do not forget that the pre-compilation only occurs at **publish**, not **build**, time!

If you are curious about the Razor view compilation process, it is controlled by instances of `ICompilationService` and `IRazorCompilationService` (ASP.NET Core 2.x no longer includes `IRazorCompilationService`) that are registered in the dependency injection framework, and the actual implementations are, respectively, `DefaultRoslynCompilationService` and `RazorCompilationService`:

- The first step, under the responsibility of `IRazorCompilationService`, translates the HTML and Razor code into C#
- The second, on charge of `ICompilationService`, compiles it into a .NET class

By default, **Roslyn** is used for parsing and compiling, which should not come as a surprise. If you want to learn more about **Roslyn**, check out this URL: `https://github.com/dotnet/roslyn`.

There are significant differences between ASP.NET Core 1.x and 2.x, as I said, it no longer includes IRazorCompilationService. Also, ASP.NET Core 2 compiles views by default upon publishing.

Suppose you want to inspect, log, or maybe even change the code produced by the view compilation process (step 1), you could write a class such as this one:

```
public class CustomRazorCompilationService : RazorCompilationService
{
  private readonly ILogger<IRazorCompilationService> _logger;

  public CustomRazorCompilationService(
    ICompilationService compilationService,
    IMvcRazorHost razorHost,
    IRazorViewEngineFileProviderAccessor fileProviderAccessor,
    ILoggerFactory loggerFactory) :
    base(compilationService, razorHost, fileProviderAccessor,
    loggerFactory)
  {
    this._logger = loggerFactory.CreateLogger<IRazorCompilationService>();
  }

  protected override GeneratorResults GenerateCode(string relativePath,
Stream inputStream)
  {
    var results = base.GenerateCode(relativePath, inputStream);
    this._logger.LogDebug($"Generated code: {results.GeneratedCode}");
    return results;
  }
}
```

The GeneratorResults class will keep a record of all warnings and errors (property ParserErrors) produced during the compilation process and, of course, also the generated code (GeneratedCode).

And for actually inspecting the generated type (step 2), you could use another class like this (slightly more complex, as DefaultRoslynCompilationService was not designed with extensibility in mind and thus does not offer virtual methods):

```
public class CustomCompilationService : ICompilationService
{
  private readonly ICompilationService _svc;
  private readonly ILogger<ICompilationService> _logger;

  public CustomCompilationService(
    CSharpCompiler compiler,
```

```
    IRazorViewEngineFileProviderAccessor fileProviderAccessor,
    IOptions<RazorViewEngineOptions> optionsAccessor,
    ILoggerFactory loggerFactory)
{
    this._svc = new DefaultRoslynCompilationService(compiler,
      fileProviderAccessor, optionsAccessor, loggerFactory);
    this._logger = loggerFactory.CreateLogger<ICompilationService>();
}

  public CompilationResult Compile(RelativeFileInfo fileInfo, string
compilationContent)
  {
    var result = this._svc.Compile(fileInfo, compilationContent);
    this._logger.LogDebug($"Generated type:
{result.CompiledType.FullName}");
    return result;
  }
}
```

The `CompilationResult` structure offers a property that exposes the generated type--`CompiledType`. It is also possible to retrieve all of the actual details of any warning or errors that occurred in the compilation process, by looking at the `CompilationFailures` collection.

To make this work, we just need to register our implementations to the DI framework, in `ConfigureServices`:

```
services.AddSingleton<ICompilationService, CustomCompilationService>();
services.AddSingleton<IRazorCompilationService,
CustomRazorCompilationService>();
```

For ASP.NET Core 2.x, there's a similar code, but the two steps are brought together, under a single interface:

```
public class CustomCompilationService : ICompilationService
{
  private readonly ICompilationService _service;
  private readonly ILogger<ICompilationService> _logger;

  public CustomCompilationService(
    CSharpCompiler compiler,
    IOptions<RazorViewEngineOptions> optionsAccessor,
    ILoggerFactory loggerFactory)
  {
    this._service = new DefaultRoslynCompilationService(compiler,
     optionsAccessor, loggerFactory);
    this._logger = loggerFactory.CreateLogger<ICompilationService>();
```

```
    }

  public CompilationResult Compile(
    RazorCodeDocument codeDocument,
    RazorCSharpDocument cSharpDocument)
  {
    var result = this._service.Compile(codeDocument, cSharpDocument);
    this._logger.LogDebug($"Generated code:
{cSharpDocument.GeneratedCode}");
    this._logger.LogDebug($"Generated type:
{result.CompiledType.FullName}");
    return result;
  }
}
```

This is slightly easier, with just one service. Likewise, we need to register our custom implementation in the DI.

 Both implementations, in version 1.x and 2.x, rely on a class named `DefaultRoslynCompilationService`, but its function changed slightly.

The class that is generated for each view exposes a property called `Html` which is of type `IHtmlHelper<T>`, `T` being the type of your model. This property has some interesting methods that can be used for rendering HTML:

- Generating links (`ActionLink`, `RouteLink`)
- Generating forms for a given model or model property (`BeginForm`, `BeginRouteForm`, `CheckBox`, `CheckBoxFor`, `Display`, `DisplayFor`, `DisplayName`, `DisplayNameFor`, `DisplayForModel`, `DisplayNameForInnerType`, `DisplayNameForModel`, `DisplayText`, `DisplayTextFor`, `DropDownList`, `DropDownListFor`, `Editor`, `EditorFor`, `EditorForModel`, `EndForm`, `Hidden`, `HiddenFor`, `Id`, `IdFor`, `IdForModel`, `Label`, `LabelFor`, `LabelForModel`, `ListBox`, `ListBoxFor`, `Name`, `NameFor`, `NameForModel`, `Password`, `PasswordFor`, `RadioButton`, `RadioButtonFor`, `TextArea`, `TextAreaFor`, `TextBox`, `TextBoxFor`, `Value`, `ValueFor`, `ValueForModel`)
- Displaying validation messages (`ValidationMessage`, `ValidationMessageFor`, `ValidationSummary`)
- Rendering anti-forgery tokens (`AntiForgeryToken`)
- Outputting raw HTML (`Raw`)

- Including partial views (`Partial`, `PartialAsync`, `RenderPartial`, `RenderPartialAsync`)
- Getting access to the context properties (`ViewContext`, `ViewBag`, `ViewData`, `TempData`) and also the base class' (`RazorPage`, `RazorPage<T>`) properties (`UrlEncoder`, `MetadataProvider`)
- A couple of configuration properties (`Html5DateRenderingMode`, `IdAttributeDotReplacement`)

We will look into these methods in more detail in the next chapter. For now, let's see how we can add our own extension (helper) methods. The easiest way is to add an extension method over `IHtmlHelper<T>`:

```
public static HtmlString CurrentUser(this IHtmlHelper<T> html)
{
   return new HtmlString(html.ViewContext.HttpContext.User.Identity.Name);
}
```

Now you can use it in every view:

```
@Html.CurrentUser()
```

Make sure that you either return `string` or `IHtmlContent` from it, otherwise you won't be able to use this syntax.

We've seen that the `ViewResult` class offers three properties that can be used to pass data from an action into a view:

- The model (`Model`): In the early days of ASP.NET MVC, it was the only mechanism that could be used; we needed to define a possibly quite complex class with all the data that we would like to make available
- The view data (`ViewData`): Now we have a strongly typed collection of random values; it has gained in popularity against the model
- The temporary data (`TempData`): Data that will only be available until the next request

These properties are eventually passed along to identically named ones in the `RazorPage<T>` class.

It is even possible, but not too common, to specify the view engine (an instance of `IViewEngine`) that should be used by the view rendering process, by setting a value to the `ViewEngine` property. Normally, this is looked after automatically.

Model

By default a Razor view inherits from `RazorPage<dynamic>`, which means that the model is prototyped as `dynamic`.

This will be the type for the `Model` property. This is a flexible solution, because you can pass whatever you want in the model, but you won't get intellisense for it.

If, on the other hand, you specify a strongly typed model, either through `inherits`:

```
@inherits RazorPage<ProcessModel>
```

or the `model` directive:

```
@model ProcessModel
```

which are essentially the same, Visual Studio helps you find its properties and methods:

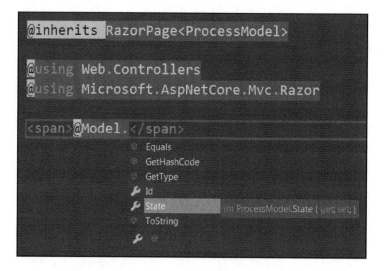

One thing to keep in mind is, you cannot pass on your controller, an anonymous type, as the view won't be able to access its properties. See the next chapter for a solution to this.

ViewBag

The view bag came as a complement for the model, but, in my perspective, has long taken over it. Why is that? Well, I guess the problem is that you need to change the model class whenever you need more properties, and it's much easier to just stick new items in the view bag.

There are two options for using the view bag:

- Through the `ViewBag` dynamic property, which is not runtime-safe:

    ```
    <script>alert('@ViewBag.Message');</script>
    ```

- Through the `ViewData` strongly-typed dictionary:

    ```
    <script>alert('@ViewData["Message"]');</script>
    ```

`ViewBag` is just a wrapper around `ViewData`, anything that is added to one can be retrieved from the other, and vice versa. A good reason for picking `ViewData` is if the stored data's name contains a space or other special character such as −, /, @, and so on.

Temporary data

Temporary data is retrieved in a similar way to `ViewData`:

```
<script>alert('@TempData["Message"]');</script>
```

View layouts

View layouts are similar to master pages in good old ASP.NET Web Forms. They define a base layout and possibly default contents that several views can use, so as to maximize reuse and offer a consistent structure:

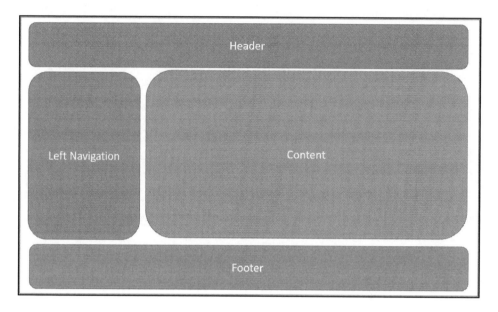

View layouts themselves are also Razor views, and they can be controlled by setting the Layout property in a view, which is defined in the RazorPage base class:

```
@{ Layout = "_Layout"; }
```

The Layout property is just the name of a view, one that can be discovered in the usual way.

The only thing that is required in a layout view is a call to the RenderBody method; this causes the actual view that is using it to be rendered. It is also possible to define section placeholders, which may be used by actual views to provide contents. A section is defined by a RenderSection call:

```
<!DOCTYPE html>
<html>
  <head><title></title>
    @RenderSection("Head", required: false)
  </head>
  <body>
```

```
    @RenderSection("Header", required: false)
    <div style="float:left">
        @RenderSection("LeftNavigation", required: false)
    </div>
    @RenderBody
    <div style="float:right">
        @RenderSection("Content", required: true)
    </div>
    @RenderSection("Footer", required: false)
  </body>
</html>
```

As you can see, `RenderSection` takes two parameters:

- A name, which must be unique among the layout
- Depending on whether the section is required, the required parameter, (the default is `true`)

There are also asynchronous versions of `RenderSection`, appropriately named `RenderSectionAsync`.

 Unlike ASP.NET Web Forms content placeholders, it is not possible to supply default content on a view layout.

If a section is defined as required, a view page that uses the layout view must declare a `section` for it:

```
@section Content
{
   <h1>Hello, World!</h1>
}
```

If no sections are defined, the Razor compilation system just takes the compiled view and inserts its contents in the location where `RenderBody` is called.

You can check whether a section is defined or not:

```
@if (IsSectionDefined("Content")) { ... }
```

The `IsLayoutBeingRendered` property tells us whether a layout view is defined, found, and is currently being rendered.

If you know that a section is defined as required in the view layout but still you do not wish to render it, you can call `IgnoreSection`:

```
@IgnoreSection(sectionName: "Content")
```

And if, for whatever reason, you decide not to include any contents of your actual view in a view layout, you can call `IgnoreBody`.

 Layouts can be nested, that is, a top level view can define one layout, which also has its own layout, and so on.

Partial views

A partial view is similar to a regular view, but it is intended to be included in the middle of one. The syntax and feature set are exactly the same. The concept is similar to that of user controls in ASP.NET Web Forms, and the idea is basically **DRY (Don't Repeat Yourself)**. By wrapping common content in a partial view, we can reference it in different places.

There are two ways by which you can include a partial view in the middle of a view, both in synchronous and asynchronous ways. The first way involves the `Partial` and `PartialAsync` methods:

```
@Html.Partial("LoginStatus")
@await Html.PartialAsync("LoginStatus")
```

You would use the asynchronous version if the view has any code that needs to run asynchronously.

 Adding code to views is generally discouraged; there are better ways, such as **View Components**, which we will talk about in a later chapter.

Another way to include partial contents is through `RenderPartial` and `RenderPartialAsync`:

```
@{ Html.RenderPartial("LoginStatus"); }
@{ await Html.RenderPartialAsync("LoginStatus"); }
```

What is the difference between the two, I hear you ask? Well, `Partial/PartialAsync` returns an `IHtmlContent`, which is essentially an encoded string, and `RenderPartial/RenderPartialAsync` directly writes to the underlying output writer, possibly resulting in a (slightly) better performance.

Partial views and view layouts are two different, complementary, mechanisms to allow reuse. They should be used together, not one instead of the other.

Passing data to partial views

Both `Partial` and `RenderPartial` offer overloads that allow us to pass a model object:

```
@Html.Partial("OrderStatus", new { Id = 100 })
@{ Html.RenderPartial("OrderStatus", new { Id = 100 }); }
```

Of course, the model declared in the `OrderStatus` view must be compatible with the passed model, which will always happen if it is declared as dynamic (the default).

For `Partial/PartialAsync`, we can also pass values for its view bag:

```
@Html.Partial("OrderStatus", new { Id = 100 }, ViewData)
@await Html.PartialAsync("OrderStatus", new { Id = 100 }, ViewData)
```

Here we are just passing along the current view bag, but it need not be the case.

Partial views can be nested, meaning, a partial view can include other partial views.

Finding partial views

The discovery of partial views is slightly different:

- If only a name is supplied (for example, `LoginStatus`), view files are discovered using the same rules as with global views
- If the view name ends with `.cshtml` (for example, `LoginStatus.cshtml`), then the view file is only looked up in the same folder as the containing view

- If the view name starts with either ~/ or / (for example, ~/Views/Status/LoginStatus.cshtml), then the view file is looked up in a folder relative to the web application root (not the wwwroot folder, mind you)
- If the view name starts with ../ (for example, ../Status/LoginStatus.cshtml), then the view engine tries to find it in a folder relative to the one of the calling views

Multiple partial views with the same name can exist, if located in different folders.

Special files

ASP.NET Core recognizes two special view files, which, if present, are treated specially:

- _ViewImports.cshtml: Used to specify Razor directives that should apply to all views (@addTagHelper, @removeTagHelper, @tagHelperPrefix, @using, @model, @inherits and @inject):

    ```
    @using Microsoft.AspNetCore.Mvc.Razor
    @using My.Custom.Namespace
    @inject IMyService Service
    ```

- _ViewStart.cshtml: Any code that is placed here will be executed for all views; for this reason, it is a good place for setting the global common layout (which, of course, can be overridden by each view), a common model or base view page:

    ```
    @{ Layout = "_Layout"; }
    ```

The Visual Studio template adds these files to the Views folder of the application, this means that they cannot be normally referenced, as this folder is outside the default search locations for views.

View options

As developers, we get to influence some of the ways views--and, in particular, Razor views--work. Normally, this is done through configuration, through extension methods AddViewOptions and AddRazorOptions, which are commonly called in sequence to AddMvc, in the ConfigureServices method:

```
services.AddMvc()
  .AddViewOptions(options =>
    {
```

```
    //global view options
})
.AddRazorOptions(options =>
{
    //razor-specific options
});
```

Through `AddViewOptions`, we can configure the following properties, of the
`MvcViewOptions` class:

- `ClientModelValidatorProviders`
  (`IList<IClientModelValidatorProvider>`): a collection of client model
  validator providers, to be used when the model is to be validated on the client-
  side; this will be discussed in the next chapter, but by default it includes a
  `DefaultClientModelValidatorProvider`, a
  `DataAnnotationsClientModelValidatorProvider` and a
  `NumericClientModelValidatorProvider`
- `HtmlHelperOptions` (`HtmlHelperOptions`): Several options related to the
  generation of HTML; this is discussed next
- `ViewEngines` (`IList<IViewEngine>`): The registered view engines; by default,
  this only contains an instance of `RazorViewEngine`

`HtmlHelperOptions` features the following properties:

- `ClientValidationEnabled` (`bool`): Whether client validation should be
  enabled or not; the default is `true`
- `Html5DateRenderingMode` (`Html5DateRenderingMode`): The format for
  rendering `DateTime` values as strings in HTML5 form fields; the default is
  `Rfc3339`, which renders a `DateTime` as `2017-08-19T12:00:00-01:00`
- `IdAttributeDotReplacement` (`string`): The string to be used instead of dots
  (`.`) when MVC renders input fields for a model; the default is `_`
- `ValidationMessageElement` (`string`): The HTML element that will be used to
  render its specific validation message; the default is `span`
- `ValidationSummaryMessageElement` (`string`): The HTML element for
  rendering the global validation summary; the default is `span`

The `AddRazorOptions` method provides features that are more specific to Razor views:

- `AdditionalCompilationReferences` (`IList<MetadataReference>`): A collection of assembly references from where ASP.NET Core elements (controllers, view components, tag helpers, and more) can be loaded; empty by default
- `AreaViewLocationFormats` (`IList<string>`): The list of folders to be searched, inside an area folder, for views; similar to `ViewLocationFormats`, but applying to areas
- `CompilationCallback` (`Action<RoslynCompilationContext>`): A callback method that is called after each element is compiled; safe to ignore, as it should only be used by advanced developers
- `CompilationOptions` (`CSharpCompilationOptions`): A set of C# compilation options
- `FileProviders` (`IList<IFileProvider>`): The collection of file providers; by default, only contains an instance of `PhysicalFileProvider`
- `ParseOptions` (`CSharpParseOptions`): A set of C# parsing options
- `ViewLocationExpanders` (`IList<IViewLocationExpander>`): the collection of view location expanders
- `ViewLocationFormats` (`IList<string>`): The locations to be searched for view files, discussed earlier

Normally, a `MetadataReference` is obtained using one of the static methods of the `MetadataReference` class:

```
var asm = MetadataReference.CreateFromFile("\Some\Folder\MyAssembly.dll");
```

The `CSharpCompilationOptions` and `CSharpParseOptions` classes are quite extensive and include mostly every setting that the compiler supports--even some that are not easily found in Visual Studio. Explaining all of them would be tedious and really off topic, but I'm going to give you just two examples:

```
services.AddMvc()
    .AddRazorOptions(options =>
        {
            //enable C# 6 syntax
options.ParseOptions.WithLanguageVersion(LanguageVersion.CSharp6);

            //add a using declaration for the System.Linq namespace
            options.CompilationOptions.Usings.Add("System.Linq");
        });
```

Areas

Areas are a way for you to segregate functionality in your website. For example, anything related to the **Admin** area goes in one place. For example, a physical folder, including its own controllers, views, and so on. In terms of views, the only thing worth mentioning is how we can configure the paths where view files can be found. This is controlled through the `AreaViewLocationFormats` collection of the `RazorViewEngineOptions` class:

```
services.AddMvc()
    .AddRazorOptions(options =>
        {
options.AreaViewLocationFormats.Add("/SharedGlobal/Areas/{2}.cshtml");
        });
```

The included values are:

- `/Areas/{2}/Views/{1}/{0}.cshtml`
- `/Areas/{2}/Views/Shared/{0}.cshtml`
- `/Views/Shared/{0}.cshtml`

Here, the `{2}` token stands for the area name, whereas `{0}` is for the view name and `{1}` for the controller name, as seen previously. Essentially, you have a similar structure as for non-area views, but you now have views that are shared globally or per area.

Dependency injection

View classes (`RazorPage<T>`) support injecting services in their constructors:

```
public class MyPage : RazorPage<dynamic>
{
  public MyPage(IMyService svc)
  {
    //constructor injection
  }
}
```

Views also support having services injected into them. Just declare an `@inject` element in the `.cshtml` file with the service type to retrieve and the local variable to hold it, probably at the beginning of the view:

```
@inject IHelloService Service
```

After this, you can use the injected `Service` variable:

```
@Service.SayHello()
```

 There may be the need to either fully qualify the type name or add a `@using` declaration for its namespace.

We've seen in the previous chapter that ASP.NET Core includes built-in mechanisms for displaying resources in different languages; this definitely includes views. Actually, there are two ways to display translated texts:

- Resources
- Translated views

Let's start with resources.

Resources

So, let's assume we have a couple of resource files (`.resx`), for languages PT and EN. Let's store them under the `Resources` folder (this can be configured, as we'll see in a moment), underneath a folder called `Views`, and inside a folder named after the controller, the views are to be served from (say, `Home`, for example). The filenames themselves must match the action names, so, for example, we might have:

- `Resources\Views\Home\Index.en.resx`
- `Resources\Views\Home\Index.pt.resx`

Before we can use them, we need to configure the localization services, in `ConfigureServices`:

```
services.AddMvc()
    .AddViewLocation(
        format: LanguageViewLocationExpanderFormat.Suffix,
        setupAction: options => {
            options.ResourcesPath = "Resources";
        });
```

The two parameters to `AddViewLocation` represent:

- `format` (`LanguageViewLocalizationExpanderFormat`): The format to use for stating the culture of the resource file
- `setupAction` (`Action<LocalizationOptions>`): The action to be taken for configuring the location mechanism, such as specifying the resources path (currently only the `ResourcesPath` property)

The two possible values of `LanguageViewLocalizationExpanderFormat` are:

- `SubFolder`: This means that every resource file should be stored under a folder named after the culture (for example, `Resources\Views\Home\en`, `Resources\Views\Home\en-gb`, `Resources\Views\Home\pt`, `Resources\Views\Home\pt-pt`, and so on)
- `Suffix`: the culture is part of the filename (for example, `Index.en.resx`, `Index.pt.resx`, and so on)

As for the `LocalizationOptions` structure, its `ResourcePath` property already has a default of `Resources`.

When it comes to actually using the values from the resource files, we need to inject into the views an instance of `IViewLocalizer` and retrieve values from it:

```
@inject IViewLocalizer Localizer
<h1>@Localizer["Hello"]</h1>
```

The `IViewLocalizer` interface extends `IHtmlLocalizer`, so it inherits all its properties and methods.

You can also use **shared resources**. A shared resource is a set of `.resx` files, identical to the ones we've seen in the last chapter, plus an empty class, and they are not tied to a specific action or controller. These should be stored in the `Resources` folder, but the namespace of this class should be set to the assembly default namespace.

```
namespace Web
{
    public class SharedResources { }
}
```

For this example, the resource files should be called `SharedResources.en.resx`, or any other culture.

Then, in your view, inject a reference to an `IHtmlLocalizer<SharedResources>`:

```
@inject IHtmlLocalizer<SharedResources> SharedLocalizer
<h1>@SharedLocalizer["Hello"]</h1>
```

Translated views

Another option is to have an entire view translated; by translated I mean that ASP.NET Core will look for a view that matches the current language before falling back to a general one.

In order to activate this feature, you need to call `AddViewLocalization`:

```
services.AddMvc()
AddViewLocalization();
```

What this does is add a **view location expander** (remember this?) called `LanguageViewLocationExpander`. What it does is duplicate the registered view locations so as to include ones with the current language as the file suffix. For example, if the initial view location formats are:

- `/Views/{1}/{0}.cshtml`
- `/Views/Shared/{0}.cshtml`

For the `pt` language, these will become:

- `/Views/{1}/{0}.pt.cshtml`
- `/Views/{1}/{0}.cshtml`
- `/Views/Shared/{0}.pt.cshtml`
- `/Views/Shared/{0}.cshtml`

Because the order matters, this effectively means that ASP.NET Core will first try to find a view ending with `.pt` (such as `Index.pt.cshtml`) and only after that, if not found, will it resort to locating the generic one (for example, `Index.cshtml`). Cool, don't you think? Of course, a translated view can be totally different than the generic one, even though this was mostly designed with translation in mind.

Razor Pages

Razor Pages were introduced in ASP.NET Core 2.0, and they follow a totally different approach from the rest of ASP.NET Core. Instead of the MVC pattern, they are self-contained files, similar to XAML controls or ASP.NET Web Forms, because they can also have a code-behind file. There is no longer a controller/view separation, as Razor Pages have all they need in a single file, although we can also specify a class for them.

In order to use Razor Pages, you need a compatible Visual Studio version, starting from 2017 Update 3, plus you need to have ASP.NET Core 2.0 installed:

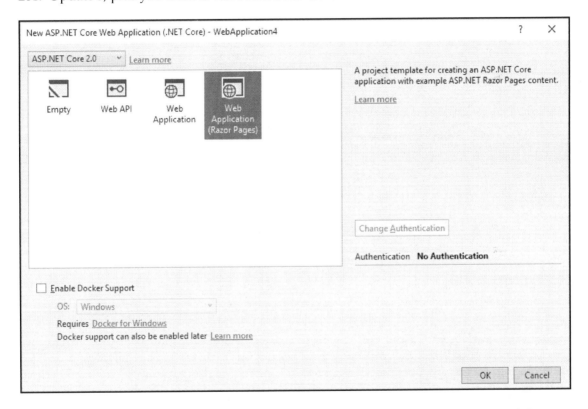

Razor Pages are physically stored in the filesystem, underneath a `Pages` folder, and they should have the same `.cshtml` extension as regular Razor views. What differentiates them is the new `@page` directive:

```
@page
@model HelloWorldModel
<!DOCTYPE html>
<html>
```

```
<head><title>Hello World</title></head>
<body>
    <h1>@Html.Raw("Hello, World!")</h1>
</body>
</html>
```

Adding an @page directive (preferably as the first line) automatically turns the .cshtml file into a Razor Page. There is no need to reference any specific NuGet package or perform any configuration because it is enabled by default.

Accessing a Razor Page is straightforward, as no routing is involved, they can be called directly, without the .cshtml extension:

- /HelloWorld
- /Admin/Settings

The only requirement is that they are located somewhere inside the Pages root folder. The Index.cshtml file is served by default, meaning, if one such file is located inside a Pages\Admin folder, it is served without having to be explicitly requested--/Admin will serve the \Pages\Admin\Index.cshml file.

 Leave the Pages prefix and the .cshtml extension out, they cannot be used in the request. Also, Razor Pages cannot start with an underscore (_).

Page model

You can use the exact same syntax as you would with a Razor view. But there's something more--a Razor Page has inherently associated with it a PageModel class, notice the @model directive pointing to HelloWorldModel. This class must inherit from PageModel, and in it, you can define methods for handling HTTP methods, such as GET or POST. The file containing the definition of the page model class must have the same physical name as the Razor Page with a .cs extension, be located in the same folder, and inherit from PageModel. So, for example, if the previous file was named HelloWorld.cshtml, then its page model would go in a HelloWorld.cshtml.cs file:

```
public class HelloWorldModel : PageModel
{
}
```

If you do not wish to specify a custom page model class, one is provided for you automatically, and you can still specify handler methods directly in the `.cshtml` file:

```
@functions
{
  public async Task<IActionResult> OnGetAsync()
  {
    if (!this.User.Identity.IsAuthenticated)
    {
      return this.RedirectToAction(actionName: "Login", controllerName:
"Account");
    }

    return this.Page();
  }
}
```

Any properties that you declare in the `PageModel`-derived class:

```
public string Message { get; set; }

public void OnGet()
{
  this.Message = "Hello, World!";
}
```

Can then be used in the `.cshtml` file:

```
<p>Message: @Model.Message</p>
```

You can even have the class declared there:

```
@page
@model IndexModel
@functions
{
  public class IndexModel : PageModel
  {
    public async Task<IActionResult> OnGetAsync()
    {
      //whatever
    }
  }
}
```

The `PageModel` class offers the following properties:

- `HttpContext` (`HttpContext`): The usual context
- `ModelState` (`ModelStateDictionary`): The model state, filled from all the value providers
- `PageContext` (`PageContext`): Offers access to the current handler method (if any), plus the value provider and view start factory collections
- `Request` (`HttpRequest`): The same value as `HttpContext.Request`, the request object
- `Response` (`HttpResponse`, from `HttpContext.Response`): The response object
- `RouteData` (`RouteData`): The route data, not normally needed
- `TempData` (`ITempDataDictionary`): Temporary data
- `Url` (`IUrlHelper`): Used for generating URLs that point to route actions, for example
- `User` (`ClaimsPrincipal`, coming from `HttpContext.User`): The current user, as determined by the authentication mechanism in use
- `ViewData` (`ViewDataDictionary`): The view bag

Page handlers

The HTTP method handlers can have several signatures:

- The name must start with `On` and be followed by the HTTP method name (`Get`, `Post`, `Put`, `Delete`, and so on)
- The return type must either be `void` or `IActionResult`
- If we are to use the asynchronous version, the method must either return `Task` or `Task<IActionResult>` and optionally have the `async` keyword applied to it, and should end with the `Async` suffix
- They can either take parameters (basic types with default values or complex types), no parameters at all, or take an `IFormCollection` parameter

You can now add methods for handling requests, either synchronously:

```
public IActionResult OnGet()
{
  if (this.HttpContext.Request.Headers["HTTP-
Referer"].Contains("google.com"))
  {
    //hey, someone found us through Google!
```

```
  }

  return this.Page();
}
```

Or in an asynchronous way:

```
public async Task<IActionResult> OnGetAsync()
{
  //...
  return this.Page();
}
```

 You cannot have both a synchronous and an asynchronous handler method, or multiple overloads for the same HTTP verb, as it will result in a runtime error.

You can even have custom handlers, which do not follow these patterns. A couple of ways to achieve that are:

- Pass a `handler` parameter in the query string, for example, `?handler=MyHandler`
- Pass the `handler` parameter in the route instead, for example, `@page "{handler?}"`
- In the `<form>`, `<input>` or `<button>` tags, set an `asp-page-handler` attribute, for example, `asp-page-handler="MyHandler"` (this uses the tag handler functionality)

This way, you can have a method such as:

```
public async Task<IActionResult> OnPostMyHandlerAsync() { ... }
```

Regardless of the name you give it, you will always have the `On` prefix and the `Async` suffix, if it is an asynchronous handler.

If you want to have your page post to multiple handlers, depending on what is clicked, it's easy:

```
<input type="submit" value="One Handler" asp-page-handler="One" />
<input type="submit" value="Another Handler" asp-page-handler="Two" />
```

You can perform tasks such as redirection by returning a proper `IActionResult`:

```
public IActionResult OnPost()
{
  return this.RedirectToPage("/Pages/Success");
}
```

Not all action results make sense though, for example, it doesn't make sense to return a `ViewResult`, as Razor Pages do not execute in the context of a controller.

If this is not required, you do not even need to return an `IActionResult`:

```
public void OnGet()
{
  //initialize everything
}
```

And these can be used as helpers for returning `IActionResults`, in pretty much the same way as the `ControllerBase` and `Controller` classes:

- Challenge (`ChallengeResult`)
- Content (`ContentResult`)
- File (`FileContentResult, FileStreamResult, VirtualFileResult`)
- Forbid (`ForbidResult`)
- LocalRedirect (`LocalRedirectResult`)
- LocalRedirectPermanent (`LocalRedirectResult`)
- LocalRedirectPermanentPreserveMethod (`LocalRedirectResult`)
- LocalRedirectPreserveMethod (`LocalRedirectResult`)
- NotFound (`NotFoundResult, NotFoundObjectResult`)
- Page (`PageResult`)
- PhysicalFile (`PhysicalFileResult`)
- Redirect (`RedirectResult`)
- RedirectPermanent (`RedirectResult`)
- RedirectPermanentPreserveMethod (`RedirectResult`)
- RedirectPreserveMethod (`RedirectResult`)
- RedirectToAction (`RedirectToActionResult`)
- RedirectToActionPermanent (`RedirectToActionResult`)
- RedirectToActionPermanentPreserveMethod (`RedirectToActionResult`)
- RedirectToActionPreserveMethod (`RedirectToActionResult`)

- `RedirectToPage` (`RedirectToPageResult`)
- `RedirectToPagePermanent` (`RedirectToPageResult`)
- `RedirectToPagePermanentPreserveMethod` (`RedirectToPageResult`)
- `RedirectToPagePreserveMethod` (`RedirectToPageResult`)
- `RedirectToRoute` (`RedirectToRouteResult`)
- `RedirectToRoutePermanent` (`RedirectToRouteResult`)
- `RedirectToRoutePermanentPreserveMethod` (`RedirectToRouteResult`)
- `RedirectToRoutePreserveMethod` (`RedirectToRouteResult`)
- `SignIn` (`SignInResult`)
- `SignOut` (`SignOutResult`)
- `StatusCode` (`StatusCodeResult`, `ObjectResult`)
- `Unauthorized` (`UnauthorizedResult`)

Some of these methods offer overloads, and each of these can return different result types.

Model binding

If you declare a property in the page model class (or one declared in a `@functions` block, for that matter) and decorate it with a `[BindProperty]` attribute, it will be bound automatically, using the same rules (binding source providers, binding attributes) as described in the previous chapter:

```
[BindProperty]
public Order Order { get; set; }
```

You will then be able to access and change any of its properties, perhaps in an **HTTP** handler method. You can also supply your own binder through the `BinderType` property. `BindProperty` can also bind on GET calls, if its `SupportsGet` property is set to `true`.

 Do notice that properties bound this way will only be so for non-GET calls (typically POST), unless you set its `SupportsGet` property. It works pretty much the same as `[ModelBinder]`, but the latter never binds on GET requests.

Also similarly to controller actions, parameters in HTTP handler methods are also automatically bound:

```
public void OnGet(int? id = null)
{
  //?id=1212
}
```

You can opt for not declaring a model as part of the handler method signature but instead updating it dynamically:

```
public void OnPost()
{
  var model = new OrderModel();
  this.TryUpdateModel(model);
}
```

A possible reason for this would be that the same page handles different requests, and consequently, different models.

Model validation

Model validation also works in pretty much the same way as in controllers:

```
public IActionResult OnPost()
{
  var model = new OrderModel();

  this.TryUpdateModel(model);

  if (this.TryValidateModel(model))
  {
    return this.RedirectToPage("/Pages/Error");
  }

  return this.Page();
}
```

Similarly to controllers, the ModelState property also keeps track of all injected values and their validation state.

Maintaining state

All of the usual ways to persist data apply also to Razor Pages.

View layouts

Razor Pages can use the same layout functionality as views, but you are advised to keep your layout pages outside the `Views\Shared` folder.

Partial views

Likewise, partial views are equally supported, in exactly the same way.

Special files

The `_ViewStart.cshtml` and `_ViewImports.cshtml` files are respected by Razor Pages and treated in the same way as for regular Razor views.

Filters

Razor Pages work with any filters except action filters, these will not be triggered, as you don't have actions. There is also a new filter, `IPageFilter`, with an asynchronous version as well, `IAsyncPageFilter`. I already talked about them in the section dedicated to filters, so I won't repeat myself.

Dependency injection

You can have dependencies injected in the constructor of your page model class, in the usual way:

```
public class HelloWorldModel : PageModel
{
  public HelloWorldPageModel(IMyService svc)
  {
    //yes, dependency injection in the constructor also works!
  }
}
```

If you decorate a property in your custom page model with the [FromServices], it will be honored, and the property will have its value set from the dependency injection framework, from its declared type.

You can also use the @inject directive, in the same way as you would in a Razor view.

Configuring options

The AddRazorPagesOptions extension method can be called subsequently to AddMvc so that we can configure some of the options of Razor Pages:

```
services.AddMvc()
  .AddRazorPagesOptions(options =>
    {
      options.RootDirectory = "RazorPages";
    });
```

The RazorPagesOptions class offers the following properties:

- Conventions (IList<IApplicationModelConvention>): the conventions to use; this will be discussed in a future chapter
- RootDirectory (string): the root directory, relative to the application root, which is normally set to /Pages

In addition, there are a few extension methods that apply to RazorPagesOptions, and basically, add one or more global filters:

- AllowAnonymousToFolder: Allows anonymous requests to all pages under a specific folder
- AllowAnonymousToPage: Allows anonymous requests for a given page
- AuthorizeFolder: Defines an authorization policy for all pages under a specific folder (will be discussed in more depth in the chapter dedicated to security)
- AuthorizePage: Defines an authorization policy for a specific page
- ConfigureFilter: Allows the configuration (adding, removing) of global filters

Page routes

Besides calling Razor Pages directly, you can also have them answer to routes. There is a new `AddPageRoute` extension method for `RazorPagesOptions` that you can leverage to add friendly routes to your pages:

```
services.AddMvc()
  .AddRazorPagesOptions(options =>
    {
       options.AddPageRoute("/Order", "My/Order/{id:int}");
    });
```

The parameters to `AddPageRoute` are:

- `pageName` (`string`): The name of a page to direct to, starting with `/`, and without the `.cshtml` suffix
- `route` (`string`): A regular route, with possible some route or query string parameters

In the view, you can then access any route or query string parameters using `HttpContext.RouteData` or `HttpContext.Request.Query`.

Interestingly, here's how you set a page (`/My/Page`) to be your default one:

```
.AddRazorPagesOptions(options =>
  {
     options.AddPageRoute("/My/Page", "");
  });
```

Moreover, you can have your Razor Page to listen to a specific route, by adding a route template parameter to the `page` directive:

```
@page "{id:int}"
```

In this case, if the Razor Page is called without the `id` parameter, which must also be of type `int`, it will not be found and an HTTP `404` error will be returned instead.

Security

Using the `AddRazorPagesOptions` extension method we can control how security can be applied to one or more pages or folders. The available methods are:

- `AllowAnonymousToPage`: Grants anonymous access to a single page
- `AllowAnonymousToFolder`: Grants anonymous access to all pages underneath a given folder
- `AuthorizePage`: Defines an authorization policy for a page
- `AuthorizeFolder`: Defines an authorization policy for all pages underneath a folder

Here's an example:

```
services.AddMvc()
  .AddRazorPagesOptions(options =>
    {
      //adds an AuthorizeAttribute with a named Policy property
      options.Conventions.AuthorizePage("/ShoppingBag", "Authenticated");
      //adds an AuthorizeAttribute
      options.Conventions.AuthorizeFolder("/Products");
      //adds an AllowAnonymousAttribute
      options.Conventions.AllowAnonymousToPage("/Login");
      options.Conventions.AllowAnonymousToFolder("/Images");
    });
```

Putting it all together

First, choosing between regular views and Razor Pages is a decision that should be made upfront--they're just too different. Having controllers and views may be more appealing to people who have worked with MVC before, and I'd say it can result in better coupling and organization, but Razor Pages are just so easy to use--no server-side code is required, and no recompilation (if the page model is not used).

On the other side, view layouts are a must; try to avoid nested (or too nested) view layouts, as it may be difficult to understand the final result. Also, partial views are also very handy, make sure you use them to avoid repeating code.

Avoid having code in views, for example, by specifying custom view classes--use filters for that purpose.

Consider the localization needs of your app upfront--it's very difficult and error-prone to refactor an existing app that does not use localization to introduce it.

Do not forget about security. The same concerns apply to Razor Pages as they do to controller actions.

Stick to the conventions in terms of folder names and the like. This will make things easier for everyone, current or future, in your team.

`_ViewImports.cshtml` and `_ViewStart.cshtml` are your friends, use them for common code that you want applied to all your pages.

Consider view compilation, it really helps in detecting some problems before they bite you.

Summary

In this chapter we covered the views feature of ASP.NET Core, using the built-in Razor engine. We saw how we can use view layouts to introduce a coherent layout and partial views for encapsulation and reuse. We learned the ways by which we can pass data from a controller to a view. Finally, we were introduced to the new Razor Pages feature of ASP.NET Core 2, which, although different from the ordinary views, shares quite a bit of functionality. In the next chapter, we will continue working with views, and in particular, with HTML forms. We will go deep into some of the topics that were introduced here.

6

Using Forms and Models

Because views are essentially HTML, nothing prevents you from manually adding your markup to it, which may possibly include values obtained from the controller, either through the model, view bag, or temporary data. ASP.NET Core, however, like previous versions, has built-in methods to assist you in generating HTML that matches your model (structure and content), displaying model validation errors and other useful model metadata.

Because all of this works on top of the model, for the framework to be able to extract any relevant information, we need to use strongly-typed views, not dynamic; this means either adding a @model or an @inherits directive to the views with the appropriate model type.

To be clear, the model is the object that you pass to the ViewResult object returned from your controller, possibly returned from the View method, and it must either match the declared @model in the view or its @inherit declaration.

In this chapter, we will cover the following topics:

- Generating forms using HTML helpers
- Using metadata to influence form generation
- Getting forms' values
- Binding forms to object models

Form context

The view context object (`ViewContext`) is available in view components (which will be discussed in a later chapter) and as a property of Razor Pages (`IRazorPage`), meaning you can access it in views. In it, besides the usual context properties (`HttpContext`, `ModelStateDictionary`, `RouteData`, `ActionDescriptor`) you also have access to the **form context** (`FormContext`) object. This object offers the following properties:

- `CanRenderAtEndOfForm` (`bool`): Indicates whether the form can render additional contents (the `EndOfFormContent`) at its end
- `EndOfFormContent` (`IList<IHtmlContent>`): A collection of contents to add at the end of the form (before the `</form>` tag)
- `FormData` (`IDictionary<string, object>`): The submitted form data
- `HasAntiforgeryToken` (`bool`): Indicates whether the form is rendering the anti-forgery token, which depends on how the `BeginForm` method was called; the default is `true`
- `HasEndOfFormContent` (`bool`): Indicates whether any end of form content has been added
- `HasFormData` (`bool`): Indicates whether the `FormData` dictionary has been used and contains data

Plus, it offers a single method, `RenderedField`, with two overloads:

- One that returns an indication of whether a form field has been rendered in the current view
- Another that sets this flag for a specific field (called by the infrastructure typically)

Developers can leverage the form context to render additional data with the form, such as validation scripts or extra fields.

Model metadata

The ASP.NET Core framework uses a **model metadata provider** to extract information from the model. This metadata provider is accessible through the `MetadataProperty` of `Html`, and is exposed as an `IModelMetadataProvider`. By default, it is set to an instance of `DefaultModelMetadataProvider`, and can be changed through the dependency injection framework.

Its contract defines only two relevant methods:

- `GetMetadataForType` (`ModelMetadata`): Returns metadata for the model type itself
- `GetMetadataForProperties` (`IEnumerable<ModelMetadata>`): Metadata for all of the public model properties

To change it, just call one of the registration methods of the dependency injection framework (`ConfigureServices`):

```
services.AddSingleton<IModelMetadataProvider,
CustomModelMetadataProvider>();
```

You never normally call these methods, they are called internally by the framework. The `ModelMetadata` class they return (which may actually be of a derived class, such as `DefaultModelMetadata`) is what should interest us more. In what ASP.NET Core is concerned, it returns:

- The display name and description of the type or property (`DisplayName`)
- The data type (`DataType`)
- The text placeholder (`Placeholder`)
- The text to display in case of a null value (`NullDisplayText`)
- The display format (`DisplayFormatString`)
- Whether the property is required (`IsRequired`)
- Whether the property is read-only (`IsReadOnly`)
- Whether the property is required for binding (`IsBindingRequired`)
- The model binder (`BinderType`)
- The binder model name (`BinderModelName`)
- The model binding source (`BindingSource`)
- The property's containing class (`ContainerType`)

These properties are used by the HTML helpers when generating HTML for the model, and they affect how it is produced.

By default, if no model metadata provider is supplied, and no attributes are present, safe or empty values are assumed for the metadata properties. It is, however, possible to override them. Let's start with looking at the display name (DisplayName) and description (Description): these can be controlled by the [Display] attribute, from the System.ComponentModel.DataAnnotations namespace. This attribute also sets the placeholder/watermark for the property (Placeholder):

```
[Display(Name = "Work Email", Description = "The work email",
    Prompt = "Please enter the work email")]
public string WorkEmail { get; set; }
```

Marking a property as required (IsRequired) is achieved through [Required]. All of the other validation attributes (inherited from ValidationAttribute) can also be supplied:

```
[Required]
[Range(1, 100)]
public int Quantity { get; set; }
```

Whether the property can be edited or not (IsReadOnly) is controlled by whether the property has a setter or not, and, if so, if it has an [Editable] attribute applied (the default value is true):

```
[Editable(true)]
public string Email { get; set; }
```

The data type (DataType) contained in a string can be defined by applying a [DataType] attribute, or one inherited from it:

```
[DataType(DataType.Email)]
public string Email { get; set; }
```

There are a few attribute classes that inherit from DataTypeAttribute and can be used instead of it:

- [EmailAddress]: same as DataType.EmailAddress
- [CreditCard]: DataType.CreditCard
- [Phone]: DataType.PhoneNumber
- [Url]: DataType.Url
- [EnumDataType]: DataType.Custom
- [FileExtensions]: DataType.Upload

`DataType` has several other possible values, I advise you to have a look at it.

The text to display if a value is null (`NullDisplayText`) and the display format (`DisplayFormatString`) are both settable through the `[DisplayFormat]` attribute:

```
[DisplayFormat(NullDisplayText = "No birthday supplied", DataFormatString =
"yyyyMMdd")]
public DateTime? Birthday { get; set; }
```

When it comes to binding, the `[ModelBinder]` can be used to specify a custom model binder type (`BinderType` property) and the name of the model to bind to (`ModelBinderName`), typically, you do not supply the name of the model, as it is assumed to be the same as the property name:

```
[ModelBinder(typeof(GenderModelBinder), Name = "Gender")]
public string Gender { get; set; }
```

Whether a property is required in the model binding (`IsBindingRequired`) process is controllable by one of `[BindRequired]`, `[BindingBehavior]` or `[BindNever]`:

```
[BindNever]  //same as [BindingBehavior(BindingBehavior.Never)]
public int Id { get; set; }
[BindRequired]  //same as [BindingBehavior(BindingBehavior.Required)]
public string Email { get; set; }
[BindingBehavior(BindingBehavior.Optional)]
public DateTime? Birthday { get; set; }
```

The `BindingSource` property is set in case we are using one of the `IBindingSourceMetadata` attributes:

- `[FromBody]`
- `[FromForm]`
- `[FromHeader]`
- `[FromQuery]`
- `[FromRoute]`
- `[FromServices]`

The default model metadata provider recognizes these attributes, but you can certainly roll out your own provider and supply properties in any other way. There may be times when you should not apply attributes to model properties, for example, when the model class is generated automatically. In that case, you can apply a `[ModelMetadataType]` attribute, probably in another file, where you specify the class that will be used to retrieve metadata attributes from:

```
public partial class ContactModel
{
  public int Id { get; set; }
  public string Email { get; set; }
}
```

You can add an attribute to this same class from another file:

```
[ModelMetadataType(typeof(ContactModelMetadata))]
public partial class ContactModel
{
}
```

And in `ContactModelMetadata` you specify the attributes you want:

```
public sealed class ContactModelMetadata
{
  [BindNever]
  public int Id { get; set; }
  [BindRequired]
  [EmailAddress]
  public string Email { get; set; }
}
```

 The `ContainerType`, of course, cannot be changed: it is inferred automatically from the property.

Models of anonymous types

Like in previous versions of ASP.NET MVC, you cannot pass an anonymous type as the model to your view. Or you can, but the view won't have access to its properties, even if the view is set to use `dynamic` as the model type. What you can do is use an extension method like this one to turn your anonymous type into an `ExpandoObject`, a common implementation of `dynamic`:

```
public static ExpandoObject ToExpando(this object anonymousObject)
```

```
{
  var anonymousDictionary =
HtmlHelper.AnonymousObjectToHtmlAttributes(anonymousObject);
  IDictionary<string, object> expando = new ExpandoObject();

  foreach (var item in anonymousDictionary)
  {
    expando.Add(item);
  }

  return expando as ExpandoObject;
}
```

This way you can use it like this in your controller:

```
return this.View(new { Foo = "bar" }.ToExpando());
```

And, in your view:

```
@Model.Foo
```

HTML helpers

HTML helpers are methods of the view's `Html` object (`IHtmlHelper`) and exist to aid in generating HTML. We may not know the exact syntax, and URLs to routes can be tricky to generate, but there are two more important reasons why we use them, HTML helpers generate the appropriate code for display and editing purposes based on the model metadata, and they also include error and description placeholders. It is important to keep in mind that they are always based on the model.

In general, the built-in HTML helpers have two overloads:

- One that takes a strongly-typed model (for example, `EditorFor(x => x.FirstName)`)
- Another that takes dynamic parameters, in the form of strings (for example, `EditorFor("FirstName")`)

Also, all take an optional parameter, `htmlAttributes`, that can be used to add any attribute to the rendered HTML element (for example, `TextBoxFor(x => x.FirstName, htmlAttributes: new { @class = "first-name" })`). For this reason, as we go through the different HTML helpers, I will skip the `htmlAttributes` parameter.

Forms

In order to submit values, we first need a form: the HTML `form` element. The `BeginForm` helper generates one for us:

```
@using (Html.BeginForm())
{
  <p>Form goes here</p>
}
```

It returns an `IDisposable` instance, therefore, it should be used in a `using` block.

This method has several overloads, and among all, it can take the following parameters:

- `actionName` (`string`): An optional name of a controller action; if present, the `controllerName` parameter must also be supplied
- `controllerName` (string): An optional name of a controller; must go along with an `actionName`
- `method` (`FormMethod`): An option HTML form method (`Get`, `Post`); if not supplied, it defaults to `Post`
- `routeName` (`string`): An optional route name (the name of a route registered through fluent configuration)
- `routeValues` (`object`): An optional object instance containing route values, specific to the routeName
- `antiForgery` (`bool?`): Indicates whether or not the form should include an anti-forgery token (more on this later on); if not supplied, it is included by default

There is another form generation method, `BeginRouteForm`, which is more focused on routes, hence it always takes a `routeName` parameter. Anything that it does can also be achieved with `BeginForm` as well.

Single line text boxes

Then we have text boxes. All of the primitive .NET types can be edited through a text box. By text box, I mean to say an `<input>` element with an appropriate `type` attribute. For that, we have the `TextBoxFor` and `TextBox` methods, the former for the strongly-typed and the other for the string version. These methods can be used like this:

```
@Html.TextBoxFor(x => x.FirstName)
@Html.TextBox("FirstName")
```

These methods have several overloads taking the following parameter:

- `format` (`string`): An optional format string, for the cases where the type to render implements `IFormattable`

The `TextBox`* HTML helper renders an `<input>` tag with a value of `type` that depends on the actual type of the property and its data type metadata (`DefaultModelMetadata.DataTypeName`):

- `text`: For string properties without any particular `DataType`
- `date`, `datetime`: For `DateTime` properties, depending on the presence of a `DataType` with a value of either `Date` or `DateTime`
- `number`: For numeric properties
- `email`: For string properties when associated with a `DataType` attribute of `EmailAddress`
- `url`: String properties with a `DataType` of `Url`
- `time`: `TimeSpan` properties or string properties with a `DataType` of `Time`
- `tel`: String properties with a `DataType` of `PhoneNumber`

Multi-line text boxes

If we want instead to render multi-line text boxes, we must use the `TextArea` and `TextAreaFor` methods. These render HTML `textarea` elements and their parameters are:

- `rows` (`int`): The rows to generate (`textarea rows` attribute)
- `columns` (`int`): The (`cols` attribute)

Passwords

Passwords (`<input type="password">`) are produced by one of the `Password` and `PasswordFor` methods. The only optional value they can take is the initial password:

- `value` (`string`): the initial password

Dropdowns

The `DropDownList` and `DropDownListFor` methods render a `<select>` element, with values specified in the form of a collection of `SelectListItem` items. The parameters are:

- `selectList` (`IEnumerable<SelectListItem>`): The list of items to display
- `optionLabel` (`string`): The default "empty" item

The `SelectListItem` class exposes the following properties:

- `Disabled` (`bool`): Indicates whether or not the item is available; default is `false`
- `Group` (`SelectListGroup`): An optional group
- `Selected` (`bool`): Indicates whether or not the item is selected; there can be only one item marked as selected, therefore, the default is `false`
- `Text` (`string`): The textual value to display
- `Value` (`string`): The value to use

The `SelectListGroup` class offers two properties:

- `Name` (`string`): The mandatory group name, used to group together multiple list items
- `Disabled` (`bool`): Indicates whether the group is disabled or not, it is `false` by default

There are two helper methods, `GetEnumSelectList` and `GetEnumSelectList<>`, that return in the form of an `IEnumerable<SelectListItem>`, the names and values of enumeration fields. This can be useful if we wish to use them to feed a drop-down list.

List boxes

The `ListBox` and `ListBoxFor` methods are similar to their drop-down list counterparts, the only difference is that the generated `<select>` element has its `multiple` attribute set to `true`. It only takes a single parameter:

- `selectList` (`IEnumerable<SelectListItem>`): The items to show

Radio buttons

As for radio buttons, we have the `RadioButton` and `RadioButtonFor` methods, which render an `<input>` with a `type` of `radio`:

- `value` (`object`): The value to use for the radio button
- `isChecked` (`bool?`): Indicates whether the radio button is checked or not (default)

The radio button group name will be the name of the property to which it is being generated, for example:

```
@Html.RadioButtonFor(m => m.Gender, "M" ) %> Male
@Html.RadioButtonFor(m => m.Gender, "F" ) %> Female
```

Checkboxes

Checkboxes are contemplated too, by means of the `CheckBox`, `CheckBoxFor` and `CheckBoxForModel` methods: this time they render an `<input>` tag with a `type` of `checkbox`. The sole parameter is:

- `isChecked` (`bool?`): Indicates whether the checkbox is checked or not; the default is `false`

Again, the group name will come from the property, as for radio buttons.

Hidden values

`Hidden`, `HiddenFor` and `HiddenForModel` render an `<input type="hidden">` element. The model or its properties can be explicitly overridden with this parameter:

- `value` (`object`): A value to include in the hidden field

Links

If we want to generate hyperlinks (`<a>`) to specific controller actions, we can use the `ActionLink` method. It has several overloads which accept the following parameters:

- `linkText` (`string`): The link text
- `actionName` (`string`): The action name
- `controllerName` (`string`): The controller name, must be supplied together with an `actionName`
- `routeValues` (`object`): An optional value (a POCO class or a dictionary) containing route values
- `protocol` (`string`): The optional URL protocol (for example, `http`, `https`, and so on)
- `hostname` (`string`): The optional URL hostname
- `fragment` (`string`): The optional URL anchor (for example, `#anchorname`)
- `port` (`int`): The optional URL port

As we can see, this method can generate links for either the same host as the web app or a different one.

Another option is to use a route name, and for that purpose, there is the `RouteLink` method; the only difference is that instead of the `actionName` and `controllerName` parameters, it takes a `routeName`:

- `routeName` (`string`): the name of a route for which to generate the link

Labels

The `Label`, `LabelFor` and `LabelForModel` render a `<label>` element with either a textual representation of the model or an optional text:

- `labelText` (`string`): the text to add to the label

Raw HTML

Renders HTML-encoded contents. Its sole parameter is:

- `value` (`string`, `object`): contents to display, after HTML encoding

IDs, names, and values

These are often useful to extract some properties from the generated HTML elements, the generated `id` and `name`. This is commonly required for JavaScript.

- `Id`, `IdFor`, `IdForModel`: Returns the value for the `id` attribute
- `Name`, `NameFor`, `NameForModel`: The value for the `name` attribute
- `DisplayName`, `DisplayNameFor`, `DisplayNameForModel`: The display name for the given property
- `DisplayText`, `DisplayTextFor`: The display text for the property or model
- `Value`, `ValueFor`, `ValueForModel`: The first non-null value from the view bag

Generic editor and display

We've seen that we can use templates for individual model properties, or the model itself. To render display templates, we have the `Display`, `DisplayFor`, and `DisplayForModel` methods. All of them accept the following optional parameters:

- `templateName` (`string`): The name of a template that will override the one in the model metadata (`DefaultModelMetadata.TemplateHint`)
- `additionalViewData` (`object`): An object or `IDictionary` that is merged into the view bag
- `htmlFieldName` (`string`): The name of the generated HTML `<input>` field

A property is only rendered, in display mode, if its metadata states it as such (`DefaultModelMetadata.ShowForDisplay`).

As for edit templates, the methods are similar: `Editor`, `EditorFor` and `EditorForModel`; these take exactly the same parameters as their display counterparts. It is important to mention that editors will only be generated for properties that are defined, as per their metadata, to be editable (`DefaultModelMetadata.ShowForEdit`).

Utility methods and properties

The `IHtmlHelper` class also exposes a few other utility methods:

- `Encode`: HTML-encodes a string using the configured HTML encoder
- `FormatValue`: Renders a formatted version of the passed value

Plus, it also exposes the following context properties:

- `IdAttributeDotReplacement`: The dot replacement string used for generating ID values (from `MvcViewOptions.HtmlHelperOptions.IdAttributeDotReplacement`)
- `Html5DateRenderingMode`: The HTML5 date rendering mode (from `MvcViewOptions.HtmlHelperOptions.Html5DateRenderingMode`)
- `MetadataProvider`: The model metadata provider
- `TempData`: Temporary data
- `ViewData` / `ViewBag`: The strongly/loosely typed view bag
- `ViewContext`: All of the view's context, including the HTTP context (`HttpContext`), route data (`RouteData`), the form context (`FormContext`) and the parsed model (`ModelStateDictionary`)

Validation messages

Validation messages can be displayed for individual validated properties or as a summary for all the model. For displaying individual messages, we use the `ValidationMessage` and `ValidationMessageFor` methods, which accept the following single optional attribute:

- `message` (`string`): An error message that will override the one from the validation framework

For the validation summary we have `ValidationSummary` and it accepts these parameters:

- `excludePropertyErrors` (`bool`): If set, display only model-level (top) errors, not errors for individual properties
- `message` (`string`): A message to display with the individual errors
- `tag` (`string`): The HTML tag to use, which overrides `MvcViewOptions.HtmlHelperOptions.ValidationSummaryMessageElement`)

Custom helpers

Some HTML elements have no corresponding HTML helper, for example, **button**. It is easy to add one, though; let's create an extension method over `IHtmlHelper`:

```
public static class HtmlHelperExtensions
{
  public static IHtmlContent Button(this IHtmlHelper html, string text)
  {
    return html.Button(text, null);
  }

  public static IHtmlContent Button(this IHtmlHelper html, string text,
object htmlAttributes)
  {
    return html.Button(text, null, null, htmlAttributes);
  }

  public static IHtmlContent Button(
    this IHtmlHelper html,
    string text,
    string action,
    object htmlAttributes)
  {
    return html.Button(text, action, null, htmlAttributes);
  }

  public static IHtmlContent Button(this IHtmlHelper html, string text,
string action)
  {
    return html.Button(text, action, null, null);
  }

  public static IHtmlContent Button(
    this IHtmlHelper html,
    string text,
    string action,
    string controller)
  {
    return html.Button(text, action, controller, null);
  }

  public static IHtmlContent Button(
    this IHtmlHelper html,
    string text,
    string action,
    string controller,
    object htmlAttributes)
```

```
  {
    if (html == null)
    {
      throw new ArgumentNullException(nameof(html));
    }

    if (string.IsNullOrWhiteSpace(text))
    {
      throw new ArgumentNullException(nameof(text));
    }

    var builder = new TagBuilder("button");
    builder.InnerHtml.Append(text);

    if (htmlAttributes != null)
    {
      foreach (var prop in
  htmlAttributes.GetType().GetTypeInfo().GetProperties())
      {
        builder.MergeAttribute(prop.Name,
          prop.GetValue(htmlAttributes)?.ToString() ?? string.Empty);
      }
    }

    var url = new UrlHelper(new ActionContext(
      html.ViewContext.HttpContext,
      html.ViewContext.RouteData,
      html.ViewContext.ActionDescriptor));

    if (!string.IsNullOrWhiteSpace(action))
    {
      if (!string.IsNullOrEmpty(controller))
      {
        builder.Attributes["formaction"] = url.Action(action, controller);
      }
      else
      {
        builder.Attributes["formaction"] = url.Action(action);
      }
    }

    return builder;
  }
}
```

This extension method uses the common guidelines for all the other HTML helpers:

- Several overloads, for each of the possible parameters
- Has a parameter of type `object` called `htmlAttributes`, which is used for any custom HTML attributes that we wish to add
- Uses the `UrlHelper` class to generate proper route links for the controller action, if supplied
- Returns an instance of `IHtmlContent`

Using it is simple:

```
@Html.Button("Submit")
```

Or, with a specific action and controller:

```
@Html.Button("Submit", action: "Validate", controller: "Validation")
```

Or even, with some custom attributes:

```
@Html.Button("Submit", new { @class = "save" })
```

Since ASP.NET Core does not offer any HTML helper for submitting the form, I hope you find this useful!

Templates

When the `Display`, `DisplayFor<T>` or `DisplayForModel` HTML helper methods are called, the ASP.NET Core framework renders the target property (or model) value, in a way that is specific to that property (or model class) and can be affected by its metadata. For example, the `ModelMetadata.DisplayFormatString` is used for rendering the property in a desired format. But suppose we want to have a slightly more complex HTML, for example, in the case of composite properties? Enter `display templates`.

Display templates are a Razor feature; basically, they are partial views, stored in a folder called `DisplayTemplates` under `Views\Shared`, and their model is set to target a .NET class. Let's imagine, for a moment, that we have a `Location` class that stores `Latitude` and `Longitude` values:

```
public class Location
{
  public decimal Latitude { get; set; }
  public decimal Longitude { get; set; }
}
```

If we want to have a custom display template for this, we could have a partial view like this:

```
@model Location
<div><span>Latitude: @Model.Latitude</span> - <span>Longitude:
@Model.Longitude</span></div>
```

So, this file is stored in `Views\Shared\DisplayTemplates\Location.cshtml`, but now you need to associate the `Location` class to it, which you can do by applying a `[UIHint]` to a property of that type:

```
[UIHint("Location")]
public Location Location { get; set; }
```

The `[UIHint]` attributes accepts a view name, the only difference is that it is only searched in the `Views\Shared\DisplayTemplates` folder.

Similar to display templates, we have **editor templates**. Editor templates are rendered by `Editor`, `EditorFor` or `EditorForModel`, and the main difference to display templates is that the partial view files are stored in `Views\Shared\EditorTemplates`. Of course, in these templates you would probably add HTML editor elements, even with custom JavaScript. For the case of the `Location` class, we could have:

```
@model Location
<div>
  <span>Latitude: @Html.TextBoxFor(x => x.Latitude)</span>
  <span>Longitude: @Html.TextBoxFor(x => x.Longitude)</span>
</div>
```

There can be only one `[UIHint]` attribute specified, which means that both templates--display and editor--must use the same name.

Model binding

ASP.NET Core tries automatically to populate (set values of their properties and fields) any parameters of an action method, it does that because it has a built-in (although configurable) **model binder provider**, which on its hand creates a **model binder**. These model binders know how to bind data from the many binding sources (discussed previously) to POCO classes, in many formats.

The model binder provider interface is `IModelBinderProvider`, and the model binder, unsurprisingly, is `IModelBinder`. The model binder providers are registered in the `ModelBinderProviders` collection of `MvcOptions`:

```
services.AddMvc(options =>
    {
      options.ModelBinderProviders.Add(new CustomModelBinderProvider());
    });
```

The included providers are:

- `BinderTypeModelBinderProvider`: Custom model binder (`IModelBinder`)
- `ServicesModelBinderProvider`: [FromServices]
- `BodyModelBinderProvider`: [FromBody]
- `HeaderModelBinderProvider`: [FromHeader]
- `SimpleTypeModelBinderProvider`: Basic types using a type converter
- `CancellationTokenModelBinderProvider`: `CancellationToken`
- `ByteArrayModelBinderProvider`: Deserializes from Base64 strings into a byte array
- `FormFileModelBinderProvider`: [FromForm]
- `FormCollectionModelBinderProvider`: IFormCollection
- `KeyValuePairModelBinderProvider`: KeyValuePair<TKey, TValue>
- `DictionaryModelBinderProvider`: IDictionary<TKey, TValue>
- `ArrayModelBinderProvider`: Arrays of object
- `CollectionModelBinderProvider`: Collections of objects (ICollection<TElement>, IEnumerable<TElement> or IList<TElement>)
- `ComplexTypeModelBinderProvider`: Nested properties (for example, `TopProperty.MidProperty.BottomProperty`)

To cut a long story short, these providers help in assigning values to the following types:

- Simple properties using type converters
- POCO classes
- Nested POCO classes
- Arrays of POCO classes
- Dictionaries
- Collections of POCO classes

For example, if you had a model of:

```
public class Order
{
  public int Id { get; set; }
  public int CustomerId { get; set; }
  public OrderState State { get; set; }
  public DateTime Timestamp { get; set; }
  public List<OrderDetail> Details { get; set; }
}

public enum OrderState
{
  Received,
  InProcess,
  Sent,
  Delivered,
  Cancelled,
  Returned
}

public class OrderDetail
{
  public int ProductId { get; set; }
  public int Quantity { get; set; }
}
```

Here we have properties of different types, including primitive types, enumerations, and collections of POCO classes. When we generate a form for one such model--perhaps using the HTML helpers that were described before--you will get HTML form elements containing values such as:

```
Id=43434
CustomerId=100
State=InProcess
Timestamp=2017-06-15T20:00:00
Details[0]_ProductId=45
Details[0]_Quantity=1
Details[1]_ProductId=47
Details[1]_Quantity=3
```

Notice the _ character separating child property names--it is configured to replace dots (.) in the `MvcViewOptions.HtmlHelper.IdAttributeDotReplacement` property. As you can see, ASP.NET Core can bind even somewhat complex cases.

Model validation

We all know that client-side validation--meaning, validating a page without having to post its contents--is nowadays what we expect from a web app. However, it may not be sufficient: for example for the (granted, few) cases where JavaScript is disabled. In this case, we need to ensure we validate our data on the server-side before actually doing anything with it. ASP.NET Core supports both scenarios, let's see how.

Server-side validation

The result of validating a submitted model is always available in the `ModelState` property of the `ControllerBase` class, and it is also present in the `ActionContext` class. Using the built-in validators, essentially based on `System.ComponentModel.DataAnnotations`, the following validations are performed:

- Validation based on attributes (`ValidationAttribute`-derived)
- Validation based on the `IValidatableObject` interface

Validation is executed when a form is posted or when explicitly invoked, by a call to `TryValidateModel`. The `ModelState` property is of type `ModelStateDictionary`, which exposes the following properties:

- `Item` (`ModelStateEntry`): Access to individual model properties' state
- `Keys` (`KeyEnumerable`): The collection of model properties' names
- `Values` (`ValueEnumerable`): The model properties' values
- `Count` (`int`): The count of model properties
- `ErrorCount` (`int`): The error count
- `HasReachedMaxErrors` (`bool`): Whether or not the found errors have reached the configured maximum
- `MaxAllowedErrors` (`int`): The configured maximum number of errors (see the following *Configuration* section next)
- `Root` (`ModelStateEntry`): The root object's model state
- `IsValid` (`bool`): Whether or not the model is valid
- `ValidationState` (`ModelValidationState`): The validation state for the model (`Unvalidated`, `Invalid`, `Valid` or `Skipped`)

Validation based on attributes is associated with the property to which the validation attribute is located at (some validation attributes can also be applied to classes), the property's name will be the key and the property's value will be the value in the `ModelStateDictionary`. For each property, once a validator fails, any other eventual validators will not be fired, the model state will be immediately invalid.

Configuration

There are a couple of configuration options available through the `AddMvc` method, as part of the `MvcOptions` class:

- `MaxModelValidationErrors` (`int`): The maximum number of validation errors before no more validation is performed (the default is `200`)
- `ModelValidatorProviders` (`IList<IModelValidatorProvider>`): The registered model validation providers; by default it contains an instance of `DefaultModelValidatorProvider` and one of `DataAnnotationsModelValidatorProvider`

These built-in providers basically do the following:

- `DefaultModelValidatorProvider`: If a property has any attribute that implements `IModelValidator`, use it for validation
- `DataAnnotationsModelValidatorProvider`: Hooks any `ValidatorAttributes` that the property to validate may have

Data annotations validation

The `System.ComponentModel.DataAnnotations` offers the following validation attributes:

- `[Compare]`: Compares two properties to see if they have the same value
- `[CreditCard]`: The string property must have a valid credit card format
- `[CustomValidation]`: Custom validation through an external method
- `[DataType]`: Validates a property against a specific data type (`DateTime`, `Date`, `Time`, `Duration`, `PhoneNumber`, `Currency`, `Text`, `Html`, `MultilineText`, `EmailAddress`, `Password`, `Url`, `ImageUrl`, `CreditCard`, `PostalCode`, `Upload`)

- [EmailAddress]: Checks if the string property is a valid email address
- [MaxLength]: The maximum length of a string property
- [MinLength]: The minimum length of a string property
- [Phone]: Checks that the string property has a phone-like structure (US only)
- [Range]: The maximum and minimum values of a property
- [RegularExpression]: Uses a regular expression to validate a string property
- [Remote]: Uses a controller action to validate a model
- [Required]: Checks if the property has a value set
- [StringLength]: Checks the maximum and minimum lengths of a string; same as one [MinLength] and one [MaxLength], but using this you only need one attribute
- [Url]: Checks that the string property is a valid URI

All of these attributes are hooked automatically by the registered DataAnnotationsModelValidatorProvider.

For custom validation, we have two options:

- Inherit from ValidationAttribute and implement its IsValid method:

```
[AttributeUsage(AttributeTargets.Property, AllowMultiple = false,
 Inherited = true)]
public sealed class IsEvenAttribute : ValidationAttribute
{
  protected override ValidationResult IsValid(object value,
   ValidationContext validationContext)
  {
    if (value != null)
    {
      try
      {
        var convertedValue = Convert.ToDouble(value);
        var isValid = (convertedValue % 2) == 0;

        if (!isValid)
        {
          return new ValidationResult(this.ErrorMessage,
             new[] { validationContext.MemberName });
        }
      }
      catch { }
    }
```

```
        return ValidationResult.Success;
    }
}
```

- Implement a validation method:

```
[CustomValidation(typeof(ValidationMethods), "ValidateEmail")]
public string Email { get; set; }
```

In this `ValidationMethods` class, add the following method:

```
public static ValidationResult ValidateEmail(string email,
ValidationContext context)
{
  if (!string.IsNullOrWhiteSpace(email))
  {
    if (!Regex.IsMatch(email, @"^([\w\.\-]+)@([\w\-]+)((\.(\w){2,3})+)$"))
    {
      return new ValidationResult("Invalid email", new[] {
        context.MemberName });
    }
  }

  return ValidationResult.Success;
}
```

A couple of notes:

- This validation attribute **only** checks for valid emails, it **does not** check for required values
- The `ValidationContext` attribute has some useful properties, such as the current member name being validated (`MemberName`), its display name (`DisplayName`) and the root validating object (`ObjectInstance`)
- `ValidationResult.Success` is `null`

The signature of the validation method can vary:

- The first parameter can either be strongly (for example, `string`) or loosely typed (for example, `object`), but it must be compatible with the property to be validated
- It can be `static` or instance
- It can take the `ValidationContext` parameter or not

Why choose one or the other? The `[CustomValidation]` attribute potentially promotes reuse, by having a set of shared methods that can be used in different contexts.

 `[CustomValidation]` can be applied to either a property or the whole class.

Error messages

There are three ways by which you can set the error message to display, in the case of a validation error:

- `ErrorMessage`: A plain old error message string, with no magic attached
- `ErrorMessageString`: A format string that can take tokens (for example, `{0}`, `{1}`) that depend on the actual validation attribute; token `{0}` is usually the name of the property being validated
- `ErrorMessageResourceType` + `ErrorMessageResourceName`: It is possible to ask for the error message to come from a string property (`ErrorMessageResourceName`) declared in an external type (`ErrorMessageResourceType`); this is the common approach if you would like to localize your error messages

Self-validation

You would implement `IValidatableObject` (also supported by `DataAnnotationsValidatorProvider`) if the validation you need involves several properties of a class, similar to what you would achieve with applying `[CustomValidation]` to the whole class. We say that the class is self-validatable. The `IValidatableObject` interface specifies a single method, `Validate`, and here is a possible implementation:

```
public class ProductOrder : IValidatableObject
{
    public int Id { get; set; }
    public DateTime Timestamp { get; set; }
    public int ProductId { get; set; }
    public int Quantity { get; set; }
    public decimal Price { get; set; }

    public IEnumerable<ValidationResult> Validate(ValidationContext context)
    {
```

```
if (this.Id <= 0)
{
  yield return new ValidationResult("Missing id", new [] { "Id" });
}

if (this.ProductId <= 0)
{
  yield return new ValidationResult("Invalid product", new [] {
    "ProductId" });
}

if (this.Quantity <= 0)
{
  yield return new ValidationResult("Invalid quantity", new [] {
    "Quantity" });
}

if (this.Timestamp > DateTime.Now)
{
  yield return new ValidationResult("Order date is in the future",
    new [] { "Timestamp" });
}
  }
}
```

Custom validation

Yet another option for custom validation involves hooking a new model validator provider and a bespoke model validator. Model validator providers are instances of IModelValidatorProvider, such as this one:

```
public sealed class IsEvenModelValidatorProvider : IModelValidatorProvider
{
  public void CreateValidators(ModelValidatorProviderContext context)
  {
    if (context.ModelMetadata.ModelType == typeof(string)
        || context.ModelMetadata.ModelType == typeof(int)
        || context.ModelMetadata.ModelType == typeof(uint)
        || context.ModelMetadata.ModelType == typeof(long)
        || context.ModelMetadata.ModelType == typeof(ulong)
        || context.ModelMetadata.ModelType == typeof(short)
        || context.ModelMetadata.ModelType == typeof(ushort)
        || context.ModelMetadata.ModelType == typeof(float)
        || context.ModelMetadata.ModelType == typeof(double))
    {
        if (context.Results.Any(x => x.Validator is IsEvenModelValidator)
== false)
```

```
      {
        context.Results.Add(new ValidatorItem
        {
          Validator = new IsEvenModelValidator(),
          IsReusable = true
        });
      }
    }
  }
}
```

This checks if the target property (`context.ModelMetadata`) is one of the expected types (numbers or strings) and then it adds an `IsEvenModelValidator`. When validation is triggered, this validator will be called.

For the sake of completion, here is its code:

```
public sealed class IsEvenModelValidator : IModelValidator
{
  public IEnumerable<ModelValidationResult> Validate(ModelValidationContext
context)
  {
    if (context.Model != null)
    {
      try
      {
        var value = Convert.ToDouble(context.Model);
        if ((value % 2) == 0)
        {
          yield break;
        }
      }
      catch { }
    }

    yield return new ModelValidationResult(
      context.ModelMetadata.PropertyName,
      $"{context.ModelMetadata.PropertyName} is not even.");
  }
}
```

This validator code tries to convert a number to a `double` (because it's the more generic) and then checks if the number is even. If the value is `null` or not convertible, it just returns an empty result.

Client-side model validation

Because server-side validation requires a post, sometimes it's more useful and provides a better user experience to perform it on the client-side. Let's see how we can do this.

All of the built-in validators also include client-side behavior; what this means is that, if you are using jQuery's unobtrusive validation--included by default in the ASP.NET Core templates--you get it automatically. Unobtrusive validation requires the following JavaScript modules:

- jQuery itself (`jquery-xxx.js`): `https://jquery.com/`
- jQuery validation (`jquery.validate.js`): `https://jqueryvalidation.org/`
- jQuery validate unobtrusive (`jquery.validate.unobtrusive.js`): `https://github.com/aspnet/jquery-validation-unobtrusive`

The actual filenames may vary slightly (minimized versus normal version, or include a version number), but this is it. They are installed by default into `wwwroot\lib\jquery`, `wwwroot\lib\jquery-validation` and `wwwroot\lib\jquery-validation-unobtrusive`.

Behind the scene, the included validators add HTML5 attributes (`data-*`) to each property to validate HTML form elements, and, when the form is about to be submitted, force a validation to occur. Client-side validation will only be performed if it is enabled (more on this on the next topic).

Configuration

Client validation providers are configured through the `AddViewOptions` method, which takes a lambda that exposes an `MvcViewOptions`:

- `ClientModelValidatorProviders` (`IList<IClientModelValidatorProvider>`): The registered client model validators; by default, it contains one `DefaultClientModelValidatorProvider`, one `DataAnnotationsClientModelValidatorProvider`, and one `NumericClientModelValidatorProvider`
- `HtmlHelperOptions.ClientValidationEnabled` (`bool`): Whether or not client-side validation is enabled; the default is `true`, meaning, it is

- `ValidationMessageElement` (`string`): The HTML element used for inserting the validation error messages for each validated property; the default is `span`
- `ValidationSummaryMessageElement` (`string`): The HTML element used for inserting the validation error messages summary for the model; the default is `span`

The included `IClientModelValidatorProviders` have the following purpose:

- `DefaultClientModelValidatorProvider`: If the validation attribute implements `IClientModelValidator`, uses it for the validation, regardless of having a specific client model validator provider
- `NumericClientModelValidatorProvider`: Restricts text boxes to only contain numeric values
- `DataAnnotationsClientModelValidatorProvider`: Adds support for all the included data annotations validators

Custom validation

You can certainly roll out your own client-side validator; the core of it is the `IClientModelValidator` and the `IClientModelValidatorProvider` interfaces. Picking up on the `IsEvenAttribute` we saw earlier, let's see how we can achieve the same validation on the client side.

First, let's register a **client model validator provider**:

```
services.AddMvc()
    .AddViewOptions(options =>
        {
            options.ClientModelValidatorProviders.Add(new
IsEvenClientModelValidatorProvider());
        });
```

The code for the `IsEvenClientModelValidatorProvider` goes like this:

```
public sealed class IsEvenClientModelValidatorProvider :
IClientModelValidatorProvider
{
  public void CreateValidators(ClientValidatorProviderContext context)
  {
    if (context.ModelMetadata.ModelType == typeof(string)
        || context.ModelMetadata.ModelType == typeof(int)
        || context.ModelMetadata.ModelType == typeof(uint)
        || context.ModelMetadata.ModelType == typeof(long)
```

```
          || context.ModelMetadata.ModelType == typeof(ulong)
          || context.ModelMetadata.ModelType == typeof(short)
          || context.ModelMetadata.ModelType == typeof(ushort)
          || context.ModelMetadata.ModelType == typeof(float)
          || context.ModelMetadata.ModelType == typeof(double))
      {
          if
(context.ModelMetadata.ValidatorMetadata.OfType<IsEvenAttribute>().Any())
          {
              if (!context.Results.Any(x => x.Validator is
IsEvenClientModelValidator))
              {
                context.Results.Add(new ClientValidatorItem
                {
                  Validator = new IsEvenClientModelValidator(),
                    IsReusable = true
                });
              }
          }
      }
    }
  }
}
```

This requires some explaining. The `CreateValidators` infrastructure method is called to give a chance for the client model validator provider to add custom validators. If the property currently being inspected (`context.ModelMetadata`) is of one of the supported types (`context.ModelMetadata.ModelType`), numbers or strings, and simultaneously contains an `IsEvenAttribute` and does not contain any `IsEvenClientModelValidator`, we add one to the validators collection (`context.Results`), in the form of a `ClientValidatorItem` that contains an `IsEvenClientModelValidator`, which is safe to reuse (`IsReusable`) as it doesn't keep any state.

Now, let's see what the `IsEvenClientModelValidator` looks like:

```
public sealed class IsEvenClientModelValidator : IClientModelValidator
{
  public void AddValidation(ClientModelValidationContext context)
  {
    context.Attributes["data-val"] = true.ToString().ToLowerInvariant();
    context.Attributes["data-val-iseven"] = this.GetErrorMessage(context);
  }

  private string GetErrorMessage(ClientModelValidationContext context)
  {
    var attr = context
        .ModelMetadata
        .ValidatorMetadata
```

```
        .OfType<IsEvenAttribute>()
        .SingleOrDefault();

    var msg = attr.FormatErrorMessage(
        context.ModelMetadata.PropertyName);
        return msg;
  }
}
```

It works like this:

1. Two attributes are added to the HTML element that is used for the editing of the model property:
   - `data-val`: Meaning, the element should be validated
   - `data-val-iseven`: The error message to use in case the element is invalid, for the `iseven` rule

2. The error message is retrieved from the `IsEvenAttribute`'s `FormatErrorMessage` method; we know there is an `IsEvenAttribute`, otherwise we wouldn't be here.

Finally, we need to add somehow a JavaScript validation code, perhaps in a separate `.js` file:

```
(function ($) {
  var $jQval = $.validator;
  $jQval.addMethod('iseven', function (value, element, params) {
    if (!value) {
      return true;
    }

    value = parseFloat($.trim(value));

    if (!value) {
      return true;
    }

    var isEven = (value % 2) === 0;
      return isEven;
    });

    var adapters = $jQval.unobtrusive.adapters;
    adapters.addBool('iseven');
}) (jQuery);
```

What we are doing here is registering a custom jQuery validation function under the name iseven, which, when fired, checks if the value is empty and tries to convert it into a floating point number (this works for both integers and floating point numbers). Finally, it checks if this value is even or not, and returns appropriately. It goes without saying, this validation function is hooked automatically by the unobtrusive validation framework, so you do not need to be worried.

 The error message is displayed in both the element-specific error message label and in the error message summary, if it is present in the view.

You may find the process to be a bit convoluted, in which case, you may be happy to know that you can add together the validation attribute and the IClientModelValidator implementation: it will work just the same, and it is because of the included DefaultClientModelValidatorProvider. It is, however, advisable to separate them because of the *Single Responsibility Principle* and the *Separation of Concerns*.

AJAX

AJAX is a term coined long ago to represent a feature of modern browsers by which asynchronous HTTP requests can be done, via JavaScript, by the browser, without a full page reload.

ASP.NET Core does not offer any support for AJAX, which doesn't mean that you can't use it--it is just the case that you need to do it manually.

This example uses jQuery to retrieve values in the form and send them to an action. Make sure the jQuery library is included in either the view file or the layout:

```
$('#submit').click(function(evt) {
  evt.preventDefault();

  var payload = $('form').serialize();

  $.ajax({
    url: '@Url.Action("Save", "Repository")',
    type: 'POST',
    data: payload,
    success: function (result) {
      //success
    },
    error: function (error) {
```

```
        //error
    }
  });
});
```

This bit of JavaScript code does a couple of things:

1. Binds a click event handler to an HTML element with an ID of `submit`.
2. Serializes all `form` elements.
3. Creates a POST AJAX request to a controller action named `Save` in a controller called `Repository`.
4. If the AJAX call succeeds, the `success` function is called, otherwise, an `error` is called instead.

 The URL to the controller action is generated by the `Action` method. It is important not to have it hardcoded but instead rely on this HTML helper to return the proper URL.

Validation

One of the included validation attributes, `[Remote]`, uses AJAX to perform validation on the server-side transparently. When applied to a property of the model, it takes a `controller` and an `action` parameter that must refer to an existing controller action:

```
[Remote(action: "CheckEmailExists", controller: "Validation")]
public string Email { get; set; }
```

This controller action must have a structure similar to this one, minus, of course, the parameters to the action:

```
[AcceptVerbs("Get", "Post")]
public IActionResult CheckEmailExists(string email)
{
  if (this._repository.CheckEmailExists(email))
  {
    return this.Json(false);
  }

  return this.Json(true);
}
```

Essentially, it must return a JSON-formatted value of `true`, if the validation succeeds, or `false`, otherwise.

 This validation can be used for both a simple property of a primitive type (like `string`) but also for any POCO class.

Restrictions

In previous (pre-Core) versions of ASP.NET MVC, there was an attribute, `[AjaxOnly]`, that could be used to restrict an action to only be callable by AJAX. While it is no longer present, it is very easy to bring it back:

```
[AttributeUsage(AttributeTargets.Method, AllowMultiple = false, Inherited =
true)]
public sealed class AjaxOnlyAttribute : Attribute, IResourceFilter
{
  public void OnResourceExecuted(ResourceExecutedContext context)
  {
  }

  public void OnResourceExecuting(ResourceExecutingContext context)
  {
    if (context.HttpContext.Request.Headers["X-Requested-With"] !=
    "XMLHttpRequest")
    {
      context.Result = new StatusCodeResult((int)HttpStatusCode.NotFound);
    }
  }
}
```

This attribute implements the **resource filter** interface, `IResourceFilter`, which will be discussed in the chapter dedicated to filters, and basically what it does is check for the presence of a specific header (`X-Requested-With`) that is an indication that the current request is being done by AJAX. If not, it sets the response result, thus short-circuiting any other possible filters. To apply it, just place it next to an action that you want to restrict:

```
[AjaxOnly]
public IActionResult AjaxOnly(Model model) { ... }
```

For an overview of AJAX and the `XMLHttpRequest` object, please see https://developer.mozilla.org/en/docs/Web/API/XMLHttpRequest.

Contents

According to the best practices, your AJAX endpoints should return data; in the modern world, when it comes to web apps, this data is normally in the form of JSON. Thus, you will most likely use the `JsonResult` class to return contents to the client code. As for sending the data to the server, if you use jQuery, it will take care of everything for you, and it just works. Otherwise, you will need to serialize data to a proper format--perhaps JSON too, set the appropriate content type header, and off you go.

Uploading files

File uploading in HTTP requires two things:

- You must use the `POST` verb
- The `multipart/form-data` encoding must be used in the form

Where ASP.NET Core is concerned, the included model binders know how to bind any posted files to an `IFormFile` object (or collection of objects). For example, if you have a form of:

```
@using (Html.BeginForm("SaveForm", "Repository", FormMethod.Post,
  new { enctype = "multipart/form-data" }))
{
  <input type="file" name="file" />
  <input type="submit" value="Save"/>
}
```

You can retrieve the file in an action method like this one:

```
[HttpPost("[controller]/[action]")]
public IActionResult SaveForm(IFormFile file)
{
  var length = file.Length;
  var name = file.Name;
  //do something with the file
  return this.View();
}
```

But the HTML file upload specification, (`https://www.w3.org/TR/2010/WD-html-markup-20101019/input.file.html`), also mentions the possibility to submit multiple files at once--it is the `multiple` attribute. In that case, you can just declare your parameter as an array of `IFormFile` instances (a collection will also work):

```
public IActionResult SaveForm(IFormFile[] file) { ... }
```

The `IFormFile` interface gives you everything you need to manipulate these files:

- `ContentType` (`string`): The content type of the posted file
- `ContentDisposition` (`string`): The inner content disposition header, containing the HTML input name and selected file name
- `Headers` (`IHeaderDictionary`): Any headers sent with the file
- `Length` (`long`): The length, in bytes, of the posted file
- `Name` (`string`): The HTML name of the input element that originated the file upload
- `FileName` (`string`): The temporary filename, in the filesystem, where the posted file was saved

By using the `CopyTo` and `CopyToAsync` you can easily copy the contents of the posted file, as arrays of bytes, from the source `Stream` to another. `OpenReadStream` allows you to peek at the actual file contents.

The default file upload mechanism makes uses of a temporary file in the filesystem, but you can roll out your mechanism. For additional information, please refer to this post by Microsoft: `https://docs.microsoft.com/en-us/aspnet/core/mvc/models/file-uploads`.

Direct access

There is also the possibility of accessing directly the `HttpContext.Request.Form.Files` collection; this collection is prototyped as the `IFormFileCollection`, and, guess what, it exposes a collection of `IFormFile`. Yet another possibility would be to declare an action parameter of type `IFormCollection`, which will contain exactly the same as `HttpContext.Request.Form`. Other than curiosity, I don't see any obvious reason why you would want to do that, unless you are working with a very dynamic user interface.

Putting it all together

For validation you should probably stick to data annotations attributes and `IValidatableObject` implementations, if need be--these are used in a plethora of other .NET APIs and are pretty much the standard for validation.

Do implement client-side validation and AJAX, as it provides a much better user experience, but never forget to validate also on the server-side!

There is probably no need for custom model binders, as the included ones seem to cover most cases.

Display and editor templates are very handy and you should try to use them as it may reduce the code you need to add every time, especially if you want to reuse it.

Summary

In this chapter we've seen how we can work with models--produce HTML for them including with templates, validate it on the front and back-end, see the validation error messages and bind your model to and from HTML form elements.

In the next chapter we talk about securing access and usage of views and forms.

7
Security

Security is one of the hottest topics in web applications. Everything seems to be moving to the web and we've had reports of significant security breaches in major websites. People expect the sites they use to be secure and reliable, and this chapter is all about that. Throughout the chapter, we will be talking about different topics, but all have in common security, from different points of view.

We will cover the following topics in this chapter:

- Authentication
- Authorization
- Anti-forgery
- CORS
- HTTPS
- Data protection

Authentication

Authentication is the process by which you tell your application who you are; from this moment on, the application will know you, at least, for a certain period of time.

Authentication is not the same as, although it is related to, authorization. You probably need authentication if you have resources that require authorization to access them.

The general authorization flow is as follows:

1. Someone requests access to a protected resource.
2. The framework checks that the user is not authorized (or authenticated) and redirects them to a login page, issuing a 302 code.
3. The user supplies their credentials.
4. The credentials are checked and, if they are valid, the user is directed to the requested resource (HTTP 302) with a cookie that identifies them as being logged in.
5. Otherwise, the framework redirects to the failed login page.
6. Access to the protected resource is now granted.

In ASP.NET Core, we use the [Authorize] attribute or some filter to restrict access to a resource, either through a controller as a whole or some specific action methods:

```
//whole controller is protected
[Authorize]
public class AdminController { }

public class SearchController
{
  //only this method is restricted
  [Authorize]
  public IActionResult Admin() { ... }
}
```

But, if we don't do anything else, when we try to access one of these resources we will end up with a 401 Unauthorized error code. What we need is some middleware that is capable of intercepting this error code and proceeding accordingly.

Windows authentication

ASP.NET Core, because it is platform-agnostic, does not natively support Windows authentication. Probably the best way to achieve this, if we so need it, is to use IIS/IIS Express as a **reverse proxy**, handling all the requests and directing them to ASP.NET Core.

For IIS Express, we need to configure the launch settings in the project's Properties\launchSettings.json file as follows, with the changes in **bold**:

```
"iisSettings": {
  "windowsAuthentication": true,
  "anonymousAuthentication": false,
  "iisExpress": {
```

```
    "applicationUrl": "http://localhost:5000/",
    "sslPort": 0
  }
}
```

For IIS, we need to make sure the `AspNetCoreModule` is enabled for our website.

In any case, we need to configure Windows authentication in the `IISOptions` class, in the `ConfigureServices` method:

```
services.Configure<IISOptions>(options =>
options.ForwardWindowsAuthentication = true);
```

Finally, the `AspNetCoreModule` makes use of a `Web.config` file, which is not needed or used by ASP.NET Core itself; make sure it is deployed and that it includes the following content:

```
<?xml version="1.0" encoding="utf-8"?>
 <configuration>
    <system.webServer>
        <aspNetCore forwardWindowsAuthToken="true"
processPath="%LAUNCHER_PATH%"
            arguments="%LAUNCHER_ARGS%" />
        <handlers>
            <add name="aspNetCore" path="*" verb="*"
modules="AspNetCoreModule"
                resourceType="Unspecified" />
        </handlers>
    </system.webServer>
 </configuration>
```

And that's it. The `[Authorize]` attribute will require authenticated users and will be happy with Windows authentication. The `HttpContext.User` will be set to an instance of `WindowsPrincipal` and any Windows groups will be available as roles and also as claims (`ClaimTypes.Role`). The Windows name will be set in `ClaimsIdentity.Name` in the form **domain\user**.

In any place where you want to get the current Windows authentication, you can just do this:

```
var identity = WindowsIdentity.GetCurrent();
```

And, for example, if you want to know if the current user belongs to a specific role, such as the built-in **Administrators**, you can do this:

```
var principal = new WindowsPrincipal(identity);
var isAdmin = principal.IsInRole(WindowsBuiltInRole.Administrator);
```

Custom authentication

ASP.NET Core does not include any authentication provider, unlike previous versions of ASP.NET, which shipped with support for Windows and SQL-based authentication--the membership provider. This means that we have to implement everything manually--or not quite, as we will see in a moment.

The way to implement this flow manually changed slightly from ASP.NET Core 1.x to 2.x. Let's start with 1.x first.

ASP.NET Core 1.x authentication

So, we need to register a couple of services related to cookie-based authentication, in `ConfigureServices`:

```
services.AddCookieAuthentication();
```

And then add a cookie authentication middleware to the pipeline (`Configure`):

```
app.UseCookieAuthentication(new CookieAuthenticationOptions()
{
  AuthenticationScheme = "Cookies",
  LoginPath = "/Account/Login/",
  AccessDeniedPath = "/Account/AccessDenied",
  LogoutPath = "/Account/Logout",
  AutomaticAuthenticate = true,
  AutomaticChallenge = true,
  SlidingExpiration = true,
  ExpireTimeSpan = TimeSpan.FromDays(14),
  ReturnUrlParameter = "ReturnUrl"
});
```

Essentially, what this means is the following:

- `AuthenticationScheme` (`string`): Just a regular name to identify this authentication scheme
- `LoginPath` (`PathString`): The path to redirect to if trying to access a protected resource while not being authenticated
- `AccessDeniedPath` (`PathString`): The path to redirect if access is not granted
- `LogoutPath` (`PathString`): The logout path
- `AutomaticAuthenticate` (`bool`): Whether to set the identity (`HttpContext.User`) automatically; the default is `true`
- `AutomaticChallenge` (`bool`): Whether to handle automatic challenge; the default is `true`
- `SlidingExpiration` (`bool`): Whether to prolong the authentication cookie expiration each time a request is made and more than half the expiration time has elapsed; the default is `true`
- `ExpireTimeSpan` (`TimeSpan`): The duration of the authentication cookie; the default is **14 days**
- `ReturnUrlParameter` (`string`): The name of the query string parameter that will hold the original URL, the one of the protected resource, when the middleware redirects to the login page; this will be used, if we so wish, to restore the navigation to it

A sample implementation of an authentication controller could look like this:

```
public class AccountController : Controller
{
  private readonly IOptions<CookieAuthenticationOptions> _options;

  public AccountController(IOptions<CookieAuthenticationOptions> options)
  {
    this._options = options;
  }

  [HttpGet]
  [AllowAnonymous]
  public IActionResult Login()
  {
    return this.View();
  }

  [HttpPost]
  [AllowAnonymous]
```

```
public async Task<IActionResult> PerformLogin(
  string username,
  string password,
  string returnUrl)
{
  if (this.ValidateCredentials(username, password)
  {
    var claim = new Claim(ClaimTypes.NameIdentifier, username,
ClaimValueTypes.String);
    var user = new ClaimsIdentity(new [] { claims }, "Cookies",
ClaimTypes.NameIdentifier, ClaimTypes.Role);

    await this.HttpContext.Authentication.SignInAsync("Cookies", new
ClaimsPrincipal(user));

    return this.Redirect(returnUrl);
  }

  return this.Redirect(this._options.Value.AccessDeniedPath);
}

[HttpGet]
public async Task<IActionResult> Logout()
{
  await this.HttpContext.Authentication.SignOutAsync("Cookies");
  return this.RedirectToRoute("Default");
}

[HttpGet]
[AllowAnonymous]
public IActionResult AccessDenied()
{
  return this.View();
}
}
```

Here's a brief explanation:

- We leverage the **dependency injection (DI)** framework to inject into this
  controller the CookieAuthenticationOptions instance, the very same passed
  to the UseCookieAuthentication call, and we store it in a field
- The Login method corresponds to the LoginPath property of
  CookieAuthenticationOptions and is called to return the login form; this
  method can be called even by unauthorized users

- The `PerformLogin` action is called via a form post and receives as its parameters the username, password, and return URL; internally, it calls some credentials validation method (not shown here) and, depending on its result, it either sets the current identity and returns the original requested URL or the failed URL
- The `Logout` method logs the current user out (by clearing the authentication cookie) and redirects them to the default route

A very simple login form could look like this:

```
@using (Html.BeginForm("PerformLogin", "Account", FormMethod.Post))
{
  <p>Username: @Html.TextBox("username")</p>
  <p>Password: @Html.Password("password")</p>
  @Html.Hidden("ReturnUrl",
Html.ViewContext.HttpContext.Request.Query["ReturnUrl"])
  <button>Login</button>
}
```

Pretty straightforward, don't you think? The only thing maybe worth mentioning is the usage of a hidden field to store the value for the `ReturnUrl` query string parameter: this is required to pass to the `PerformLogin` action.

 You could set other claims in the `ClaimsPrincipal` instance, such as a list of roles, but let's leave it for now.

ASP.NET Core 2.x authentication

In ASP.NET Core 2, things changed a bit. First, the method used to register the services is still `AddCookieAuthentication`, but this time it takes two parameters:

```
services.AddCookieAuthentication(CookieAuthenticationDefaults.Authenticatio
nScheme, options =>
{
  options.LoginPath = "/Account/Login/";
  options.AccessDeniedPath = "/Account/Forbidden/";
  options.LogoutPath = "/Account/Logout";
  options.ReturnUrlParameter = "ReturnUrl";
});
```

We keep the `UseAuthentication` method in `Configure`, but this time without parameters:

```
app.UseAuthentication();
```

The changes in the `AccountController` are minor--we must call the `SignInAsync` and `SignOutAsync` extension methods over the `HttpContext` instance instead of calling the **old** versions in `HttpContext.Authorization`:

```
[HttpPost]
[AllowAnonymous]
public async Task<IActionResult> PerformLogin(
   string username,
   string password,
   string returnUrl)
{
   //...
   await this.HttpContext.SignInAsync("Cookies", new ClaimsPrincipal(user));
   //...
}

[HttpGet]
public async Task<IActionResult> Logout()
{
   await this.HttpContext.SignOutAsync("Cookies");
   //..
}
```

Before using these new methods, add a `using` statement for the `Microsoft.AspNetCore.Authentication` namespace.

Identity

Because you shouldn't have to deal with low-level authentication yourself, there are a number of packages that assist you in that task. The one that Microsoft recommends is **Microsoft Identity** (`http://github.com/aspnet/identity`).

Identity is an extensible library for doing username-password authentication and storing user properties. It is modular and, by default, it uses Entity Framework Core for the data store persistence. Of course, because Entity Framework itself is quite extensible, it can use any of its data providers (SQL Server, SQLite, Redis, and so on). The NuGet package for Identity with Entity Framework Core is `Microsoft.AspNetCore.Identity.EntityFrameworkCore`. Identity is installed by default with the Visual Studio templates for *ASP.NET Core Web Applications*, if we choose to use authentication through **Individual User Accounts**. This shows the Visual Studio screen where we can select the authentication method:

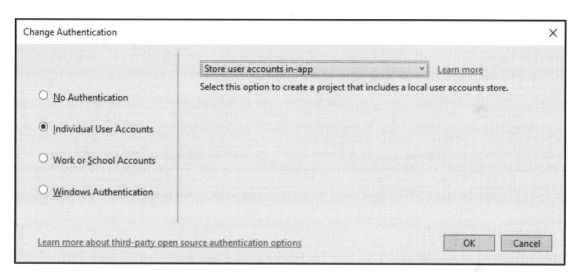

Identity supports both user properties and roles. In order to use Identity, we first need to register its services:

```
services.AddEntityFramework()
    .AddSqlServer()
    .AddDbContext<ApplicationDbContext>(options =>
options.UseSqlServer(Configuration["Data:DefaultConnection:ConnectionString
"]));

services.AddIdentity<ApplicationUser, IdentityRole>()
    .AddEntityFrameworkStores<ApplicationDbContext>()
    .AddDefaultTokenProviders();
```

By all means, do replace the connection string key (`Data:DefaultConnection:ConnectionString`) in the configuration to whatever suits you best, and make sure it points to a valid configuration value.

Identity supports a large number of options when it comes to security; these can be configured on an `IdentityOptions` instance:

```
services.Configure<IdentityOptions>(options =>
    {
        options.Lockout.DefaultLockoutTimeSpan = TimeSpan.FromMinutes(30);
        options.Lockout.MaxFailedAccessAttempts = 10;
        options.Cookies.ApplicationCookie.ExpireTimeSpan =
TimeSpan.FromDays(150);
        options.Cookies.ApplicationCookie.LoginPath = "/Account/Login";
        options.Cookies.ApplicationCookie.LogoutPath = "/Account/Logout";
        options.Cookies.ApplicationCookie.AccessDeniedPath =
"/Account/AccessDenied";
    });
```

I won't go through all of the available options; please refer to the Identity site for the full picture: `https://docs.microsoft.com/en-us/aspnet/core/security/authentication/identity`.

The Identity registration code (first listing) mentioned the `ApplicationDbContext` and `ApplicationUser` classes. A skeleton of these classes is added automatically when we create a project using the Visual Studio template that uses custom authentication, but I'm adding them here for your reference:

```
public class ApplicationDbContext : IdentityDbContext<ApplicationUser,
ApplicationRole, string>
{
  public ApplicationDbContext(DbContextOptions options) : base(options) { }
}

public class ApplicationUser : IdentityUser
{
  //add your custom properties here
}

public class ApplicationRole : IdentityRole
{
  //add your custom properties here
}
```

Nothing fancy here, as you can see. The only thing worth mentioning is that you can add your own custom properties to the `ApplicationUser` and `ApplicationRole` classes and these will be persisted and retrieved as part of the login process.

Now, picking up on the previous authentication example, let's see how it goes with Identity:

```
public class AccountController : Controller
{
  private readonly IOptions<IdentityOptions> _options;
  private readonly UserManager<ApplicationUser> _userManager;
  private readonly RoleManager<ApplicationRole> _roleManager;
  private readonly SignInManager<ApplicationUser> _signInManager;

  public AccountController(IOptions<IdentityOptions> options,
    UserManager<ApplicationUser> userManager,
    RoleManager<ApplicationRole> roleManager,
    SignInManager<ApplicationUser> signInManager)
  {
    this._options = options;
    this._signInManager = signInManager;
    this._userManager = userManager;
    this._roleManager = roleManager;
  }

  [HttpPost]
  [AllowAnonymous]
  public async Task<IActionResult> PerformLogin(
    string username,
    string password,
    string returnUrl)
  {
    var result = await this._signInManager.PasswordSignInAsync(username,
password, isPersistent: true, lockoutOnFailure: false);

    if (result.Succeeded)
    {
      return this.Redirect(returnUrl);
    }
    else if (result.IsLockedOut)
    {
      return this.RedirectToAction("Account", "LockedOut");
    }

    return
this.Redirect(this._options.Value.Cookies.ApplicationCookie.AccessDeniedPat
h);
  }

  [HttpGet]
  [AllowAnonymous]
  public IActionResult LockedOut()
```

```
    {
      return this.View();
    }

    [HttpGet]
    public async Task<IActionResult> Logout()
    {
      await this._signInManager.SignOutAsync();
      return this.RedirectToRoute("Default");
    }

    private async Task<ApplicationUser> GetCurrentUserAsync()
    {
      //the current user properties
      return await this._userManager.GetUserAsync(this.HttpContext.User);
    }

    private async Task<ApplicationRole> GetUserRoleAsync(string id)
    {
      //the role for the given user
      return await this._roleManager.FindByIdAsync(id);
    }
  }
```

As you can see, it is pretty similar to the previous code, but this is just a teaser, as Identity supports lots of other features, such as:

- User registration, including email activation codes
- Assigning roles to users
- Account locking after a number of failed login attempts
- Two-factor authentication
- Password retrieval
- External authentication providers

Please consult the Identity site for more information: `https://www.asp.net/identity`.

Using JWT

JSON Web Tokens (JWT) are an open standard, defined in RFC 7519, for representing claims securely between two connecting parties using HTTP for communication. The spec is available at `https://tools.ietf.org/html/rfc7519`.

Using JWT tokens is similar to using cookies for authentication, but cookies are usually associated with human interaction, whereas JWT tokens are more common in machine-to-machine scenarios, like web services.

Let's have a look at a full example. Before we delve into the code, make sure you add the `Microsoft.AspNetCore.Authentication.JwtBearer` NuGet package.

We first need to generate, and make available to the client, a JWT token. We can produce one through an action method, like this one:

```
[Route("/token")]
[HttpPost]
public IActionResult CreateToken(string username, string password)
{
  if (this.IsValidCredentials(username, password) == true)
  {
    return new ObjectResult(this.GenerateToken(username));
  }

  return this.BadRequest();
}
```

Let's forget about the `IsValidCredentials` method (it should be pretty straightforward to check if a credential set is valid) and focus on the `GenerateToken` method instead:

```
private string GenerateToken(string username)
{
    var claims = new Claim[]
        {
            new Claim(ClaimTypes.Name, username),
            new Claim(JwtRegisteredClaimNames.Nbf,
                new
DateTimeOffset(DateTime.UtcNow).ToUnixTimeSeconds().ToString()),
            new Claim(JwtRegisteredClaimNames.Exp,
                new
DateTimeOffset(DateTime.UtcNow.AddDays(1)).ToUnixTimeSeconds().ToString()),
        };

    var token = new JwtSecurityToken(
        new JwtHeader(new SigningCredentials(
            new SymmetricSecurityKey(Encoding.UTF8.GetBytes("at-least-16-
character-secret-key")),
                SecurityAlgorithms.HmacSha256)),
        new JwtPayload(claims));

    return new JwtSecurityTokenHandler().WriteToken(token);
}
```

This code allows anyone knowing a valid username/password pair to request a JWT token, which lasts 1 day. The secret key, of course, can come from configuration and should not really be hardcoded.

Now, to set up the authentication, we need to go to `ConfigureServices`; this is how it looks in ASP.NET Core 2.x:

```
services.AddAuthentication(options =>
    {
      options.DefaultAuthenticateScheme =
JwtBearerDefaults.AuthenticationScheme;
      options.DefaultChallengeScheme =
JwtBearerDefaults.AuthenticationScheme;
    }).AddJwtBearer(JwtBearerDefaults.AuthenticationScheme, options =>
    {
      options.TokenValidationParameters = new TokenValidationParameters
        {
          ValidateAudience = false,
          ValidateIssuer = false,
          ValidateIssuerSigningKey = true,
          IssuerSigningKey = new SymmetricSecurityKey(
            Encoding.UTF8.GetBytes("at-least-16-character-secret-key")),
          ValidateLifetime = true,
          ClockSkew = TimeSpan.FromMinutes(5)
        };
    });
```

And this goes in `Configure`:

```
app.UseAuthentication();
```

As for ASP.NET Core 1.x, the method is similar; in `ConfigureServices`, just add authentication support:

```
services.AddAuthentication(options =>
    {
      options.SignInScheme = JwtBearerDefaults.AuthenticationScheme;
    });
```

And in `Configure`, add all the actual options:

```
var options = new JwtBearerOptions();
options.TokenValidationParameters = new TokenValidationParameters
    {
      ValidateAudience = false,
      ValidateIssuer = false,
      ValidateIssuerSigningKey = true,
      IssuerSigningKey = new SymmetricSecurityKey(
```

```
        Encoding.UTF8.GetBytes("at-least-16-character-secret-key")),
        ValidateLifetime = true,
        ClockSkew = TimeSpan.FromMinutes(5)
    };
    app.UseJwtBearerAuthentication(options);
```

Now, any requests for action methods with the [Authorize] attribute will be checked for the JWT token and will only be accepted if it is valid! To make sure this happens, you need to send the authorization token with all requests (including AJAX calls); it is the Authorization header and it looks like this:

```
Authorization: Bearer <my-long-jwt-authorization-token>
```

You can play and generate valid JWT tokens using a number of public sites, such as https://jwt.io/. Of course, you need to find a way to store the token for the duration of the request (HTML local storage, for example); if the token was tampered with or its timeout was reached, you will get an authorization error.

If you wish, you can instruct ASP.NET Core to use a different authentication validation provider, for example, you can have both a cookie and a JWT-based authorization providers. You only need to use the AuthenticationSchemes property of the [Authorize] attribute, like this, for JWT:

```
[Authorize(AuthenticationSchemes = JwtBearerDefaults.AuthenticationScheme)]
```

or this, to use cookies:

```
[Authorize(AuthenticationSchemes =
CookieAuthenticationDefaults.AuthenticationScheme)]
```

IdentityServer

IdentityServer is an open source implementation of the **OpenID Connect** and **OAuth 2.0** protocols for ASP.NET. The version we are interested in, IdentityServer4, was designed specifically for ASP.NET Core; its source code is made available at https://github.com/ IdentityServer/IdentityServer4 and its documentation at http://docs. identityserver.io/. It is so popular that it is in fact Microsoft's recommended implementation for service federation and single sign-on.

IdentityServer, loosely speaking, can be used for authentication as a service, meaning it can accept requests for authentication, validate them against any number of data stores and grant access tokens.

We won't go into the details of setting up IdentityServer, as it can be quite complex and has a huge number of features. What we are interested in is how we can use it to authenticate users. We will need the `Microsoft.AspNetCore.Authentication.OpenIdConnect` and `IdentityServer4.AccessTokenValidation` NuGet packages, but the configuration changes slightly from ASP.NET Core 1.x to 2.x.

ASP.NET Core 1.x

In the `Configure` method, add the cookie authentication and OpenID Connect middleware to the pipeline:

```
JwtSecurityTokenHandler.DefaultInboundClaimTypeMap.Clear();

app.UseCookieAuthentication(new CookieAuthenticationOptions
    {
        AuthenticationScheme = "Cookies"
    });

app.UseOpenIdConnectAuthentication(new OpenIdConnectOptions
    {
        ClientId = "MasteringAspNetCore",
        SignInScheme = "Cookies",
        //change the IdentityServer4 URL
        Authority = "https://servername:5000",
        //uncomment the next line if not using HTTPS
        //RequireHttpsMetadata = false
    });
```

 Make sure you set the `Authority` URL and the `ClientId` property according to your setup. If you want to use HTTP instead of HTTPS, you will have to set the `RequireHttpsMetadata` to `false`.

ASP.NET Core 2.x

In ASP.NET Core 2.x, it is slightly different: we set all configuration in the `ConfigureServices` method:

```
services.AddCookieAuthentication("Cookies");

services.AddOpenIdConnectAuthentication(options =>
    {
        options.ClientId = "MasteringAspNetCore";
        //change the IdentityServer4 URL
        options.Authority = "https://servername:5000";
```

```
    //uncomment the next line if not using HTTPS
    //options.RequireHttpsMetadata = false;
});
```

Then add the authentication middleware, in `Configure`:

```
JwtSecurityTokenHandler.DefaultInboundClaimTypeMap.Clear();

app.UseAuthentication();
```

> For additional information, consult the wiki article at `https://social.technet.microsoft.com/wiki/contents/articles/37169.secure-your-netcore-web-applications-using-identityserver-4.aspx` and the IdentityServer Identity documentation at `http://docs.identityserver.io/en/release/quickstarts/6_aspnet_identity.html`.

Azure AD

With everything moving to the cloud, it should come as no surprise that ASP.NET Core also supports authentication with Azure AD. When you create a new project, you have the option to select **Work or School Accounts** for authentication and then enter the details of your Azure cloud:

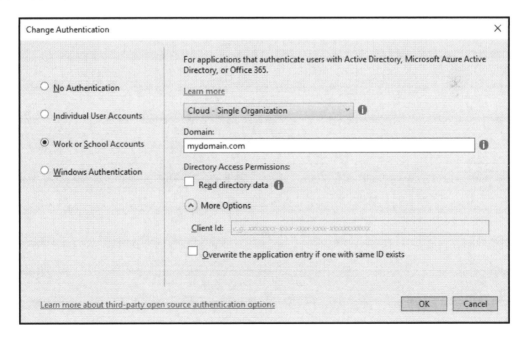

Note: You must enter a valid domain!

Essentially, the wizard adds the following two NuGet packages to the project-- `Microsoft.AspNetCore.Authentication.Cookies` and `Microsoft.AspNetCore.Authentication.OpenIdConnect` (Azure authentication is based on OpenID). It also adds the following entry to the configuration file `appsettings.json`:

```
"Authentication": {
  "AzureAd": {
    "AADInstance": "https://login.microsoftonline.com/",
    "CallbackPath": "/signin-oidc",
    "ClientId": "<client id>",
    "Domain": "mydomain.com",
    "TenantId": "<tenant id>"
  }
}
```

The authentication uses cookies, so a similar entry is added to the `ConfigureServices` method:

```
services.AddAuthentication(options =>
    options.SignInScheme =
CookieAuthenticationDefaults.AuthenticationScheme
);
```

Finally, the OpenID middleware is added to the pipeline in `Configure`:

```
app.UseOpenIdConnectAuthentication(new OpenIdConnectOptions
    {
        ClientId = this.Configuration["Authentication:AzureAd:ClientId"],
        Authority = this.Configuration["Authentication:AzureAd:AADInstance"]
+ this.Configuration["Authentication:AzureAd:TenantId"],
        CallbackPath =
this.Configuration["Authentication:AzureAd:CallbackPath"]
    });
```

The relevant methods in the `AccountController` class are described next (from the original listing presented at the beginning of the chapter):

```
[HttpGet]
public async Task<IActionResult> Logout()
{
  var callbackUrl = this.Url.Action("SignedOut", "Account", values: null,
protocol: this.Request.Scheme);
    return this.SignOut(new AuthenticationProperties { RedirectUri =
callbackUrl },
      CookieAuthenticationDefaults.AuthenticationScheme,
      OpenIdConnectDefaults.AuthenticationScheme);
}

[HttpGet]
public IActionResult SignedOut()
{
  return this.View();
}

[HttpGet]
public IActionResult SignIn()
{
  return this.Challenge(new AuthenticationProperties { RedirectUri = "/" },
      OpenIdConnectDefaults.AuthenticationScheme);
}
```

Social logins

Another option for keeping and maintaining user credentials yourself is to use authentication information from third parties, such as social networking apps. This is an interesting option because you don't require users to go through the account creation process, you just trust the external authentication provider for that. This mechanism is based on providers and there are a number of ones made available by Microsoft; you must be aware that all of these rely on Identity, so you need to configure it first (`UseIdentity`). When you create your project, make sure you choose to use authentication and select individual accounts. This will ensure that the proper template is used and the required files are present in the project.

 For more information please consult `https://docs.microsoft.com/en-us/aspnet/core/security/authentication/social/`.

Facebook

The Facebook provider is available as the
`Microsoft.AspNetCore.Authentication.Facebook` NuGet package. You will need to create a developer account with Facebook first and then use the application ID and user secret when registering the provider in the `Configure` method:

```
app.UseFacebookAuthentication(new FacebookOptions()
    {
        AppId = Configuration["Authentication:Facebook:AppId"],
        AppSecret = Configuration["Authentication:Facebook:AppSecret"]
    });
```

 Facebook login details are available here: `https://docs.microsoft.com/en-us/aspnet/core/security/authentication/social/facebook-logins`.

Twitter

Twitter is another popular social networking site and the provider for it is available as `Microsoft.AspNetCore.Authentication.Twitter`. You will also need to register your application in the Twitter developer site. Its configuration goes like this:

```
app.UseTwitterAuthentication(new TwitterOptions()
    {
        ConsumerKey = Configuration["Authentication:Twitter:ConsumerKey"],
        ConsumerSecret =
Configuration["Authentication:Twitter:ConsumerSecret"]
    });
```

 Twitter login details are available here: `https://docs.microsoft.com/en-us/aspnet/core/security/authentication/social/twitter-logins`.

Google

The Google provider is contained in the NuGet package
`Microsoft.AspNetCore.Authentication.Google`. Again, you will need to create a developer account and register your app beforehand. The Google provider is configured like this:

```
app.UseGoogleAuthentication(new GoogleOptions()
    {
```

```
ClientId = Configuration["Authentication:Google:ClientId"],
ClientSecret = Configuration["Authentication:Google:ClientSecret"]
});
```

For more information about the Google provider, please consult: `https://docs.microsoft.com/en-us/aspnet/core/security/authentication/social/google-logins`.

Microsoft

Of course, Microsoft makes available a provider for its own authentication service; it is included in the `Microsoft.AspNetCore.Authentication.MicrosoftAccount` NuGet package, and the configuration goes like this:

```
app.UseMicrosoftAccountAuthentication(new MicrosoftAccountOptions()
    {
      ClientId = Configuration["Authentication:Microsoft:ClientId"],
      ClientSecret = Configuration["Authentication:Microsoft:ClientSecret"]
    });
```

Go to `https://docs.microsoft.com/en-us/aspnet/core/security/authentication/social/microsoft-logins` for more information.

Binding security

We know that ASP.NET Core automatically binds submitted values to model classes; what would happen if we hijacked a request and asked ASP.NET to bind a different user or role than the one we have? For example, consider if we have a method that updates the user profile using this model:

```
public class User
{
  public string Id { get; set; }
  public bool IsAdmin { get; set; }
  //rest of the properties go here
}
```

If this model is committed to the database, it is easy to see that if we pass a value of `IsAdmin=true`, then we would become administrators instantly! To prevent this situation, we should do either of the following:

- Move out sensitive properties from the `public` model, the one that is retrieved from the data sent by the user
- Apply `[BindNever]` attributes to these sensitive properties:

```
[BindNever]
public bool IsAdmin { get; set; }
```

In the latter case, we need to populate these properties ourselves, using the right logic.

> As a rule of thumb, never use as the MVC model the domain classes that you use in your O/RM; it is better to have a clear distinction between the two and map them yourself (even if with the help of some tool such as Automapper), taking care of sensitive properties.

Cookie security

The `CookieAuthenticationOptions` class has a few properties that can be used for extra security:

- `CookieHttpOnly` (`bool`): Whether the cookie should be HTTP-only or not (see https://www.owasp.org/index.php/HttpOnly); the default is `false`. If not set, then the `HttpOnly` flag is not sent.
- `CookieSecure` (`CookieSecurePolicy`): Whether the cookie should be sent only over HTTPS (`Always`), always (`None`), or according to the request (`SameAsRequest`), which is the default; if not set, the `Secure` flag is not sent.
- `CookiePath` (`string`): An optional path to which the cookie applies; if not set, it defaults to the current application path.
- `CookieDomain` (`string`): An optional domain for the cookie; if not set, the site's domain will be used.
- `DataProtectionProvider` (`IDataProtectionProvider`): An optional data protection provider, used to encrypt and decrypt the cookie value; by default, it is `null`.

- `CookieManager` (`ICookieManager`): An optional storage for cookies; it might be useful, for example, to share cookies between applications (see `https://docs.microsoft.com/en-us/aspnet/core/security/data-protection/compatibility/cookie-sharing`); the default is `null`.

The same properties are available in Identity.

 The HTTP Cookie specification is available at `https://tools.ietf.org/html/rfc6265`.

Authorization

So, let's say you want to mark either a whole controller or specific actions as requiring authentication. The easiest way is to add an `[Authorize]` attribute to it. Just like that, if you try to access the protected controller or resource, you will be returned a `401 Authorization Required` error.

Roles

If we want to go a little further in the authorization process, we can request that a protected resource--controller or action--only be accessible when the authenticated user is in a given role. Roles are just claims and are supported by any authentication mechanism:

```
[Authorize(Roles = "Admin")]
public IActionResult Admin() { ... }
```

It is possible to specify multiple roles, separated by commas; in this case, access will be granted if the current user is in at least one of these roles:

```
[Authorize(Roles = "Admin,Supervisor")]
```

If you ever want to know by code whether the current user belongs to a specific role you can use the `ClaimsPrincipal` instance's `IsInRole` method:

```
var isAdmin = this.HttpContext.User.IsInRole("Admin");
```

Policies

Policies are a far more flexible way to grant authorization; here we can use whatever rule we want, not just the rule belonging to a certain role or being authenticated.

To use policies, we need to decorate the resources to protect (controllers, actions) with the [Authorize] attribute and the Policy property:

```
[Authorize(Policy = "EmployeeOnly")]
```

Policies are configured through the AddAuthorization method, in an AuthorizationOptions class.

```
services.AddAuthorization(options =>
    {
        options.AddPolicy("EmployeeOnly", policy =>
policy.RequireClaim("EmployeeNumber"));
    });
```

This code is requiring that the current user has a specific claim, but we can think of other examples, such as, only allowing local requests:

```
options.AddPolicy("LocalOnly", builder =>
{
  builder.RequireAssertion(ctx =>
  {
    if (ctx.Resource is AuthorizationFilterContext mvcContext)
    {
      var remoteIp = mvcContext.HttpContext.Connection.RemoteIpAddress;
      var localIp = mvcContext.HttpContext.Connection.LocalIpAddress;
      var allow = remoteIp.Equals(localIp) ||
IPAddress.IsLoopback(remoteIp);
      return allow;
    }

    return false;
  });
});
```

You can also use policies for specific claims or roles, for being authenticated, or even for having a specific username:

```
options.AddPolicy("Sample", builder =>
    {
        //a specific username
        builder.RequireUserName("admin");
        //being authenticated
```

```
    builder.RequireAuthenticatedUser();
    //a claim with one of three options
    builder.RequireClaim("Option", "A", "B", "C");
    //of of two roles
    builder.RequireRole("Admin", "Supervisor");
});
```

The sky is the limit, you can use whatever logic you want to grant or deny access. The `Resource` property is prototyped as `object`, which means it can take any value, if called as part of the MVC authorization filter, it will always be an instance of `AuthorizationFilterContext`.

Authorization handlers

Authorization handlers are a way to encapsulate business validations in classes. There is an Authorization API composed of the following:

- `IAuthorizationService`: The entry point for all the authorization checks
- `IAuthorizationHandler`: An implementation of an authorization rule
- `IAuthorizationRequirement`: The contract for a single authorization requirement, to be passed to an authorization handler
- `AuthorizationHandler<TRequirement>`: An abstract base implementation of `IAuthorizationHandler` that is bound to a specific `IAuthorizationRequirement`

We implement an `IAuthorizationHandler` (perhaps subclassing from `AuthorizationHandler<TRequirement>`) and we define our rules in there:

```
public class DayOfWeekAuthorizationHandler :
AuthorizationHandler<DayOfWeekRequirement>
{
  protected override Task HandleRequirementAsync(
    AuthorizationHandlerContext context, DayOfWeekRequirement requirement)
  {
    if ((DayOfWeek) context.Resource == requirement.DayOfWeek)
    {
      context.Succeeed(requirement);
    }
    else
    {
      context.Fail();
    }
```

```
      return Task.CompletedTask;
  }
}

public class DayOfWeekRequirement : IAuthorizationRequirement
{
  public DayOfWeekRequirement(DayOfWeek dow)
  {
    this.DayOfWeek = dow;
  }

  public DayOfWeek DayOfWeek { get; }
}
```

An authorization pipeline can take a number of requirements, and for the authorization to succeed, all of the requirements must too. This is a very simple example by which we have a requirement for a specific day of the week, and the authorization handler either succeeds or fails depending on whether the current day of the week matches the given requirement.

The IAuthorizationService class that is registered with the dependency injection framework, DefaultAuthorizationService, is smart enough to let us have an IAuthorizationHandler that is an IAuthorizationRequirement at the same time, or, to put this another way, looks something like this:

```
public class DayOfWeekRequirementHandler : IAuthorizationRequirement,
IAuthorizationHandler
{
  public DayOfWeekRequirementHandler(DayOfWeek dow)
  {
    this.DayOfWeek = dow;
  }

  public DayOfWeek DayOfWeek { get; }

  public Task HandleAsync(AuthorizationHandlerContext context)
  {
    if ((DayOfWeek) context.Resource == requirement.DayOfWeek)
    {
      context.Succeeed(this);
    }
    else
    {
      context.Fail();
    }

    return Task.CompletedTask;
  }
}
```

```
      }
```

We would fire a check for permission using this code:

```
IAuthorizationService authSvc = ...;

if (authSvc.AuthorizeAsync(
  user: this.User,
  resource: DateTime.Today.DayOfWeek,
  requirement: new DayOfWeekRequirementHandler(DayOfWeek.Monday)
) { ... }
```

An authorization handler can also be bound to a policy name:

```
services.AddAuthorization(options =>
    {
      options.AddPolicy("DayOfWeek", builder =>
      {
        builder.AddRequirements(new
DayOfWeekRequirementHandler(DayOfWeek.Friday));
      });
    });
```

In this case, the previous call would be the following instead:

```
if (await authSvc.AuthorizeAsync(
    user: this.User,
    resource: DateTime.Today.DayOfWeek,
    policyName: "DayOfWeek"
) { ... }
```

The parameters to these two overloads are the following:

- user (ClaimsPrincipal): The current logged-in user
- policyName (string): A registered policy name
- resource (object): Any object that will be passed to the authorization pipeline
- requirement (IAuthorizationRequirement): One or more requirements that will be passed along to the authorization handler

Final word: If we ever want to override the default authorization handler, we can do so very easily in ConfigureServices:

```
services.AddSingleton<IAuthorizationHandler, CustomAuthorizationHandler>();
```

Resource-based authorization

We can leverage the authorization handlers to have resource-based authorization. Basically, we ask the authorization service to check for permission to access a given resource and policy. We call one of the `AuthorizeAsync` methods of the `IAuthorizationService` instance:

```
IAuthorizationService authSvc = ...;

if (await authSvc.AuthorizeAsync(this.User, resource, "Policy")) { ... }
```

The `IAuthorizationService` is normally obtained from the dependency injection framework. The `AuthorizeAsync` method takes the following parameters:

- user (`ClaimsPrincipal`): The current user
- resource (`object`): A resource to check for permission against the `policyName`
- policyName (`string`): The name of the policy for which to check permission for the `resource`

This method can be called in both the controller and a view to check for fine-grained permissions. What it will do is execute the `AuthorizationPolicy` registered under the policy name passing it the resource, which in its turn will call all the registered authorization handlers.

A typical example of a fine-grained authorization check would be to ask for edit permission on a given record, for example, in a view:

```
@inject IAuthorizationService authSvc
@model Order

@{
    var order = Model;
  }

@if (await authSvc.AuthorizeAsync(User, order, "Order.Edit"))
{
  @Html.EditorForModel()
}
else
{
  @Html.DisplayForModel()
}
```

Here, we are checking a policy named `Order.Edit` which is expecting a resource of type `Order`. All of its requirements are run and, if they all succeed, then we are entitled to edit the order; otherwise, we just display it.

Anonymous access

If, for any reason, when using access control, you want to allow access to specific controllers or a specific action in a controller, you can apply to it the `[AllowAnonymous]` attribute. It will bypass any security handlers and execute the action. Of course, in the action or view, you can still perform explicit security checks.

Anti-forgery

Cross-Site Request Forgery (**CSRF** or **XSRF**) attacks are one of the most common hacks by which a user is tricked into performing some action in one of the sites to which they are logged in. For example, imagine you have just visited your e-banking site and then you go to a malicious site, without having logged out; some JavaScript on the malicious site could have the browser post to the e-banking site an instruction to transfer some amount of money to another account. Realizing that this is a serious problem, Microsoft has long supported an anti-forgery package, `Microsoft.AspNetCore.Antiforgery`, which implements a mixture of the *Double Submit Cookie* and *Encrypted Token* Pattern described in the OWASP cheat sheet:

`(https://www.owasp.org/index.php/Cross-Site_Request_Forgery_(CSRF)_Prevention_Cheat_Sheet#CSRF_Specific_Defense)`.

OWASP is the **Open Web Application Security Project** and it aims to provide a not-for-profit repository of best practices related to security on the web. It lists common security problems and explains how to address them.

The anti-forgery framework does the following:

- Generates a hidden field with an anti-forgery token on every form (could also be a header)
- Sends a cookie with the same token
- Upon post back, checks that it received an anti-forgery token as part of the payload, and that it is identical to the anti-forgery cookie

The `BeginForm` method, by default, outputs an anti-forgery token when it produces a `<form>` tag, unless called with the `antiforgery` parameter set to `false`.

You will need to register the required services by calling `AddAntiforgery`:

```
services.AddAntiforgery(options =>
    {
        options.FormFieldName = "__RequestVerificationToken";
    });
```

The possible options are as follows:

- `CookieName` (`string`): The name of the cookie to replace the default one; this is automatically generated with a prefix of `.AspNetCore.Antiforgery`.
- `CookiePath` (`PathString?`): An optional path to restrict the applicability of the cookie; the default is `null`, meaning, no path setting will be sent with the cookie
- `CookieDomain` (`string`): An optional domain to restrict (or augment) the applicability of the cookie; the default is `null`, so no domain setting will be set
- `FormFieldName` (`string`): The name of the hidden form field where the anti-forgery token is to be stored; the default is `__RequestVerificationToken`, and this is required
- `HeaderName` (`string`): The header name that will store the token; the default is `RequestVerificationToken`
- `RequireSsl` (`bool`): True if the anti-forgery cookie is to be sent only using HTTPS; the default is `false`
- `SuppressXFrameOptionsHeader` (`bool`): Whether or not the `X-Frame-Options` header should be sent; the default is `false`, which means that a value of `SAMEORIGIN` will be sent

The anti-forgery service is registered under the `IAntiforgery` interface.

There are number of attributes that can be used to control the default behavior:

- `[ValidateAntiforgeryToken]`: Adds anti-forgery validation to a specific controller or action
- `[IgnoreAntiforgeryToken]`: Disables anti-forgery validation on a specific controller or action, if it has been globally enabled
- `[AutoValidateAntiforgeryToken]`: Adds anti-forgery validation to any unsafe requests (`POST`, `PUT`, `DELETE`, `PATCH`)

All of these can be added as global filters besides as attributes:

```
services.AddMvc(options =>
    {
       options.Filters.Add(new AutoValidateAntiforgeryTokenAttribute());
    });
```

The difference between `[ValidateAntiforgeryToken]` and `[AutoValidateAntiforgeryToken]` is that the latter is designed to be used as a global filter; there is no need to apply it everywhere explicitly.

Check out `https://docs.microsoft.com/en-us/aspnet/core/security/anti-request-forgery` for a more in-depth explanation of the anti-forgery options available.

What if you want to use it with AJAX, to also protect these kinds of requests? Well, first you need to get a token from the server and the name of the header to use, so that you can add it to each AJAX request. You can do it in an action method:

```
[HttpGet("GetXsrfToken")]
public IActionResult GetXsrfToken()
{
   IAntiForgery antiforgery = ...; //get it from DI
   var token = antiforgery.GetAndStoreTokens(this.HttpContext);   //will issue a cookie

   return this.Json(new { token = token.RequestToken, header = token.HeaderName });
}
```

And in the AJAX call, just add this headers, for example, using jQuery:

```
var header = {};
header[xsrf.header] = xsrf.token;
$.ajax({
  type: 'POST',
  url: url,
  headers: header })
  .done(function(data) { ... });
```

Here, `xsrf` is the response to the `GetXsrfToken` action method.

HTML encoding

The views engine in ASP.NET Core uses HTML encoders to render HTML, in an effort to prevent script injection attacks. The `RazorPage` class, the base for all Razor views, features an `HtmlEncoder` property of type `HtmlEncoder`. By default, it is obtained from dependency injection as a `DefaultHtmlEncoder`, but you can set it to a different instance, probably not needed. We ask for content to be encoded explicitly by using the Razor syntax `@("...")`:

```
@("<div>encoded string</div>")
```

This will render an HTML-encoded string of the following:

```
&lt;div&gt;encoded string&lt;/div&gt;
```

You can also explicitly do it using the `Encode` method of the `IHtmHelper` object:

```
@Html.Encode("<div>encoded string</div>")
```

Lastly, if you have a helper method that returns a value of `IHtmlContent`, it will automatically be rendered using the registered `HtmlEncoder`.

 If you want to learn more about script injection, please consult `https://www.owasp.org/index.php/Code_Injection`.

HTTPS

The usage of HTTPS is becoming more and more common these days; not only is the performance penalty that existed in the early days now gone, but it is also significantly cheaper to get a certificate; in some cases, it may even be free, for example, **Let's Encrypt** (`https://letsencrypt.org`) offers such certificates. Plus, search engines such as Google boost results for sites served through HTTPS. Of course, ASP.NET Core fully supports HTTPS.

Hosting

The way to go depends on whether we are connecting to the ASP.NET Core host (such as Kestrel) directly or through a reverse proxy such as IIS Express. IIS Express is the light version of IIS that you can run locally for development purposes. It offers all the features of full-blown IIS, but not quite the same performance and scalability.

IIS Express

If we are to use IIS Express, we just need to configure its settings to enable SSL:

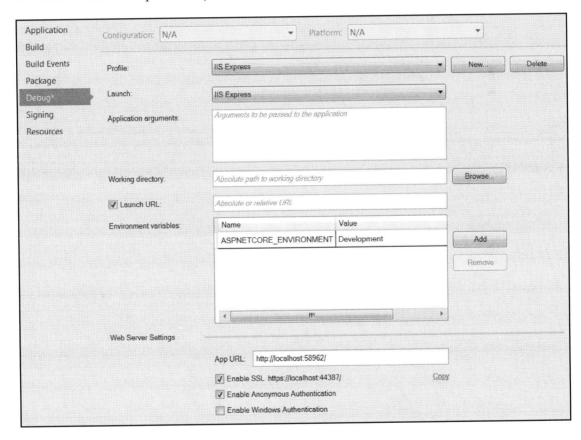

Kestrel

If, on the other hand we are going with Kestrel, things are a bit different. First, we will need the `Microsoft.AspNetCore.Server.Kestrel.Https` NuGet package and a certificate file. In the bootstrap code, it is used implicitly:

ASP.NET Core 1.x

```
var host = new WebHostBuilder()
    .UseConfiguration(config)
    .UseKestrel(options =>
        {
            options.UseHttps("certificate.pfx", "password");
        })
    .UseContentRoot(Directory.GetCurrentDirectory())
    .UseIISIntegration()
    .UseUrls("https://*:443")
    .UseStartup<Startup>()
    .Build();
```

ASP.NET Core 2.x

Seasoned developers will recognize this as ASP.NET Core 1.x code; the code for ASP.NET Core 2 will look like this instead:

```
WebHost.CreateDefaultBuilder(args)
    .UseKestrel(options =>
        {
            options.Listen(IPAddress.Any, 443, listenOptions =>
                {
                    listenOptions.UseHttps("certificate.pfx", "password");
                });
        })
    .UseStartup<Startup>()
    .Build();
```

The two listings are essentially the same:

- A certificate is loaded from a file called `certificate.pfx` protected by a password of `password`
- Both listen on port `443` for any of the local IP addresses

WebLisTener

For WebListener, we will need the `Microsoft.AspNetCore.Server.WebListener`
package, and instead of `UseKestrel` we call `UseWebListener`:

```
.UseWebListener()
.UseUrls("https://+:443")
```

This is the same in both ASP.NET Core 1.x and 2.x.

> Using HTTPS with WebListener requires some extra steps; I recommend
> you have a look at `https://blogs.msdn.microsoft.com/timomta/2016/`
> `11/04/how-do-i-set-up-a-net-core-weblistener-with-ssl/`.

Restricting HTTP

This makes sure that we are running on HTTPS, but we may need something else. For
example, we may require that all calls are made through HTTPS, and all others are rejected.
For that we can use a global filter, `RequireHttpsAttribute`:

```
services.Configure<MvcOptions>(options =>
    {
        options.SslPort = 443;
        options.Filters.Add(new RequireHttpsAttribute());
    });
```

We also need to tell MVC which port we are using for HTTPS, just for cases where we use a
non-standard one (`443` is the standard).

Redirecting to HTTPS

ASP.NET Core includes a redirection middleware. It is similar in functionality to the
ASP.NET IIS Rewrite module (see `https://www.iis.net/learn/extensions/url-rewrite-`
`module`). Its description is beyond the scope of this chapter, but it is sufficient to explain how
we can force a redirect from HTTP to HTTPS:

```
var options = new RewriteOptions()
    .AddRedirectToHttps();
app.UseRewriter(options);
```

This simple code in `Configure` registers the redirection middleware and instructs it to redirect all traffic coming to HTTP to the HTTPS protocol. It's as simple as that.

CORS

Cross-Origin Resource Sharing (CORS) is essentially the ability to request a resource from one domain from a page being served by a different domain, think of a page at `http://mysite.com` requesting a JavaScript file from `http://javascriptdepository.com`. Modern browsers forbid this by default, but it is possible to enable it on a case-by-case basis.

 If you want to learn more about CORS, please consult `https://developer.mozilla.org/en/docs/Web/HTTP/Access_control_CORS`.

ASP.NET Core supports CORS servicing. You first need to register the required services (in `ConfigureServices`):

```
services.AddCors();
```

Or, a slightly more complex example involves defining a policy:

```
services.AddCors(options =>
    {
        options.AddPolicy("CorsPolicy", builder =>
            builder
                .AllowAnyOrigin()
                .AllowAnyMethod()
                .AllowAnyHeader()
                .AllowCredentials()
        );
    });
```

A policy can take specific URLs; there is no need to support any origin:

```
builder
    .WithOrigins("http://mysite.com", "http://myothersite.com")
```

A more complete example, with headers, methods, and origins would be:

```
var policy = new CorsPolicy();
policy.Headers.Add("*");
policy.Methods.Add("*");
policy.Origins.Add("*");
policy.SupportsCredentials = true;
```

```
services.AddCors(options =>
    {
      options.AddPolicy("CorsPolicy", policy);
    });
```

The `Headers`, `Methods` and `Origins` collections contain all values that should be allowed explicitly; adding * to them is the same as calling `AllowAnyHeader`, `AllowAnyMethod` and `AllowAnyOrigin`. Setting `SupportsCredentials` to `true` means that an `Access-Control-Allow-Credentials` header will be returned, meaning that the application allows sending login credentials from a different domain. Beware of this setting because it means that a user in a different domain can try to log in to your app, probably even as the result of malicious code. Use this judiciously.

And then, add the CORS middleware in `Configure`, which will result in globally allowing CORS requests:

```
app.UseCors(builder => builder.WithOrigins("http://mysite.com"));
```

Or, with a specific policy:

```
app.UseCors("CorsPolicy");
```

All of this requires the `Microsoft.AspNetCore.Cors` NuGet package, mind you. You can add as many URLs as you like, using the `WithOrigins` method, and it can be called sequentially with all the addresses that are to be granted access. You can restrict it to specific headers and methods too:

```
app.UseCors(builder =>
  builder
      .WithOrigins("http://mysite.com", "http://myothersite.com")
      .WithMethods("GET")
);
```

One thing to keep in mind is that `UseCors` must be called before `UseMvc`!

If, on the other hand, you want to enable CORS on a controller-by-controller or action-by-action basis, you can use the `[EnableCors]` attribute:

```
[EnableCors("CorsPolicy")]
public class HomeController : Controller { ... }
```

Here you need to specify a policy name, never individual URLs.

Or, if you need to specify different CORS policies per local path (area, controller), you can use this approach:

```
//in ConfigureServices
services.AddCors(options =>
    {
        options.AddPolicy("Foo", /* something */);
        options.AddPolicy("Bar", /* something */);
    });

//in Configure
app.Map("/foo", options =>
    {
        options.UseCors("Foo");
    });

app.Map("/bar", options =>
    {
        options.UseCors("Bar");
    });
```

Data protection

ASP.NET Core uses **data protection providers** to protect data that is exposed to third parties, such as cookies. The interface `IDataProtectionProvider` defines its contract and ASP.NET Core ships with a default instance registered in the dependency injection framework of `KeyRingBasedDataProtector`:

```
services.AddDataProtection();
```

The data protection provider is used by the cookies authentication and also the cookie temp data provider APIs. A data protection provider exposes a method, `CreateProtector`, that is used to retrieve a protector instance, which can then be used to protect a string:

```
var protector = provider.CreateProtector("MasteringAspNetCore");
var input = "Hello, World";
var output = protector.Protect(input);
//CfDJ8AAAAAAAAAAAAAAAAAAAA...uGoxWLjGKtm1SkNACQ
```

You can certainly use it for other purposes, but for the two I presented before, you just need to pass a provider instance to the `CookiesAuthenticationOptions` instance, in the `Configure` method (for ASP.NET Core 1.x):

```
app.UseCookieAuthentication(new CookieAuthenticationOptions
{
  AuthenticationScheme = CookieAuthenticationDefaults.AuthenticationScheme,
  DataProtectionProvider = provider
});
```

And in ASP.NET Core 2.x, in `ConfigureServices`:

```
services.AddCookieAuthentication(CookieAuthenticationDefaults.Authenticatio
nScheme, options =>
{
  options.DataProtectionProvider = instance;
});
```

The `CookieTempDataProvider` class already receives an instance of `IDataProtectionProvider` in its constructor, so when the dependency injection framework builds it, it passes in the registered instance.

 Data protection providers are a big topic, and one that is outside the scope of this book. For more information, please consult `https://docs.microsoft.com/en-us/aspnet/core/security/data-protection/`.

Static files

There is no way to protect static files on ASP.NET Core; it goes without saying; however, that doesn't mean that you can't do it. Essentially, you have the following two options:

- Keeping the files that you want to serve outside the `wwwroot` folder and using a controller action to retrieve them; this action should enforce any security mechanism you want
- Using a middleware component to check access to your files and optionally restrict access to them

Using an action to retrieve files

So, you want to use an action method to retrieve a file. Either decorate this action method with an [Authorize] attribute or check for fine-grained access inside of it (IAuthorizationService.AuthorizeAsync):

```
[Authorize]
[HttpGet]
public IActionResult DownloadFile(string filename)
{
  var path = Path.GetDirectoryName(filename);
  //uncomment this if fine-grained access is not required
  if (this._authSvc.AuthorizeAsync(this.User, path, "Download"))
  {
    var contentType = "application/octet-stream";

    new FileExtensionContentTypeProvider().TryGetContentType("filename",
out contentType);

    var realFilePath = Path.Combine("ProtectedPath", filename);

    return this.File(realFilePath, contentType);
  }

    return this.Challenge();
}
```

This will only allow GET requests by authenticated users and the download policy is checked for the path of the file to retrieve. Then the requested file is combined with a ProtectedPath in order to get the real filename.

Using middleware to enforce security

You know about the ASP.NET Core/OWIN pipeline. Each middleware component in it can affect the others, even by preventing their execution. This other option will intercept any file. Let's add a configuration class and an extension method:

```
public class ProtectedPathOptions
{
  public PathString Path { get; set; }
  public string PolicyName { get; set; }
}

public static IApplicationBuilder UseProtectedPaths(
  this IApplicationBuilder app,
```

```
    params ProtectedPathOptions [] options)
{
    app.UseMiddleware<ProtectedPathsMiddleware>(options);
    return app;
}
```

Next, the code for the actual middleware component; this needs to be added quite early in the pipeline (`Configure` method):

```csharp
public class ProtectedPathsMiddleware
{
    private readonly RequestDelegate _next;
    private readonly IEnumerable<ProtectedPathOptions> _options;
    private readonly IAuthorizationService _authSvc;

    public ProtectedPathsMiddleware(
        RequestDelegate next,
        IAuthorizationService authSvc,
        IEnumerable<ProtectedPathOptions> options)
    {
        this._next = next;
        this._options = options ?? Enumerable.Empty<ProtectedPathOptions>();
        this._authSvc = authSvc;
    }

    public async Task Invoke(HttpContext context)
    {
        foreach (var option in this._options)
        {
            if (context.Request.Path.StartsWithSegments(option.Path))
            {
                if (!await this._authSvc.AuthorizeAsync(
                    context.User,
                    context.Request.Path,
                    option.PolicyName))
                {
                    await context.Authentication.ChallengeAsync();
                    return;
                }
            }
        }
        await this._next.Invoke(context);
    }
}
```

This middleware goes through all registered path protection options and checks whether the policy they specify is satisfied by the request path. If not, they challenge the response, redirecting to the login page.

To activate this, you need to add this middleware to the pipeline, in the `Configure` method:

```
app.UseProtectedPaths(new ProtectedPathOptions { Path = "/A/Path",
PolicyName = "APolicy" });
```

If, by any chance, you need to lock down your app, meaning bring it offline, you can do so by adding an `app_offline.htm` file to the root of your app (not the `wwwroot` folder!). If this file exists, it will be served, and any other requests will be ignored. This is an easy way to temporarily disable access to your site, without actually changing anything.

Putting it all together

Do use authorization attributes to protect sensitive resources of your application. It's better to use policies than actual named claims or roles, because it's so much easier to change a policy configuration, and you can do pretty much everything.

Use identity for authentication rather than rolling out your own mechanism. If your requirements so allow it, use social logins, as this is probably widely accepted, since most people use social networking apps.

Be careful with binding sensitive data to your model; prevent it from happening automatically and use different models for MVC and the actual data storage.

Always HTML-encode data that comes from a database, to prevent the possibility that some malicious user has inserted JavaScript into it.

Beware of static files as they are not protected by default. Use one of the two solutions; probably, I'd go with actions for retrieving the files.

Finally, consider moving the entirety of your site to HTTPS, as it significantly reduces the chances of eavesdropping your data.

Summary

This was quite an extensive topic that covered many aspects of security. If you stick to these recommendations, your app will be somewhat safer, but this is not enough. Always follow the security recommendation rules for the APIs you use, and make sure you know what their implications are.

In the next chapter, we will be talking about reusable components.

8
Reusable Components

This chapter covers the reusable components of ASP.NET Core. By reusable, I mean to say that they can potentially be used across different projects, or in the same project in different places, with different parameters, yielding possibly distinct results. We will be covering view components and **tag helpers**, which are new in ASP.NET Core, tag helper components (new in ASP.NET Core 2), and partial views, our old friends.

In this chapter, we will cover the following topics:

- View components
- Tag helpers
- Tag helper components
- Partial views

View components

View components are new in ASP.NET Core. You can think of them as replacements for partial views (which are still around) and the `RenderAction` method for returning child actions (which are gone). No more being tied to controllers; they are reusable because they can be loaded from external assemblies (that is, not the assembly of the web app) and they are better suited than partial views to render complex HTML.

Discovering view components

View components are discovered in one of the following ways:

- Inheriting from the `ViewComponent` class
- Adding a `[ViewComponent]` attribute
- Adding the `ViewComponent` suffix to a class

Most likely, you will be inheriting from `ViewComponent`, as this class offers a couple of useful methods. View components can be loaded from external assemblies, if the web app has references to them or they are registered as application parts:

```
services.AddMvc()
    .ConfigureApplicationPartManager(options =>
        {
            options.ApplicationParts.Add(new AssemblyPart(
                typeof(MyViewComponent).GetTypeInfo().Assembly));
        })
```

For POCO view components, you won't get easy access to the ambient context of your request. If you have to choose, please opt for inheriting from `ViewComponent` because otherwise you will need to get into extra work for getting all the references (`HttpContext`, and more) you need. I describe this in the dependency injection topic later.

Using view components

View components are called from views, and there are two different syntaxes:

- **Code syntax** lets you pass parameters of complex types but the code must be syntactically valid:

    ```
    @await Component.InvokeAsync("MyViewComponent", new { Parameter = 4, OtherParameter = true })
    ```

The `InvokeAsync` method takes a view component name and an optional parameter containing the parameters to be passed to the view component's `InvokeAsync` method; this method can take any number of parameters, and return an instance of `IViewComponentResult`.

- **Markup**, using the tag helpers syntax (more on this in a moment); notice the `vc` namespace:

    ```
    <vc:my-view-component parameter="4" otherParameter="true"/>
    ```

Pascal-cased class and method parameters for tag helpers are translated into lower-kebab case, which you can read about here: http:// stackoverflow.com/questions/11273282/whats-the-name-for-dash-separated-case/12273101#12273101.

You would choose the code syntax if you have complex parameters that cannot be represented easily in attributes. The namespace, by the way, is configurable.

Yet another option is to return a view component from a controller action, in the form of a `ViewComponentResult`:

```
public IActionResult MyAction()
{
  return this.ViewComponent("MyViewComponent");
}
```

This is very similar to returning a partial view, only in view components all of the contents need to be generated by code, that is, if you want to return custom HTML, you will likely need to build by concatenating strings.

View component results

View components returns an instance of `IViewComponentResult`, of which there are three implementations in ASP.NET Core, each returned by a method of the `ViewComponent` class:

- `Content` (`ContentViewComponentResult`): Returns string content.
- `View` (`ViewViewComponentResult`): Returns a partial view.
- The third implementation is `HtmlViewComponentResult`, which is similar to `ContentViewComponentResult`, but returns encoded HTML instead. There is no method that creates an instance of this class but you can instantiate one yourself.

 The rules for discovering partial view files are identical to the ones described earlier in the chapter dedicated to views.

The `IViewComponentResult` interface only specifies a single method, in both asynchronous (`ExecuteAsync`) and synchronous versions (`Execute`). It takes as its sole parameter an instance of `ViewComponentContext`, which has the following properties:

- `Arguments` (`IDictionary<string, object>`): The named properties of the object passed to the `InvokeAsync` method
- `HtmlEncoder` (`HtmlEncoder`): The HTML output encoder
- `ViewComponentDescriptor` (`ViewComponentDescriptor`): Describes the current view component
- `ViewContext` (`ViewContext`): All of the view context, including the current view object, the HTTP context, route data, model, the form context, and the action descriptor
- `ViewData` (`ViewDataDictionary`): The view data from the controller
- `Writer` (`TextWriter`): Used for writing directly to the output stream

Since you have access to all of the context, you can do pretty much what you want, such as, accessing headers, cookies, and request parameters, but you wouldn't use view component results for redirection, only for rendering HTML.

Dependency injection

You can register view components as services by calling the `AddViewComponentsAsServices` extension method on top of the `AddMvc` method in `ConfigureServices`:

```
services.AddMvc()
    .AddViewComponentsAsServices();
```

View components support constructor injection so you can declare any registered types in the constructor:

```
public class MyViewComponent : ViewComponent
{
  private readonly ILoggerFactory loggerFactory;

  public MyViewComponent(ILoggerFactory loggerFactory)
  {
    this._loggerFactory = loggerFactory;
  }
}
```

A common need is to get hold of the current `HttpContext`; if you need it in a POCO controller, you need to inject an `IHttpContextAccessor` instance:

```
public class MyViewComponent
{
  public MyViewComponent(IHttpContextAccessor httpAccessor)
  {
    this.HttpContext = httpAccessor.HttpContext;
  }

  public HttpContext HttpContext { get; }
}
```

Tag helpers

Tag helpers, again, are new in ASP.NET Core. A tag helper is a mechanism to add server-side processing to a regular HTML/XML tag; you can think of it as similar to ASP.NET Web Forms' server-side controls, although there are several differences. Tag helpers are registered on Razor views and when any tag on the view matches a tag helper, it is fired. They are an alternative, arguably a simpler one, to HTML helpers as they result in much cleaner markup, without code blocks.

Tag helpers' functionality is specified through the `ITagHelper` interface, of which the `TagHelper` abstract base class offers a base implementation. Its life cycle includes two methods:

- `Init`: Called when the tag helper is being initialized, prior to any possible child
- `ProcessAsync`: The actual processing of a tag helper

A tag helper, on the view side, is nothing more than a regular tag, and as such it can contain other tags, which themselves may also be tag helpers. Let's see an example:

```
<time></time>
```

As you can see, nothing more than a plain XML tag--not HTML because there is no such tag on any version of HTML.

In order to add custom server-side behavior, we define a tag helper class:

```
public class TimeTagHelper : TagHelper
{
  public override Task ProcessAsync(TagHelperContext context,
TagHelperOutput output)
  {
```

```
        var time = DateTime.Now.ToString();

        output.Content.Append(time);

        return base.ProcessAsync(context, output);
    }
}
```

Tag helpers are recursive, meaning tag helpers declared inside other tag helpers are all processed.

We'll see in a moment what we need to do to have ASP.NET Core recognize this; for now, let's have a look at the parameters to the ProcessAsync method.

TagHelperContext contains the context as seen from the tag helper; it includes these properties:

- AllAttributes (ReadOnlyTagHelperAttributeList): All of the attributes declared in the view for this tag helper
- Items (IDictionary<string, object>): A free-form collection of items used to pass context to other tag helpers on the current request
- UniqueId (string): A unique identifier for the current tag helper

As for TagHelperOutput, it allows the return of content to the view, but also the return of any contents that have been declared inside the tag. It exposes the following properties:

- IsContentModified (bool): A read-only flag that says whether the contents have been modified or not
- Order (int): The order by which the tag helper is processed
- PostElement (TagHelperContent): The following tag element
- PostContent (TagHelperContent): The contents following the current tag
- Content (TagHelperContent): The current tag's contents
- PreContent (TagHelperContent): The contents prior to the current tag
- PreElement (TagHelperContent): The previous tag element
- TagMode (TagMode): The tag mode (SelfClosing, StartTagAndEndTag and StartTagOnly), which is used to define how the tag should be validated in the markup (allowing inner content = SelfClosing, only the tag with no self content = StartTagOnly)
- TagName (string): The name of the tag in the view
- Attributes (TagHelperAttributeList): The original list of attributes of the tag; this can be modified

For example, imagine that you had this tag instead:

```
<time format="yyyy-MM-dd">Current date is: {0}</time>
```

Here, you need to access both an attribute (`format`) but also the content of the `<time>` tag. Let's see how we can achieve this:

```csharp
public class TimeTagHelper : TagHelper
{
  public string Format { get; set; }

  public override void Process(TagHelperContext context, TagHelperOutput output)
  {
    var content =
output.GetChildContentAsync().GetAwaiter().GetResult().GetContent();
    var time = DateTime.Now.ToString(this.Format);

    output.TagName = "span";
    output.Content.Append(string.Format(content, time));

    base.Process(context, output);
  }
}
```

We can see that we are doing a couple of things:

- Getting the value of the `Format` attribute
- Getting all the tag's content
- Setting the target tag name to `span`
- Using the content and the format to output a string with the formatted timestamp

This is essentially the way to go for getting contents and attributes. You can also add attributes to the output, by adding values to `output.Attributes`, change the output tag name (`output.TagName`), or prevent any content being generated at all (method `output.SuppressOutput`).

When outputting contents, we can either return plain strings, which will be encoded as per the view's `HtmlEncoder` instance, or return already encoded contents, in which case, instead of `Append`, we would call `AppendHtml`:

```csharp
output.Content.Append("<p>hello, world!</p>");
```

Besides appending, we can also replace all of the contents; for that, we call \t/SetHtmlContent, or even clear everything (Clear or SuppressOutput).

An [OutputElementHint] attribute can be used to provide a hint as to what tag will be output--this is useful so that Visual Studio knows to give hints about attributes of some other element, such as IMG:

```
[OutputElementHint("img")]
```

This way, when you add your custom tag in markup, Visual Studio will suggest all of the IMG element's attributes, such as, SRC, and more.

We can use the context.Items collection to pass data from one tag helper to the other-- remember that the Order property defines which will be processed first.

Understanding the properties of a tag helper

Any public properties in the tag helper class can be set through the view. By default, the same name in either lowercase or the same case will be used, but we can give a property a different name to be used in the view by applying a [HtmlAttributeName] attribute:

```
[HtmlAttributeName("time-format")]
public string Format { get; set; }
```

In this case, the attribute must now be declared as time-format.

If, on the other hand, we do not want to allow setting a property's value through the view's markup, we can apply the [HtmlAttributeNotBound] attribute to it.

Properties of basic types can be specified in the markup, plus a couple of others that can be converted from strings (Guid, TimeSpan, DateTime) and any enumerations as well.

We can use Razor expressions (code) to pass code-generated values to tag attributes:

```
<time format="GetTimeFormat()">Time is {0}</format>
```

Finally, it is worth mentioning that we can get Visual Studio Intellisense for the view's model if we use a property of type ModelExpression:

```
public ModelExpression FormatFrom { get; set; }
```

This is what it would look like:

For actually retrieving the value for the property, we need to analyze the Name and Metadata properties of ModelExpression.

Restricting applicability

A tag helper can be restricted in a few ways:

- It can target a specific element, either a known HTML tag or a custom XML tag
- The target tag is contained inside of another tag
- The target tag has certain attributes, with possibly a specific format
- The tag has a specific structure

Many restrictions can be specified, in terms of several [HtmlTargetElement] attributes:

```
//matches any a elements
[HtmlTargetElement("a")]
//matches any a elements contained inside a div tag
[HtmlTargetElement("a", ParentTag = "div")]
//matches any a elements that target a JavaScript file ending in .js
[HtmlTargetElement("a", Attributes = "[href$='.js']")]
//matches any a elements that target a link starting with ~
[HtmlTargetElement("a", Attributes = "[href^='~']")]
//matches any a elements with a value for the name attribute
[HtmlTargetElement("a", Attributes = "name")]
//matches any a elements with a specific id
[HtmlTargetElement("a", Attributes = "id='link'")]
//matches any a elements that do not have any inner contents (e.g., <a/>)
[HtmlTargetElement("a", TagStructure = TagStructure.WithoutEndTag)]
```

So, we have the following properties:

- `ParentTag` (`string`): The name of a parent tag
- `Attributes` (`string`): A comma-separated list of attributes and optional values
- `TagStructure` (`TagStructure`): The format of the tag, the default being `Unspecified`

`TagStructure` specifies whether the tag is self-closing (`WithoutEndTag`) or may have contents (`NormalOrSelfClosing`).

If a tag helper is found that does not match its applicability rules, an exception is thrown at runtime. Multiple rules can be specified at the same time and different tag helpers can match the same rules.

If you target `*`, it will apply to any element.

Discovering tag helpers

A tag helper needs to implement the `ITagHelper` interface. Tag helpers need to be explicitly added, and a good place to do so is the `_ViewImports.cshtml` file. Anything placed here will apply to all views.

The `addTagHelper` directive adds a specific assembly and tag helpers, where `*` can mean all of the included:

```
@addTagHelper *, Microsoft.AspNetCore.Mvc.TagHelpers
```

If we want to prevent a specific tag helper from being used, we apply one or more `removeTagHelper` directives:

```
@removeTagHelper Microsoft.AspNetCore.Mvc.TagHelpers.AnchorTagHelper,
Microsoft.AspNetCore.Mvc.TagHelpers
```

If we want to make the usage of tag helpers explicit, we can force them to have a prefix, by means of a `tagHelperPrefix` directive:

```
@tagHelperPrefix asp:
```

Finally, we also have the option to disable any tag helpers that may exist that target a certain tag. We just prefix it with the `!` character:

```
<!a href="...">link</a>
```

Dependency injection

Tag helpers are instantiated by the dependency injection mechanism, which means that they can take registered services in the constructor.

Neither the `Init` or the `Process` or `ProcessAsync` methods offer access to the execution context, but, similarly to POCO controllers and view components, we can have the `ViewContext` injected:

```
[ViewContext]
public ViewContext ViewContext { get; set; }
```

From here we have access to the `HttpContext`, `ActionDescriptor`, route and view data, and so on.

Included tag helpers

The following tag helpers are included in the `Microsoft.AspNetCore.Mvc.TagHelpers` assembly:

- `AnchorTagHelper` (`<a>`)
- `CacheTagHelper` (`<cache>`)
- `DistributedCacheTagHelper` (`<distributed-cache>`)
- `EnvironmentTagHelper` (`<environment>`)
- `FormActionTagHelper` (`<form>`)
- `FormTagHelper` (`<form>`)
- `ImageTagHelper` (`<img>`)
- `InputTagHelper` (`<input>`)
- `LabelTagHelper` (`<label>`)
- `LinkTagHelper` (`<link>`)
- `OptionTagHelper` (`<option>`)
- `RenderAtEndOfFormTagHelper` (`<form>`)
- `ScriptTagHelper` (`<script>`)
- `SelectTagHelper` (`<select>`)
- `TextAreaTagHelper` (`<textarea>`)
- `ValidationMessageTagHelper` (`<span>`)
- `ValidationSummaryTagHelper` (`<div>`)

Some of these basically translate URLs that start with ~ to the server-specific address, or add controller and action attributes, that are in turn translated to controller action URLs:

```
<a asp-controller="Account" asp-action="Logout">Logout</a>
<form asp-controller="Account" asp-action="Login">
</form>
```

For example, you can have your application deployed under / or under some virtual path such as /admin; if you do not know this upfront, you can't just hardcode your links to point to /, but, instead, you can use ~, and the ASP.NET Core framework will make sure it is set to the right path.

However, some others are quite powerful and offer very interesting features.

The <a> tag

This tag helper offers some properties for anchors that allow you to target specific actions of specific controllers, Razor pages, or named routes:

```
<a
  asp-action="ActionName"
  asp-controller="ControllerName"
  asp-page="RazorPageName"
  asp-route="RouteName"
  asp-area="AreaName">...</a>
```

If you add the asp-action but not the asp-controller attribute it will default to the current controller.

The <cache> tag

This tag helper caches the contents declared inside of it in the memory cache (any instance of IMemoryCache registered in the dependency injection framework). The only options we have are the duration to keep the cache, and whether it is relative, absolute, or sliding. Let's see the most basic example:

```
<cache expires-after="TimeSpan.FromMinutes(5)">
@DateTime.Now
</cache>
```

This will keep the string inside the `<cache>` tag in the memory cache for a certain amount of time. We also have the following properties:

- `enabled` (`bool`): Whether it is enabled (default) or not
- `expires-after` (`TimeSpan`): A value for relative expiration
- `expires-on` (`DateTime`): Absolute expiration
- `expires-sliding` (`TimeSpan`): Sliding expiration, meaning, it is identical to relative expiration, but it will restart every time the cache is hit
- `priority` (`CacheItemPriority`): A priority for the cache, the default being `Normal`
- `vary-by` (`string`): An arbitrary (and possibly dynamic) string value to vary the cache by
- `vary-by-cookie` (`string`): A comma-separated list of cookie names to vary the cache by
- `vary-by-header` (`string`): A comma-separated list of header names to vary the cache by
- `vary-by-query` (`string`): A comma-separated list of query string parameter names to vary the cache by
- `vary-by-route` (`string`): A comma-separated list of route data parameters to vary the cache by
- `vary-by-user` (`bool`): Whether to vary the cache per the logged-in user name (default is `false`)

Exactly one of `expires-after`, `expires-on`, or `expires-sliding` must be supplied, but the default is 20 minutes. For `vary-by`, it is common to set a model value, such as an order or product ID, for example:

```
<cache vary-by="@ProductId">
...
</cache>
```

The <distributed-cache> tag

This one is identical to the <cache> tag helper but it uses distributed cache instead (IDistributedCache). It adds another property to the ones supplied by <cache>:

- name (string): A unique name for the distributed cache entry; each entry should have it's own

The <environment> tag

This one is also very handy--the ability to add contents depending on the environment that is running (for example, Development, Staging, Production, and so on):

```
<environment names="Development,Staging">
    <script src="development/file.js"></script>
</environment>
<environment names="Production">
    <script src="production/file.js"></script>
</environment>
```

Starting in ASP.NET Core 2, besides names, we also have two new attributes: include and exclude. include is exactly the same as names, whereas exclude does what you think: it will show the contents for all environments except those listed here (comma-separated).

The <form> tag

The form tag helper can be used instead of IHtmlHelper.BeginForm(). Both offer the same features, including posting to specific controller actions and adding anti-forgery tokens as hidden fields (see the chapter on security). See this example:

```
<form asp-controller="Home" asp-antiforgery="false" asp-action="Process">
```

Anti-forgery is turned on by default.

The <script> tag

The script tag helper allows test, default, and fallback values to be specified for the source property. The test is a JavaScript expression; let's see an example:

```
<!-- if the current browser does not have the window.Promise property load
a polyfill -->
<script asp-fallback-test="window.Promise" src="file.js" asp-fallback-
src="polyfill.js"></script>
```

It can also be used to load all files in a folder at once (with some possible exceptions):

```
<script asp-src-include="~/app/**/*.js" asp-src-
exclude="~/app/services/**/*.js"></script>
```

Finally, it can also be used to bust caching, by adding a version number to local scripts; this version will reflect the file's timestamp:

```
<script src="~/file.js" asp-append-version="true"></script>
```

You might have noticed the leading ~ in the `src` attribute: it is automatically replaced by the root folder of your application; for example, if your app is deployed in /, it will be /, but if it is /virtualPath, then ~ is replaced by /virtualPath.

The <link> tag

The link tag helper can suffix a local URL with a version, so as to make it cache-friendly:

```
<link rel="stylesheet" href="~/css/site.min.css" asp-append-
version="true"/>
```

Similarly to the script tag helper, it can also include contents conditionally:

```
<link rel="stylesheet" href="file.css" asp-fallback-href="otherfile.css"
    asp-fallback-test-class="hidden" asp-fallback-test-
property="visibility"
    asp-fallback-test-value="hidden" />
```

The <select> tag

The select tag helper knows how to retrieve items from a model property of an enumerable type or also from a collection of `SelectListItem` objects:

```
@functions
{
  IEnumerable<SelectListItem> GetItems()
  {
    yield return new SelectListItem { Text = "Red", Value = "#FF0000" };
    yield return new SelectListItem { Text = "Green", Value = "#00FF00" };
    yield return new SelectListItem { Text = "Blue", Value = "#0000FF",
Selected = true };
  }
}
<select asp-items="GetItems()"/>
```

Validation message and summary

The `ValidationMessageTagHelper` and `ValidationSummaryTagHelper` tag helpers merely add the validation message for any model properties, in a <span> tag and for the whole model, in a <div>. For example, say you would like to get the current validation message for the `Email` model property, you would do the following:

```
<span asp-validation-for="Email"/>
```

And for the whole model:

```
<div asp-validation-summary/>
```

Tag helper components

Tag helper components were introduced in ASP.NET Core 2.0. They are a way to use DI for inserting markup in the output. Imagine, for example, inserting JavaScript or CSS files at a specific location in your views.

Tag helper components must implement `ITagHelperComponent` and are registered in the DI framework (`ConfigureServices` method):

```
services.AddSingleton<ITagHelperComponent, HelloWorldTagHelperComponent>();
```

The `ITagHelperComponent` interface only specifies a method, `ProcessAsync`. Each registered tag helper component will have its `ProcessAsync` method called for every tag found on the current view--including layouts--giving it a chance to inject custom tag helpers:

```
public class HelloWorldTagHelperComponent : TagHelperComponent
{
  public override Task ProcessAsync(TagHelperContext context,
TagHelperOutput output)
  {
    if (context.TagName.ToLowerInvariant() == "head")
    {
      output.Content.AppendHtml("<script>window.alert('Hello,
World!')</script>");
    }

    return Task.CompletedTask;
  }
}
```

This example inserts a custom JavaScript at the end of the current tag's content.

The `TagHelperComponent` class implements `ITagHelperComponent` and offers virtual methods that we can override as we please. Like the `ITagHelper` interface, we have the same two methods, `Init` and `ProcessAsync`; and they are used in the same way.

`ProcessAsync` takes two parameters, which are the same as the ones the `ITagHelper` interface's `ProcessAsync` method takes.

Tag helper components, being instantiated by the DI framework, fully support constructor injection.

Partial views

We already covered partial views in the previous chapter. Although they are a very interesting mechanism for reusing content, they have a catch--they cannot be reused across assemblies. But fortunately, there is a way around it: the idea is to mark the view's `.cshtml` file as an embedded resource:

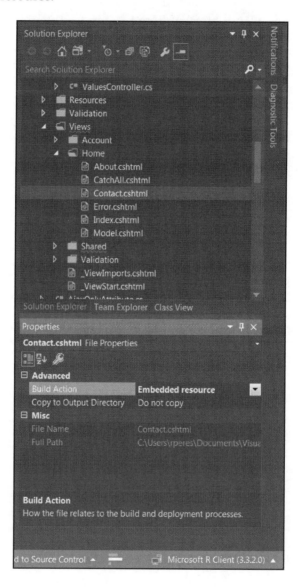

Then, we just need to use a file provider that knows how to retrieve file contents from assembly embedded resources. Do add the `Microsoft.Extensions.FileProviders.Embedded` NuGet package for this example.

When registering the MVC services in `ConfigureServices`, we need to register another **file provider**, `EmbeddedFileProvider`, passing it the assembly that contains the embedded resource:

```
services.AddMvc()
    .AddRazorOptions(options =>
    {
        var assembly = typeof(MyViewComponent).GetTypeInfo().Assembly;
        var embeddedFileProvider = new EmbeddedFileProvider(assembly,
"ReusableComponents");
        options.FileProviders.Add(embeddedFileProvider);
    });
```

In this case, the `MyViewComponent` class is hosted on the same assembly where the view is embedded, and its default namespace is `ReusableComponents`. When trying to load a file, ASP.NET Core will go through all the registered file providers until one returns a non-null result.

Partial views versus view components

These two mechanisms are similar, but you would choose partial views if you have a somewhat big chunk of HTML that you want to render, as in view components you would need to manipulate strings and return them by code.

Putting it all together

Always use the supplied base classes for view components, tag helpers and tag helper components, as they make your life easier.

Do prefer tag helpers to HTML helpers whenever possible. Write your own tag helpers as they are much easier to read than code. Tag helper components are very useful for inserting code automatically in specific locations.

The `<cache>`, `<distributed-cache>` and `<environment>` tag helpers are very interesting and will help you a lot.

Partial views are preferable to view components when you have a template that you wish to render, which is easier to code in HTML. View components are all about code, and it's harder to implement HTML by string concatenation.

Tag helper components are a very nice way to inject HTML elements anywhere, from a centralized location. Use this for common CSS and JavaScript.

Summary

In this chapter we looked at techniques for reusing components across projects. Code reuse is almost always a good idea and you can use view components with parameters to help achieve this. In the next chapter, we will be covering filters, a process to intercept and possibly modify requests and responses.

9
Filters

Filters in ASP.NET Core are an interception mechanism by which we can execute code before, instead, or after a request is processed. Think of it as a way to add custom steps to the pipeline without actually doing so, it remains unchanged but instead we have a finer-grained control over what we are intercepting. They are useful for implementing cross-cutting operations, such as access control, caching, or logging. Here, we will be discussing the following:

- The different filter types
- How to apply them
- Specialized filters, such as action and Razor page filters

Types of filters

Filters are an interception mechanism. In ASP.NET Core 2, we have the following filters:

- **Authorization** (IAuthorizationFilter, IAsyncAuthorizationFilter): Controls whether the user performing the current request has permission to access the specified resource; if not, then the rest of the pipeline is short-circuited and an error message is returned
- **Resource** (IResourceFilter, IAsyncResourceFilter): These execute after a request is authorized but before action selection and model binding; these are new in ASP.NET Core
- **Action** (IActionFilter, IAsyncActionFilter): Executed before and after the action method is called
- **Result** (IResultFilter, IAsyncResultFilter): Occur before and after the actual execution of an action result (the IActionResult.ExecuteResultAsync method)

- **Exception** (IExceptionFilter, IAsyncExceptionFilter): Called when an exception is thrown in the course of the action being processed
- **Page** (IPageFilter, IAsyncPageFilter): Occur before and after a Razor Page handler method is called; new in ASP.NET Core 2

Filters of these kinds have pre-and post-methods, called, respectively, before and after the target event--Authorization, resource, action, result, and page. The pre-version always ends in **executing** and the post version in **executed**. For example, for action filters, the methods are called OnActionExecuting and OnActionExecuted. Authorization and exception filters, of course, only offer a single method, OnAuthorization and OnException, respectively, but you can think of them as post-event methods.

The only base class for all filters is IFilterMetadata, which offers no methods or properties, and is just meant as a marker interface. Because of this, the ASP.NET Core framework must check the concrete type of a filter to try to identity the known interfaces that it implements.

Synchronous versus asynchronous

Each filter type offers both a synchronous and an asynchronous version, the latter having an Async prefix. The difference between the two is that in the async version, only the pre method is defined, and it is called asynchronously; for action filters, the synchronous version offers OnActionExecuting/OnActionExecuted and the asynchronous version a single OnActionExecutionAsync. Only exception filters do not offer an asynchronous version.

Filter scope

Filters can be applied at different levels:

- **Global**: Global filters apply to all controllers and actions, and thus also capture any exceptions thrown; global filters are added through the AddMvc method, to the Filters collection of the MvcOptions class:

```
services.AddMvc(options =>
    {
      options.Filters.Add(new AuthorizeAttibute());
    });
```

- **Controller**: Controller-level filters are generally added through resources applied to the controller class, and apply to any actions called upon them:

```
[Authorize]
public class HomeController : Controller
{
}
```

- **Action**: These filters only apply to the action method where they are declared:

```
public class HomeController
{
  [Authorize]
  public IActionResult Index() { ... }
}
```

The Filters collection of MvcOptions can take either a filter type or an instance of a filter. Use the filter type if you want the filter to be built using the dependency injection framework.

Execution order

Filters are called in the following order:

1. Authorization
2. Resource
3. Action
4. Page
5. Result

Exception and page filters, of course, are special, so are only called, respectively, in the occurrence of an exception or when calling a Razor Page.

Depending on how the filters are applied, we can influence this order; for example, for global filters, filters of the same type are ordered according to the index in the MvcOptions.Filters collection:

```
options.Filters.Insert(0, new AuthorizeAttribute());  //first one
```

For attribute filters, the `IOrderedFilter` interface provides an `Order` property which can be used to order attributes of the same scope (global, controller, or action):

```
[Cache(Order = 1)]
[Authorize(Order = 0)]
[Log(Order = 2)]
public IActionResult Index() { ... }
```

Applying filters through attributes

Any of the filter interfaces can be implemented by a regular attribute (`Attribute` class) and it will then act as a filter; there are a couple of abstract base attribute classes, `ActionFilterAttribute` (action and result filters), `ResultFilterAttribute` (result filters), and `ExceptionFilterAttribute` (exception filters), that can be subclassed to implement this behavior. These classes implement both the synchronous and asynchronous versions and also support ordering by implementing `IOrderedFilter`. So, if you want to have a filter attribute that handles actions and results, you can inherit from `ActionFilterAttribute` and implement just one or more of its virtual methods:

- `OnActionExecuting`
- `OnActionExecuted`
- `OnActionExecutionAsync`
- `OnResultExecuting`
- `OnResultExecuted`
- `OnResultExecutionAsync`

For example, if you wish to override some behavior on the abstract `ActionFilterAttribute` to do something before an action is invoked:

```
public class LogActionAttribute : ActionFilterAttribute
{
  public LogActionAttribute(ILoggerFactory loggerFactory)
  {
  }

  public override void OnActionExecuting(ActionExecutingContext context)
  {
    var logger = loggerFactory.CreateLogger(context.Controller.GetType());
    logger.Trace($"Before {context.ActionDescriptor.DisplayName}");
  }
}
```

Factories and providers

A **filter factory** is just an instance of a class that creates filters; the only requisite is that it implements IFilterFactory, which, because it inherits from IFilterMetadata, can also be used as a global filter or in a custom attribute. Why would you do that? Well, because when the filter factory runs you will probably know something more from the current execution context:

```
public class CustomFilterFactory : IFilterFactory
{
    public bool IsReusable => true;

    public IFilterMetadata CreateInstance(IServiceProvider serviceProvider)
    {
      var httpContextAccessor =
serviceProvider.GetService<IHttpContextAccessor>();
      var httpContext = httpContextAccessor.HttpContext;
      //do something with the context
      return new CustomFilter();
    }
}
```

For registering this custom filter factory globally, we use:

```
services.AddMvc(options =>
    {
      options.Filters.Insert(0, new CustomFilterFactory());
    });
```

Implementing IFilterFactory in an attribute is equally trivial, so I won't show it here.

The contract for a filter factory is simple:

- IsReusable (bool): Tells the framework if it is safe to reuse the filter factory across requests
- CreateInstance: This method returns a filter

The CreateInstance method takes an IServiceProvider instance as its sole parameter and returns a IFilterMetadata object, meaning you can return any kind of filter you want (or even another filter factory).

A **filter provider** (IFilterProvider) is the actual implementation that is registered in the dependency injection framework as part of the MVC configuration and is the one that fires all the different filter behaviors. The default implementation is DefaultFilterProvider.

The IFilterProvider interface has a single property:

- Order (int): The order by which the provider will be executed

And it offers two methods:

- OnProvidersExecuting: Called to inject filters in its context parameter
- OnProvidersExecuted: Called after all filters have been executed

Dependency injection

The ways we've seen so far to add filters--globally through the Filters collection or by means of attributes--are not dependency injection-friendly, in the first case, you add an already instantiated object, and for attributes, they are static data that is not instantiated by the DI framework. But we have the [ServiceFilter] attribute--it accepts as its sole required parameter the Type of a filter class (of any kind) and it uses the DI framework to instantiate it; what's more, it even allows ordering:

```
[ServiceFilter(typeof(CacheFilter), Order = 2)]
[ServiceFilter(typeof(LogFilter), Order = 1)]
public class HomeController : Controller
{
}
```

The LogFilter class, for example, might look like this:

```
public class LogFilter : IAsyncActionFilter
{
  private readonly ILoggerFactory _loggerFactory;

  public LogFilter(ILoggerFactory loggerFactory)
  {
    this._loggerFactory = loggerFactory;
  }

  public Task OnActionExecutionAsync(ActionExecutingContext context,
ActionExecutionDelegate next)
  {
    var logger =
this._loggerFactory.CreateLogger(context.Controller.GetType());
```

```
    logger.LogTrace($"{context.ActionDescriptor.DisplayName} action
called");
    return Task.CompletedTask;
  }
}
```

The `ILoggerFactory` is passed in the controller by the DI framework, as usual.

There is another special attribute, `[TypeFilter]`, which, given a certain `Type` and some optional arguments, tries to instantiate it:

```
[TypeFilter(typeof(CacheFilter), Arguments = new object[] { 60 * 1000 * 60
})]
```

These arguments are passed as parameters to the constructor of the filter type. This time, no dependency injection is used; it will just pass along any values it receives when attempting to build the concrete type, in the same way as `Activator.CreateInstance` does.

If you want, you can change the default filter provider by supplying your own implementation for the `IFilterProvider` service:

```
services.AddSingleton<IFilterProvider, CustomFilterProvider>();
```

 This process is complex, because you need to return filters coming from the global repository (`MvcOptions`), attributes applied to the class, the method, and more, so you better know what you're doing. If in doubt, keep the existing implementation.

The other way is to use the `RequestServices` service locator:

```
var svc = context.HttpContext.RequestServices.GetService<IMyService>();
```

This is available in every filter that exposes the `HttpContext` object.

Context

You can pass context from one filter to the others by using the `HttpContext.Items` collection, for example:

```
public class FirstFilter : IActionFilter
{
  public void OnActionExecuting(ActionExecutingContext context)
  {
  }
```

```
    public void OnActionExecuted(ActionExecutedContext context)
    {
      context.HttpContext.Items["WasFirstFilterExecuted"] = true;
    }
}

public class SecondFilter : IActionFilter
{
  public void OnActionExecuted(ActionExecutedContext context)
  {
  }

  public void OnActionExecuting(ActionExecutingContext context)
  {
    if (context.HttpContext.Items["WasFirstFilterExecuted"] == true)
    {
      //proceed accordingly
    }
  }
}
```

Authorization filters

This kind of filter is used to authorize the current user. The most notorious authorization attribute is [Authorize] and it can be used for common checks, such as being authenticated, belonging to a given role, or fulfilling a given policy. This attribute does not implement either IAuthorizationFilter or IAsyncAuthorizationFilter, but instead it implements IAuthorizeData, which lets us specify either role names (Roles), a custom policy name (Policy), or authentication schemes (AuthenticationSchemes). This attribute is handled by a built-in filter called AuthorizeFilter that is added by default when we add the authorization middleware (AddAuthorization).

Other things that you can check in an authorization attribute include, for example:

- Validating the source IP or domain of the client
- Verifying if a given cookie is present
- Validating the client certificate

So, for custom authorization, we either need to implement IAuthorizationFilter or IAsyncAuthorizationFilter; the first one exposes a single method, OnAuthorization. The context object passed to the OnAuthorization method exposes the HttpContext, ModelState, RouteData, and ActionDescriptor for the current request and MVC action; you can use any of these to perform your own custom authorization. If you do not wish to authorize the access, you can return an UnauthorizedResult in the context's Result property:

```
public void OnAuthorization(AuthorizationFilterContext context)
{
  var entry =
Dns.GetHostEntryAsync(context.HttpContext.Connection.RemoteIpAddress)
      .GetAwaiter()
      .GetResult();

  if (!entry.HostName.EndsWith(".MyDomain",
StringComparison.OrdinalIgnoreCase))
  {
    context.Result = new UnauthorizedResult();
  }
}
```

In this case, if the request does not come from a known domain, it is denied access.

The AuthorizationFilterContext class has the following properties:

- ActionDescriptor (ActionDescriptor): The descriptor of the action to be called
- Filters (IList<IFilterMetadata>): The filters bound to this request
- HttpContext (HttpContext): The HTTP context
- ModelState (ModelStateDictionary): The model state (unused for authorization filters)
- Result (IActionResult): An optional result to return to the client, bypassing the request pipeline
- RouteData (RouteData): Route data of the request

 You may be tempted to add a global filter that requires users to be authenticated everywhere; in this case, keep in mind that at least the entry page and the action that takes credentials need to allow anonymous access.

As for `IAsyncAuthorizationFilter`, its `OnAuthorizationAsync` method also takes an `AuthorizationFilterContext` parameter, the only difference being that it is called asynchronously.

 A word of caution: if you implement both `IAuthorizationFilter` and `IAsyncAuthorizationFilter`, only the async version will be used.

Authorization policies

In the previous chapter, we talked about authorization handlers. They can be added as global filters too, through the `AuthorizeFilter` class, which is a filter factory. Here's one example:

```
services.AddMvc(options =>
    {
      var policy = new AuthorizationPolicyBuilder()
          .RequireAssertion(ctx => true) //let everything pass
          .Build();

      options.Filters.Add(new AuthorizeFilter(policy));
    });
```

Resource filters

In resource filters, you can apply similar logic to authorization filters but it executes slightly after authorization filters, and you have more information. For example, when resource filters execute, the user has already logged in (if using authentication). Common usages for resource filters are:

- Logging
- Caching
- Throttling
- Modifying model binding

The `IResourceFilter` interface defines two methods:

- `OnResourceExecuting`: Called before the request reaches the action
- `OnResourceExecuted`: After the action is executed

Each of these methods takes a single parameter of type `ResourceExecutingContext` and `ResourceExecutedContext`, respectively, for pre and post-events. `ResourceExecutingContext` offers these properties, which reflect the context prior to the resource being processed:

- `Result` (`IActionResult`): If you wish to short-circuit the request pipeline, you can set a value here, and all the other filters and middleware will be bypassed (except the `OnResourceExecuted` method), returning this result; if you want to return a POCO value, wrap it in `ObjectResult`
- `ValueProviderFactories` (`IList<IValueProviderFactory>`): Here you can inspect, add, or modify the collection of value provider factories to be used when providing values to the target action's parameters

As for `ResourceExecutedContext`, we have this:

- `Canceled` (`bool`): Whether or not a result was set in `OnResourceExecuting`
- `Exception` (`Exception`): Any exception thrown during the processing of the resource
- `ExceptionDispatchInfo` (`ExceptionDispatchInfo`): The exception dispatch object, used for capturing the stack trace of an exception and optionally re-throwing it, while preserving this context
- `ExceptionHandled` (`bool`): Whether the exception was handled or not (if there was one), the default being `false`; if not handled, then the framework will re-throw it
- `Result` (`IActionResult`): The action set by the `OnExecuting` method, which can also be set here

If an exception is thrown during the processing of the resource (in the action method or in another filter), and it is not explicitly marked as handled (`ExceptionHandled`) by the resource filter, it will be thrown by the framework, resulting in an error. If you want to know more, consult the documentation for `ExceptionDispatchInfo` here: `https://msdn.microsoft.com/en-us/library/system.runtime.exceptionservices.exceptiondispatchinfo.aspx`

The async alternative, `IAsyncResourceFilter`, only declares a single method, `OnResourceExecutionAsync`, taking two parameters--one `ResourceExecutingContext` (the same as for the `OnResourceExecuting` method) and one of type `ResourceExecutionDelegate`; this one is interesting, as you can use it to inject other middleware at runtime to the pipeline.

 Again, do not implement the synchronous and asynchronous interfaces at the same time, as only the asynchronous interface will be used.

Understanding action filters

Action filters are invoked before and after an action method is called, so they can be used, for example, to:

- Cache results
- Modify parameters
- Modify results

Now, we already have the parameters to the action method, which come from the value providers. Here the filter interfaces are `IActionFilter` and `IAsyncActionFilter`. The synchronous one offers two methods, `OnActionExecuting` and `OnActionExecuted`, for pre-and post-event notifications. `OnActionExecuting` takes a single parameter of type `ActionExecutingContext`, offering the following properties:

- `Result` (`IActionResult`): Set a value here to short-circuit the request processing pipeline and return a value to the client, without actually executing the action
- `ActionArguments` (`IDictionary<string, object>`): The parameters to the action method
- `Controller` (`object`): The target controller instance

 You may be wondering why the `Controller` property is not prototyped as `ControllerBase` or `Controller`: do not forget that we can have POCO controllers!

The `ActionArguments` parameter has entries for each parameter of the target action method, and its values have been provided by the registered value providers.

The post-event method, `OnActionExecuted`, takes a parameter of type `ActionExecutedContext`, which exposes the following properties:

- `Canceled` (`bool`): Whether or not a result was set in `OnActionExecuting`
- `Controller` (`object`): The controller instance
- `Exception` (`Exception`): Any exception thrown during the processing of the resource
- `ExceptionDispatchInfo` (`ExceptionDispatchInfo`): The exception dispatch object, used for capturing the stack trace of an exception and optionally re-throwing it, while preserving this context
- `ExceptionHandled` (`bool`): Whether the exception was handled or not (if there was one), the default being `false`; if not handled, then the framework will re-throw it
- `Result` (`IActionResult`): The action set by the `OnExecuting` method, which can also be set here

As for `IAsyncActionFilter`, it offers a single method, `OnActionExecutionAsync`, taking two parameters, in the same fashion as `OnResourceExecutionAsync`: `ActionExecutingContext` and `ActionExecutionDelegate`. The `ActionExecutionDelegate` instance points to the next action filter method in the pipeline.

Result filters

Result filters let you execute custom actions before and after the result is processed, in case an action executes with success. Action results are represented by `IActionResult`, and we can have code run before and after `ExecuteResultAsync` is called. Common usages for result filters include:

- Caching (as before)
- Interception (modification of the response)
- Adding response headers
- Result formatting

The `IResultFilter` interface defines the `OnResultExecuting` and `OnResultExecuted` methods. The first takes as its sole parameter an instance of `ResultExecutingContext`, which offers the following properties:

- `Cancel` (`bool`): Whether or not to cancel the processing of the result
- `Result` (`IActionResult`): The result to process in case we want to bypass the returned result's execution
- `Controller` (`object`): The controller instance

As for the post-event method, `OnResultExecuted`, we have the following properties on `ResultExecutedContext`:

- `Canceled` (`bool`): Whether or not a result was set in `OnResultExecuting`
- `Controller` (`object`): The controller instance
- `Exception` (`Exception`): Any exception thrown during the processing of the resource
- `ExceptionDispatchInfo` (`ExceptionDispatchInfo`): The exception dispatch object, used for capturing the stack trace of an exception and optionally re-throwing it, while preserving this context
- `ExceptionHandled` (`bool`): Whether the exception was handled or not (if there was one), the default being `false`; if not handled, then the framework will re-throw it
- `Result` (`IActionResult`): The action set by the `OnResultExecuting` method, but which can also be set here

These are exactly the same as in `ResourceExecutedContext`. As usual, we also have an asynchronous version of result filters, `IAsyncResultFilter`, which, following the same pattern, offers a single method called `OnResultExecutionAsync` that has two parameters--one of type `ResultExecutingContext`:

- `Cancel` (`bool`): Whether or not to cancel the processing of the result
- `Result` (`IActionResult`): The result to process in case we want to bypass the returned result's execution
- `Controller` (`object`): The controller instance

And the other is a `ResultExecutionDelegate`, which will point to the next delegate of type `IAsyncResultFilter` in the pipeline. Here is a simple example of a result filter:

```
public class CacheFilter : IResultFilter
{
  private readonly IMemoryCache _cache;

  public CacheFilter(IMemoryCache cache)
  {
    this._cache = cache;
  }

  private object GetKey(ActionDescriptor action)
  {
    //generate a key and return it
  }

  public void OnResultExecuted(ResultExecutedContext context)
  {
  }

  public void OnResultExecuting(ResultExecutingContext context)
  {
    var key = this.GetKey(context.ActionDescriptor);
    string html;

    if (this._cache.TryGetValue<string>(key, out html))
    {
      context.Result = new ContentResult { Content = html, ContentType =
"text/html" };
    }
    else
    {
      if (context.Result is ViewResult)
      {
        //get the rendered view, maybe using a TextWriter, and store it in
the cache
      }
    }
  }
}
```

When this filter runs it checks if there is an entry in the cache for the current action and parameters, and, if so, it just returns it as the result.

Exception filters

These are the easiest to understand: whenever there's an exception under the scope of an exception filter (action, controller, or global), its `OnException` method is called. This is pretty useful for logging errors, as you can imagine.

The `OnException` method takes a parameter of type `ExceptionContext`:

- `Exception` (`Exception`): Any exception thrown during the processing of the resource
- `ExceptionDispatchInfo` (`ExceptionDispatchInfo`): The exception dispatch object, used for capturing the stack trace of an exception and optionally re-throwing it, while preserving this context
- `ExceptionHandled` (`bool`): Whether the exception was handled or not (if there was one), the default being `false`; if not handled, then the framework will re-throw it
- `Result` (`IActionResult`): Possibly an action result, if one was set, but can also be set here

There is no `Controller` property because the exception may have been thrown outside of a controller.

The asynchronous interface `IAsyncExceptionFilter` has a single method declared, `OnExceptionAsync`, and it also receives a parameter of type `ExceptionContext`. The behavior is exactly the same as its synchronous counterpart, but it is called in another thread.

Caught exceptions are propagated unless the `ExceptionHandled` property is set to `true`. If you do handle the exception, it is your responsibility to return a result (the `Result` property).

Page filters

This is a new one for Razor Pages. Basically, we can have custom actions being fired before or after a Razor Page's model method. As for the other filters, it is available in synchronous (`IPageFilter`) and asynchronous flavors (`IAsyncPageFilter`). Starting with the synchronous version, it declares three methods:

- `OnPageHandlerSelected`: Called after the framework selects a target handler method for the processing of the request, giving developers a chance to change this
- `OnPageHandlerExecuting`: Called before the handler is invoked
- `OnPageHandlerExecuted`: Called after the handler is invoked

`OnPageHandlerSelected` takes a parameter of type `PageHandlerSelectedContext`, and this class offers the following properties:

- `ActionDescriptor` (`CompiledPageActionDescriptor`): Describes the handler and model classes
- `HandlerMethod` (`HandlerMethodDescriptor`): The method that will be called, and can be changed
- `HandlerInstance` (`object`): The instance that will handle the request

The pre-event handler, `OnPageHandlerExecuting`, takes a single parameter of type `PageHandlerExecutingContext`, with the following properties:

- `ActionDescriptor` (`CompiledPageActionDescriptor`): The handler and model classes
- `Result` (`IActionResult`): The result to return, in case we want to override the default processing of the page
- `HandlerArguments` (`IDictionary<string, object>`): The arguments to be passed to the handler method
- `HandlerMethod` (`HandlerMethodDescriptor`): The method that will be called on the handler instance
- `HandlerInstance` (`object`): The instance that will handle the request

As for the post-event, OnPageHandlerExecuted, we have a parameter of type PageHandlerExecutedContext:

- ActionDescriptor (CompiledPageActionDescriptor): The handler and model classes
- Canceled (bool): Whether or not the current processing has been canceled, by setting a result in the pre-event
- HandlerMethod (HandlerMethodDescriptor): The method that will be called on the handler instance
- HandlerInstance (object): The instance that will handle the request
- Exception (Exception): Any exception thrown during the processing of the resource
- ExceptionDispatchInfo (ExceptionDispatchInfo): The exception dispatch object, used for capturing the stack trace of an exception and optionally re-throwing it
- ExceptionHandled (bool): Whether the exception was handled or not; the default is false, meaning the framework will re-throw it
- Result (IActionResult): The result to return, in case we want to override the default processing of the page

Finally, the asynchronous interface offers two asynchronous methods, which are the counterparts to OnPageHandlerSelected--now called OnPageHandlerSelectionAsync--and OnPageHandlerExecuted--now OnPageHandlerExecutionAsync. OnPageHandlerSelectionAsync has as its single parameter an instance of PageHandlerSelectedContext and OnPageHandlerExecutionAsync takes two parameters--PageHandlerExecutingContext and PageHandlerExecutionDelegate. PageHandlerExecutionDelegate is, again, a delegate that points to the next method of the same type in the pipeline, if one exists.

Putting it all together

In general, always prefer the asynchronous versions of each filter method, because they are inherently more scalable--a thread does not block while filters are being invoked. Do not mix, on the same class, a synchronous and an asynchronous version of a filter interface because only the asynchronous version is called.

Use dependency injection through the [ServiceFilter] attribute if you need to inject dependencies into your filters. For global filters, add the filter type to the MvcOptions.Filters collection in AddMvc rather than a filter instance.

Beware of each filter's intended purpose: do not use a resource filter for authorization. Use action filters if you need to intercept action parameters or do caching, and result filters for modifying the output or the format of a result. Exception filters are crucial for logging failures; these are safe to have at a global level. Apply authorization filters for protecting any sensitive resources and choose the best authorization (roles, policies, or merely being authenticated).

Also pay attention to the scope of the filter--carefully opt for global, controller, or action, whatever best suits your needs.

Summary

In this chapter, we've looked at the interception mechanisms of ASP.NET Core. In the next one, we will be looking at the logging, diagnostics, tracing, and health monitoring that ASP.NET Core has to offer.

10
Logging, Tracing, and Diagnostics

Logging is an essential feature of any non-trivial application. In this chapter, we will have a look at some of the options we have to hand for adding logging to our apps.

We will cover the following topics in this chapter:

- The .NET Core common logging framework
- Custom logging middleware
- The diagnostics feature
- Telemetry using Microsoft Azure AppInsights
- ASP.NET Core health checks

Common logging

Logging is an integral part of .NET Core, which provides several abstractions to support it; needless to say, it is fully pluggable and extensible. The infrastructure classes, interfaces, abstract base classes, enumerations, and so on are contained in the `Microsoft.Extensions.Logging.Abstractions` NuGet package and the built-in implementations in `Microsoft.Extensions.Logging`. When you log a message, it is routed to all registered logging providers. Now, there were some changes from ASP.NET Core 1.x to 2.x, so we will need to have a look at them separately. Let's start first with what is common to both versions.

Using logging

We register the logging services by a call to `AddLogging` in the `ConfigureServices` method. This is actually done by other methods, such as `AddMvc`, so there is usually no need to call it manually, except, of course, if we are not using MVC. No harm in doing so, though:

```
services.AddLogging();
```

In order to log in .NET Core, you need an instance of the `ILogger` (or `ILogger<T>`) interface. You normally inject one into your class--controller, view component, tag helper, middleware--using the **dependency injection** (DI) framework, that fully supports it:

```
public class HomeController : Controller
{
  private readonly ILogger<HomeController> _logger;

  public HomeController(ILogger<HomeController> logger)
  {
    this._logger = logger;
  }
}
```

But you can also request one from the `ILoggerFactory`:

```
var logger1 = loggerFactory.CreateLogger<MyClass>();
//or
var logger2 = loggerFactory.CreateLogger("MyClass");
```

The category name is taken from the full type name of the generic class parameter.

The `ILogger` interface only offers three methods, plus a number of extension methods. The core methods are as follows:

- `BeginScope`: Starts a block to which all logs made inside of it are related
- `IsEnabled`: Checks whether a given log level is enabled to be logged
- `Log`: Writes a log message to a specific log level, with an event ID and optional formatter

Log levels are defined in the `LogLevel` enumeration as follows:

Level	Numeric value	Purpose
Trace	0	Logs that contain the most detailed messages. These messages may contain sensitive application data.
Debug	1	Logs that are used for interactive investigation during development. These logs should primarily contain information useful for debugging and have no long-term value.
Information	2	Logs that track the general flow of the application. These logs should have long-term value.
Warning	3	Logs that highlight an abnormal or unexpected event in the application flow, but do not otherwise cause the application execution to stop.
Error	4	Logs that highlight when the current flow of execution is stopped due to a failure. These should indicate a failure in the current activity, not an application-wide failure.
Critical	5	Logs that describe an unrecoverable application or system crash, or a catastrophic failure that requires immediate attention.
None	6	Specifies that a logging category should not write any messages.

As you can see, these log levels have increasing numeric values, starting with the most verbose and potentially uninteresting (except for debugging purposes) and ending in the most severe. The logging framework is designed so that we can filter out levels below a given one, so as to avoid unnecessary clutter in the logging. To check whether a given level is enabled or not, we use `IsEnabled`.

The `Log` generic method is usually the most interesting one, and it takes these parameters:

- `logLevel` (`LogLevel`): The desired log level
- `eventId` (`EventId`): A event ID
- `state` (`TState`): The state to log
- `exception` (`Exception`): An exception to log
- `formatter` (`Func<TState, Exception, string>`): A formatting function based on the state and the possible exception

Each log entry has the following information:

- Log level
- Timestamp
- Category
- State or exception
- Event ID
- Scope name (if called from inside a scope)

When we request a logger instance from `ILoggerFactory`--which is normally done automatically by declaring an `ILogger<T>` in the constructor of a class--the `T` parameter is the category name--it is the same as the fully qualified type name.

By far the most usual message kind that we want to log is strings (or exceptions), so there are a few extension methods that do just that:

- `LogTrace`
- `LogDebug`
- `LogInformation`
- `LogWarning`
- `LogError`
- `LogCritical`

As you can see, all of these methods are bound to a specific log level, and each has three overloads, for taking a combination of these parameters:

- `message` (`string`): A message to log, with optional parameter placeholders (for example, `{0}`, `{1}`, and so on)
- `parameters` (`params object []`): The optional parameters for the message to log
- `eventId` (`EventId`): A correlation ID
- `exception` (`Exception`): An exception to log, if there is one

Every one of the three overloads takes the `message` plus its optional `parameters`, another one takes the `eventId`, and the other takes the `exception`. We can see that they dropped the `formatter` parameter; this is because it uses the default string formatting behavior.

What is the event ID used for, I hear you ask? Well, it is a correlation id, an identifier that is possibly unique among requests, and which correlates several logging messages together, so that someone analyzing them can find out that they are related. Event IDs are essentially a number plus an optional name. If not supplied, it is not used.

A scope merely includes the given scope name in all the logging messages until the scope is ended. Because `BeginScope` returns an `IDisposable`, calling its `Dispose` method ends the scope.

Logging providers

A logging provider is a class that implements the `ILoggerProvider` interface. Logging providers need to be registered with the logging framework so that they can be used. Normally this is done by either the `ILoggerFactory.AddProvider` method or an extension method supplied by the provider.

Microsoft ships .NET Core with the following providers:

Provider	NuGet package	Purpose
Azure App Services	`Microsoft.Extensions.Logging.AzureAppServices`	Logs to Azure Blobs or to filesystem
Console	`Microsoft.Extensions.Logging.Console`	Logs to the console
Debug	`Microsoft.Extensions.Logging.Debug`	Logs using `Debug.WriteLine`
EventLog	`Microsoft.Extensions.Logging.EventLog`	Logs to the Windows Event Log
EventSource	`Microsoft.Extensions.Logging.EventSource`	Logs to **Event Tracing for Windows (ETW)**
TraceSource	`Microsoft.Extensions.Logging.TraceSource`	Logs using `TraceSource`

You may not be so familiar with **Event Tracing for Windows**. It is a complex subject, and you can read about it here: `https://msdn.microsoft.com/en-us/library/windows/desktop/bb968803.aspx`. It is also, at least for now, Windows-specific.

Normally, we register these providers in the `Startup` class of ASP.NET Core, during its bootstrap, but we can also do it earlier, in the `Program` class; this has the benefit of capturing some early events that may be raised before `Startup` comes along. For that, we need to add an extra step to the `WebHostBuilder` call:

```
new WebHostBuilder()
    .ConfigureLogging(options =>
        {
          options
             .AddConsole()
             .AddDebug();
        })
```

The way to add these providers in the `Startup` class changed from ASP.NET Core 1.x to 2.x. Let's look at 1.x first.

ASP.NET Core 1.x

Inside `Configure`, from the reference to the `ILoggerFactory` instance, we register all the providers we're interested in:

```
loggerFactory
    .AddConsole()
    .AddDebug();
```

All of the built-in providers offer extension methods over `ILoggerFactory` with the format Addxxxx, and while some may take additional parameters such as the Azure App Services one--all can also take a single parameter that is the minimum level to log, for example:

```
.AddConsole(LogLevel.Information)
```

ASP.NET Core 2.x

In ASP.NET Core 2, the configuration of the logging mechanism is done earlier, in the `ConfigureServices` method, when we register the logging providers to the DI framework:

```
services
    .AddLogging(options =>
        {
          options.AddConsole()
             .AddDebug();
        });
```

Azure App Services logging has, of course, much more to it than the other built-in providers. For a good introduction to it, outside the scope of this book, please have a look at `https://blogs.msdn.microsoft.com/webdev/2017/04/26/asp-net-core-logging`.

There are several other providers for .NET Core out there, including the following:

Provider	NuGet package	Source
AWS	`AWS.Logger.AspNetCore`	`https://github.com/aws/aws-logging-dotnet`
Elmah.io	`Elmah.Io.Extensions.Logging`	`https://github.com/elmahio/Elmah.Io.Extensions.Logging`
Log4Net	`log4net`	`https://github.com/apache/logging-log4net`
Loggr	`Loggr.Extensions.Logging`	`https://github.com/imobile3/Loggr.Extensions.Logging`
NLog	`NLog`	`https://github.com/NLog`
Serilog	`Serilog`	`https://github.com/serilog/serilog`

Of these packages, `Serilog` can do structured logging--something else besides just strings.

Log filtering

We can restrict logging based on the following criteria:

- Log level
- Category name

This means, for some providers, we can log events for levels up to and including a certain one, for categories starting with some name.

While this is common for both ASP.NET Core 1.x and 2.x, there are some changes.

ASP.NET Core 1

Some of the providers can take a configuration section and use it to configure the minimum logging for each category. Imagine your JSON configuration file looks like this:

```
{
    "Logging": {
        "IncludeScopes": true,
        "Console": {
            "LogLevel": {
                "Default": "Warning",
                "System": "Critical",
                "Microsoft": "Critical"
            },
            "Debug": {
                "LogLevel": {
                    "Default": "Trace",
                    "System": "Critical",
                    "Microsoft": "Critical"
                }
            }
        }
    }
}
```

Here we are configuring the logging default levels for the `Debug` and the `Console` providers, both for any category (**Default**) and for categories starting with the names `System` or `Microsoft`. These will include logs produced by any class under the `System.*` or `Microsoft.*` namespaces, such as, `System.Data.SqlClient.SqlConnection`. By default, we are including scope information in the logs.

This can also be achieved in code, per provider:

```
loggerFactory.AddConsole((category, level) =>
    {
        if (category.StartsWith("Microsoft") ||
category.StartsWith("System"))
        {
            return level >= LogLevel.Critical;
        }
        return level >= LogLevel.Warning;
    });
```

For setting the minimum logging level and whether or not to include scopes, there is another extension method:

```
loggerFactory.AddConsole(
    minLevel: LogLevel.Warning,
    includeScopes: true);
```

Other providers offer similar methods.

ASP.NET Core 2

In ASP.NET Core 2, we can configure default global filters, per category and log level; the lambda expression lets us return a Boolean value whether or not the log should be processed:

```
services
    .AddLogging(options =>
        {
            options.AddFilter((category, logLevel) => logLevel >=
LogLevel.Warning);
        });
```

Or just per category, here the lambda just takes the category name:

```
services
    .AddLogging(options =>
        {
            options.AddFilter("Microsoft", LogLevel.Warning);
        });
```

If we want to filter per a specific provider, we add it as a generic template method to `AddFilter`:

```
services
    .AddLogging(options =>
        {
            options.AddFilter<ConsoleLoggerProvider>("Microsoft",
LogLevel.Warning);
                //or, with a lambda
            options.AddFilter<ConsoleLoggerProvider>((categoryName, logLevel)
=> true);
        });
```

Or even per provider, category and log level:

```
services
    .AddLogging(options =>
    {
      options.AddFilter<ConsoleLoggerProvider>("System", logLevel =>
          logLevel >= LogLevel.Warning);
      //same as this
      options.AddFilter((provider, category, logLevel) =>
      {
          //you get the picture
      });
    });
```

Additionally, providers can be configured in the `Program` class, as part of the host building process:

```
var builder = new WebHostBuilder()
    .ConfigureLogging((hostingContext, logging) =>
        {
logging.AddConfiguration(hostingContext.Configuration.GetSection("Logging")
);
            logging.AddConsole(LogLevel.Warning);
            logging.AddDebug();
        })
    //rest goes here
```

Custom providers

A provider that does not come out of the box is one that writes to a file. A (somewhat simple) file logging provider could look like this:

```
public sealed class FileLoggerProvider : ILoggerProvider
{
  private readonly Func<string, LogLevel, bool> _func;

  public FileLoggerProvider(Func<string, LogLevel, bool> func)
  {
    this._func = func;
  }

  public FileLoggerProvider(LogLevel minimumLogLevel) :
    this((category, logLevel) => logLevel >= minimumLogLeve)
  {
  }
```

```csharp
  public ILogger CreateLogger(string categoryName)
  {
    return new FileLogger(categoryName, this._func);
  }

  public void Dispose()
  {
  }
}

public sealed class FileLogger : ILogger
{
  private readonly string _categoryName;
  private readonly Func<string, LogLevel, bool> _func;

  public FileLogger(string categoryName, Func<string, LogLevel, bool> func)
  {
    this._categoryName = categoryName;
    this._func = func;
  }

  public IDisposable BeginScope<TState>(TState state)
  {
    return new EmptyDisposable();
  }

  public bool IsEnabled(LogLevel logLevel)
  {
    return this._func(this._categoryName, logLevel);
  }

  public void Log<TState>(
    LogLevel logLevel,
    EventId eventId,
    TState state,
    Exception exception,
    Func<TState, Exception, string> formatter)
  {
    if (this.IsEnabled(logLevel) == true)
    {
      var now = DateTime.UtcNow;
      var today = now.ToString("yyyy-MM-dd");
      var fileName = $"{this._categoryName}_{today}.log";
      var message = formatter(state, exception);

      File.AppendAllText(fileName, $"{message}\n");
    }
  }
```

```
  }

  internal sealed class EmptyDisposable : IDisposable
  {
    public void Dispose() { }
  }

  public static class LoggerFactoryExtensions
  {
    public static ILoggerFactory AddFile(
      this ILoggerFactory loggerFactory,
      Func<string, LogLevel, bool> func)
    {
      loggerFactory.AddProvider(new FileLoggerProvider(func));
      return loggerFactory;
    }

    public static ILoggerFactory AddFile(
      this ILoggerFactory loggerFactory,
      LogLevel minimumLogLevel)
    {
      return AddFile(loggerFactory, (category, logLevel) => logLevel >=
minimumLogLevel);
    }
  }
}
```

This example is composed of the following:

- A logger factory class, `FileLoggerFactory`, that is responsible for creating actual loggers
- The `FileLogger` class, that logs to a file
- A helper class, `EmptyDisposable`, that is used to mock scopes
- Some extension methods in the `LoggerFactoryExtensions` class, to make registering the file provider easier

The `FileLoggerFactory` class needs to take a single parameter that is the minimum log level to accept, which is then passed along to any created logger. The file to be created has a name in the format `{categoryName}-{yyyy-MM-dd}.log`, where `categoryName` is the value passed to the `CreateLogger` method and `yyyy-MM-dd` is the current date. Simple, don't you think?

Dependency injection

As we've seen, we can inject into our classes either a logger or the logger factory itself. Passing the logger is by far the most common scenario, but we can also pass the logger factory if we want to do some additional configuration, such as register a new logging provider.

 Be warned: you cannot inject an ILogger instance, only an ILogger<T>, where T is an actual type--class or struct, abstract or concrete, it doesn't matter.

In ASP.NET Core 2, you do not need to call AddLogging explicitly in your ConfigureServices method, as the logging services are automatically registered.

Logging attributes

An interesting usage of the filter mechanism explained in the previous chapter is to add logging through filter attributes. Depending on where we want to add this logging, we could use resource, result, or action filters, but I'm going to give an example with action filters, as these have the ability to inspect both the model that is going to be passed to the action method and also the result of its invocation.

The following code shows an attribute that, when applied to a class or a method, will cause a log message to be issued:

```
[AttributeUsage(AttributeTargets.Method | AttributeTargets.Class,
AllowMultiple = true,
    Inherited = true)]
public sealed class LoggerAttribute : ActionFilterAttribute
{
  public LoggerAttribute(string logMessage)
  {
    this.LogMessage = logMessage;
  }

  public string LogMessage { get; }
  public LogLevel LogLevel { get; set; } = LogLevel.Information;

  private EventId _eventId;

  private string GetLogMessage(ModelStateDictionary modelState)
  {
    var logMessage = this.LogMessage;
```

```
    foreach (var key in modelState.Keys)
    {
      logMessage = logMessage.Replace("{" + key + "}",
modelState[key].RawValue?.ToString());
    }

    return logMessage;
  }

  private ILogger GetLogger(HttpContext context, ControllerActionDescriptor
action)
  {
    var logger = context
      .RequestServices
      .GetService(typeof(ILogger<>)
      .MakeGenericType(
        action.ControllerTypeInfo.UnderlyingSystemType)) as ILogger;
       return logger;
  }

  public override void OnActionExecuted(ActionExecutedContext context)
  {
    var cad = context.ActionDescriptor as ControllerActionDescriptor;
    var logMessage = this.GetLogMessage(context.ModelState);
    var logger = this.GetLogger(context.HttpContext, cad);
    var duration = TimeSpan.FromMilliseconds(Environment.TickCount -
this._eventId.Id);

    logger.Log(this.LogLevel, this._eventId,
        $"After {cad.ControllerName}.{cad.ActionName} with {logMessage} and
result {context.HttpContext.Response.StatusCode} in {duration}", null,
(state, ex) => state.ToString());

    base.OnActionExecuted(context);
  }

  public override void OnActionExecuting(ActionExecutingContext context)
  {
    var cad = context.ActionDescriptor as ControllerActionDescriptor;
    var logMessage = this.GetLogMessage(context.ModelState);
    var logger = this.GetLogger(context.HttpContext, cad);

    this._eventId = new EventId(Environment.TickCount,
$"{cad.ControllerName}.{cad.ActionName}");

    logger.Log(this.LogLevel, this._eventId, $"Before
{cad.ControllerName}.{cad.ActionName} with {logMessage}", null, (state, ex)
=> state.ToString());
```

```
      base.OnActionExecuting(context);
    }
  }
```

This attribute can be applied either to an action method or to a controller class, and it needs to take a log message parameter. This parameter can take model names enclosed in brackets (for example, {email}) that will then be replaced in the logging message. It uses as the event ID the number of milliseconds elapsed since the system restarted (Environment.TickCount) and as the event name, a combination of controller and action names; this event ID is reused in the pre and post events. A message is logged with the provided log level before and after each action method is called. Here is an example declaration:

```
[Logger("Method called with {email}", LogLevel.Information)]
public IActionResult AddToMailingList(string email) { ... }
```

This may be handy if we wish to add custom logging transparently to some action methods to log out model values.

Custom logging middleware

We've seen earlier how we can write custom middleware to perform actions before and after the rest of the pipeline. A simple middleware class to log all requests can be written as follows:

```
public class LoggingMiddleware
{
  private readonly RequestDelegate _next;
  private readonly ILoggerFactory _loggerFactory;

  public LoggingMiddleware(RequestDelegate next, ILoggerFactory
loggerFactory)
  {
    this._next = next;
    this._loggerFactory = loggerFactory;
  }

  public async Task Invoke(HttpContext context)
  {
    var logger = this._loggerFactory.CreateLogger<LoggingMiddleware>();
    using (logger.BeginScope<LoggingMiddleware>(this))
    {
      logger.LogInformation("Before request");
      await this._next.Invoke(context);
```

```
        logger.LogInformation("After request");
    }
  }
}
```

Notice that the category of the logger is set to the `LoggingMiddleware` type's full name and we are starting a scope for each invocation, which is here just as an example. The way to register this middleware is by calling `UseMiddleware` in `Configure`:

```
app.UseMiddleware<LoggingMiddleware>();
```

ASP.NET Core provides a feature, `IHttpRequestIdentifierFeature`, that generates a unique ID per each request. This id may help you correlate events that happen in the context of a request. Two ways to get it, but the same value:

```
//using the TraceIdentifier property in ASP.NET Core 2.x
var id1 = this.HttpContext.TraceIdentifier;
//accessing the feature in earlier versions of ASP.NET Core
var id2 =
this.HttpContext.Features.Get<IHttpRequestIdentifierFeature>().TraceIdentif
ier;
```

A trace identifier is just an opaque reference like `0HL8VHQLUJ7CM:00000001` that is guaranteed to be unique among requests.

Diagnostics

I already mentioned the diagnostics functionality of ASP.NET Core in `Chapter 5`, *Views*. Diagnostics is comparable to logging, but it has some advantages:

- It can do structured logging, that is, it can call methods in the trace loggers that take parameters, not just strings
- It's easy to plug in new adapters, merely by adding an attribute to a class; even classes in referenced assemblies can be used

Please refer to `Chapter 5`, *Views*, for a wider explanation. Here I am going to cover a Microsoft package, `Microsoft.AspNetCore.MiddlewareAnalysis`. When it is used, it traces all middleware component that executes on the pipeline, through the diagnostics feature. It is configured by a simple call to `AddMiddlewareAnalysis`:

```
services.AddMiddlewareAnalysis();
```

Then, we register a listener for a couple of new events:

- `Microsoft.AspNetCore.MiddlewareAnalysis.MiddlewareStarting`: Called when the middleware is starting
- `Microsoft.AspNetCore.MiddlewareAnalysis.MiddlewareFinished`: Called when the middleware has finished
- `Microsoft.AspNetCore.MiddlewareAnalysis.MiddlewareException`: Called whenever an exception occurs while the middleware is executed

Here is how to register the diagnostic source listener:

```
public void Configure(
  IApplicationBuilder app,
  IHostingEnvironment env,
  DiagnosticListener diagnosticListener)
{
  var listener = new TraceDiagnosticListener();
  diagnosticListener.SubscribeWithAdapter(listener);

  //rest goes here
}
```

The `TraceDiagnosticListener` class has methods that will be automatically wired to these events:

```
public class TraceDiagnosticListener
{
[DiagnosticName("Microsoft.AspNetCore.MiddlewareAnalysis.MiddlewareStarting
")]
    public virtual void OnMiddlewareStarting(HttpContext httpContext,
string name)
    {
      //called when the middleware is starting
    }

[DiagnosticName("Microsoft.AspNetCore.MiddlewareAnalysis.MiddlewareExceptio
n")]
    public virtual void OnMiddlewareException(Exception exception, string
name)
```

```
    {
        //called when there is an exception while processing a middleware
component
    }

[DiagnosticName("Microsoft.AspNetCore.MiddlewareAnalysis.MiddlewareFinished
")]
    public virtual void OnMiddlewareFinished(HttpContext httpContext,
string name)
    {
        //called when the middleware execution finishes
    }
}
```

Note that this is called for both middleware classes (refer to the `Chapter 1`, *Getting Started with ASP.NET Core*) or for middleware that is added to the pipeline as a custom delegate:

```
app.Properties["analysis.NextMiddlewareName"] = "MyCustomMiddleware";
app.Use(async (context, next) =>
    {
      //do something
      await next();
    });
```

Notice the line where we set the `analysis.NextMiddlewareName` property--because this middleware does not have a name--it is an anonymous delegate--the property is used for the `name` parameter of each of the `TraceDiagnosticListener` class' methods.

If you want to visually analyze all this activity, you can add another Microsoft package, `Microsoft.AspNetCore.Diagnostics.Elm`. This stands for **Error Logging Middleware**, and is added in the usual way; first, by registering services (`ConfigureServices` method):

```
services.AddElm();
```

Then, by adding the middleware to the pipeline (`Configure`):

```
app.UseElmPage();
app.UseElmCapture();
```

You may want to add these just for development. After you do, when you access /elm, you will get a nice trace of what is going on:

You can see all the events that take place when a request is processed, all of these come from the diagnostic feature.

If you want to set the URL that ELM uses, or filter the results, you can certainly do so:

```
var options = serviceProvider.GetService<IOptions<ElmOptions>>();
options.Value.Path = "_Elm";
options.Value.Filter = (name, logLevel) =>
    {
        return logLevel > LogLevel.Information;
    };
```

Telemetry

When you create an ASP.NET project using Visual Studio, you are presented with the option to add support for **Application Insights (AI)**. AI is an Azure service that lets you monitor your web application for availability, performance, and usage, including errors. When you add support for AI to your web app, you can go to the AI console and monitor the behavior of your application in real time, see how it behaved recently, and even get notified in case something unusual happens. Here, we won't cover AI in full, but just give you an overview of how to use it in your ASP.NET Core projects. The following screenshot shows a typical combined view displaying response and page load times:

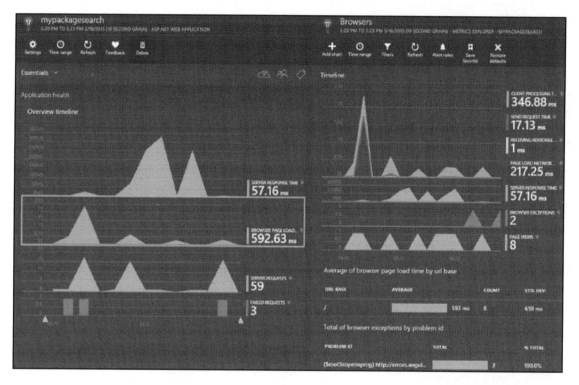

Before you can use AI, you need to have a working Azure account (`https://portal.azure.com`) and you need to create an AI resource. You can create one from inside Visual Studio:

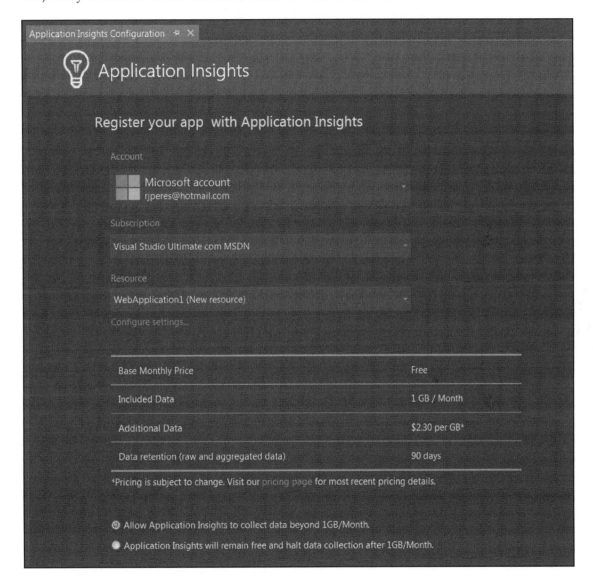

For detailed instructions, please consult `https://github.com/Microsoft/ApplicationInsights-aspnetcore/wiki/Getting-Started-with-Application-Insights-for-ASP.NET-Core`. AI relies on the `Microsoft.ApplicationInsights.AspNetCore` NuGet package and you will need to add a configuration setting with the instrumentation key that is provided to you in the AI console, once you create an AI resource. If you use a JSON configuration file, you will need something like this:

```
{
  "ApplicationInsights": {
    "InstrumentationKey": "11111111-2222-3333-4444-555555555555"
  }
}
```

In any case, you will need to register the AI services, directly from your configuration:

```
services.AddApplicationInsightsTelemetry(this.Configuration);
```

Or you can pass the instrumentation key directly:

```
services.AddApplicationInsightsTelemetry(
    instrumentationKey: "11111111-2222-3333-4444-555555555555");
```

For more advanced options, you can pass in an instance of `ApplicationInsightsServiceOptions`:

```
services.AddApplicationInsightsTelemetry(new
ApplicationInsightsServiceOptions
    {
        InstrumentationKey = "11111111-2222-3333-4444-555555555555",
        DeveloperMode = true,
        EnableDebugLogger = true
    });
```

When running in development, it is often useful to use the developer mode of AI as you can see results immediately (not in batches).

ASP.NET Core 1.x

For ASP.NET Core 1.x, you need to explicitly enable request and exception telemetry, in the `Configure` method:

```
app.UseApplicationInsightsRequestTelemetry();
app.UseApplicationInsightsExceptionTelemetry();
```

Now, in the `_ViewImports.cshtml` partial view, inject the telemetry configuration object:

```
@inject Microsoft.ApplicationInsights.Extensibility.TelemetryConfiguration
TelemetryConfiguration
```

And in a view layout (such as `_Layout.cshtml`), render the AI JavaScript code:

```
@Html.ApplicationInsightsJavaScript(TelemetryConfiguration)
```

ASP.NET Core 2.x

In ASP.NET Core 2.x, you do need to enable exception and request telemetry explicitly, it is done for you automatically, and the code for `_ViewImports.cshtml` is also different:

```
@using Microsoft.ApplicationInsights.AspNetCore
@inject JavaScriptSnippet snippet
```

In the layout view (probably `_Layout.cshtml`):

```
@Html.Raw(snippet.FullScript)
```

Custom events

You can send custom data using the `TelemetryClient` API. Essentially, you build an instance of `TelemetryClient`:

```
var client = new TelemetryClient();
client.InstrumentationKey =
this.Configuration["ApplicationInsights:InstrumentationKey"];
```

You have the following methods, from the documentation (https://docs.microsoft.com/en-us/azure/application-insights/app-insights-api-custom-events-metrics):

- `TrackPageView`: Pages
- `TrackEvent`: User actions and custom events
- `TrackMetric`: Performance measurements
- `TrackException`: Exceptions

- `TrackRequest`: Frequency and duration of server requests for performance analysis
- `TrackTrace`: Diagnostic log messages
- `TrackDependency`: Duration and frequency of calls to external components that your app depends on

You can call one of its `Track*` methods, such as `TrackEvent`:

```
client.TrackEvent("Product added to basket");
```

You can also call a specific metric:

```
client.TrackMetric("TotalCost", 100.0);
```

You can request information:

```
var now = DateTimeOffset.Now;
var timer = Stopwatch.StartNew();
//issue call
client.TrackRequest("Searching for product", now, timer.Elapsed, "OK",
true);
```

To send an exception:

```
client.TrackException(ex);
```

To send dependency (any called code that is not our own) elapsed time (similar to request tracking):

```
var success = false;
var startTime = DateTime.UtcNow;
var timer = Stopwatch.StartNew();
var id = Guid.NewGuid();

try
{
  success = orderService.ProcessOrder();
}
finally
{
  timer.Stop();
  telemetry.TrackDependency("Order Service", $"Order id {id}", startTime,
timer.Elapsed, success);
}
```

To send a custom trace message:

```
client.TrackTrace("Processing order", SeverityLevel.Warning, new
Dictionary<string,string> { {"Order", id} });
```

Or even a page view:

```
client.TrackPageView("ShoppingBag");
```

You can also group together several related events, inside a scope:

```
using (var operation = telemetry.StartOperation<RequestTelemetry>("Order
Processing"))
{
  //one or more of Track* methods
}
```

Because AI batches data to send, at any point you can force this to be flushed to Azure:

```
client.Flush();
```

All of these events will be made available in the AI console:

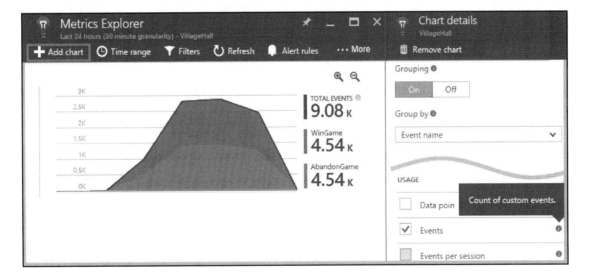

The AppInsights dashboard can display different visualizations of events:

Health checking

Microsoft has been working on a health checking framework for ASP.NET Core called `Microsoft.AspNetCore.HealthChecks`. It provides a standard and pluggable way to check the state of services on which your app depends and it includes checkers for the following:

- SQL Server databases
- HTTP endpoints
- Azure storage services
- Memory status

This is not a feature of ASP.NET itself, but since normally any complex web app has external dependencies, this may come in handy for checking their statuses before taking some actions.

After adding the core NuGet package, you will need to add the ones for the checks that you're interested in, such as SQL Server or HTTP. We register those in the `ConfigureServices` method:

```
services.AddHealthChecks(checks =>
{
  checks
    .AddUrlCheck("GitHub", "https://github.com")
    .AddSqlCheck("Database", "Data Source=.;Integrated Security=SSPI;")
    .AddWorkingSetCheck(1024);
});
```

In this example we are registering three checks:

- One for the GitHub site
- Another one for a database connection
- The final one for the working set memory for the current process

We can then have an instance of `IHealthCheckService` injected into our classes and see if everything is `OK`:

```
var </span>timedTokenSource = new
CancellationTokenSource(TimeSpan.FromSeconds(3));
var checkResult = await
_healthCheck.CheckHealthAsync(timedTokenSource.Token);

if (checkResult.CheckStatus != CheckStatus.Healthy)
{
  //Houston, we have a problem
}
```

This code waits for at most three seconds while checking the status of all the registered health checks. The result can be one of the following:

- `Unknown`: The status is unknown, possibly due to a timeout
- `Unhealthy`: At least one of the services is not `OK`
- `Healthy`: Everything seems to be `OK`
- `Warning`: Everything is `OK`, but with some warnings

There is much more to it, including the following:

- Iterating through all of the registered health checks
- Check groups
- Custom health checks
- Exposing our app as an health server

 All of this, however, is outside the scope of this book, so I advise you to take a look at the source code for the `Microsoft.AspNetCore.HealthChecks` package.

Putting it all together

Common logging is a must-have in .NET Core. The infrastructure, although limited--does not support structure logging out of the box, for example--is built-in, pluggable, and DI-friendly. Use it for most common logging uses. Please explore all the logging providers available to see whether there is one that meets your requirements. Special hosting providers, such as Azure or AWS, offer their own packages, which you should leverage for best results.

Diagnostic tracing offers the advantage that you can call methods with discrete parameters, which is an advantage as it can lead to more meaningful logs. You can use it to see exactly what middleware is being executed and how much time each step takes.

The other options shown, adding middleware or action filters, are also probably worth exploring, especially action filters.

Telemetry is essential for enterprise applications working 24/7, because it gives you an overview of how things behave during long periods of time and you can set alerts to respond to emergency situations.

Summary

In this chapter, we had a look at the different logging and diagnostic options available in ASP.NET Core. In the next chapter, we will see how we can perform unit tests for all the features discussed in the previous chapters.

11
Testing

In the previous chapters, we saw how to build things. We all know that we should be testing our applications before we consider them done. What happens is, applications evolve and stuff that used to work at some point in time may no longer work now. Because of that, we set up tests that can run automatically and check whether everything is still working as it should. In this chapter, we will have a look at two approaches for executing these tests.

We will cover the following topics in this chapter:

- Unit testing principles
- Using xUnit
- Mocking objects
- Assertions
- User interface tests
- Integration tests

Unit testing

Unit tests are not new. Essentially, a unit test is designed to test a feature of your system, in isolation, to prove that it is working as it should. The **F.I.R.S.T Principles of Unit Testing** (https://github.com/ghsukumar/SFDC_Best_Practices/wiki/F.I.R.S.T-Principles-of-Unit-Testing) state that they should be the following:

- **Fast**: They should execute fast, meaning, they shouldn't do any complex or lengthy operations
- **Isolated/Independent**: A unit test should not depend on other systems and should provide results independent of any specific context

- **Repeatable**: A unit test should yield the same result whenever it executes, if nothing changed on the implementation
- **Self-validating**: They should be self-sufficient, that is, should not require any manual inspection or analysis
- **Thorough/Timely**: They should cover all the important stuff, even if not required to be 100% of the code

In a nutshell, a unit test should run fast so that we don't have to wait a long time for the results and should be coded so that the essential features are tested and do not depend on external variables; also, they should not produce any side effects and it should be possible to repeat them and get the same results all the time.

Some people even advocate starting to implement unit tests before the actual code. This has the benefit that the code is testable, after all it was designed with testing in mind, and once we have implemented it we already have the unit tests to go along. It is called **Test-Driven Design** (**TDD**). While I am not a die-hard defender of TDD, I see advantages in it. Development using TDD usually goes in a cycle known as **Red-Green-Refactor**, which means that tests are first red, meaning they fail, then they are green, they pass, and only then, when all is working properly, do we need to refactor the code so as to improve it. Read more about TDD here: `https://technologyconversations.com/2014/09/30/test-driven-development-tdd`.

We usually rely on unit test frameworks to help us perform these tests and get their results. There are several such frameworks for .NET Core, including the following:

- **MSTest**: This is Microsoft's own test framework; it is open source and is made available at `https://github.com/Microsoft/testfx`
- **xUnit**: A popular framework that is even used by Microsoft; also available at `https://xunit.github.io`
- **NUnit**: One of the oldest unit test frameworks; available at `http://nunit.org`

They are all open source and their features are similar, so let's pick one, xUnit. You can find a good comparison of the three frameworks here: `https://xunit.github.io/docs/comparisons.html`.

A note: if you prefer to start your projects from the console instead of Visual Studio, dotnet has templates for both MSTest and xUnit, just pick one:

```
dotnet new xunit
dotnet new mstest
```

xUnit

In order to use xUnit, you need to add a couple of NuGet packages:

- xunit
- xunit.runner.visualstudio
- Microsoft.NET.Test.Sdk

The first is the framework itself, the other two are required for the Visual Studio integration; yes, all of these frameworks integrate nicely with Visual Studio! Visual Studio 2017 even provides an xUnit test project template, which is even nicer!

Let's create a unit test project; because we will be targeting ASP.NET Core features, .NET Core Apps, we need to create a unit test project that also targets .NET Core Apps, netcoreapp2.0 or netcoreapp1.0. In this project, we add a reference to our web app and we create a class. Let's call it ControllerTests.

In this class, we add this code:

```
public class ControllerTests
{
  [Fact]
  public void CanExecuteIndex()
  {
    var controller = new HomeController();
    var result = controller.Index();

    Assert.NotNull(result);
  }
}
```

This is a very simple test, we are creating a `HomeController` instance, executing its `Index` method and checking that no exception is thrown (implicit, otherwise the test would fail) and that its result is not null. Notice the `[Fact]` attribute in the `CanExecuteIndex` method: it is an indication that this method contains a unit test, and it is captured by the **Test Explorer** feature of Visual Studio:

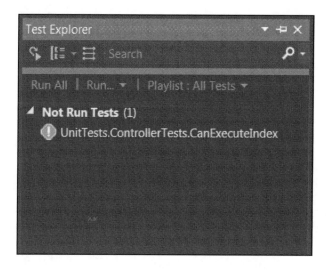

Visual Studio will be able to find any test method provided that the following is true:

- They are declared in a non-abstract class
- They are public
- They have either the `[Fact]` or `[Theory]` attributes (more on this in a second)

From here, you can run or debug your tests; try placing a breakpoint inside the `CanExecuteIndex` method. It is called automatically by Visual Studio and it considers that the test passes if no exception is thrown. Controllers are usually good candidates for unit testing, but you should also unit test your services and business objects as well. Remember, focus on the most critical classes first, and if you have the resources, time, developers, proceed to the less critical code.

Besides `[Fact]`, you have another option for declaring a method to be a unit test, `[Theory]`. This one is even more interesting, as you can supply parameters to your test method, and xUnit will take care of calling it with them! See for yourself:

```
[Theory]
[InlineData(1, 2, 3)]
[InlineData(0, 10, 10)]
public void Add(int x, int y, int z)
```

```
{
  Assert.Equals(x + y, z);
}
```

This example is a bit simple, but I think you get the picture! `[InlineData]` should have as many parameters as the method it is declared on. As we have two `[InlineData]` we have two datasets, so the method will be called twice, one for each of the values in one of the `[InlineData]` attributes.

Or, if you want to test an action method model you could have the following:

```
var controller = new ShoppingController();
var result = controller.ShoppingBag();
var viewResult = Assert.IsType<ViewResult>(result);
var model = Assert.IsType<ShoppingBag>(viewResult.ViewData.Model);
```

You can have as many test methods as you like, and you can run one or more from the Visual Studio Test Explorer. Each of your methods should be responsible for testing one feature, so make sure you don't forget that! Normally, unit tests are set up according to **Arrange-Act-Assert** (**AAA**), meaning first we setup (arrange) our objects, then we call some code upon them (act) and then we check its results (assert). Do keep this mnemonic in mind!

If the class where you have the unit tests implements `IDisposable`, its `Dispose` method will be called automatically at the end of all tests. Also, the constructor of the class will be run, of course, so it needs to be public and have no parameters. You can add any instance fields and they will be made available to all of the test methods.

There are several utility methods in the xUnit `Assert` class that will throw an exception if a condition is not met:

- `All`: All items in the collection match a given condition
- `Collection`: All items in the collection match all of the given conditions
- `Contains`: The collection contains a given item
- `DoesNotContain`: A collection does not contain a given item
- `DoesNotMatch`: A string does not match a given regular expression
- `Empty`: The collection is empty
- `EndsWith`: A string ends with some content
- `Equal`: Two collections are equal (contain exactly the same elements)
- `Equals`: Two items are equal
- `False`: The expression is false

- `InRange`: A comparable value is in a range
- `IsAssignableFrom`: An object is assignable from a given type
- `IsNotType`: An object is not of a given type
- `IsType`: An object is of a given type
- `Matches`: A string matches a given regular expression
- `NotEmpty`: A collection is not empty
- `NotEqual`: Two objects are not equal
- `NotInRange`: A comparable value is not in a range
- `NotNull`: Value is not null
- `NotSame`: Two references are not the same object
- `NotStrictEqual`: Verifies that two objects are not equal, using the default comparer (`Object.Equals`)
- `Null`: Checks that a value is null
- `ProperSubset`: Verifies that a set is a proper subset (is contained) of another set
- `ProperSuperset`: Verifies that a set is a proper superset (contains) of another set
- `PropertyChanged`/`PropertyChangedAsync`: Verifies that a property was changed
- `Raises`/`RaisesAsync`: Verifies that an action raises an event
- `RaisesAny`/`RaisesAnyAsync`: Verifies that an action raises one of the given events
- `Same`: Two references point to the same object
- `Single`: The collection contains one and only one item
- `StartsWith`: Verifies that a string starts with another string
- `StrictEqual`: Verifies if two objects are equal, using the default comparer (`Object.Equals`)
- `Subset`: Verifies that a set is a subset (is contained) of another set
- `Superset`: Verifies that a set is a superset (contains) of another set
- `Throws`/`ThrowsAsync`: Verifies that an action throws an exception
- `ThrowsAny`/`ThrowsAnyAsync`: Verifies that an action throws one of the given exceptions
- `True`: The expression is true

Essentially all these methods are variations of `True`; you want to assert that some condition is true or not. Do not have lots of assertions in your unit test method, make sure only the essential is tested, like, check that a method returns a non-empty or non-null collection in a test, and have other test check for the correctness of the values returned. If you want to test different scenarios or return values, create another unit test.

Injecting dependencies

It may not always be as simple; for example, the class you wish to test may contain dependencies. By far, the best way to inject dependencies into your controller is through its controller. Here is an example for a controller that does logging:

```
ILogger<HomeController> logger = ...;
var controller = new HomeController(logger);
```

Fortunately, the `RequestServices` property of the `HttpContext` is itself settable, meaning, you can build your own instance with the services that you want:

```
var services = new ServiceCollection();
services.AddSingleton<IMyService>(new MyServiceImplementation());

var serviceProvider = services.BuildServiceProvider();

controller.HttpContext.RequestServices = serviceProvider;
```

If your code depends on the current user being authenticated or possessing certain claims, you need to set up an `HttpContext` object, which you can do like this:

```
controller.ControllerContext = new ControllerContext
{
  HttpContext = new DefaultHttpContext
  {
    User = new ClaimsPrincipal(new ClaimsIdentity(new Claim[]
    {
      new Claim(ClaimTypes.Name, "username")
    }, "Password"))
  }
};
```

This way, inside your controller, the `HttpContext` and `User` properties will be initialized properly. In the `DefaultHttpContext` class's constructor, you can also pass along a collection of features (the `HttpContext.Features` collection):

```
var features = new FeatureCollection();
features.Set<IMyFeature>(new MyFeatureImplementation());

var ctx = new DefaultHttpContext(features);
```

By using a custom features collection, you can inject values for lots of features, such as the following:

- **Sessions:** `ISessionFeature`
- **Cookies:** `IRequestCookiesFeature`, `IResponseCookiesFeature`
- **Request:** `IHttpRequestFeature`
- **Response:** `IResponseCookiesFeature`
- **Connections:** `IHttpConnectionFeature`

Either by providing your own implementation in the features collection or by assigning values to the existing one, you can inject values for your tests, so as to simulate real-life scenarios. For example, suppose your controller needs a specific cookie:

```
var features = new FeatureCollection();
var cookies = new RequestCookieCollection(new Dictionary<string, string> {
{ "username", "dummy" } });
features.Set<IRequestCookiesFeature>(new RequestCookiesFeature(cookies));

var context = new DefaultHttpContext(features);
```

One of the challenges of dependencies is that because we are executing a limited subset of our system, it may not be easy to get proper functioning objects, we may need to replace them with substitutes. We will see now how we can get over this.

Mocking

Mocks, fakes, and stubs are similar concepts that essentially mean that an object is substituted with another one that mimics its behavior. Why would we do that? Well because we are testing our code in isolation, and we are assuming that third party code works as advertised, so we do not care about it, so we can just replace these other dependencies with dummies.

For a comparison of these terms, please see `https://blog.pragmatists.`
`com/test-doubles-fakes-mocks-and-stubs-1a7491dfa3da`.

We use mocking frameworks for this purpose, and there are a few available for .NET Core as well, such as the following:

- **Moq**: `https://github.com/moq/moq4`
- **NSubstitute**: `http://nsubstitute.github.io`
- **FakeItEasy**: `https://fakeiteasy.github.io`

Let's pick **Moq**. In order to use it, add the `Moq` NuGet package to your project. Then, when you need to mimic the functionality of a given type, you can create a mock of it and set up its behavior:

```
//create the mock
var mock = new Mock<ILogger<HomeController>>();
//setup an implementation for the Log method
mock.Setup(x => x.Log(LogLevel.Critical, new EventId(), "", null, null));

//get the mock
ILogger<HomeController> logger = mock.Object;
//call the mocked method with some parameters
logger.Log(LogLevel.Critical, new EventId(2), "Hello, Moq!", null, null);
```

You set up a method by passing an expression consisting of a method or property call with appropriate parameter types, regardless of its actual value. You can pass the mocked object as a dependency of your services or controllers, run your tests and then make sure that the mocked method was called:

```
mock.Verify(x => x.Log(LogLevel.Critical, new EventId(), "", null, null));
```

It is also possible to set up a response object, for example, if we are mocking `HttpContext`:

```
var mock = new Mock<HttpContext>();
mock.Setup(x => x.User).Returns(new ClaimsPrincipal(new
ClaimsIdentity(new[] { new
    Claim(ClaimTypes.Name, "username") }, "Password", ClaimTypes.Name,
"Admin")));

var context = mock.Object;
var user = context.User;

Assert.NotNull(user);
Assert.True(user.Identity.IsAuthenticated);
```

```
Assert.True(user.HasClaim(ClaimTypes.Name, "username"));
```

Here you can see that we are supplying the return value for a call to the `User` property, and we are returning a pre-built `ClaimsPrincipal` object with all the bells and whistles.

Of course, there's so much more about Moq, but I think this should be enough to get you started.

Assertions

Your unit test will fail if any exception is thrown. So you can either roll out your own exception-throwing code or you can rely on one of the assertion methods provided by your unit test framework, all offer similar methods.

 For more complex scenarios, it may pay off to use an assertion library. `FluentAssertions` is one such library that happens to play nicely with .NET Core. Get it from NuGet as `FluentAssertions` and from GitHub at `https://github.com/fluentassertions/fluentassertions`.

With it, you can have assertions such as the following:

```
int x = GetResult();
x
  .Should()
  .BeGreaterOrEqualTo(100)
  .And
  .BeLessOrEqualTo(1000)
  .And
  .NotBe(150);
```

As you can see, you can combine lots of expressions related to the same object type, numeric values have comparisons, strings have matches, and more. You can also throw in property change detection:

```
svc.ShouldRaisePropertyChangeFor(x => x.SomeProperty);
```

Or execution time as well:

```
svc
  .ExecutionTimeOf(s => s.LengthyMethod())
  .ShouldNotExceed(500.Milliseconds());
```

There's a lot more to it, so I advise you to have a look at the documentation made available at `http://fluentassertions.com`.

User interface

The unit tests we've seen so far are for testing APIs, like business methods, logic, and more. But it is also possible to test user interface. Let's see how using Selenium, it is a portable software-testing framework for web applications and there is a .NET port of it, `Selenium.WebDriver`. Besides this one, we will need one of:

- `Selenium.Chrome.WebDriver`: for Chrome
- `Selenium.Firefox.WebDriver`: for Firefox
- `Selenium.WebDriver.MicrosoftWebDriver`: for IE and Edge

We start by creating a driver:

```
using (var driver = (IWebDriver) new
ChromeDriver(Environment.CurrentDirectory))
{
  //...
}
```

Notice the `Environment.CurrentDirectory` parameter; it specifies the path where the driver can find the `chromedriver.exe` file, `geckodriver.exe` for Firefox or `MicrosoftWebDriver.exe`, in the case of IE/Edge. These executables are added automatically by the NuGet packages. Also, if you don't dispose of the driver, the window will remain open after the unit test finishes. You can also call `Quit` at any time, to close the browser.

Now, we can navigate to some page:

```
driver
  .Navigate()
  .GoToUrl("http://www.google.com");
```

And find some element from its name:

```
var elm = driver.FindElement(By.Name("q"));
```

Besides the name, we can also search by:

- **Id**: `By.Id`
- **CSS class**: `By.ClassName`
- **CSS selector**: `By.CssSelector`
- **Tag name**: `By.TagName`
- **Link text**: `By.LinkText`
- **Partial link text**: `By.PartialLinkText`
- **XPath**: `By.XPath`

Once we find an element, we can access its properties:

```
var attr = elm.GetAttribute("class");
var css = elm.GetCssValue("display");
var prop = elm.GetProperty("enabled");
```

Send keystrokes:

```
elm.SendKeys("asp.net");
```

Or click:

```
elm.Click();
```

As we know, page loading can take some time, so we can configure the default time to wait for it, probably before we do a `GoToUrl`:

```
var timeouts = driver.Manage().Timeouts();
timeouts.ImplicitWait = TimeSpan.FromSeconds(1);
timeouts.PageLoad = TimeSpan.FromSeconds(5);
```

`ImplicitWait` is just a time that Selenium waits before searching for an element, `PageLoad` I'm sure you can understand.

If we need to wait for some period of time, like until some AJAX request finishes, we can do this:

```
var waitForElement = new WebDriverWait(driver, TimeSpan.FromSeconds(5));
var logo =
waitForElement.Until(ExpectedConditions.ElementIsVisible(By.Id("hplogo")));
```

The condition passed to `ExpectedConditions` can be one of:

- `AlertIsPresent`
- `AlertState`
- `ElementExists`
- `ElementIsVisible`
- `ElementSelectionStateToBe`
- `ElementToBeClickable`
- `ElementToBeSelected`
- `FrameToBeAvailableAndSwitchToIt`
- `InvisibilityOfElementLocated`
- `InvisibilityOfElementWithText`
- `PresenceOfAllElementsLocatedBy`
- `StalenessOf`
- `TextToBePresentInElement`
- `TextToBePresentInElementLocated`
- `TextToBePresentInElementValue`
- `TitleContains`
- `TitleIs`
- `UrlContains`
- `UrlMatches`
- `UrlToBe`
- `VisibilityOfAllElementsLocatedBy`

As you can see, you have a wealth of conditions that you can use. If the condition is not met before the timer expires, then the value returned by `Until` is `null`.

Hopefully, with this you will be able to write unit tests that can check the UI aspects of your sites. Of course they need to point to a live environment, so in this case the tests won't be self-contained. When we talk about integration tests we will see how to overcome this.

Using the command line

The `dotnet` command line tool is the Swiss army knife of .NET Core development, and as such it has full support for running unit tests. If you are on the project folder where you have your unit tests, just run `dotnet test`, and off you go:

```
C:\Users\Projects\MyApp\UnitTests>dotnet test
Build started, please wait...
Build completed.

Test run for
C:\Users\Projects\MyApp\UnitTests\bin\Debug\netcoreapp2.0\UnitTests.dll(.NE
TCoreApp,Version=v2.0)

Microsoft (R) Test Execution Command Line Tool Version 15.3.0-
preview-20170628-02
Copyright (c) Microsoft Corporation. All rights reserved.

Starting test execution, please wait...
[xUnit.net 00:00:00.3769248] Discovering: UnitTests
[xUnit.net 00:00:00.4364853] Discovered:  UnitTests
[xUnit.net 00:00:00.4720996] Starting:    UnitTests
[xUnit.net 00:00:00.5778764] Finished:    UnitTests

Total tests: 10. Passed: 10. Failed: 0. Skipped: 0.
Test Run Successful.
Test execution time: 1,0031 Seconds
```

Since the project is setup to use xUnit (the `xunit.runner.visualstudio` package), `dotnet` is happy to use it automatically.

If you wish to see all the tests that are defined, run `dotnet test --list-tests` instead.

Limitations of unit tests

As useful as unit tests are, keep in mind that they are used essentially for regression testing, and they have some limitations:

- You cannot test some ASP.NET features, such as filters or views, for example

- External systems are mocked, so you only have a limited view of a small part of the system
- They generally do not cover user interfaces, although some frameworks exist that can do it (at this time, not for .NET Core)

In the next section, we will see how we can overcome the first two.

Integration testing

Microsoft makes available as part of ASP.NET Core the `Microsoft.AspNetCore.TestHost` NuGet package. Essentially, it lets us host a web application so that we can execute tests over it as we would in a real-life server, taking out, of course, performance and scalability issues.

In your unit test project, create a class like this:

```
public class IntegrationTests
{
  private readonly TestServer _server;
  private readonly HttpClient _client;

  public IntegrationTests()
  {
    var asm = typeof(Startup).GetTypeInfo().Assembly.GetName().Name;
    var path = PlatformServices.Default.Application.ApplicationBasePath;
    var contentPath = Path.GetFullPath(Path.Combine(path,
$@"..\..\..\..\{asm}"));

    this._server = new TestServer(new WebHostBuilder()
      .UseContentRoot(contentPath)
      .UseStartup<Startup>()
      .UseEnvironment("Development"));

    this._client = this._server.CreateClient();
  }

  [Fact]
  public async Task CanInvokeController()
  {
    var response = await this._client.GetAsync("/Home/About");

    response.EnsureSuccessStatusCode();

    var content = await response.Content.ReadAsStringAsync();
```

```
        Assert.Contains("Welcome", content);
    }
}
```

So, what do we have here? Well, we are setting up a `TestServer` using the same `Startup` class that is used for the proper app, we get an HTTP client reference to point to it and we issue a request. After we get the response we validate its status code (`EnsureSuccessStatusCode` checks that we don't have a `4xx` or `5xx`) and we actually have a look at the returned contents. Mind you, here we do not work with `IActionResults` or the likes, but with HTTP responses. We need to set up the content root to be the one of the target project, because in case we are returning a view, `TestServer` needs to know from where to get the view files, hence the nasty hardcoded string that points to the referenced project/assembly's root folder (not it's `wwwroot`).

The advantage of this approach is that we are really testing our controllers (and all their services) in a web-like scenario, meaning filters will be run, configuration will be loaded as usual, and all that jazz. This plays nicely with unit tests, as you can see from this example.

 Notice that in this example, the unit test method is asynchronous; this is supported by xUnit and the other unit test frameworks.

Putting it all together

You definitely should have unit tests for your apps. Whether you follow TDD strictly or not these can be very useful, especially for regression tests. Most continuous integration tools out there fully support running unit tests. Just don't try to cover everything, focus on the critical parts of your app and if time allows, then proceed to the other parts. It is unreasonable to think that we will have 100% coverage in most projects, so we need to make decisions. Mocking frameworks play an essential role here as they allow us to simulate third-party services nicely.

Automated integration tests as we saw here allow us to test features that aren't available in unit tests, and these cover another part of our needs.

Summary

This chapter covered ways to test our apps, either parts of them in isolation or the system as a whole. We didn't cover client-side unit tests, as these will be discussed in the next chapter.

12
Client-Side Development

Client-side development is the counterpart to server-side development; in modern web applications, one cannot exist without the other. Although this book is primarily about ASP.NET Core, a server-side technology, chances are we will be working with JavaScript or CSS. Visual Studio (and Visual Studio Code too) includes some features that make our life easier and ASP.NET Core introduced interoperability with Node.js, something that wasn't possible earlier, including built-in package managers for NPM and Bower (see `https://webtooling.visualstudio.com/package-managers`) and task runners for Gulp and Grunt (`https://webtooling.visualstudio.com/task-runners`). Continue reading to see what all this is about.

We will cover the following topics in this chapter:

- Using Bower
- Using Node.js
    - Calling Node from .NET Core
    - Pre-compiling views
    - Using WebPack
    - SPA templates
- Using Gulp
- Using Grunt
- Using TypeScipt
- Using Less
- Putting it all together

Using Bower

Bower is a package manager for client-side libraries. It is similar to NuGet, but for JavaScript and CSS. You may recall that in recent versions of Visual Studio, its templates for ASP.NET applications used to include libraries such as jQuery; well this is no longer the case, as NuGet is left for .NET, and JavaScript and CSS now use Bower. Visual Studio 2017 supports it: `https://webtooling.visualstudio.com/package-managers/bower`. Take a look at the following screenshot:

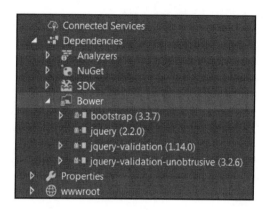

Bower is free and open source and its site is `https://bower.io`. It is a Node.js tool, but that is transparent to us. Visual Studio has a user interface for managing Bower packages very similar to that of NuGet:

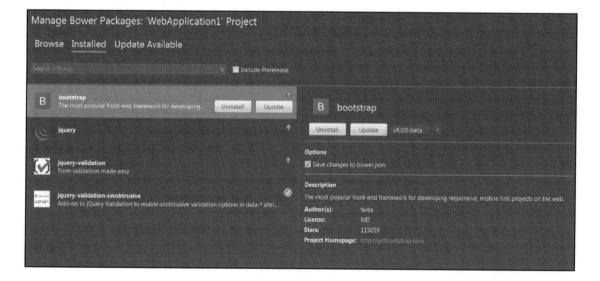

The actual settings are stored in a `bower.json` file:

```
bower.json
Schema: http://json.schemastore.org/bower
{
    "name": "asp.net",
    "private": true,
    "dependencies": {
        "bootstrap": "3.3.7",
        "jquery": "2.2.0",
        "jquery-validation": "1.14.0",
        "jquery-validation-unobtrusive": "3.2.6"
    }
}
```

That's pretty much it; by adding a reference to a Bower-stored package, Visual Studio makes sure it is downloaded when the project is either run or deployed, its assets are stored underneath a `lib` folder below `wwwroot`. Mind you, the deployment structure does not include the version, so it's difficult to tell, without looking at the `bower.json` file, which version we have.

It is curious that, although Bower is still up and running, their authors now actually recommend the usage of **yarn** (`https://yarnpkg.com`) and **WebPack** (`https://webpack.js.org`) for new projects that include front-end instead of Bower. As of now, Visual Studio does not yet offer direct support for these.

For additional information on how to use Bower and Visual Studio together, please refer to `https://webtooling.visualstudio.com/package-managers/bower`.

Using Node.js

Most of you will be familiar with **Node.js** by now, it is essentially JavaScript on the server-side. It is an open-source project that, at least for now, uses Chrome's V8 JavaScript engine to run JavaScript out of the context of a browser. It has become extremely popular arguably due to its use of the JavaScript language, some may not agree, but essentially because of its speed and the huge amount of libraries made available through **Node Package Manager (NPM)**, currently more than 550,000. You can find more information about Node.js and NPM on their sites, `https://nodejs.org` and `https://www.npmjs.com`, and about the Visual Studio support for NPM here: `https://webtooling.visualstudio.com/package-managers/npm`.

You can install the Node.js support for Visual Studio through the VS installer tool, but you will also need to have Node.js itself installed, which you can get from `https://nodejs.org`. After you have it installed, you get Visual Studio templates for creating Node.js projects:

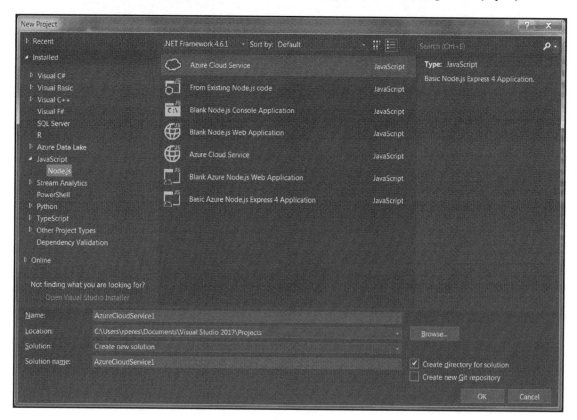

You can also add Node.js files to an ASP.NET Core project, but unlike Bower, there is no obvious NPM explorer in Visual Studio until you add a `package.json` file and reference some package; the NPM node appears under project **Dependencies**:

Node.js files are kept in a `node_modules` folder outside `wwwroot`; this is because these files are usually not meant to be served to the browser. You need to explicitly restore the packages before you can use them.

Calling Node from .NET Core

Steve Sanderson, of Knockout.js (`http://knockoutjs.com/`) fame, started a pet project called *NodeServices* a few years ago. It was made available as `Microsoft.AspNetCore.NodeServices` a few years ago from NuGet, and it is now part of the ASP.NET Core ecosystem. In a nutshell, it allows us to call Node.js code from ASP.NET Core. Just think about it, we get all the benefits of both ASP.NET Core and Node.js (and NPM) at the same time!

In order to use NodeServices, we need to register its services in `ConfigureServices`:

```
services.AddNodeServices();
```

After this, we can inject an instance of `INodeServices` into our components, controllers, view components, tag helpers, middleware classes, and more. This interface exposes a single method, `InvokeAsync`, which we can use to invoke one of the modules that we have locally installed. An example might be:

```
var result = nodeServices.InvokeAsync<int>("Algebra.js", 10, 20);
```

The `Algebra.js` file would then need to export a default module, something along these lines:

```
module.exports = function(callback, a, b) {
    var result = a + b;
    callback(null, result);
};
```

NodeServices expects the default export to return a function that takes a callback, implicitly passed by `InvokeAsync`, and any number of parameters. Make note of this, these parameters should be of primitive types, but you can pass along a JSON-formatted object and have your Node.js code convert it. You can do pretty much whatever you want from your Node.js code, including referencing other modules. At the end of the default export you call the implicit callback function with an optional error parameter and the value to return to .NET Code; if you pass an error, the .NET code will raise an exception.

Pre-compiling views

Some **Single Page Application (SPA)** client-side technologies, such as Angular or React, have view templates that can be pre-compiled on the server-side, thus decreasing the startup speed; behind the scene this uses Node.js. It turns out that you can leverage NodeServices to precompile your views for ASP.NET Core.

What you need is the `Microsoft.AspNetCore.SpaServices`. After you add a reference to it you have two options:

- Explicitly compile your templates in code (possibly in a controller)
- Add a tag helper that compiles it when the view is accessed

For the first option we need to get hold of an `ISpaPrerenderer` instance, which we can get from the dependency injection framework:

```
var result = await prerenderer.RenderToString("./Node/PrerenderPage.js");
this.ViewData["PrerenderedHtml"] = result.Html;
this.ViewData["PrerenderedGlobals"] =
result.CreateGlobalsAssignmentScript();
```

Then in your view, you need something like this:

```
@Html.Raw(ViewData["PrerenderedHtml"])
<script>@Html.Raw(ViewData["PrerenderedGlobals"])</script>
```

The two calls are for injecting the HTML and any JavaScript code that the compiled template may define. An example script might be:

```
var createServerRenderer = require('aspnet-
prerendering').createServerRenderer;
module.exports = createServerRenderer(function(params) {
  return new Promise(function (resolve, reject) {
   var message = 'The HTML was returned by the prerendering function. '
    + 'The boot function received the following params:'
    + '<pre>' + JSON.stringify(params, null, 4) + '</pre>';
   resolve({
     html: '<h1>Hello, world!</h1>' + message,
     globals: { data: { version: process.version } }
   });
  });
});
```

As you can see, you will need the `aspnet-prerendering` NPM package first; make sure it is registered in your `package.json` file. When the code is rendered you will have a global data variable with a field of version.

The other option is to add a tag helper (needs registration first) that points to a template to be compiled on the server and rendered to the HTML result:

```
<div id="react-app" asp-prerender-module="main-server" asp-prerender-
data="{}">Loading...</div>
```

This will execute the `main-server.js` file using Node.js on the server; if you noticed the `asp-prerender-data` attribute, it is optional and allows you to pass any arbitrary value to the script. In the previous code example, it is the parameter passed as the parameter to the `createServerRenderer` function.

To register the SPA tag helpers, add this to your `_ViewImports.cshtml` file:

```
@addTagHelper "*, Microsoft.AspNetCore.Mvc.TagHelpers"
@addTagHelper "*, Microsoft.AspNetCore.SpaServices"
```

Using WebPack

WebPack is now very popular as the *de facto* standard for bundling and transpiling JavaScript. Using WebPack you can have your application build automatically your views whenever the code changes on the server, without the need to explicitly reload. It is open source and available at `https://webpack.github.io`.

You will need the `aspnet-webpack` NPM package and to register the WebPack middleware:

```
if (env.IsDevelopment())
{
  //should be called before UseStaticFiles
  app.UseWebpackDevMiddleware();
}

app.UseStaticFiles();
```

If you wish to enable **Hot Module Replacement (HMR)**, do this instead:

```
app.UseWebpackDevMiddleware(new WebpackDevMiddlewareOptions {
  HotModuleReplacement = true
});
```

You will need to install the `webpack-hot-middleware` NPM module first.

 To learn more about WebPack's HMR, please have a look at `https://webpack.github.io/docs/hot-module-replacement.html`.

SPA templates

There's another package, `Microsoft.AspNetCore.SpaTemplates`, where you can find templates for the `dotnet new` command. With this installed, you will be able to create skeleton apps for:

- **Angular 2** (angular)
- **Aurelia** (aurelia)
- **Knockout** (knockout)
- **React** (react)
- **React+Redux** (reactredux)
- **Vue** (vue)

Just do the following:

```
dotnet new --install Microsoft.AspNetCore.SpaTemplates::*
```

You will get all of the templates. Then, for example do the following:

```
dotnet new angular
dotnet restore
npm install
```

You will get a nice project skeleton using Angular waiting to be complete!

Using Gulp

Gulp is a popular build tool for client-side assets. It is open source and it is available from `https://gulpjs.com`. Gulp allows you to define tasks in pure JavaScript.

Visual Studio automatically recognizes any build tasks declared in the `gulpfile.js` file. However, you need first to install the `gulp` NPM module. All tasks defined in `gulpfile.js` will show up in the **Task Runner Explorer** window:

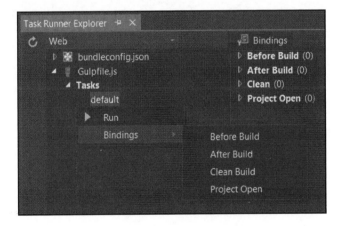

From there you can run any of the tasks or set them for pre or post-build execution. For more info, have a look at `https://webtooling.visualstudio.com/task-runners/gulp`.

Using Grunt

Grunt is an alternative build library to Gulp. Grunt is also open source and is available from `https://gruntjs.com`. You also need to install the `grunt` NPM module before using it.

Grunt relies on a `gruntfile.js` file, which Visual Studio also automatically recognizes:

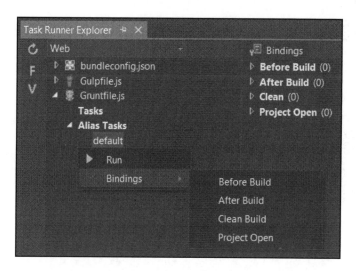

It allows you to define tasks that Visual Studio can trigger, for example, should you wish to minimize all `.js` files so that you can distribute them, you could define a `uglify` task using the `grunt-contrib-uglify` NPM module:

```
module.exports = function(grunt) {
  grunt.initConfig({
    pkg: grunt.file.readJSON('package.json'),
    uglify: {
      options: {
        banner: '/*! <%= pkg.name %> <%= grunt.template.today("yyyy-mm-dd") %> */\n'
      },
      build: {
        src: 'src/<%= pkg.name %>.js',
        dest: 'build/<%= pkg.name %>.min.js'
      }
    }
  });

  grunt.loadNpmTasks('grunt-contrib-uglify');
```

```
    grunt.registerTask('default', ['uglify']);
};
```

This example registers a task called `uglify` that takes a source package name from a JSON file and minimizes it, adding a header (a banner) with the package name and the current day.

For more information on how to use Grunt with Visual Studio, checkout `https://webtooling.visualstudio.com/task-runners/grunt`.

Using TypeScript

TypeScript is a JavaScript object-oriented superset. It is an open-source language developed by Microsoft that offers features that exist in other non-scripted object-oriented languages such as modules, classes, interfaces, strong typing, templates, different visibility levels, method overloading, and so on. By coding in TypeScript, you get all the benefits of these languages but, after the code is transpiled (cross-language compiled), you still get your daddy's JavaScript, which you can use in both the client and the server-side (Node.js). See more about TypeScript in `https://www.typescriptlang.org` and get it from GitHub at `https://github.com/Microsoft/TypeScript`. Alternatively, if you want to play with it a bit first, you should try the TypeScript Playground: `http://www.typescriptlang.org/play`.

Visual Studio has two extensions, **TypeScript Build for Microsoft Visual Studio** and **TypeScript for Microsoft Visual Studio**, both installable with the **TypeScript SDK** (`https://www.microsoft.com/en-us/download/details.aspx?id=55258`) which can be used to assist you in creating TypeScript code and turning it into JavaScript. You add a TypeScript file to your project by clicking **Add New Item | Visual C# | ASP.NET Core | Web | Scripts | TypeScript File**. As you add TypeScript contents and you save the file, Visual Studio automatically transpiles it to a corresponding JavaScript file. Remember that you do not use the TypeScript (`.ts`) files directly, but the JavaScript ones (`.js`):

It is also possible to create a TypeScript project on its own, but only for targeting Node.js, it would be pointless to have a TypeScript project for the web outside the scope of an ASP.NET project. You can create a Node.js TypeScript project from Visual Studio using the default templates:

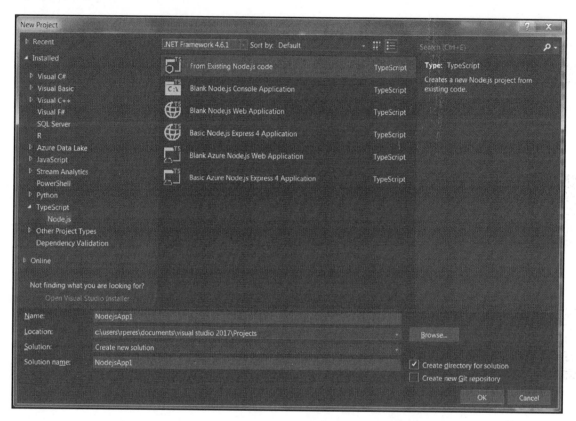

Using Less

Less is a CSS preprocessor built on top of Node.js. It features its own syntax, close to CSS, but augments it with variables, nested rules, and mixins. Less lets you separate your style definitions across several files, having one reference others as needed and using variables and mixins, similar to imports, to avoid repetition. Less is available freely from `http://lesscss.org`.

Because Less is an NPM module, you need to install it before you can use it (`gulp-less` package for Gulp, `grunt-less-bundle` for Grunt). Visual Studio already provides templates for Less files:

However, you need to add it to some task in Gulp or Grunt to wire up Less to your deployment; here is an example Gulp task using **gulp-less**:

```
/* Compile a less file */
gulp.task('compile-less', function() {
  gulp.src('./src/style.less')
    .pipe(less())
    .pipe(gulp.dest('./dist/css/'));
});
```

Alternatively, you can use an extension such as **Web Compiler**, by **Mads Kristensen**, to compile and minify your .less files directly from the Visual Studio Solution Explorer.

 Have a look at https://docs.microsoft.com/en-us/aspnet/core/client-side/less-sass-fa to see how you can leverage Less in order to have a more consistent, maintainable and readable CSS stylesheet.

Putting it all together

You've seen that Node.js and NPM are getting more and more important, even for those of us using ASP.NET and ASP.NET Core, because of its rich wealth of packages. Some of the tools that we've talked about in this chapter rely on it. Because you can now invoke Node.js from ASP.NET Core, you can benefit from its many available packages and thriving community. Even if you are not much of a JavaScript person, I truly advise you to try to get into it.

Using Less instead of writing CSS can prove valuable in the long run, as it promotes code maintainability and reuse.

Gulp is probably more widely used than Grunt nowadays and is perhaps a safer bet. Use Gulp for your client-side build needs, such as minification, bundling, and linting (flagging code that does not follow the recommended best practices).

Unless you really need to, avoid using Bower as it seems to be going nowhere.

Summary

In this chapter, we covered some of the client-side technologies for which Visual Studio offers first-class support. We did not go into great detail, as this is a huge topic and one that seems to be changing very fast, but I left some clues for you, dear reader, to explore and find out more for yourself.

13
Improving the Performance and Scalability

This chapter talks about the different optimizations that we can apply to ASP.NET Core applications so that they perform faster and are able to handle more simultaneous connections. These two concepts, performance, and scalability, are different and, in fact, to some degree, they are conflicting; one must apply the right level of optimization to find the sweet spot. Let's go through some of the available techniques.

We will cover the following topics in this chapter:

- Profiling: how to gain insights into what your application is doing
- Hosting choices and how to tweak your host for best performance
- Bundling and minimization
- Caching
- Compressing responses

Profiling

As Lord Kelvin once famously said, *If you cannot measure it, you cannot improve it*. With that in mind, we need to measure our application to see where its problems are. There are some applications, known as profilers, that can give us the means to do this. Let's have a look at some of the free choices that we have.

CoreProfiler

CoreProfiler is available from `https://github.com/teddymacn/CoreProfiler` and from the NuGet package `CoreProfiler.Web`; it is a port of NanoProfiler. It can profile ASP.NET Core Web apps and ADO.NET connections, by wrapping any `DbConnection` instance. You can create scopes, including nested ones, and you will be able to see how long they took to execute. It is a simple profiler, so don't expect it to do much more than give times. Consider the following screenshot:

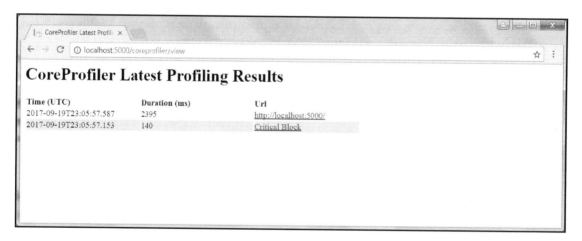

MiniProfiler

Another open-source profiler is **MiniProfiler**, available from `http://miniprofiler.com/dotnet/AspDotNetCore` and from NuGet as `MiniProfiler.AspNetCore.Mvc`. This one is not released, so you will need to get the latest pre-release version. The following screenshot shows the console with details about the request and also any database calls:

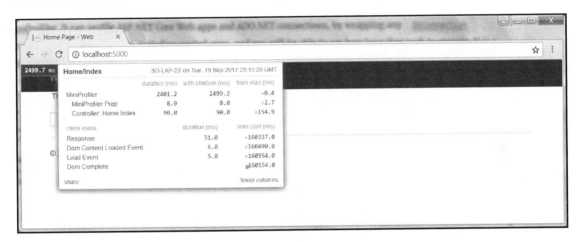

Stackify Prefix

Stackify Prefix is not an open-source product, but rather one that is maintained by the well-known **Stackify** (`https://stackify.com`). It can be downloaded from `https://stackify.com/prefix` and at this time it is not available with NuGet. It offers more features than the other two, so might be worth taking a look at:

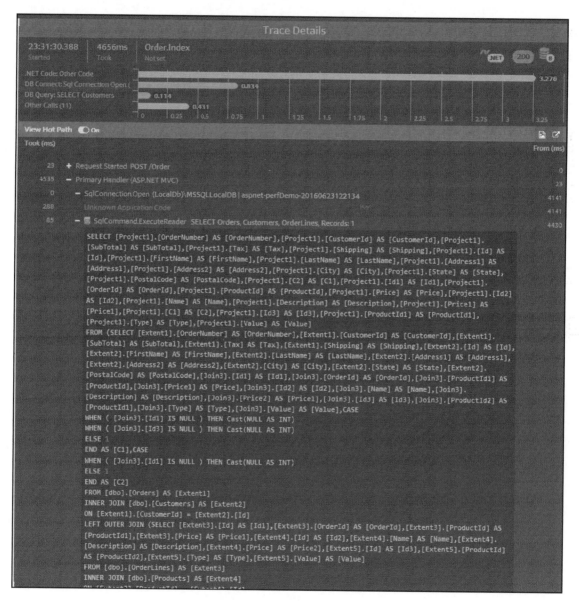

Hosting

Hosting is the process that is used to run your ASP.NET Core application. In ASP.NET Core, you have two out-of-the-box hosting choices:

- **Kestrel**: The cross-platform host which is set by default
- **WebListener (HTTP.sys in ASP.NET Core 2.x)**: A Windows-only host

If you want your application to run on different platforms, not just on Windows, then Kestrel should be your choice, but if you need to target only Windows, then WebListener/HTTP.sys may offer better performance as it makes usage of native Windows system calls. You have to make this choice. By default, the Visual Studio template (or the ones used by the `dotnet` command) uses Kestrel, which is appropriate for most common scenarios.

Choosing the best host

You should compare the two hosts to see how well they behave in stress situations. Kestrel is the default one and is included in the `Microsoft.AspNetCore.Server.Kestrel` NuGet package. If you want to try WebListener, you need to add a reference to the `Microsoft.AspNetCore.Server.WebListener` package, in ASP.NET Core 1.x, or `Microsoft.AspNetCore.Server.HttpSys`, in ASP.NET Core 2. For ASP.NET Core 2, they are also both included in the `Microsoft.AspNetCore.All metapackage`.

In order to use WebListener in ASP.NET Core 1.x, change the code in your `Main` method to be like this:

```
var host = new WebHostBuilder()
    .UseContentRoot(Directory.GetCurrentDirectory())
    .UseWebListener()
    .UseIISIntegration()
    .UseStartup<Startup>()
    .Build();

host.Run();
```

And for ASP.NET Core 2.x:

```
WebHost.CreateDefaultBuilder(args)
    .UseStartup<Startup>()
    .UseHttpSys()
    .Build();
```

Tuning

Both hosts, Kestrel and WebListener/HTTP.sys, support tuning some of their parameters. Let's see some of them.

Maximum number of simultaneous connections

For Kestrel, it goes like this:

```
.UseKestrel(options =>
    {
        options.Limits.MaxConcurrentConnections = null;
        options.Limits.MaxConcurrentUpgradedConnections = null;
    })
```

MaxConcurrentConnections specifies the maximum number of connections that can be accepted; if set to null, there will be no limit, except, of course, system resource exhaustion. MaxConcurrentUpgradedConnections is the maximum number of connections that can be migrated from HTTP or HTTPS; for example, to WebSockets. null is the default value, meaning, no limit.

For Kestrel (in ASP.NET Core 1.x), it goes like this:

```
.UseWebListener(options =>
    {
        options.MaxAccepts = 40;
        options.ListenerSettings.RequestQueueLimit = 20;
    })
```

An explanation of this code is in order:

- MaxAccepts: It is equivalent to MaxConcurrentConnections. The default is 0, for no limit.
- RequestQueueLimit: It is also possible to specify the maximum queued requests in HTTP.sys.

For HTTP.sys, WebListener's replacement in ASP.NET Core 2.x, it is similar:

```
.UseHttpSys(options =>
    {
        options.MaxAccepts = 40;
        options.MaxConnections = null;
        options.RequestQueueLimit = 1000;
    })
```

This code sets some common performance-related options for the HTTP.sys host:

- `MaxAccepts` specifies the maximum number of concurrent accepts
- `MaxConnections` is the maximum number of concurrent accepts, where the default is `null`, to use the machine-global settings from the Registry, and -1 means an infinite number of connections
- `RequestQueueLimit` is the maximum number of requests that can be queues by HTTP.sys

Limits

Similarly to HTTP.sys, Kestrel also allows the setting of some limits, even a few more than HTTP.sys:

```
.UseKestrel(options =>
    {
        options.Limits.MaxRequestBodySize = 30 * 1000 * 1000;
        options.Limits.MaxRequestBufferSize = 1024 * 1024;
        options.Limits.MaxRequestHeaderCount = 100;
        options.Limits.MaxRequestHeadersTotalSize = 32 * 1024;
        options.Limits.MaxRequestLineSize = 8 * 1024;
        options.Limits.MaxResponseBufferSize = 64 * 1024;
        options.Limits.MinRequestBodyDataRate.BytesPerSecond = 240;
        options.Limits.MaxResponseDataRate.BytesPerSecond = 240
    })
```

Explaining this code is simple:

- `MaxRequestBodySize`: The maximum allowed size for a request body
- `MaxRequestBufferSize`: The size of the request buffer
- `MaxRequestHeaderCount`: The maximum number of request headers
- `MaxRequestHeadersTotalSize`: The total acceptable size of the request headers
- `MaxRequestLineSize`: The maximum number of lines in the request
- `MaxResponseBufferSize`: The size of the response buffer
- `MinRequestBodyDataRate.BytesPerSecond`: The maximum request throughput
- `MaxResponseDataRate.BytesPerSecond`: The maximum response throughput

Timeouts

Whenever the application is waiting for some external event--waiting for a request to arrive entirely, waiting for a form to be submitted, waiting for a connection to be established, and so on it can only wait for a certain period of time; this is so that it does not affect the global functioning of the application. When it elapses, we have a timeout, after which the application either gives up and fails or starts again. Kestrel allows the specifying of some timeouts:

```
.UseKestrel(options =>
    {
        options.Limits.KeepAliveTimeout = TimeSpan.FromMinutes(2);
        options.Limits.RequestHeadersTimeout = TimeSpan.FromSeconds(30);
    })
```

As for the two properties being set, here is some information:

- `KeepAliveTimeout` is the client connection timeout in keep-alive connections; 0, the default, is forever
- `RequestHeadersTimeout` is the time to wait for headers to be received; the default is also 0

For WebListener, the properties are:

```
.UseWebListener(options =>
    {
        options.Timeouts.DrainEntityBody = TimeSpan.FromSeconds(0);
        options.EntityBody = TimeSpan.FromSeconds(0);
        options.HeaderWait = TimeSpan.FromSeconds(0);
        options.IdleConnection = TimeSpan.FromSeconds(0);
        options.MinSendBytesPerSecond = 0;
        options.RequestQueue = TimeSpan.FromSeconds(0);
    })
```

These properties have this purpose:

- `DrainEntityBody` is the time allowed in keep-alive connections to read all the request bodies
- `EntityBody` is the maximum time for each individual body to arrive
- `HeaderWait` is the maximum time to parse all request headers
- `IdleConnection` is the time before an idle connection is shut down
- `MinSendBytesPerSecond` is the minimum send rate, in bytes per second
- `RequestQueue` is the time allowed for queued requests to remain in the queue

For HTTP.sys, it is the same:

```
.UseHttpSys(options =>
    {
        options.Timeouts.DrainEntityBody = TimeSpan.FromSeconds(0);
        options.EntityBody = TimeSpan.FromSeconds(0);
        options.HeaderWait = TimeSpan.FromSeconds(0);
        options.IdleConnection = TimeSpan.FromSeconds(0);
        options.MinSendBytesPerSecond = 0;
        options.RequestQueue = TimeSpan.FromSeconds(0);
    })
```

Bundling and minification

Bundling means that several JavaScript or CSS files can be combined together, so as to minimize the number of requests that the browser sends to the server. Minification is a technique that removes unnecessary blanks from CSS and JavaScript files and changes the function and variable names so that they are smaller. When combined, these two techniques can result in much less data to transmit, which will result in faster load times.

A default project created by Visual Studio performs bundling automatically when the application is run or deployed. The actual process is configured by the `bundleConfig.json` file, which has a structure similar to this one:

```
[
  {
    "outputFileName": "wwwroot/css/site.min.css",
    "inputFiles": [
      "wwwroot/css/site.css"
    ]
  },
  {
    "outputFileName": "wwwroot/js/site.min.js",
    "inputFiles": [
        "wwwroot/js/site.js"
    ],
    "minify": {
      "enabled": true,
      "renameLocals": true
    },
    "sourceMap": false
  }
]
```

We can see two different groups, one for CSS and the other for JavaScript, each resulting in a file (the `outputFileName`). Each takes a set of files, which can include wildcards (`inputFiles`), and it is possible to specify whether the result is to be minified (`enabled`) and functions and variables renamed so as to be smaller (`renameLocals`). For JavaScript files it is possible to automatically generate a source map file (`sourceMap`). You can read about source maps here: `https://developer.mozilla.org/en-US/docs/Tools/Debugger/How_to/Use_a_source_map`. Mind you, this behavior is actually not intrinsic to Visual Studio, but rather it is produced by the **Bundler & Minifier** extension by Mads Kristensen, available from the Visual Studio gallery: `https://marketplace.visualstudio.com/items?itemName=MadsKristensen.BundlerMinifier`.

Other options exist, such as adding the `BuildBundlerMinifier` NuGet package, also from Mads Kristensen, which adds a command line option to `dotnet`, allowing us to perform bundling and minification from the command line at build time. Yet another option is to use Gulp, Grunt, or WebPack, but since these are JavaScript solutions rather than ASP.NET Core ones, I won't discuss them here. For Gulp and Grunt, please refer to `Chapter 12`, *Client-Side Development*, and for WebPack, please see `https://webpack.github.io`.

Asynchronous actions

Asynchronous calls are a way to increase the scalability of your application. Normally, the thread that handles the request is blocked while it is being processed, meaning this thread will be unavailable to accept other requests. By using asynchronous actions, another thread from a different pool is assigned the request, and the listening thread is returned to the pool, waiting to receive other requests. Controllers, Razor Pages, tag helpers, view components, and middleware classes can perform asynchronously.

For controllers, just change the signature of the action method to be like this (notice the `async` keyword and the `Task<IActionResult>` return type):

```
public async Task<IActionResult> Index() { ... }
```

In Razor Pages, it is similar (notice the `Async` suffix, the `Task<IActionResult>` return type, and the `async` keyword):

```
public async Task<IActionResult> OnGetAsync() { ... }
```

For tag helpers and tag helper components, override the `ProcessAsync` method instead of `Process`:

```
public override async Task ProcessAsync(TagHelperContext context,
TagHelperOutput output) { ... }
```

In view components, implement an `InvokeAsync` method, like this one:

```
public async Task<IViewComponentResult> InvokeAsync(/* any parameters */) {
... }
```

And also make sure to invoke it asynchronously in your views:

```
@await Component.InvokeAsync("MyComponent", /* any parameters */)
```

Finally, in a middleware class:

```
public async Task Invoke(HttpContext httpContext) { ... }
```

That is not all; you should also prefer asynchronous API methods instead of blocking ones, especially those that do I/O, database or network calls.

 Keep in mind, however, that asynchronicity is not a panacea for all your problems, it is simply a way to make your application more responsive.

Caching

Caching is one of the optimizations that can have a greater impact on the performance of a site. By caching responses and data you do not have to fetch them again, process them, and send them to the client. Let's see a couple of ways by which we can achieve this.

Caching data

By caching your data you do not need to go and retrieve it again and again, whenever it is needed. You need to consider a couple of things:

- For how long will it be kept in the cache?
- How can you invalidate the cache, if you so need it?
- Do you need it to be distributed across different machines?
- How much memory will it take? Will it grow forever?

There are usually three ways to specify the cache duration:

- **Absolute**: The cache will expire at a predefined point in time
- **Relative**: The cache will expire some time after it is created
- **Sliding**: The cache will expire some time after it is created, but, if accessed, this time will be extended by the same amount

In-memory cache

The easiest way to achieve caching is by using the built-in implementation of `IMemoryCache`, available in the NuGet package `Microsoft.Extensions.Caching.Memory` (it also comes in the `Microsoft.AspNetCore.All` metapackage). As you can guess, it is a memory-only cache, suitable for single-server apps. In order to use it, you need to register its implementation in `ConfigureServices`:

```
services.AddMemoryCache();
```

After that, you can inject the `IMemoryCache` implementation into any of your classes--controllers, middleware, tag helpers, view components, and more. You have essentially three operations:

- Add an entry to the cache (`CreateEntry`, `Set`)
- Get an entry from the cache (`Get`, `GetOrCreate`, `TryGetValue`)
- Remove an entry from the cache (`Remove`)

Adding an entry requires that you give it a name, a priority, and a duration. The name can be any object and the duration can either be specified as a relative, sliding or an absolute time. Here's an example:

```
//relative expiration in 30 minutes
cache.Set("key", new MyClass(), TimeSpan.FromMinutes(30));

//absolute expiration for next day
cache.Set("key", new MyClass(), DateTimeOffset.Now.AddDays(1));

//sliding expiration
var entry = cache.CreateEntry("key");
entry.SlidingExpiration = TimeSpan.FromMinutes(30);
entry.Value = new MyClass();
```

Or, you can also combine the two strategies:

```
//keep item in cache as long as it is requested at least once every 5
minutes
// but refresh it every hour
var options = new MemoryCacheEntryOptions()
    .SetSlidingExpiration(TimeSpan.FromMinutes(5))
    .SetAbsoluteExpiration(TimeSpan.FromHours(1));

var entry = cache.CreateEntry("key");
entry.SetOptions(options);
```

When using the sliding expiration option, it will be renewed whenever the cache item is accessed. Using Set will create a new item or replace any existing item with the same key. You can also use GetOrCreate to either add one if no item with the given key exists or to return the existing one:

```
var value = cache.GetOrCreate("key", (entry) =>
    {
        entry.AbsoluteExpirationRelativeToNow = TimeSpan.FromMinutes(30);
        return new MyClass();
    });
```

Priority controls when an item is evicted from the cache, due to out of memory situations; The possible values are:

- High: Try to keep an item in memory for as long as its possible
- Low: It's OK to evict the item from memory when it is necessary
- NeverRemove: Never evict an item from memory unless its duration is reached
- Normal: Use the default algorithm

It is possible to pass a collection of expiration tokens, this is essentially a way to have cache dependencies. You create a cache dependency in a number of ways, such as from a cancellation token:

```
var cts = new CancellationTokenSource();
var entry = cache.CreateEntry("key");
entry.ExpirationTokens.Add(new CancellationChangeToken(cts.Token));
```

Or from a configuration change:

```
var ccts = new
ConfigurationChangeTokenSource<MyOptions>(this.Configuration);
var entry = cache.CreateEntry("key");
entry.ExpirationTokens.Add(ccts.GetChangeToken());
```

Or even from a change in a file (or directory):

```
var fileInfo = new FileInfo(@"C:\Some\File.txt");
var fileProvider = new PhysicalFileProvider(fileInfo.DirectoryName);
var entry = cache.CreateEntry("key");
entry.ExpirationTokens.Add(fileProvider.Watch(fileInfo.Name));
```

And if you want to combine many, so that the cache item expires when any of the change tokens does, you can use a `CompositeChangeToken`:

```
var entry = cache.CreateEntry("key");
entry.ExpirationTokens.Add(new CompositeChangeToken(new List<IChangeToken>
{
    /* one */,
    /* two */,
    /* three */
}));
```

You can also register a callback that will be called automatically when an item is evicted from the cache:

```
var entry = cache.CreateEntry("key");
entry.RegisterPostEvictionCallback((object key, object value,
EvictionReason reason, object state) => { /* do something */ }, "/* some
optional state object */");
```

This can be used as a simple scheduling mechanism: you can add another item with the same callback so when the item expires it will add the item again and again. The key and value parameters are obvious; the reason parameter will tell you why the item was evicted and it can be one of the following:

- None: No reason is known
- Removed: The item was explicitly removed
- Replaced: The item was replaced
- Expired: The expiration time was reached
- TokenExpired: An expiration token was fired
- Capacity: The maximum capacity was reached

The `state` parameter will contain any arbitrary object, including `null`, that you pass to `RegisterPostEvictionCallback`.

In order to get an item from the cache, two options exist:

```
//return null if it doesn't exist
var value = cache.Get<MyClass>("key");

//return false if the item doesn't exist
MyClass value;
var exists = cache.TryGetValue<MyClass>("key", out value);
```

As for removing, it couldn't be simpler:

```
cache.Remove("key");
```

A side note: it is not possible to iterate through the items in the cache from the `IMemoryCache` instance, but you can count them, by downcasting to `MemoryCache` and using its `Count` property.

Distributed cache

ASP.NET Core ships with two distributed cache providers:

- **Redis:** Available as NuGet package `Microsoft.Extensions.Caching.Redis`
- **SQL Server**: Available from `Microsoft.Extensions.Caching.SqlServer`

The core functionality is made available through the `IDistributedCache` interface. You need to register one or another implementation in `ConfigureServices`. For Redis this is:

```
services.AddDistributedRedisCache(options =>
{
  options.Configuration = "serverName";
  options.InstanceName = "InstanceName";
});
```

For SQL Server it is:

```
services.AddDistributedSqlServerCache(options =>
{
  options.ConnectionString = @"<Connection String>";
  options.SchemaName = "dbo";
  options.TableName = "CacheTable";
});
```

Once you do that, you will be able to inject a `IDistributedCache` instance, which offers four operations:

- Add or remove an item (`Set`, `SetAsync`)
- Retrieve an item (`Get`, `GetAsync`)
- Refresh an item (`Refresh`, `RefreshAsync`)
- Remove an item (`Remove`, `RemoveAsync`)

As you can see, it is similar to `IMemoryCache`, but not quite the same--for once, it offers asynchronous and synchronous versions for all operations. Also, it does not feature all of the options that exist for in-memory cache, such as priorities, expiration callbacks or expiration tokens. But the most important difference is that all items need to be stored as byte arrays, meaning you have to serialize any objects you want to store in the cache beforehand. A special case is strings, where there are extension methods that work directly with strings.

So, in order to add an item, you need to do this:

```
using (var stream = new MemoryStream())
{
  var formatter = new BinaryFormatter();
  formatter.Serialize(stream, new MyClass());

  cache.Set("key", formatter.ToArray(), new DistributedCacheEntryOptions
  {
    //pick only one of these
    //absolute expiration
    AbsoluteExpiration = DateTimeOffset.Now.AddDays(1),
    //relative expiration
    AbsoluteExpirationRelativeToNow = TimeSpan.FromMinutes(60),
    //sliding expiration
    SlidingExpiration = TimeSpan.FromMinutes(60)
  });
}
```

As you can see, it does support absolute, relative, and sliding expiration. If you want to use strings, it's simpler:

```
cache.SetString("key", str, options);
```

To retrieve an item, you also need to deserialize it afterward:

```
var bytes = cache.Get("key");
using (var stream = new MemoryStream(bytes))
{
  var formatter = new BinaryFormatter();
  var data = formatter.Deserialize(stream) as MyClass;
}
```

And for strings:

```
var data = cache.GetString("key");
```

Refreshing is easy; if the item uses sliding expiration, then it is renewed:

```
cache.Refresh("key");
```

And the same goes for removing:

```
cache.Remove("key");
```

The asynchronous versions are identical except that they end with the `Async` suffix and return a `Task` object, which you can then await.

As you may know, `BinaryFormatter` is only available from .NET Core 2.0 onward, so, for versions of .NET Core prior to that, you need to come up with your own serialization mechanism. A good one might be `MessagePack`, available from NuGet.

Caching action results

By caching action results you instruct the browser, after the first execution, to keep the supplied result for a period of time. This can result in a dramatic performance improvement; as no code needs to be run, the response comes directly from the browser's cache. The process is specified in an RFC here: `https://tools.ietf.org/html/rfc7234#section-5.2`. We can apply caching to action methods by applying the `[ResponseCache]` attribute, to either the controller or the action method. It can take some parameters:

- `Duration` (`int`): The cache duration in seconds; it is mapped to the `max-age` value in the `Cache-control` header
- `Location` (`ResponseCacheLocation`): Where to store the cache (one of `Any`, `Client` or `None`)
- `NoStore` (`bool`): Do not cache the response

- `VaryByHeader` (`string`): A header that will make the cache vary; for example, `Accept-Language` causes a response to be cached for each requested language; see https://www.w3.org/International/questions/qa-accept-lang-locales
- `VaryByQueryKeys` (`string[]`): Any number of query string keys that will make the cache vary
- `CacheProfileName` (`string`): The name of a cache profile; more on this in a moment

The cache locations have the following meanings:

- `Any`: Cached on the client and in any proxies; sets the `Cache-control` header to `public`
- `Client`: Cached on the client only; `Cache-control` is set to `private`
- `None`: Nothing is cached; `Cache-control` and `Pragma` are both set to `no-cache`

But before we can use it, we need to register the needed services in `ConfigureServices`:

```
services.AddResponseCaching();
```

It is possible to configure some options by passing a delegate:

```
services.AddResponseCaching(options =>
  {
    options.MaximumBodySize = 64 * 1024 * 1024;
    options.SizeLimit = 100 * 1024 * 1024;
    options.UseCaseInsensitivePaths = false;
});
```

The available options are:

- `MaximumBodySize` (`int`): The maximum cacheable response; the default is 64 KB
- `SizeLimit` (`int`): Maximum size of all the cached responses; the default is 100 MB
- `UseCaseInsensitivePaths` (`bool`): Whether or not paths should be taken as case-sensitive or not; the default is `false`

To make this work, besides registering the services, we need to add the response caching middleware (method `Configure`):

```
app.UseResponseCaching();
```

Rather than passing duration, location, and the other parameters, it is better to use **cache profiles**. Cache profiles are defined when we register the MVC services:

```
services
    .AddMvc(options =>
    {
        options.CacheProfiles.Add("Public5MinutesVaryByLanguage", new
CacheProfile
        {
            Duration = 5 * 60,
            Location = ResponseCacheLocation.Any,
            VaryByHeader = "Accept-Language"
        });
    });
```

If you wish, you could load the configuration from a configuration file. Say you have this structure:

```
{
    "CacheProfiles": {
        "Public5MinutesVaryByLanguage": {
            "Duration": 300,
            "Location": "Any",
            "VaryByHeader" : "Accept-Language"
        }
    }
}
```

You could load it using the configuration API, in `ConfigureServices`:

```
services
    .Configure<Dictionary<string,
CacheProfile>>(this.Configuration.GetSection("CacheProfiles"))
    .AddMvc(options =>
        {
            var cacheProfiles =
this.Configuration.GetSection<Dictionary<string, CacheProfile>();
            foreach (var keyValuePair in cacheProfiles)
            {
                options.CacheProfiles.Add(keyValuePair);
            }
        });
```

Using cache profiles allows us to have a centralized location where we can change the profile settings which will be used across all the applications. It's as simple then as:

```
[ResponseCache(CacheProfileName = "Public5MinutesVaryByLanguage")]
public IActionResult Index() { ... }
```

Response caching also depends on a host (WebListener and HTTP.sys) setting, which is enabled by default. It is called `EnableResponseCaching`:

```
.UseWebListener(options =>
    {
       options.EnableResponseCaching = true;
    })
```

It has the same name in both WebListener and HTTP.sys.

Caching views

By using the included tag helpers, `<cache>` and `<distributed-cache>`, you are able to cache parts of your views. As you can infer from their names, `<cache>` requires a registered instance of `IMemoryCache` and `<distributed-cache>` requires `IDistributedCache`. I have already talked about these two tag helpers in Chapter 8, *Reusable Components*, so I won't go over them again. Just two examples, one for in-memory caching:

```
<cache expires-sliding="TimeSpan.FromMinutes(30)">
    ...
</cache>
```

And another for distributed caching:

```
<distributed-cache name="redis" expires-sliding="TimeSpan.FromMinutes(30)">
    ...
</distributed-cache>
```

Do not forget that you need to register an instance of either the `IMemoryCache` or `IDistributedCache`. These tag helpers, unfortunately, cannot take cache profiles.

Compressing responses

Response compression is available from the
`Microsoft.AspNetCore.ResponseCompression` package, or
`Microsoft.AspNetCore.All`, for ASP.NET Core 2.x. Essentially, for browsers that
support it, it can compress the response before sending it through the wire, thus minimizing
the amount of data that will be sent, at the expense of consuming some time compressing it.
If a browser supports response compression, it should send an `Accept-Encoding: gzip,`
`deflate` header.

We first need to register the response compression services in `ConfigureServices`:

```
services.AddResponseCompression();
```

A more elaborate version allows you to specify the actual compression provider
(`GzipCompressionProvider` is the one included) and the compressable file types:

```
services.AddResponseCompression(options =>
    {
        options.Providers.Add<GzipCompressionProvider>();
        options.MimeTypes =
ResponseCompressionDefaults.MimeTypes.Concat(new[] { "image/svg+xml" });
    });

services.Configure<GzipCompressionProviderOptions>(options =>
    {
        options.Level = CompressionLevel.Fastest;
    });
```

The only option to `GzipCompressionProviderOptions` is the compression level, of which
there are three options:

- `None`: No compression, this is the default
- `Fastest`: The fastest compression method
- `Optimal`: The compression method that offers the best compression, but
  potentially takes more time

You can see that you can also configure the file types to compress. As a note, the following content types are automatically compressed:

- `text/plain`
- `text/css`
- `application/javascript`
- `text/html`
- `application/xml`
- `text/xml`
- `application/json`
- `text/json`

Finally you need to add the response compression middleware, in the `Configure` method:

```
app.UseResponseCompression();
```

Now, whenever a response is of one of the configured mime types, it will be automatically compressed and the response headers will include a `Content-Encoding: gzip` header.

Note you can rollout your own compression implementation by implementing the `ICompressionProvider` interface and registering it in the `AddResponseCompression` method.

 The Deflate compression method is not supported in ASP.NET Core 2.x, only GZip. Read about Deflate from its RFC (`https://tools.ietf.org/html/rfc1951`) and about GZip here (`https://tools.ietf.org/html/rfc1952`).

Putting it all together

Using response caching in action methods and views is essential, but it must be used judiciously, because you do not want your contents to become outdated. Use cache profiles for action methods, as they provide a centralized location, which makes it easier to make changes. Have as many profiles as needed.

Distributed caching can help if you need to share data among a cluster of servers, but be warned that transmitting data over the wire can take some time, even if, trivially, it is faster than retrieving it from a database, for example. It can also take a lot of memory and thus cause other unforeseeable problems.

Bundling and minification are also quite handy because they can greatly reduce the amount of data to be transmitted, which can be even more important for mobile browsers.

Asynchronous operations should also be your first choice; some modern APIs don't even allow otherwise. It can greatly improve the scalability of your app.

Finally, do use a profiler to identify the bottlenecks. Stackify Prefix is a very good choice.

The choice of the host greatly depends on the deployment needs--if it is non-Windows, we have no choice other than Kestrel. On both Kestrel and WebListener/HTTP.sys, there are a great number of parameters that you can tweak to your needs, but be warned that playing with these can result in poor performance.

Summary

In this chapter, we've looked at some ways by which we can improve the performance and scalability of an application. This is not an exhaustive list, and there is a lot that can be done in the code, especially when it comes to fetching data. Use your best judgement and experiment with things before applying them in production. In the next chapter, we will be covering real-time communication.

14

Real-Time Communication

Microsoft SignalR is a library for doing real-time communication between the client and the server. It allows the server to call the client on its own initiative, not as a result of a request. It leverages well-known technologies such as AJAX, WebSockets and Server-Sent Events, but in a transparent manner--you do not need to know what it's using, it basically just works, regardless of the browser you have, and it supports quite a lot of browsers, including mobile. Let's explore this technology and see what it has to offer, essentially:

- How to send messages from the client to the server
- How to broadcast messages from the server to all/some clients
- How to send messages from outside a hub

Setting up SignalR

You need to install the `Microsoft.AspNetCore.SignalR` package; at the time of the writing of this book, only a pre-release version exists. You also need a JavaScript library that is made available through **NPM (Node Package Manager)** as `@aspnet/signalr-client`. Once you install it, you need to copy the JavaScript file, either the minimized or the debug version to some folder under `wwwroot`, as it needs to be retrieved by the browser. The file containing the SignalR library is called `signalr-client-1.0.0-alpha1-final.js` (the version may differ) or `signalr-client-1.0.0-alpha1-final.min.js` (for the minimized version) and it is available under `node_modules\@aspnet\signalr-client\dist\browser`.

Unlike previous pre-Core versions, it does not need any other library, such as jQuery, but it can happily coexist with it. Just add a reference to the `signalr-client-1.0.0-alpha1-final.js` file before using the code.

 Warning: SignalR requires ASP.NET Core 2.x.

Hosting a hub

A **hub** is a concept that SignalR uses for clients to come together in a well-known location. From the client-side, it is identified as a URL, such as `http://serverName/chat`. On the server, it is a class that inherits from `Hub` and must be registered with the ASP.NET Core pipeline. Here's a simple example for a chat hub:

```
[Authorize]
public class ChatHub : Hub
{
    public async Task Send(string message)
    {
        await this.Clients.All.InvokeAsync("Send",
this.Context.User.Identity.Name, message);
    }
}
```

The `Send` message is meant to be callable by JavaScript only, and it must only be so by an authenticated client--see the `[Authorize]` attribute. This method is asynchronous. We must register this hub in a well-known endpoint, in the `Configure` method:

```
app.UseSignalR(routes =>
{
    routes.MapHub<ChatHub>("chat");
});
```

A single note--`UseSignalR` must be called before `UseMvc`!

And also register its services, in the `ConfigureServices` method:

```
services.AddSignalR();
```

The `Hub` class exposes two virtual methods, `OnConnectedAsync` and `OnDisconnectedAsync`, which are fired, you guessed it, whenever a client connects or disconnects. `OnDisconnectedAsync` takes as its parameter an `Exception`, which will only be not null if an error occurred when disconnecting.

In order to call a `hub` instance, we must first initialize the SignalR framework:

```
var logger = new signalR.ConsoleLogger(signalR.LogLevel.Information);
var hub = new
signalR.HttpConnection(`http://${document.location.host}/chat`, { logger:
logger });
```

Here we are calling an endpoint named `chat` on the same host from where the request is being served--notice the usage of JavaScript's new string interpolation, from EcmaScript 2015 (`https://developer.mozilla.org/en-US/docs/Web/JavaScript/Reference/Template_literals`). Now, to the communication itself, we need to start it:

```
var connection = new signalR.HubConnection(hub, logger);

connection.onclose(e => {
  console.log('Chat connection closed');
});

connection.on('Send', (user, message) => {
  console.log(`Message from ${user}: ${message}`);
});

connection.start().catch(err => {
  console.log('Error creating the connection to the chat hub');
});
```

I'm also using `arrow` functions, of which you can find out more by reading this article: `https://developer.mozilla.org/en-US/docs/Web/JavaScript/Reference/Functions/Arrow_functions`. This is just syntax, and it can be achieved with anonymous functions.

As a remark, you can pass additional query string parameters that may be later caught in the hub:

```
var hub = new
signalR.HttpConnection(`http://${document.location.host}/chat?key=value`, {
logger: logger });
```

It is sometimes useful, as there is no much ways to pass data from the client to a hub other than, of course, calling its methods. The way to retrieve these values is:

```
var value =
this.Context.Connection.GetHttpContext().Query["key"].SingleOrDefault();
```

Now, we can start sending messages:

```
function send(message) {
   connection.invoke('Send', message);
}
```

Essentially, this method asynchronously calls the `Send` method of the `ChatHub` class, and any response will be received by the `'Send'` listener, which we registered previously (see `connection.on('Send')`).

In a nutshell, the flow is:

1. A connection is created on the client-side (`signalR.HubConnection`) using a hub address (`signalR.HttpConnection`) which must be mapped to a .NET class inheriting from `Hub`.
2. An event handler is added for some event (`connection.on()`).
3. The connection is started (`start()`).
4. Clients send messages to the hub (`connection.invoke()`), using the name of a method declared in the `Hub` class.
5. The method on the `Hub` class broadcasts a message to all/some of the connected clients.
6. When a client receives the message, it raises an event to all subscribers of that event name (the same declared in `connection.on()`).

 Note that the client can call any method on the `Hub` class, and this, in turn, can raise any other event on the client.

Communication protocols

SignalR supports the following communication protocols:

- **WebSockets**: In browsers that support it; probably the most performant one, read more about WebSockets here: `https://developer.mozilla.org/en-US/docs/Web/API/WebSockets_API`
- **Server-sent events**: Another HTTP standard, it allows the client to continuously poll the server, giving the impression that the server is communicating directly to it; see `https://developer.mozilla.org/en-US/docs/Web/API/Server-sent_events`
- **AJAX long polling**: Also known as AJAX Comet, it is a technique by which the client keeps an AJAX request alive, possibly for a long time, until the server provides an answer, which is when it returns and issues another long request

Usually, `signalR` determines the best protocol to use, but you can force one, from the client:

```
var transportType = signalR.TransportType.ServerSentEvents;
var hub = new
signalR.HttpConnection('http://${document.location.host}/chat',
  { transport: transportType });
```

Or the server:

```
app.UseSignalR(routes =>
{
  routes.MapHub<ChatHub>("chat", opt =>
  {
    opt.Transports = TransportType.LongPolling |
TransportType.ServerSentEvents;
  });
});
```

Forcing one protocol may be required in operating systems where, for example, WebSockets is not supported, such as Windows 7. The client and server-side configuration must match, that is, if the server does not have a specific protocol enabled, setting it on the client-side won't work.

You can transmit any kind of object using SignalR, not just primitive types. They are just turned into JSON and deserialized on the other end.

SignalR context

The SignalR context is made available through the `Context` property. In it you will find:

- `Connection` (`HubConnectionContext`): Low-level connection information; you can get a reference to the current `HttpContext` from it (`GetHttpContext()`) as well as metadata stuff (`Metadata`); it is also possible to terminate the connection (`Abort()`)
- `ConnectionId` (`string`): The one and only connection ID that uniquely identifies a client on this hub
- `User` (`ClaimsPrincipal`): The current user, if using authentication

The `Context` property is available when any of the `hub` methods is called, including `OnConnectedAsync` and `OnDisconnectedAsync`.

Message targets

A SignalR message can be sent to one of:

- **All**: All connected clients will receive it
- **Group**: Only clients in a certain group will receive it
- **Client**: Only a specific client

Clients are identified by a connection ID, that can be obtained from the `Hub` class's `Context` property:

```
var connectionId = this.Context.ConnectionId;
```

And users can be added to any number of groups (and removed as well, of course):

```
await this.Groups.AddAsync(this.Context.ConnectionId, "MyFriends");
await this.Groups.RemoveAsync(this.Connection.ConnectionId, "MyExFriends");
```

To send a message to a group, replace the `All` property by a `Group` call:

```
await this.Clients.Group("MyFriends").InvokeAsync("Send", message);
```

Or, similarly to a specific client:

```
await this.Clients.Client(this.Context.ConnectionId).InvokeAsync("Send",
message);
```

Groups are maintained internally by SignalR, but, of course, nothing prevents you from having your own helper structures.

Communicating from the outside

It is possible to send messages into a hub from the outside of it. This does not mean accessing an instance of, for example, the ChatHub class, but only its connected clients. You can do this by injecting an instance of IHubContext<ChatHub> using the built-in dependency injection framework:

```
private readonly IHubContext<ChatHub> _context;

[HttpGet("Send/{message}")]
public IActionResult Send(string message)
{
    this._context.Clients.All.Invoke("Send", this.User.Identity.Name,
message);
}
```

As you can see, you are responsible for sending all parameters to the clients. It is also, of course, possible to send to a group or directly to a client.

Imagine you want to send a recurring message to all clients; you could write code like this in your Configure method (or from somewhere where you have a reference to the service provider):

```
TimerCallback callback = (x) => {
    var hub = serviceProvider.GetService<IHubContext<TimerHub>>();
    hub.Clients.All.InvokeAsync("Notify", DateTime.Now);
};

var timer = new Timer(callback);
timer.Change(TimeSpan.FromSeconds(0), TimeSpan.FromSeconds(1));
```

The `Timer` will fire every second and broadcast the current time to a hypothetical `TimerHub`. This `TimerHub` class need not have any methods, it only needs to exist and be registered in both the server:

```
app.UseSignalR(routes =>
    {
        routes.MapHub<TimerHub>("timer");
    });
```

As well as the client-side:

```
var timerHub = new
signalR.HttpConnection(`http://${document.location.host}/timer`,
  { logger: logger });
var timerConnection = new signalR.HubConnection(timerHub, logger);

timerConnection.on('Notify', (time) => {
  console.log(`time: ${time}`);
});

timerConnection.start().catch(err => {
  console.log('Error starting the timer hub');
});
```

Do not restrict the transport types unless you have a very good reason for doing so, such as browser or operating system incompatibilities.

Summary

You can use SignalR to perform the kind of tasks that you used AJAX for--calling server-side code and getting responses asynchronously. The advantage is that you can use it for having the server reach out to connected clients on its own, when it needs to broadcast some information. SignalR is a very powerful technology because it essentially adapts to whatever your server and client supports. It makes server-to-client communication a breeze. Although the current version is not release-quality, it is stable enough for you to use in your projects. We are reaching the end of the book, so, in the next chapter we will have a look into some of the APIs that weren't covered in previous chapters.

15
Other Topics

In this chapter, we will cover some topics that could find no place elsewhere. This is because, although important, there was no ideal location for them in the other chapters. This includes:

- Areas
- Static files
- Application lifetime events
- Conventions
- Embedded resources
- Hosting extensions
- URL rewriting

Some of these topics are quite important, namely, areas and static files. Let's see what they are all about.

Areas

An area is a way to physically separate your app's contents, in a logical way. For example, you can have an area for the administration and **normal** for the other stuff. It is particularly useful in big projects. Each area has its own controllers and views. They were also discussed in Chapter 3, *Routing*.

In order to use areas, we need to create an Areas folder in our app, at the same level as Controllers and Views. Underneath it, we will create an area folder, for example, Admin, and inside it we need to have a structure similar to the one we have in the root, with Controllers and Views folders.

Usage

Controllers are created just the same, but we need to add an [Area] attribute:

```
[Area("Admin")]
public class ManageController : Controller
{
}
```

 It is OK to have multiple controllers with the same name, provided they are in different namespaces (of course), and in different areas as well.

The views for this controller will be automatically located from the Areas/Admin/Views/Manage folder; this is because the built-in **view location expander** (read about it in Chapter 5, *Views*), already looks at the folders under Areas. What we need to do is just register a route for this, before the default (or any bespoke one), in the Configure method:

```
app.UseMvc(routes =>
{
  routes.MapRoute(
    name: "areas",
    template: "{area:exists}/{controller=Home}/{action=Index}");

  routes.MapRoute(
    name: "default",
    template: "{controller=Home}/{action=Index}/{id?}");
});
```

Routes now have an additional built-in template token, [area], that you can use in your routes, in pretty much the same way as [controller] and [action]:

```
[Route("[area]/[controller]/[action]")]
```

Tag and HTML helpers

The included tag helpers (<a>, <form>, and more) recognize the attribute asp-area, which can be used to generate the proper URL to a controller under a specific area:

```
<a asp-controller="Manage" asp-action="Index" asp-
area="Admin">Administration</a>
```

However, this is not the case with HTML helpers, where you need to provide the route `area` parameter explicitly:

```
@Html.ActionLink(
    linkText: "Administration",
    actionName: "Index",
    controllerName: "Manage",
    routeValues: new { area = "Admin" } )
```

Working with static files and folders

ASP.NET Core can serve static files, and even respects folders. The default template in Visual Studio, for both ASP.NET Core 1.x and 2.x, includes the `Microsoft.AspNetCore.StaticFiles` NuGet package, which is also included in the `Microsoft.AspNetCore.All` metapackage. Also, the code to initialize the host--Kestrel or WebListener/HTTP.sys--defines as the root folder for static files, `Directory.GetCurrentDirectory()`, but you can change that in the `Program` class, where the host is initialized:

```
.UseContentRoot("some.folder")
```

Directory browsing

Directory browsing can be enabled for the whole app; it's just a matter of calling `UseDirectoryBrowser` without any parameters (in `Configure`):

```
app.UseDirectoryBrowser();
```

 Beware: if you do this, instead of running the default action of the default controller, you will end up with a file listing of the files on the root folder!

But you may want to expose your root folder under a virtual path:

```
app.UseDirectoryBrowser("/virtualPath");
```

Notice the leading /, it is required. Notice that if you don't include support for static files-- up next--you won't be able to download any of them, an HTTP 404 error will be returned instead.

Digging a little further, it is possible to specify what files are to be returned and how to render them; this is through an overload of `UseDirectoryBrowser` that takes a `DirectoryBrowserOptions` parameter. This class has these properties:

- `RequestPath` (`string`): The virtual path
- `FileProvider` (`IFileProvider`): A file provider from which to obtain the directory contents; the default is `null`, and a `PhysicalFileProvider` will be used in that case

An example of configuring a root directory:

```
app.UseDirectoryBrowser(new DirectoryBrowserOptions
{
  RequestPath = "/resources",
  FileProvider = new EmbeddedFileProvider(Assembly.GetEntryAssembly())
});
```

This very simple example exposes all of the current app's assembly embedded resources under the `/resources` virtual path.

Static files

In order to serve (allow the download of) static files we need to call `UseStaticFiles`:

```
app.UseStaticFiles();
```

Again, it is possible to set the virtual root to be some arbitrary folder:

```
app.UseStaticFiles("/files");
```

Meaning, even if a `FooBar.txt` file is stored under `wwwroot`, it will only be accessible as `/files/FooBar.txt`.

There is another overload of `UseStaticFiles` that takes a `StaticFileOptions` parameter. This has the following properties:

- `DefaultContentType` (`string`): The default content type for unknown files; the default is `null`
- `ServeUnknownFileTypes` (`bool`): Whether or not to serve files with unknown MIME types; the default is `false`

- ContentTypeProvider (IContentTypeProvider): Used to get the MIME type for a given extension
- FileProvider (IFIleProvider): The file provider used to retrieve the file's contents; by default it is null, which means that a PhysicalFileProvider is used
- OnPrepareResponse (Action<StaticFileResponseContext>): A handler that can be used to intercept the response, like, setting default headers or plainly rejecting it
- RequestPath (string): The virtual base path

For files, it is important to set the content (MIME) type; this is inferred from the file's extension, and we can choose to allow downloading unknown file types (those without registered MIME types for their extension) or not:

```
app.UseStaticFiles(new StaticFileOptions
    {
        DefaultContentType = "text/plain",
        ServeUnknownFileTypes = true
    });
```

Here we are allowing downloading any files with unknown extensions and serving them with the content type text/plain. If the ServeUnknownFileTypes is not set to true and you try to download one such file, you will receive an HTTP 404 error.

But there is a class that knows about the common file extensions, it is FileExtensionContentTypeProvider, and it implements IContentTypeProvider, which means we can assign it to the ContentTypeProvider property of StaticFileOptions:

```
var provider = new FileExtensionContentTypeProvider();
provider.Mappings[".myext"] = "my/ext";

app.UseStaticFiles(new StaticFileOptions
    {
        ContentTypeProvider = provider,
        DefaultContentType = "text/plain",
        ServeUnknownFileTypes = true
    });
```

As you can see, we are adding a new extension and its associated MIME type to the built-in list. If you are curious, you can iterate over it to see what it contains or start from scratch by calling Clear. The extensions need to take the ., and they are caseinsensitive.

As with directory browsing, we can specify the `IFileProvider` that will be used to retrieve the actual file contents, by setting the `FileProvider` property.

And if we want to set a custom header with all files, or implement security, conspicuously absent from static files handling, we can do something along these lines:

```
app.UseStaticFiles(new StaticFileOptions
    {
        OnPrepareResponse = ctx =>
            {
                ctx.Context.Response.Headers.Add("X-SENDER", "ASP.NET Core");
            };
    });
```

Of course, we can also return an HTTP error code, redirect, or any other kind of operation.

Default documents

If we enable directory browsing, we may as well serve a default document, if it exists. For that we need to add some middleware, by calling `UseDefaultFiles`, always before `UseStaticFiles`:

```
app.UseDefaultFiles();
app.UseStaticFiles();
```

Needless to say, the default documents can be configured by passing an instance of `DefaultFilesOptions`. This class contains:

- `DefaultFileNames` (`IList<string>`): The ordered list of default files to serve
- `RequestPath` (`string`): The virtual path
- `FileProvider` (`IFileProvider`): The file provider from which to obtain the files list; `null` by default

In case you are interested, the default filenames are:

- `default.htm`
- `default.html`
- `index.htm`
- `index.html`

An example for configuring a single default document is as follows:

```
app.UseDefaultFiles(new DefaultFilesOptions
    {
        DefaultFileNames = new [] { "document.html" };
    });
```

If a file called `document.html` exists in any browseable folder, it will be served, and the folder's contents will not be listed.

Security

As I mentioned earlier, security is absent from static file handling, but we can implement our own mechanism, using the `OnPrepareResponse` handler of `StaticFileOptions` as the basis:

```
app.UseStaticFiles(new StaticFileOptions
    {
        OnPrepareResponse = ctx =>
            {
                //check if access should be granted for the current user and
file
                if (AccessIsGranted(ctx.File, ctx.Context.User) == false)
                {
                    ctx.Context.Response.StatusCode = (int)
HttpStatusCode.Forbidden;
                    ctx.Context.Abort();
                }
            };
    });
```

If you want to serve files from outside the `wwwroot` folder, pass a custom `IFileProvider`; maybe an instance of `PhysicalFileProvider` that is set to use a different root.

Application lifetime events

ASP.NET Core exposes events for the whole application life cycle. You can hook to these events so as to be notified of when they are about to happen. The entry point to this is the `IApplicationLifetime` interface, which you can get from the dependency injection framework. It exposes the following properties:

- `ApplicationStarted` (`CancellationToken`): Raised when the host is fully started and is ready to wait for requests

- `ApplicationStopping` (`CancellationToken`): Raised when the application is about to stop, in what is known as a graceful shutdown; some requests may still be in process
- `ApplicationStopped` (`CancellationToken`): Raised when the application is fully stopped

Each of these properties is a `CancellationToken`, which means that they can be passed along any methods that take one such parameter, but, more interestingly, it means that we can add our own handlers to it:

```
IApplicationLifetime events = ...;
events.ApplicationStopping.Register(
    callback: state =>
        {
            //application is stopping
        },
    state: "some state");
```

The `state` parameter is optional; if not supplied, the `callback` parameter does not take any parameters.

There are some ways to cause a graceful shutdown; one of them is by calling the `IApplicationLifetime` interface's `StopApplication` method, others include adding an `app_offline.htm` file.

If you want to have events at the start or end of a request, you're better off by using a filter. Read about filters in `Chapter 9`, *Filters*.

Embedded resources

Since the original versions of .NET, it has been possible to embed contents inside the assembly, including binary files. For that, we can use Visual Studio to set the **Build Action** property in the property explorer of Visual Studio:

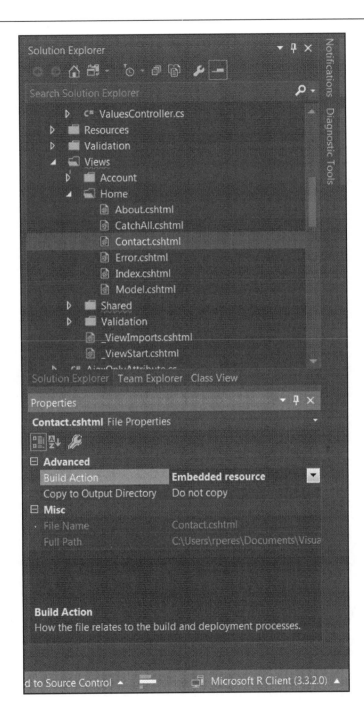

Then, to retrieve an embedded resource, you will need an instance of
EmbeddedFileProvider. This class belongs to the
Microsoft.Extensions.FileProviders.Embedded package and implements the
IFileProvider interface, meaning it can be used in any API that expects an
IFileProvider. You initialize an EmbeddedFileProvider by passing it an assembly:

```
var embeddedProvider = new
EmbeddedFileProvider(Assembly.GetEntryAssembly());
```

An optional base namespace can also be passed:

```
var embeddedProvider = new
EmbeddedFileProvider(Assembly.GetEntryAssembly(), "My.Assembly");
```

This base namespace is the one specified in the project properties:

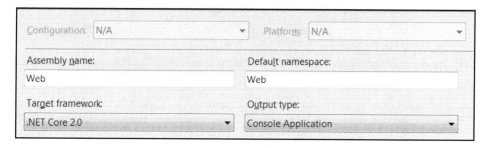

It is up to you to know what is inside an embedded resource; for example, it may be text or
binary contents.

Hosting extensions

We are now going to talk about a mechanism to automatically load classes from other
assemblies and another one for spawning background threads automatically.

Hosting startup

There is an interface, IHostingStartup, that exposes a single method:

```
public class CustomHostingStartup : IHostingStartup
{
  public void Configure(IWebHostBuilder builder)
  {
```

```
    }
  }
```

This can be used, at host startup time, to inject additional behavior into the host. The `IWebHostBuilder` is exactly the same instance being used in the `Program.Main` method. So how is this class loaded? In one of two ways:

- By adding a `[HostingStartup]` attribute at the assembly level, we can specify one or more `IHostingStartup`-implementing classes that should be loaded automatically from the application's assembly.
- By setting a value to the `ASPNETCORE_HOSTINGSTARTUPASSEMBLIES` environment variables, which can be a semicolon-separated list of assembly names and/or fully qualified type names. For each assembly name, the hosting framework will detect any `[HostingStartup]` attributes, and for the type names, if they implement `IHostingStartup`, they will be loaded automatically.

This is a great mechanism for loading classes such as plugins, and in fact, it is the way that some Microsoft packages actually work, such as Application Insights.

Hosted services

The `IHostedService` interface defines a contract for a background task. By implementing this interface in a concrete class, we can spawn workers in the background of our app. It has two methods:

```
public class BackgroundHostedService : IHostedService
{
  public async Task StartAsync(CancellationToken cancellationToken)
  {
    //start some asynchronous task
  }

  public async Task StopAsync(CancellationToken cancellationToken)
  {
    //stop the asynchronous task
  }
}
```

`StartAsync` and `StopAsync` are, of course, called automatically when the hosted service starts and stops, respectively. They both take a `CancellationToken` parameter that can be used to pass along other asynchronous operations, which will then be cancelled should the hosted service be cancelled too.

Hosted services need to be registered into the dependency injection framework:

```
services.AddSingleton<IHostedService, BackgroundHostedService>();
```

These hosted services start as soon as the `Configure` method finishes.

Custom conventions

ASP.NET Core has some built-in conventions that are, in fact, classes that implement well-known interfaces and are registered by default. It is possible to change these conventions, by replacing or registering new convention classes. The convention interfaces are:

- `IApplicationModelConvention`: This provides access to application-wide conventions, allowing you to iterate over each of the following levels, that is, controller model, action model, and parameter model
- `IControllerModelConvention`: These are conventions that are specific to a controller, but also allow you to evaluate lower levels (action model)
- `IActionModelConvention`: This lets you make changes to action-level conventions, as well as on any parameters of the actions (parameter model)
- `IParameterModelConvention`: This is specific to parameters only
- `IPageRouteModelConvention`: Razor Pages (ASP.NET Core 2.x); this lets us customize the default routes to Razor Pages
- `IPageApplicationModelConvention`: Razor Pages (ASP.NET Core 2.x); this allows the customization of Razor models

From higher to lower scope we have: Application > Controller > Action > Parameter.

Non-Razor conventions are registered through the `Conventions` collection of `MvcOptions`:

```
services
    .AddMvc(options =>
        {
            options.Conventions.Add(new CustomConvention());
        });
```

So, this goes for `IApplicationModelConvention`, `IControllerModelConvention`, `IActionModelConvention`, and `IParameterModelConvention`. The Razor conventions are configured on a similar collection on the `RazorPagesOptions`:

```
services
    .AddMvc()
    .AddRazorPagesOptions(options =>
```

```
{
    options.Conventions.Add(new CustomRazorConvention());
});
```

It is also possible to apply custom conventions by having a custom attribute implement one of the convention interfaces and applying it at the right level:

- IControllerModelConvention: Controller class
- IActionModelConvention: Action method
- IParameterModelConvention: Action method parameter

So, what can we do with custom conventions? Some examples follow:

- Register new controllers and add attributes to existing ones dynamically
- Set a route prefix for all or some controllers dynamically
- Define authorization for action methods dynamically
- Set the default location for parameters in action methods dynamically

If you wanted to add a new controller to the list of registered ones, we would do something like this:

```
public class CustomApplicationModelConvention : IApplicationModelConvention
{
    public void Apply(ApplicationModel application)
    {
        application.Controllers.Add(new ControllerModel(typeof(MyController),
            new List<object> { { new AuthorizeAttribute() } }));
    }
}
```

Or, if we want to have a [Route] attribute to all controllers with a certain prefix (Prefix):

```
foreach (var applicationController in application.Controllers)
{
    foreach (var applicationControllerSelector in
applicationController.Selectors)
    {
        applicationControllerSelector.AttributeRouteModel =
            new AttributeRouteModel(new RouteAttribute("Prefix"));
    }
}
```

This could also go in an `IActionModelConvention` implementation, but serves to show that you can apply conventions at all levels from `IApplicationModelConvention`.

Now, adding an `[Authorize]` attribute to certain action methods, ending in `Auth`:

```
foreach (var controllerModel in application.Controllers)
{
  foreach (var actionModel in controllerModel.Actions)
  {
    if (actionModel.ActionName.EndsWith("Auth"))
    {
      var policy = new AuthorizationPolicyBuilder()
          .RequireAuthenticatedUser()
          .Build();
      actionModel.Filters.Add(new AuthorizeFilter(policy));
    }
  }
}
```

Finally, setting the source for parameters to be the service provider whenever their name ends in `Svc`:

```
foreach (var controllerModel in application.Controllers)
{
  foreach (var actionModel in controllerModel.Actions)
  {
    foreach (var parameterModel in actionModel.Parameters)
    {
      if (parameterModel.ParameterName.EndsWith("Svc"))
      {
        if (parameterModel.BindingInfo == null)
        {
          parameterModel.BindingInfo = new BindingInfo();
        }
        parameterModel.BindingInfo.BindingSource = BindingSource.Services;
      }
    }
  }
}
```

For Razor Pages, it is somewhat different, as there is no relation between the two convention interfaces; that is, they are used for totally different purposes. Two examples follow:

- Setting all page model properties to be automatically bound to the service provider
- Setting the root of all pages

For the first example, we need an `IPageApplicationModelConvention` implementation:

```
public class CustomPageApplicationModelConvention :
IPageApplicationModelConvention
{
  public void Apply(PageApplicationModel model)
  {
    foreach (var property in model.HandlerProperties)
    {
      if (property.BindingInfo == null)
      {
        property.BindingInfo = new BindingInfo();
      }
      property.BindingInfo.BindingSource = BindingSource.Services;
    }
  }
}
```

What it does is automatically set as the binding source for any properties in a page model class the dependency injection; this would be analogous to setting a `[FromServices]` attribute on them.

And for setting a custom route prefix, an `IPageRouteModelConvention`:

```
public class CustomPageRouteModelConvention : IPageRouteModelConvention
{
  public void Apply(PageRouteModel model)
  {
    foreach (var selector in model.Selectors)
    {
      if (selector.AttributeRouteModel == null)
      {
        selector.AttributeRouteModel = new AttributeRouteModel(new
RouteAttribute("Foo"));
      }
      else
      {
        selector.AttributeRouteModel = AttributeRouteModel
          .CombineAttributeRouteModel(selector.AttributeRouteModel,
            new AttributeRouteModel(new RouteAttribute("Foo")));
      }
    }
  }
}
```

Here, what we are doing is setting the `[Route]` attribute for all Razor Pages to start with `Foo`.

URL rewriting

Convenient as MVC routing is, there are, however, times when we need to present different URLs to the public, or, the other way, be able to accept a URL that the public knows about. Enter URL rewriting.

URL rewriting is not new, it's been around since ASP.NET Web Forms, natively, and, in a more advanced way, through the IIS URL Rewrite module (see `https://www.iis.net/downloads/microsoft/url-rewrite`). ASP.NET Core offers similar functionality through the `Microsoft.AspNetCore.Rewrite` package, let's see how it works.

Essentially, URL rewriting is a feature by which you can turn request URLs into something different, based on a set of pre-configured rules. Microsoft suggests some situations where this may come in handy:

- Moving or replacing server resources temporarily or permanently while maintaining stable locators for those resources
- Splitting request processing across different apps or across areas of one app
- Removing, adding, or reorganizing URL segments on incoming requests
- Optimizing public URLs for **Search Engine Optimization** (**SEO**)
- Permitting the use of friendly public URLs to help people predict the content they will find by following a link
- Redirecting insecure requests to secure endpoints
- Preventing image hotlinking

The `Microsoft.AspNetCore.Rewrite` package can be configured through code but it can also accept a IIS Rewrite Module configuration file (`https://docs.microsoft.com/en-us/iis/extensions/url-rewrite-module/creating-rewrite-rules-for-the-url-rewrite-module`). Because after all ASP.NET Core is cross-platform, Apache's `mod_rewrite` (`http://httpd.apache.org/docs/current/mod/mod_rewrite.html`) configuration is also supported, alongside IIS.

URL rewriting is different from URL redirect--in the latter, the server sends a `3xx` status code upon receiving a request that should be redirected, and it's up to the client to follow that request; in URL rewriting, the request is processed immediately by the server without another round-trip, but the application sees it differently, according to the rewrite rules. `Microsoft.AspNetCore.Rewrite` supports both situations.

To start with, there is the `RewriteOptions` class, which is used to define all rules. There are a couple of extension methods for it:

- `AddRedirect`: Adds a URL redirect rule with an optional status code (3xx)
- `AddRewrite`: Adds a URL rewrite rule
- `Add(Action<RewriteContext>)`: Adds a delegate that can be used to produce a rewrite or redirect rule on the fly
- `Add(IRule)`: Adds an implementation of `IRule` which defines a runtime rule, in a way similar to the `Action<RewriteContext>` delegate

Then there are two extension methods that are specific to Apache and IIS:

- `AddApacheModRewrite`: Reads from a `mod_rewrite` configuration file
- `AddIISUrlRewrite`: Reads from an IIS URL Rewrite Module configuration file

These two either take a file provider (`IFileProvider`) and a path or a `TextReader` that is already pointing to an open file.

Finally, there are two methods for forcing HTTPS:

- `AddRedirectToHttps`: Tells the client to ask for the same request but this time using the HTTPS protocol instead of HTTP
- `AddRedirectToHttpsPermanent`: This is analogous to the previous one except it sends a `301 Moved Permanently` instead of a `302 Found`

These methods will force a redirect to HTTPS if the request was for HTTP, for any resource on the server.

URL redirection

First, an example, for URL redirection:

```
.AddRedirect("redirect-rule/(.*)", "redirected/$1",
StatusCodes.Status307TemporaryRedirect);
```

The first parameter is a regular expression that should match the request, and in it we can specify captures (inside parenthesis); the second parameter is the redirection URL, notice that we can make use of the captures defined on the first parameter. The third parameter is optional, and, if not used, it defaults to `302 Found`.

Read about HTTP redirection in the HTTP specification here: `https://www.w3.org/Protocols/rfc2616/rfc2616-sec10.html#sec10.3`.

URL rewrite

Next, an internal rewrite. An example of `AddRewrite` could be:

```
.AddRewrite(@"^rewrite-rule/(\d+)/(\d+)", "rewritten?var1=$1&var2=$2",
skipRemainingRules: true);
```

Here we are instructing `Microsoft.AspNetCore.Rewrite` to turn any path components after `rewrite-rule` that are made up of digits (this also uses regular expressions) into query string parameters. If a match for the first parameter is found, the third parameter (`skipRemainingRules`) instructs the rewriting middleware to stop processing any other rules and just use this one. The default for the `skipRemainingRules` parameter is `false`.

Runtime evaluation

The extensions that take an `Action<RewriteContext>` or an `IRule` are actually the same: the first just wraps the passed delegate in a `DelegateRule`, a specific implementation of `IRule`. This interface merely defines a single method:

```
void ApplyRule(RewriteContext context)
```

`RewriteContext` offers a couple of properties from which you can access the context and set the response:

- `HttpContext` (`HttpContext`): The current HTTP context
- `StaticFileProvider` (`IFileProvider`): The current file provider to use for checking the existence of static files and folders
- `Logger` (`ILogger`): A logger
- `Result` (`RuleResult`): The rule evaluation result, which must be set; the default is `ContinueRules`, which instructs the middleware to continue processing other requests, and the other possible values are `EndResponse` (which does what you think it does) and `SkipRemainingRules`, which holds off from processing other rules and just applies the current one

To use an `IRule` or a delegate, we use one of:

```
.Add(new RedirectImageRule("jpg", "png"));
```

Or:

```
.Add((ctx) =>
    {
        ctx.HttpContext.Response.Redirect("/temporary_offline", permanent:
true);
        ctx.Result = RuleResult.EndResponse;
    });
```

The `RedirectImageRule` rule is something like this:

```
public sealed class RedirectImageRule : IRule
{
  private readonly string _sourceExtension;
  private readonly string _targetExtension;

  public RedirectImageRule(string sourceExtension, string targetExtension)
  {
    if (string.IsNullOrWhiteSpace(sourceExtension))
    {
      throw new ArgumentNullException(nameof(sourceExtension));
    }

    if (string.IsNullOrWhiteSpace(targetExtension))
    {
      throw new ArgumentNullException(nameof(targetExtension));
    }

    if (string.Equals(sourceExtension, targetExtension,
        StringComparison.InvariantCultureIgnoreCase))
    {
      throw new ArgumentException("Invalid target extension.",
nameof(targetExtension));
    }

    this._sourceExtension = sourceExtension;
    this._targetExtension = targetExtension;
  }

  public void ApplyRule(RewriteContext context)
  {
    var request = context.HttpContext.Request;
    var response = context.HttpContext.Response;
```

```
      if (request.Path.Value.EndsWith(this._sourceExtension,
   StringComparison.OrdinalIgnoreCase))
        {
          var url = Regex.Replace(request.Path,
   $@"^(.*)\.{this._sourceExtension}$", $@"$1\.{this._targetExtension}");
          response.StatusCode = StatusCodes.Status301MovedPermanently;
          context.Result = RuleResult.EndResponse;

          if (request.QueryString.HasValue == false)
          {
            response.Headers[HeaderNames.Location] = url;
          }
          else
          {
            response.Headers[HeaderNames.Location] = url + "?" +
   request.QueryString;
          }
        }
      }
    }
  }
```

This class turns any request for a specific image extension into another. The delegate is purposely very simple as it merely redirects to a local endpoint, ending the request processing.

HTTPS

The extensions that redirect to HTTPS, if the current request was HTTP, are straightfoward. The only options are to send a 301 Moved Permanently instead of 301 Found or the option to specify a custom HTTPS port:

```
.AddRedirectToHttps(sslPort: 4430);
```

Platform-specific

AddIISUrlRewrite and AddApacheModRewrite have identical signatures--they both can take a file provider and a path or an stream to a existing file. Here is an example of the latter:

```
using (var iisUrlRewriteStreamReader = File.OpenText("IISUrlRewrite.xml"))
{
  var options = new RewriteOptions()
      .AddIISUrlRewrite(iisUrlRewriteStreamReader)
}
```

I did not cover the format of the **IIS Rewrite Module** or the `mod_rewrite` configuration files, please refer to its documentation.

Putting it all together

In case you want to serve some files on the filesystem, always specify a virtual path for it, so as not to interfere with your controllers.

Areas are a handy way to structure your contents. They are particularly useful in big ASP.NET Core projects.

To combine the normal way of static files, directory browsing and default documents, you can just call `UseFileServer` instead of the three other methods.

Beware of unwanted file downloads, as it's not easy to apply security to them.

Resource files can be quite useful, as we do not need to distribute the files separately from the assembly, and can use the same versioning as the rest of the code. They are definitely worth considering.

Use URL rewriting when you do not wish to expose the inner structure of your site or when you wish to comply to an externally-defined URL.

Use hosted services to spawn background services automatically and have them linked to the application's lifetime.

Summary

In this chapter, we concluded our tour of the ASP.NET Core APIs. We had a look into some of the less-used features that nevertheless play an important role in ASP.NET Core.

16
Deployment

After you have implemented your application, tested it, and are happy with it, it's time to deploy it, that is make it available to the outside world, or at least part of it! In this chapter we will see how we do that and explore some of the options available, including IIS, Azure, and Docker.

In this chapter, we will cover the following topics:

- Manual deployment and real-time compilation of changes
- Deployment using Visual Studio
- Deployment to IIS
- Deployment to Azure
- Deployment to **Amazon Web Services (AWS)**
- Deployment to Docker
- Deployment as a Windows Service

Manual deployment

The `dotnet` command line tool offers the `publish` command. In a nutshell, what it does is pack everything together, get all the required dependencies from the project file, build the application and any dependent projects and then copy all output to a target folder. It offers lots of options, but the most usual ones are probably:

- `-c | --configuration`: Defines the build configuration. The default value is `Debug` and the other common option is `Release`, but of course, you can create other Visual Studio profiles

- `-r | --runtime`: Publishes the application for a given runtime, in the case of self-contained deployments; the default is to use whatever runtime is available on the target machine; see the description in **Self-contained deployments and runtimes**
- `-f | --framework`: Sets the target framework. See the following list in **Setting the target framework**
- `-o | --output`: Sets the path of the target output folder
- `-h | --help`: Displays usage information
- `-v | --verbosity`: Sets the build verbosity level; one of `q[uiet]` (no output), `m[inimal]`, `n[ormal]`, `d[etailed]`, and `diag[nostic]` (highest level), the default is `n[ormal]`
- `--force`: Forces all dependencies to be resolved even if the last restore was successful; effectively deletes all output files and tries to get them again
- `--self-contained`: Publishes the .NET Core runtime together with your application, so that it doesn't need to be installed on the target machine

For more information, please use the `help` command.

The following is an example of the `dotnet publish` command:

```
dotnet publish MyApplication -c Release -o /Output
```

It is worth mentioning that you can also pass parameters to MSBuild, by making use of the `p` flag:

```
dotnet publish /p:Foo=Bar
```

Do not forget that the target environment is defined by the `ASPNETCORE_ENVIRONMENT` environment variable, so you may want to set it before calling `dotnet publish`.

Setting the target framework

When you target a framework in an app or library, you're specifying the set of APIs that you'd like to make available to the app or library. If you target one of the .NET Standards, you are making it available on a wider set of platforms, for example Linux will not have the full .NET Framework, but it will have .NET Standard. This framework is specified in the project file, but you can override it for a particular publish.

The monikers to use for the **framework** command are:

Target framework	Name
.NET Standard	netstandard1.0 netstandard1.1 netstandard1.2 netstandard1.3 netstandard1.4 netstandard1.5 netstandard1.6 netstandard2.0
.NET Core	netcoreapp1.0 netcoreapp1.1 netcoreapp2.0
.NET Framework (aka, full framework)	net11 net20 net35 net40 net403 net45 net451 net452 net46 net461 net462 net47

For your information, I have only listed the most useful ones; you can find the full (and updated) list here: https://docs.microsoft.com/en-us/ dotnet/standard/frameworks.

Self-contained deployments and runtimes

If you specify a target **runtime** for your app, you are also setting the default of **self-contained** to **true**. What this means is that the publish package will include everything it needs to run. This has some advantages and some disadvantages:

Advantages	• You have full control on the version of .NET that your app will run on • You can be assured that the target server will be able to run your app, as you are providing the runtime
Disadvantages	• The size of the deployment package will be larger, as it includes the runtime; if you deploy many different apps with their own runtimes, this is likely to take lots of disk space • You need to specify the target platforms beforehand

The names to use with the **runtime** command are composed of:

- A target operating system moniker
- A version
- An architecture

Examples include `ubuntu.14.04-x64`, `win7-x64`, and `osx.10.12-x64`. For a full list and the general specifications, please refer to `https://docs.microsoft.com/en-us/dotnet/core/rid-catalog`.

You may want to have a look at `https://docs.microsoft.com/en-us/aspnet/core/publishing` and `https://docs.microsoft.com/en-us/dotnet/core/deploying` for a more in-depth introduction to deploying ASP.NET Core applications.

Real-time rebuilding

The `dotnet` command offers a functionality by which it can monitor in real-time any changes to the code and automatically build it, in case it changes. It is `dotnet watch`, and you can read all about it here: `https://docs.microsoft.com/en-us/aspnet/core/tutorials/dotnet-watch`. In a nutshell, to use this you need to add the `Microsoft.DotNet.Watcher.Tools` package to your project and configure it as a tool in the `.csproj` file:

```
<ItemGroup>
    <DotNetCliToolReference Include="Microsoft.DotNet.Watcher.Tools"
Version="2.0.0" />
</ItemGroup>
```

This is for version 2.0, but you can also use this in ASP.NET Core 1.x. After this, instead of issuing a `dotnet run` command, you would instead run `dotnet watch`:

```
dotnet watch run
```

Visual Studio deployment

Of course, most of the time, at least for me, we are using Visual Studio for all of our development and publishing work. All the options to `dotnet publish` are available in Visual Studio as well. We need to create a publish profile, which we can do by right-clicking the project in Visual Studio and clicking **Publish**. After this, we need to select a publish method, **File System**, **FTP**, **Web Deploy**, or **Web Deploy Package** (more on these two later):

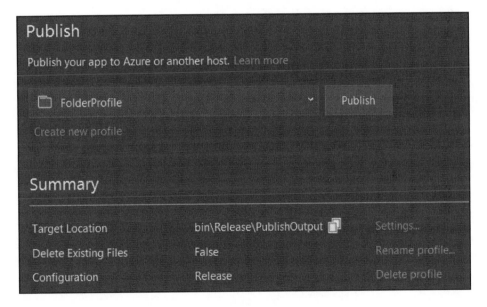

Regardless of the publish method, we can configure the common publish options by clicking on **Settings**:

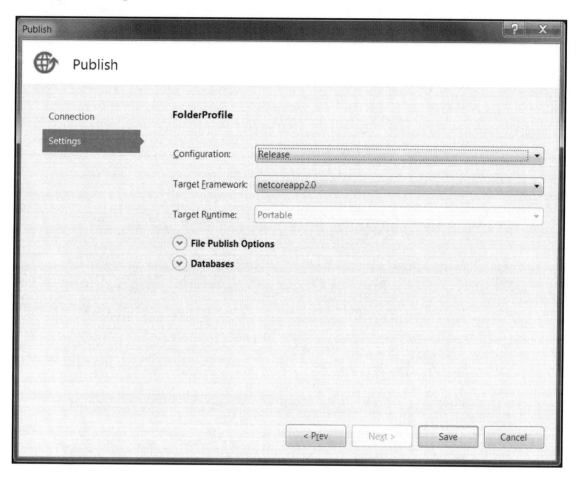

For a more in-depth guide, please refer to `https://docs.microsoft.com/en-us/aspnet/core/publishing/web-publishing-vs`. Visual Studio publish profiles are stored in the `Properties\PublishProfiles` folder:

IIS

Probably the most common server will be IIS. It actually happens that IIS merely acts as a **reverse proxy**, directing HTTP/HTTPS traffic to the .NET Core host. IIS hosting is supported from Windows 7 upwards and it requires the **ASP.NET Core Module**, installed by default with Visual Studio 2017 and the .NET Core SDK. You can download it from `https://aka.ms/dotnetcore.2.0.0-windowshosting`.

Why would you use IIS instead of Kestrel, WebListener/HTTP.sys? IIS offers some more options for you, such as:

- **Authentication**: You can easily set up Windows Authentication, for example
- **Logging**: You can configure IIS to produce logs for all accesses
- **Custom response**: IIS can serve different pages per HTTP response code
- **Security**: You can set up HTTPS for your site, and it's easy to configure SSL certificates, IIS Manager even generates dummy ones
- **Management**: Easy management, even from remote servers, using the **IIS Manager** tool

You should have IIS/IIS Manager installed on the target machine, and in your host creating code you should add support for IIS hosting, in ASP.NET Core 1.x it is like this:

```
var host = new WebHostBuilder()
    .UseKestrel()
    .UseIISIntegration();
```

ASP.NET Core 2.x already does this by default, so no change is required. It's OK to call `UseIISIntegration` regardless or not you will be using IIS, it is harmless and you should probably keep it.

You can use Visual Studio to automatically create the website for you at run or publish time, or you can do it yourself; the only two things that you need to keep in mind are:

- The application pool should not use a .NET CLR version (**no managed code**)
- The `AspNetCoreModule` module should be enabled

If you remember, two of the publish methods were **Web Deploy** and **Web Deploy Package**. **Web Deploy** makes use of the **Web Deployment Agent Service (msdepsvc)** Windows service that is installable through the Web Deployment Tool (`https://www.iis.net/downloads/microsoft/web-deploy`). If it is running, you can have Visual Studio directly connect to a remote (or local) site and install the web project there, if you select the **Web Deploy** method:

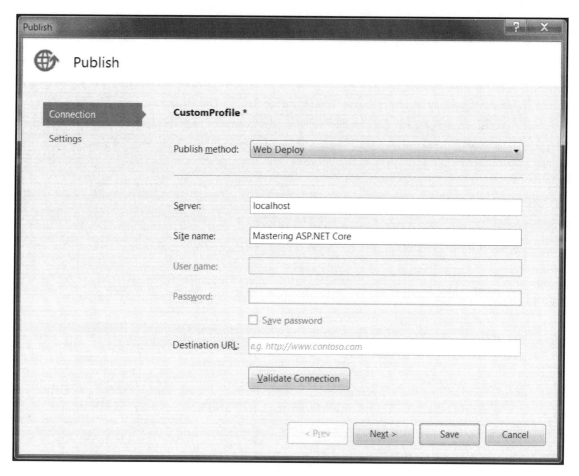

The **Web Deploy Package**, on the other hand, produces a .zip file containing a package that you can deploy through the IIS Manager console, just right-click on any site and select **Deploy | Import Server or Site Package**:

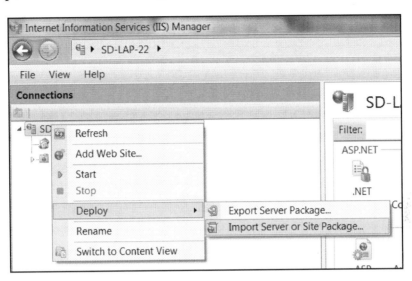

You may have noticed the Web.config file that is produced by dotnet publish (or the Visual Studio publish wizard). It is not used by ASP.NET Core, but rather by the AspNetCoreModule module. It is only required if you wish to host your app behind IIS. You can tweak some settings, like enabling output logging to a file:

```xml
<?xml version="1.0" encoding="utf-8"?>
<configuration>
  <system.webServer>
    <aspNetCore
      processPath="dotnet"
      arguments=".\MyApp.dll"
      stdoutLogEnabled="true"
      stdoutLogFile=".\logs\stdout.log" />
  </system.webServer>
</configuration>
```

Here, I changed the stdoutLogEnabled and the stdoutLogFile attributes; this should be pretty easy to understand.

Once again, for the full documentation, please refer to https://docs.microsoft.com/en-us/aspnet/core/publishing/iis.

Nginx

Nginx is a very popular reverse-proxy server for the Unix and Linux family of operating systems. Like IIS, it offers interesting features that are not provided out of the box by the ASP.NET Core hosts, like caching requests, serving files straight from the file system, SSL termination, and others. You can configure it to forward requests to an ASP.NET Core application that is running stand-alone. This application needs to be modified to acknowledge forwarded headers:

```
app.UseForwardedHeaders(new ForwardedHeadersOptions
    {
        ForwardedHeaders = ForwardedHeaders.XForwardedFor |
ForwardedHeaders.XForwardedProto
    });
```

We also need to configure Nginx to forward requests to ASP.NET Core (`/etc/nginx/sites-available/default`):

```
server
{
  listen 80;
  location /
  {
    proxy_pass http://localhost:5000;
    proxy_http_version 1.1;
    proxy_set_header Upgrade $http_upgrade;
    proxy_set_header Connection keep-alive;
    proxy_set_header Host $host;
    proxy_cache_bypass $http_upgrade;
  }
}
```

Read all about Nginx here: `https://docs.microsoft.com/en-us/aspnet/core/publishing/linuxproduction`.

Azure

Microsoft Azure is also a very strong candidate for hosting your app. When creating a publish profile, select **Azure** as the publish method:

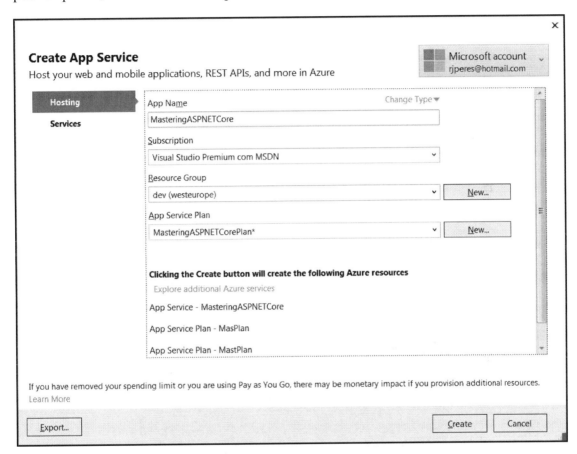

You will need to enter your credentials and select all the appropriate settings--
Subscription, **Resource Group**, **App Service Plan**, and so on.

 Of course, you need to have a working Azure subscription. There is no need for resource groups or app service plans, these can be created from inside the Visual Studio publish wizard.

If you need more info, navigate to `https://docs.microsoft.com/en-us/aspnet/core/tutorials/publish-to-azure-webapp-using-vs`.

AWS

Amazon Web Services (AWS) is Amazon's competitor to Microsoft Azure. It is a cloud provider that offers very similar features to Azure. Visual Studio can interact with it through the **AWS Toolkit for Visual Studio**, available freely from here: `https://marketplace.visualstudio.com/items?itemName=AmazonWebServices.AWSToolkitforVisualStudio2017`. You will, of course, need to have a working account with AWS.

We will see how we can deploy an ASP.NET Core app to AWS' Elastic Beanstalk, Amazon's easy to use hosting and scaling service for web apps. In order to deploy to Elastic Beanstalk, we must first create an environment using the AWS Elastic Beanstalk Console (`https://console.aws.amazon.com/elasticbeanstalk`). Then, we need to ZIP all our apps' contents, minus any third-party NuGet packages or binary outputs and upload it to AWS. Luckily, AWS Toolkit for Visual Studio does all this for us! Just right-click on the project in Solution Explorer and select **Publish to AWS Elastic Beanstalk**:

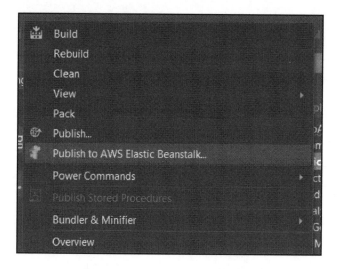

Then, you can specify all aspects of the deployment, or just stick with the defaults:

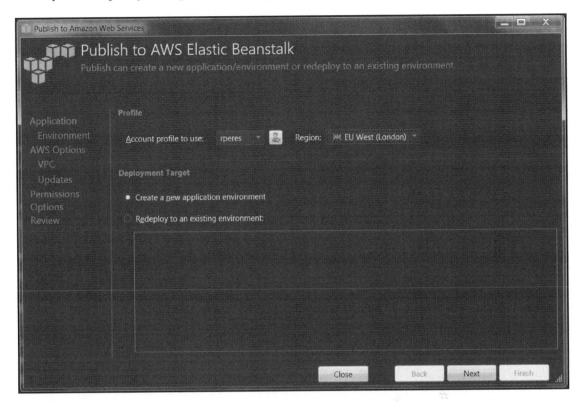

Docker

Since Visual Studio 2017, there is no longer a need to add an extension for working with Docker; it is built in.

Docker offers an excellent option when it comes to creating and destroying containers very quickly, with the same exact contents. This way you can be pretty sure that things will work as you expect them to!

To add a Docker deployment target to your project, you first need to add Docker support to it by clicking on **Project | Docker Support**. You then need to choose which operating system you will target, Windows or Linux:

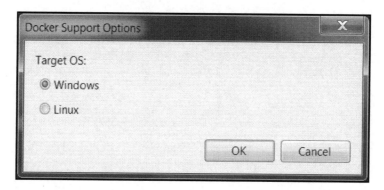

After this, you get a **Dockerfile** file added to your project. It will contain something like this:

```
FROM microsoft/aspnetcore:2.0
ARG source
WORKDIR /app
EXPOSE 80
COPY ${source:-obj/Docker/publish} .
ENTRYPOINT ["dotnet", "MyApplication1.dll"]
```

The FROM line will be different if you are targeting ASP.NET Core 1.x.

Plus, notice an extra solution folder called docker-compose, Docker Compose is the tool used to define and run multi-container Docker applications and you can read about it here: https://docs.docker.com/compose. In this folder you will find three files:

- docker-compose.ci.build.yml: A Docker Compose file to be used for **Continuous Integration (CI)**
- docker-compose.yml: Base Docker Compose file used to define the collection of images to be built and run
- docker-compose.override.yml: An override to docker-compose.yml for the Development environment

You can create files similar to docker-compose.override.yml for other environments.

The toolbar will add extra options for Docker:

You can run and even debug your app using Docker, it is transparent. Even if you have multiple Docker projects in your solution, you will be able to jump seamlessly from one to the other while debugging, which is pretty cool! When building your project, you just need to make sure that Docker is running beforehand and the Docker image (`microsoft/aspnetcore:2.0`) is available locally.

 As of now, running under Docker requires **Docker For Windows** (`https:/ /www.docker.com/docker-windows`).

For more information, jump to `https://docs.microsoft.com/en-us/aspnet/core/ publishing/docker` and `https://docs.microsoft.com/en-us/aspnet/core/publishing/ visual-studio-tools-for-docker`.

Windows Service

A different option is to host your ASP.NET Core app as a Windows Service. Of course, this is inherently not portable as Windows services are only available, well, on Windows. Anyway sometimes, especially for simple apps/APIs, this is the best option.

Start by adding the `Microsoft.AspNetCore.Hosting.WindowsServices` NuGet package. Then modify your `Program` class like this (for ASP.NET Core 1.x):

```
var host = new WebHostBuilder()
    .UseKestrel()
.UseContentRoot(Path.GetDirectoryName(Process.GetCurrentProcess().MainModul
e.FileName))
    .UseIISIntegration()
    .UseStartup<Startup>()
    .UseApplicationInsights()
    .Build();

host.RunAsService();
```

Alternatively, to make it dependent on a command-line flag, you can do something like this:

```
if (Debugger.IsAttached || args.Contains("--debug"))
{
  host.Run();
}
else
{
  host.RunAsService();
}
```

For ASP.NET Core 2.x, modify the `Main` method like this:

```
BuildWebHost(args).RunAsService();
```

Then, add `UseContentRoot` to the `BuildWebHost` body:

```
WebHost
    .CreateDefaultBuilder(args)
    .UseContentRoot(Path.GetDirectoryName(Process.GetCurrentProcess()
    .MainModule.FileName)).UseStartup<Startup>().Build();
```

Then, use `dotnet publish` to deploy your app to a folder on your machine and then register and start the service with Windows:

```
sc create MyService binPath="C:\Svc\AspNetCoreService.exe"
sc start MyService
```

The page at https://docs.microsoft.com/en-us/aspnet/core/hosting/windows-service contains all this information and more; make sure you read it.

Putting it all together

Even if it's convenient to use Visual Studio to deploy your apps, it is useful that you know how to do it using the command line, that is essentially what Visual Studio does.

Most of the time we Windows developers will be deploying to IIS; so learn how to use the Web Deployment Tools service and user interface. You can distribute the Web Deployment packages as `.zip` files quite easily.

Docker is the new (cool) kid on the block, it provides unprecedented easiness in creating containers, which you can then just pick and deploy to Azure, AWS, or other cloud providers, or just run on your local infrastructure.

A Windows Service sometimes is useful for simple things. I don't expect you, dear reader, to be making much use of them, but it's nice to know that this option is available.

Summary

This concludes our book. I hope you got a good understanding of the different hosting options available and how to use them. In particular Azure, AWS, and Docker can be quite useful; make sure you consider them as part of your deployment strategy!

Index

Made in the USA
Columbia, SC
20 February 2018